The Writers

The Writers

A History of American Screenwriters and Their Guild

MIRANDA J. BANKS

RUTGERS UNIVERSITY PRESS

NEW BRUNSWICK, NEW JERSEY, AND LONDON

LIBRARY OF CONGRESS CATALOGING-IN-PUBLICATION DATA

Banks, Miranda J., 1972–
     The writers : a history of American screenwriters and their Guild / Miranda J.
Banks.
          pages   cm
     Includes bibliographical references and index.
     ISBN 978–0–8135–7139–3 (hardcover : alk. paper) — ISBN 978–0–8135–7138–6
(pbk. : alk. paper) — ISBN 978–0–8135–7140–9 (e-book)
     1. Motion picture authorship—United States—History.   2. Writers Guild of
America—History.   3. Motion picture industry—Employees—Labor
unions—United States.   4. Television broadcasting—Employees—Labor
unions—United States.   5. Screenwriters—United States—Interviews.
     I. Title.
     PN1996.B382   2015
     812'.0309—dc23   2014014280

A British Cataloging-in-Publication record for this book is
available from the British Library.

Material used in chapter 5 was originally published in a much abbreviated form in
"The Picket Line Online: Creative Labor, Digital Activism, and the 2007–2008 Writers
Guild of America Strike," in *Popular Communication* 8 (2010): 20–33. Small portions of
the Introduction were published in "Oral History and Media Industries," in *Cultural
Studies* 8 no. 4 (2014).

Visit our website: http://rutgerspress.rutgers.edu

Visit the author's website: http://www.mirandabanks.tv

Manufactured in the United States of America

CONTENTS

ACKNOWLEDGMENTS

This book is a labor of love. At every point in this process I have been astonished by the support and generosity that I have received along the way. I am grateful to the wise and witty writers whom I interviewed, as well as to those who sat for interviews in 1978 for the Writers Guild Oral History Project. Every writer I approached agreed to be interviewed. I am not sure whether I am just incredibly lucky or have found the ideal subjects for research—probably both. The Writers Guild of America, both East and West Boards, and current and former employees have been wonderful resources. I am indebted to Geoff Betts for his help early on in securing interviews. The Writers Guild Foundation (WGF) is an invaluable resource, and it has become my home away from home the past five years. When I told Karen Pedersen, then the director of the Foundation's Shavelson-Webb Library, about my book project, she said, "Thank goodness someone is writing this book," and readily opened the vaults to me. The WGF Executive Board and Executive Director Katie Buckland have indulged my many requests. WGF Director of the Archive Joanne Lammers has been a dream partner as we combed through the archives, searching for and sharing the treasures we found. Javier Barrios and Idene Field steered me through boxes of documents, and Kevin Ott, Chris Kartje, Sandy Allyn, and Eva Gross kept me laughing during those many hours of research. Further thanks go to the WEA and WGF, as well, for granting me access to photographs from its collection for use in this book, including the two photographs on the cover.

John Caldwell continues to be my best guide to what it means to be a scholar and a professor. I am in my second decade of membership in the Cult of Caldwell, and my affection for him as a researcher, as a teacher, and as a human being continues to grow. His unwavering support through the years defines the meaning of mentorship. Jim Hosney was the first teacher who fostered my love of film and film analysis. His intellectual zeal for cinema ignited my own. I remember the day that I went to Anne Friedberg and Howard A. Rodman and told them my idea of writing a history of the Writers Guild. Anne is this book's guardian angel, and Howard has been her counterpart on the ground, willingly opening doors and mentoring me through this project.

The Writers started when I was a visiting assistant professor at the University of Southern California in the School of Cinematic Arts. There I found a wonderful mentor and friend, Ellen Seiter. Early conversations and research with her were instrumental in forming this book project. I continued to develop this research for the Nordic Media Festival and the DigiCult conference; thanks to Helle Sjøvaag and Jostein Gripsrud, respectively, for their early interest in this work. I am lucky to have found amazing support at Emerson College, in particular from Amy Ansell, Kristin Lieb, Peter Flynn, Linda Reisman, Eric Gordon, Jean Stawarz, Jim Macak, Jane Shattuc, Matt Finn, Bob Fleming, Donna Heiland, the Emerson Engagement Lab, and my VM402 seminar students. This research was funded in part by grants from the Emerson College Faculty Advancement Fund. A number of scholars offered valuable insight along the way, in particular Thomas Schatz, Vicki Mayer, Deborah Jaramillo, Alisa Perren, Allison Perlman, Bridget Conor, Nina Huntemann, Suzanne Leonard, Bambi Haggins, and Jennifer Holt. I learned a great deal from the faculty fellowships I was awarded through the Academy of Television Arts and Sciences and the National Association of Television Producers and Executives, as well as from the access I was granted by Rob Owen to the 2007 Television Critics Association press tour.

Leslie Mitchner has been the ideal editor for this book. She immediately understood the project and helped usher it through the review and publication process with enthusiasm and sage advice. I owe great thanks to the editorial board and staff at Rutgers University Press. My anonymous readers revealed themselves along the way. Many thanks to Andrew Horton for his thoughtful evaluation. Charles Wolfe was the perfect reader for this project; with his detailed notes, it has become a stronger book. I'm so grateful to Aidan O'Donohue, a talented artist and art director, who designed my cover.

Three gifted writers assisted me with this project. Gabrielle Banks was a phenomenal researcher and editor, providing essential help at critical junctures. Mojie Crigler not only transcribed dozens of interviews for me, but also devoted hours to discussing the insights we gathered from these tapes.

Alexandra Sear came late to this project, but was integral to finalizing the manuscript. I could not have dreamed of a better support team.

My friends have kept me sane, healthy, and laughing during the many years of researching and writing. In particular, I want to thank Andrea Crossan, Melissa Silverman, Joe Epstein, Jennifer Holt, Rodolfo Fernández, Claudia Bestor, Kirstin Henninger, Matt Ackley, Eloise Lawrence, Marisa Milanese, Max Brooks, and Roberta Chávez. Melissa Clark and Abbie Schiller have not only been dear friends for many years, but they also put their reputations on the line to help me with this project. Surviving the writing process was made easier through the help of Beverly Moy, Kerry Reynolds, Michelle Specht, Shannon MacDonald, Lara Traeger, and Susan Gorton. I would also like to thank Alvin Sargent, who wisely told me during my interview with him to keep getting my check-ups.

This book is dedicated to my family: Sherry Banks instilled in me a love of brilliant writers, great characters, fabulous stories, and the written word. Jeff Banks still makes me laugh more than the great comedy writers I interviewed. My grandmother, Geraldine Janis, was the first person to delight me with stories of old Hollywood. Julia and Benjamin Rosenfeld and Jonah and Gracie Banks make my time away from work much more fun. Barry Gittelson, Gavriel Rosenfeld, and Sharmon Goodman continually have encouraged my love of Los Angeles as a cultural and historic city. Erika Banks and Gabrielle Banks continue to guide me, inspire me, and ground me.

ABBREVIATIONS
USED IN THE TEXT

AAA	American Authors Authority
AFTRA	American Federation of Television and Radio Artists
ALA	Authors League of America
AMPAS	Academy of Motion Picture Arts and Sciences
AMPTP	Alliance of Motion Picture and Television Producers
CAC	Contract Adjustment Committee
CFA	Committee for the First Amendment
CSU	Conference of Studio Unions
DGA	Directors Guild of America
FCC	Federal Communications Commission
HUAC	House Un-American Activities Committee
HWM	Hollywood Writers Mobilization
IATSE	International Alliance of Theatrical Stage Employees
MBA	Minimum Basic Agreement
MCA	Music Corporation of America
MPAA	Motion Picture Association of America
MPAPAI	Motion Picture Alliance for the Preservation of American Ideals
MPPDA	Motion Picture Producers and Distributors of America
NLRB	National Labor Relations Board
OWI	Office of War Information
PGA	Producers Guild of America
RWG	Radio Writers Guild
SAG	Screen Actors Guild
SAG-AFTRA	Screen Actors Guild–American Federation of Television and Radio Artists
SP	Screen Playwrights
SWG	Screen Writers Guild
TSW	*The Screen Writer*
TWA	Television Writers Association
WGA	Writers Guild of America
WGAE	Writers Guild of America, East
WGAw	Writers Guild of America, West

The Writers

EPISODE 101

1 Baltimore Circuit Court, Pt 23: A jury trial in progress, a drug-involved homicide case
Judge Clifford Watkins, black, middle-aged, vaguely wearied, presiding as a young prosecutor
struggles to keep witnesses from backing up on their grand jury testimony. The second row of
seats in the half-empty courtroom is filled with some rough-looking characters, all staring
intently at the prosecution witnesses, who are clearly frightened. One of those in the second-row
-- Stringy Bell -- is better-dressed, more studious-looking. He writes on a legal pad as each
witness answers questions. The defendant is young, black, trying to look hard but clearly
nervous. The jury is mostly black, as is the prosecutor. In the back of the room, a rumpled, worn
Irish face stares at the proceedings impassively.
          Prosecutor. "Mr. Mitchell, did you or did you not tell the grand jury.. "
          Witness "I can't remember now. I don't know that I told anyone anything.. "
          The witness looks up at the Bell twenty feet away Bell eyefucks him coolly, writes
something on his pad. The rumpled Irishman exhales, gets up, leaves. On Judge Watkins,
watching him go.

2 State's attorney's office, Violent Crimes Unit. We follow the Irishman into the office He
greets the secretaries, moving toward the rear offices as if he owns the place. He sees another
cop, also white, on the phone, his feet up on a prosecutor's desk. The Irishman nods, listens. His
fellow detective is arguing with a contractor about the cost of pressure-treated lumber
          The Irishman sits. His pager goes off. He scans the number, frowns
          The other detective hangs up, looks to the Irishman
          "Fucking thieves."
          "You putting a deck up?"
          "Not for eight thousand I'm not. Fucking thieves."
          The detective picks up the phone again, ready to do battle. The Irishman interrupts him.
"You talked to Hansen lately?"
          "I'm with Hansen in Part 23 right now. The Marando Bennett case "
          "I know that I was just in there."
          "Yeah?" asks the detective, not really giving a shit.
          "Yeah. Your case is falling apart."
          "The fuck it is "
          The Irishman shrugs "Last two witnesses just backed all the way up."
          "The fuck you say."
          "You got Stringy Bell and his crew sitting in the second row staring them down They're
backin' up like bad sewer pipe."
          "What's Hansen doing?"
          The Irishman shrugs. The detective mulls the news over for a second, picks up the phone,
calls a second contractor, seeking another estimate

IMAGE 1 Summary notes on the pilot episode, "The Target," from David Simon's
show bible for *The Wire*.
Show Bible Collection, Writers Guild Foundation Archive, Shavelson-Webb Library,
Los Angeles

Introduction

The main reason the studios and the producers are scared of [writers] is because they know that they are crazy, that writers will do things that could be considered either suicidal or heroic, depending how you look at it—which is to act against what seems to be their best interests. . . . They are a particular breed. . . . It is the most miserable thing—you sit by yourself, wanting to kill yourself, looking at this blank screen, and who would want to do that?

—Walter Bernstein (writer of *The Front* and *Miss Evers' Boys*),
interview with the author, 16 July 2009

Screenwriters are storytellers, dream builders, and, more often than they would like, simple workaday hacks. They envision new worlds and the beings to populate them, bringing them to life through storylines and idiosyncratic details. Writers craft tales of heroism against all odds—so much so that they are sometimes swept up in the formula, becoming their own plucky protagonists in epic behind-the-scenes Hollywood dramas. Walter Bernstein, a sixty-year industry veteran and blacklist survivor, feels compelled to write by an artistic zeal and a fearless drive for individual expression. Screenwriters exist in their professional community as socially alienated intellectuals, spurned luminaries, and entertainment's most replaceable but ultimately indispensable artists. They are creative workers building widgets within a capitalist system, fabricating stories for others to bring to life. United as a labor group, these vociferous and contentious hero-makers have lived through many episodes of industry drama writ large.

The history of each unique writer in the American entertainment industry is further revealed in the thorny tale of the union that has represented them for more than eighty years. Generation by generation, writers and their union have fought to stay afloat amid evolving screen technologies, production methods, distribution models, and shifts in the industry's economy.[1] Rather than proactively bargaining for innovative contracts, the Writers Guild's labor negotiations emerge as reactions to industrial economics and national politics. At each juncture in the history of their craft, writers have grappled with traditional definitions of authorship, insider status, and creativity.

While most books on screenwriting focus on the script drafting process, often narrowing to an examination of an individual career arc, *The Writers* mines the collective experiences of writers as media practitioners and tracks the conditions of their creative labor. In the process of researching this book, I collected more than two hundred accounts of professional storytellers from in-person or historic interviews, memoirs, and archival documents. This task of patching together oral histories—each tainted by faulty memory, opinion, personal politics, and creative enhancement and omission—is, as one writer put it, "a kind of *Rashomon*."[2] The broader history I unearth is larger than the amalgamation of these narratives. In more than eighty years of American film and television history, writers have initiated action in pursuit of collective rights more frequently than any other professional group.

Five key moments in media history triggered monumental shifts in the profession: the formation of the Screen Writers Guild in 1933, the era of the blacklist, the wildfire expansion of television and the ensuing strike of 1960, battles over hyphenate roles and ownership in the 1970s and 1980s, and the strike of 2007–2008. In reviewing writers' accounts of these landmark moments, I trace three concerns that inevitably manifest themselves in each era: ownership of creative work, the adjudication of credits, and the liminal boundaries of membership and community.

Defining the Writer and the Guild

BANKS: Why do you think writers have been at the forefront of labor issues in Hollywood?

NORMAN LEAR, creator of *All in the Family*: Maybe because they're paid to think.

−Interview, 20 August 2013

Before diving into this rich and layered history, I want to specify what I mean by screenwriters, how I define the scope of their work, and what a writers' guild does. Screenwriters are practitioners who put pen to paper (or fingers to keyboard) and set a scene. I define screenwriters as industry professionals who write for screened entertainment, whether their work appears on film, television, a video game, or streaming media. They plot narrative, craft characters and give them unique voices, and devise the action that unfolds on the page and, ultimately, the screen. Irving Thalberg, the much-celebrated head of production at MGM in the 1920s and 1930s, interrogated the writer of *Street of Chance* and script doctor Lenore Coffee at a story meeting: "What's all this business about being a writer? It's just putting one word after another." To which Coffee responded, "Pardon me, Mr. Thalberg. It's putting one *right* word after another."[3]

Ideally, the work of writing is complete before the cameras roll. Writers either conceive a story idea or they are the first employees hired to flesh out someone else's vision. In most cases, they arrive long before a cast or crew. Mel Brooks, who has worked in every facet of the artistic process, hailed writing as the highest of all the creative crafts in entertainment: "It's the most splendid job . . . of all the jobs in Hollywood. The toughest job. . . . You would think the miracle would be starring or appearing in a movie, getting a movie job directing? No. The miracle is . . . getting your screenplay made into a movie. . . . Getting your dream realized. That is the biggest miracle."[4]

George Axelrod, an acclaimed playwright and novelist who adapted both *Breakfast at Tiffany's* and *The Manchurian Candidate* for the screen, declared script writing to be the most demanding form of writing. "A screenplay is the hardest single form there is. . . . It's continuous, razor-edge-of-now action. You aren't allowed any mistakes, because the audience is a fantastic entity. You can have 1,100 morons sitting in the audience, but when they come together in the darkness, an almost mystical thing happens, a kind of mass unconsciousness that is smarter than you are. They can spot a phony a mile off."[5]

But writing takes time. Although the screenwriter is a vital player in the production process, cast and crew often gripe about the protracted period of creation. Robert Towne, who scripted *Chinatown* and the film version of *Mission: Impossible*, explained why: "Until the screenwriter does his job, nobody else has a job. In other words, he is the asshole who keeps everybody else from going to work."[6] When assuming the role of producer, though, a writer works in the front office and on the set. In the world of television, writers increasingly hold producer credits. As *Cheers* showrunner Cheri Steinkellner noted, "The easiest, quickest way to get from page to stage is to just do it. To be the ultimate interpreter."[7]

The script is the first step toward a leap of faith that the cast, the crew, and ultimately the audience must willingly make to enter into the universe of a filmed narrative. Even when a writer delivers the work, the plan is only partly detailed. A screenplay does not equate to a film, nor does a television script amount to an episode. As Philip Dunne, screenwriter of *The Last of the Mohicans, How Green Was My Valley*, and *Pinky*, remarked, "The true analogy of script to picture is that of architect's blueprint to finished house. Without the first, the second could not exist. No director can make a good picture out of a bad script, and it takes a very bad director indeed to ruin a good one, though it has been done."[8] Paul Schrader, who scripted *Taxi Driver* and *Raging Bull*, echoes this analogy: "A screenwriter is not really a writer; his words do not appear on the screen. What he does is to draft out blueprints that are executed by a team."[9] Screenwriters, then, are architects who might never visit the construction site. If a writer is not also the producer on a project, often the job ends after the planning phase. Writer Charlie Kaufman parodies this phenomenon in *Adaptation* when Charlie Kaufman the character arrives on the set of *Being John Malkovich*. Not only does the crew fail to recognize him as the film's writer, they even find Charlie's presence distracting and ask him to step out of the way.

Although writers dream of crafting scripts that are ready to be shot as written, in reality they are often called back, or others are hired in their place, for multiple rewrites. Sometimes a script is purchased and then shelved. If a project moves forward, cast and crew build upon the blueprint, collaborating to realize plot and characters. In the early days of the industry, most writers worked under long-term contracts with studios. Now, more often than not, a writer works script by script. The time it takes to move from script to screen varies depending on the medium. Norman Lear found pleasure in both short and long formats: "You can have an idea on the first of the month and by the eighteenth, deliver it to . . . sixty million people [in television]. . . . But a movie, you can complete and make love to it for a year."[10]

If a writer lands on a successful television show, the work, no matter how satisfying, can become a routinized act of multitasking. Saul Turteltaub, who wrote on *Candid Camera, The Carol Burnett Show*, and *Sanford and Son*, dismissed any notion of his work as glamorous: "I'll tell you the truth, a job is a job, and having a job was the most important thing. And bringing home a check . . . and supporting my family. . . . One show led to the other. As far as the work was concerned, it was just the same work, sitting down, then at a typewriter, and typing, and turning it in, and hoping it was performed."[11] As Turteltaub acknowledged, the writing itself is creative, but the task of writing a formulaic episode each week becomes habitual. Elias Davis, writer on *M*A*S*H** and *Frasier*, provided a similar perspective: "You write for TV, you sit down and basically every week you're doing about three or four things at once. You're breaking the stories for new scripts, you're writing a script, you're rewriting another script, and you're working on a script that's onstage that week. And at the end of that week, one of those is . . . done. And then everything moves up on the checkerboard one square. . . . You come into the office every day, five days a week, sometimes six. . . . It's a lunch-pail kind of job."[12] Television writers parcel out their weeks between writing alone, hammering out scripts in the writers' room (more so if they are writing a comedy), and, if they are also producers, tweaking lines on the spot as needed. The work is varied and collaborative. And, as Turtletaub said, it is often rote.

IMAGE 2 Writing staff of *Caesar's Hour* in the office, c. 1955. Left to right front: Gary Belkin, Sheldon Keller, Mike Stewart, Mel Brooks. Back: Neil Simon, Mel Tolkin, Larry Gelbart.

Mel Tolkin Collection, Writers Guild Foundation Archive, Shavelson-Webb Library, Los Angeles

Many writers try to seek a balance, making the most of their talent and passion while complying with the needs and expectations of the executives who pay them. Feigning the former rarely works on the page. William Goldman, who wrote *Butch Cassidy and the Sundance Kid, All the President's Men*, and *The Princess Bride*, insists that writers should work only on stories they are passionate about, not ones they think will sell. "This sounds so rabbinical, but you can only write what you give a shit about. And you have got to keep doing that. For example, if you don't like special effects movies, don't try to write one, because it will suck. . . . I don't like special effects movies. . . . It would be ridiculous for me to try to write one. You have got to try to write about something you care about—that sounds really corny, but it's true."[13] Alvin Sargent, writer of *Paper Moon* and *Ordinary People*, echoed this sentiment when touting the superlative skills of a peer: "Well, I shouldn't say this because he's a friend of mine—but I wish I'd written *Cool Hand Luke*. But I can't write that stuff. There's a kind of muscle in Frank Pierson's work. He's extremely articulate. He's a very, very bright guy with a history, in every way, as a journalist, a fighting Marine. I'm a nice guy. I did write [for] *Naked City*. But in my *Naked City*, the writing was *nice*."[14]

Many television writers make their way in the industry by emulating the voice of a series creator. Courtney Lilly, writer on *Arrested Development* and *The Cleveland Show*, explained how television writing often means learning to be a brilliant mimic: "You are writing in somebody else's voice for a living. There are people that make a living with that as their primary skill set. And there are people like David E. Kelley [who originated *Ally McBeal*] who just create shows, and that's kind of their thing. . . . And the people with the most versatility are the ones that have the most opportunity to work. It is a job. It's fun, it's creative, it's great. But just like anything else, it's not like 'Ah, I've arrived! It's perfect!' It's not like that."[15] The bureaucratic structure of the industry does weigh heavily on many writers, making them feel they must disengage with their own creative visions and become team members in order to succeed.

Since very early on in motion picture writing, producers have brought in supplemental writers as specialists to doctor scripts according to their areas of expertise, whether writing action sequences, comedic scenes, genre pictures, or key revisions. Studios often view writers as interchangeable talent. There are instances of directors, actors, or cinematographers being replaced midway through a project, but they are rare. Writers, on the other hand, regularly step in for a portion of the work without necessarily getting screen credit. Sandra Tsing Loh, who worked on the television series *Clueless* and contributed dialogue to *Chicken Little*, joked that she either gets called in to do "little jewels of jobs, quick little mini-tartlets" or to work with other writers to boost the comedic elements in a feature. She describes these group punch-up sessions as "yelling funny lines at the screen" while "locked in a room with ten white male comedy writers named Josh."[16]

Studios sometimes contract ace writers to deliver several sequential drafts of a script based on a pitch. They will pay these scribes up front, knowing that to reach a shooting script the production team will need to work through multiple rewrites. While these so-called multi-step deals were once the bread-and-butter of the post–studio system era, they have become increasingly rare. Michael Oates Palmer, a writer on *The West Wing* and a WGA West board member, understands the financial incentive for the decline of step contracts. Yet he thinks the retreat "penny wise and pound foolish,"[17] arguing that contracting for a single draft of a script fails to capitalize on the collaborative process to reach the best possible version of the narrative.

Today, most writers—from novices to industry veterans—prepare "spec" (speculative) scripts, that is, uncommissioned screenplays written for possible future sale. They are gambling months or years of labor if the script goes unsold. A spec script can serve as a calling card from the writer to a prospective agent and, in turn, from the agent to a hungry producer. Some established writers draft specs for the pleasure of bringing an idea to fruition, some do it out of financial necessity, and others want to establish themselves in a different genre.

My use of the term "labor" might seem incongruent with the creative process of writing. Even though writing calls for a great psychic effort, the work of hammering words onto paper does not rise to the level of manual labor in the traditional sense. Since the 1930s, with few exceptions, professional screenwriters have been college educated. In recent generations, many have earned graduate degrees, though not necessarily in fields related to film or television. Most working writers emerge from the middle and upper middle classes; most are white; and the majority, most strikingly from the 1930s through the 1970s, have been men.[18] Today, many women make a living as professional writers, but longitudinal studies have found that their scripts are far less likely to make it to the screen.[19]

Sociologists Joan Moore and Burton Moore mapped the sweeping changes in the screenwriters' labor conditions: "The studio writer of 1923 was most often a paid employee who worked a regular day in a specified place. By 1970, the writer was most likely to be working in combination with a producer and director 'developing a property' which [would] ultimately be sold as a 'package.' . . . The director is always the writer's client—the person to whom he delivers his work and whom he must please."[20] Whereas film writers cater to the needs of a director or a producer, television writers have the additional burden, in some cases, of having to comply with the demands of a sponsor or network.

Although the work of a writer is inarguably part of an assembly-line production, it appears to the outsider more akin to white-collar labor. Andrew Ross, who studied the contemporary Silicon Valley labor force, designates these New Economy creative types as "no collar" laborers.[21] This terminology suits screenwriters in the late twentieth and early twenty-first century; they belong to the flexible hours, work from home or a coffee house economic class. It would require a carefully tailored fit for any labor organization to represent such an unwieldy cohort.

Over the years the Writers Guild has shouldered this complex task. Eighty years into its project, the Guild is the bargaining agent for writers who create film, television, news, animation, streaming media, and video game scripts for American signatory companies.[22] For the writers under its protection, the Guild convenes and mobilizes members, addresses their concerns, negotiates and enforces contracts, lobbies on behalf of its members, represents the face of screenwriters to the outside world, and preserves the craft of screenwriting.

This final directive, to preserve the art of writing, illuminates the subtle difference between a craft guild and a union. During moments of crisis, writers feel compelled to choose sides based on how they interpret the terms *guild* and *union*. Bob Barbash, writer on *Zane Grey Theater*, explained how this perception played out during a strike in 1960: "A tremendous amount of people in the Guild . . . resent the word 'union.' . . . [Every] morning I had to be carrying a picket sign in front of MGM. Now that is not a Guild. That's a union, man. When you are walking there and you are trying to stop people from crossing the line. We are an unusual group because we like to think of ourselves as [part of a] super, upper [tier of] intelligence. That we don't work on a loading dock . . . but if you are going to have a union, you are a union."[23]

IMAGE 3 The revolution will be downloaded. Rally on Hollywood Boulevard during the 2007–2008 WGA strike.

Photo by author

In contrast, the term *guild* implies a focus less on working conditions and more on championing the artistry of the profession. Agreeing on terminology is not merely semantic: it has resulted in a recurring tug-of-war across the entertainment industry between writers and sometimes even within an individual writer's mind. The battle over self-definition will be a recurring theme in this book. The internal friction is captured in the very concept of "creative labor."[24]

Writers must join the Guild if they have surpassed a certain quantity of work with a company that has signed as a contractual partner on the Guild's collective bargaining agreement. A signatory company can be as vast as a multinational corporation or as limited as a small pro-union production company. An associate writer amasses units to gain full membership, and today writers must belong to either the WGA East (which uses the acronym WGAE) or the Writers Guild West (which prefers WGAw), depending on geography. The Guild's stated objectives are voluminous. It contracts minimum rates for specific types of work, determines writers' screen credits, ensures payment of residuals, provides pensions and health

benefits for members, engages in national policy debates that concern writers' interests, and provides continuing education for members and the
community. Some writers have seen their induction into the Guild as a sign
of having "made it" in the industry. Others have felt membership to be a
weighty burden foisted upon them. And still others have paid little attention to what membership means. Then there are those who view membership as a life raft. Barbara Corday, creator of *Cagney & Lacey*, expressed deep
gratitude for the benefits afforded to veteran writers: "First of all, having
residuals. Lifetime medical insurance as a backup to Medicare, as a secondary insurance. How many people outside of Congress have things like that?
It's just *phenomenal.*"[25]

Corralling this disparate group of workers, however, is an arduous task.
The Guild brings together thousands of individuals who predominantly perform solitary work. As Hal Kanter, creator of the series *Julia*, noted in the
1970s, "We writers are, collectively, a strange group of creatures and it's a
frequent source of amazement to me that the Guild is such a well-run zoo!"[26]
John Furia Jr., writer of *The Singing Nun* and president of the WGAw from 1973
to 1975, laughed as he pointed out, "We are the most individualistic group
to band together."[27] Phyllis White, who worked on writing teams for various
television series from the 1950s through the 1980s, noted the paradox of
singular writers with unique voices aligning for a collective cause: "It's a
Guild of individuals as no other union is. You've got the Teamsters and there
are a certain number of Teamsters who do the same job. . . . They do the
same hours. They do the same thing. We don't. . . . Trying to amalgamate
this group . . . [of] nearly 5,000 into one union now is horrendous. It's amazing that it works at all."[28]

The Guild's daunting task is further complicated by the reality that
many writers also hold membership in at least one other trade union.
Specifically, the other groups that negotiate with signatory companies
include the Directors Guild of America (DGA), which represents directors,
assistant directors, unit production managers, and production associates;
the Screen Actors Guild–American Federation of Television and Radio
Artists (SAG-AFTRA), which represents actors, extras, broadcast journalists,
and puppeteers, among others; and the International Alliance of Theatrical
Stage Employees (IATSE), which represents a diverse set of industry workers,
from electricians to set carpenters, makeup artists, prop masters, cinematographers, editors, and art directors.

Peer organizations, studios, and the press regard the Writers Guild as the *enfant terrible* of the industry. Although writers have not consistently mobilized for social justice or workers' rights, the Writers Guild has always been the most politicized among its fellow organizations. Many chalk up this reputation to writers' eccentric personalities. But the reason writers are better equipped to drum up support for an issue is that every Guild member performs the same labor: putting words on paper. The other three organizations service vastly larger constituencies with needs so diverse that a united front proves tricky—especially when it comes time to negotiate with the monolithic Alliance of Motion Picture and Television Producers (AMPTP).

The AMPTP is a powerful bargaining unit that digests the concerns of hundreds of production companies, networks, and studios and then delivers a proposal—representing the united group's interests—to the negotiating table. Whereas in standard bargaining a union tries to garner advantage by playing one company off against others, the AMPTP positions itself so that the various unions must jostle with each other, grabbing for scraps at the table. This tactic, called "reverse pattern bargaining," forces each guild into what one member called "a kind of a chess game between the three unions."[29]

Since its formation, the Writers Guild has gone on strike six times, in 1959–1960, 1973, 1981, 1985, 1988, and 2007–2008. Three of these industry-wide walkouts were protracted, lasting for many months. SAG has endured a total of five strikes. In marked comparison, DGA's members have walked out only one time since the guild's formation in 1936. That strike, in 1987, lasted three hours and five minutes. IATSE has never once gone on strike over filmed entertainment.[30] In 1945, members of the short-lived Conference of Studio Unions (CSU) picketed their employers and literally took a beating. Despite screaming matches, lost jobs, and finger pointing among its members, the Guild still enjoys greater cohesion than other entertainment unions.

Three Recurring Themes

As I interviewed writers and began weaving their individual recollections into the larger narrative of the American media industry, I noticed three overarching issues. I will call attention to them in the following chapters, and so I want to pause here and explain each one briefly. They are: the shifting definitions of ownership and authorship, the meaning of a writer's name on a screen credit, and the perception of writers being outsiders within their own professional communities.

Authorship, Ownership, and Control

Writers are at once creative artists and employees. Frank Pierson, former president of WGAw and of the Academy of Motion Picture Arts and Sciences and writer of *Cool Hand Luke* and *Dog Day Afternoon*, explained the absurdity of work-for-hire rules, which have plagued writers since the earliest days of cinema. "Work-for-hire says that Pope Julius II and so on painted the Sistine Chapel ceiling and Mad King Ludwig of Bavaria wrote Wagner's operas. . . . [T]he employer is deemed to be the author. And that's the source of our problem."[31] Long before the time of Guild's first contract, writers had lost control of copyright. The US Copyright Act of 1909 states: "the word 'author' shall include an employer in the case of works made for hire."[32] As creative workers churning out stories for studios, writers have no ownership. Not until 1960, after a long-fought battle, did they begin to receive residual payments for subsequent screenings of their work. Profit participation for creative workers began in the 1950s: the writers' pay rate is generally at 2 to 10 percent of net profit points, although a minority of writers have brokered deals for gross point profits. Screenwriters are paid for a script and for rewrites (plus a production bonus if and when a film based on the script starts principal photography) and for residuals on ancillary sales.

Unless a special clause has been written into the contract, writers have no creative control over their work once it has been purchased. Erik Barnouw, a documentary film writer and the president of the Radio Writers Guild (RWG) from 1947 to 1949, recalled his disappointment when he grasped his loss: "I remember the first time I discovered that something I had written for *Cavalcade of America* was copyrighted, and it said on the copyright card: 'Author: DuPont Company.' I remember, I came face to face with the realization that DuPont was the author of what I had written."[33] David Harmon, whose career as a television writer spanned more than thirty years, from *The Man Behind the Badge* to *Hotel*, offered a similar story: "I discovered, much to my chagrin, when I got out here, that I no longer owned what I wrote. In New York, I leased it to the studios for one showing. I come out here and find out Harry Cohn [president of Columbia Pictures] is the author, which put me into shock."[34]

When television writers joined the Guild, they were dismayed by their lesser role within the media hierarchy, but they were in a much better position regarding control of authorial rights. Ernest Kinoy, a writer on *Goodyear Playhouse* and the miniseries *Roots*, explained the complex differences in notions of authorship and creative control between film and television writers as they united under one umbrella guild in the 1950s:

> You hired a [film] writer like you hired a carpenter. And they were interchangeable. . . . The project was considered the property (emotional property, let alone legal) of the producer. . . . In New York, in live television, the concept of the playwright and the author lay philosophically behind . . . the writer. It was his play. . . . [Screenwriters] felt that we were neophytes and lesser in prestige. . . . And no screenwriter would demean himself by working in television. We felt that they came out of the Hollywood tradition, in which the position of the writer was in fact demeaned. The truth was probably somewhere in between."[35]

Hortense Powdermaker admitted in 1967 that she had been disdainful of film writers in her 1950 anthropological study *Hollywood, the Dream Factory* precisely for their lack of authorial control. She was incensed that prosperity for a writer necessitated a loss of integrity.

> Although closer by temperament and profession to the writers than to any other group in Hollywood, I failed to identify with them. . . . I was indignant at the writers . . . and horrified when I found gifted writers (whose work before coming to Hollywood had been literature) working on admittedly mediocre scripts and taking them seriously. But was this any different from the actor taking his role in a mediocre film with seriousness? Obviously not. For both it was a way of preserving some measure of self-respect. But at the time I did not see this. I wrote that the writers had become "soft," that they sacrificed their integrity as artists for monetary rewards.[36]

The notion of giving up ownership for financial security infuriated Powdermaker, and many others as well. The idea of selling one's soul—and setting aside one's artistry—for money is a popular myth in Hollywood. At various periods in time, challenging this classic conception of screenwriting was reason enough for writers to fight the studios for more control over and credit for their work.

In my conversations with writers, this lack of creative control—at least for those who did not also carry a secondary role as a producer or director—led to a kind of frustrated sense of entitlement. In the 1930s and 1940s, writers worked under exclusive contract for a specific Hollywood studio, making substantial sums of money, but they had little autonomy; for example, writers could be loaned out to other studios for particular projects with little choice in the matter. As Max Wilk describes in *Schmucks with Underwoods*, "You came as a pencil for hire, at sums heretofore unheard of for pencils. You brought no plots, dreams, or high intentions. If you wrote a good movie it was because you were lucky enough to get on the payroll of a classy boss. Class or not, the boss called the shots and you did as bid. You were a sort of literary errand boy with an oil magnate's income."[37] Playwrights, on the other hand, controlled their own writing and, as pointed out by Stirling Silliphant, screenwriter of *In the Heat of the Night*, also paid their own bills.

> If you sit in a New York cold water flat and you write your play and no one is paying your rent and giving you any money you, by god's right [you] have the ownership of that material. You have created it. But when you are living out here and some producer calls you in and says this is a show we have sold, these are the characters, give us an idea for a story and you have got an assignment? There is a hell of a lot of difference between being subsidized to write that kind of crap than there is subsidizing yourself and writing out of your gut and selling it. The man that sits in the cold water flat and writes out of his gut is entitled to anything he can get. The man who is hired to perform a professional job is, in my opinion and you might as well face it, no different than a plumber, a bricklayer, or anyone else. All the aesthetics cloud the issues. He is a hired professional writer.[38]

Screenwriters in the contract era were hired scribes, producing subsidized writing or writing on assignment. In giving up authorial control and by writing for film, they could make more money than most of them ever could by writing plays or novels.

With the end of contract labor, the work of the writer was transformed. For some writers, the need to pitch and sell their ideas was decidedly unappealing, outside the confines of what they had experienced as the nature of the job. Interviewed in 1978, Maurice Tombragel, a writer on *Walt Disney's*

THE WORLD:

Training to be a surgeon is like no other job.

After 4 years of college and 4 years of med school, if you're smart enough and tough enough to be accepted into a surgical residency, you have seven more years of training to go. 7 more years at the bottom of the surgical food chain. 7 more years as a grunt, as a soldier. You work at a crazed pace -- 60 hours on, 18 hours off. You make $28,000 a year. You rarely see your non-doctor friends, your refrigerator never has any food, you can't remember the last time you had a date or got your hair cut. You're sleep-deprived, nutrition deprived, you smoke too much, drink too much caffeine and when you get those 18 hours off, you either sleep your life away or you party far too hard -- desperate to get squeeze a week's worth of living into one day. You eat, sleep and breathe surgery.

And you love it. Because it's a turn on. Because the upside is amazing. Because, even while you are training, you stand at the front line of humanity. You reach into a body and hold a beating heart in your hands. You stop the destruction of bullets. You remove bad kidneys and replace them with new ones. You remove the left side of a baby's damaged brain and two years later, she's playing on a swing set. It's power, pure and simple. And that kind of power --the power to change fate -- makes you special. Ask anybody who has ever had to go under the knife -- a good surgeon is the equal of God. And the best surgeons know it. Deep down, they think that not even God is their equal. Because god kills indiscriminately -- surgeons get to choose. They decide who lives and who dies. Surgeons have cornered the market on arrogance.

But while you're God with a scalpel in hand, without the scalpel, you're as human as anybody. You're a real person trying to lead a real life while doing the a job that makes having a real life next to impossible.

How do you date when you're never at home? And even if you do manage to date, exactly how do you keep a relationship going? What if you're married to someone you never have time be with? Raising a child who only sees you two night a week? Have a family member sick with something that no surgery can repair? So what if you're saving 20 lives a week when you can't fix your own life?

So what we want to do is...tell the story of:

IMAGE 4 Shonda Rhimes's early pitch outline for "Under the Knife/Cutting Edge," an early draft of what would become the series *Grey's Anatomy*.

Anatomy of a Script Collection, Writers Guild Foundation Archive, Shavelson-Webb Library, Los Angeles

Wonderful World of Color, expressed his distaste for what he called the new job description of the writer-auteur: "Today you have to be an auteur. You not only have to create your material . . . you have got to raise the money for it, you have to direct it, you produce it. You are the one-man show . . . [doing] a picture today. And the writers that I knew . . . we just couldn't do that nor were [we] interested in doing it. . . . To sit down and write something, fine. To try to sell it? Just leave me alone. I don't even want to go on a set. I don't want to even be involved in the studio."[39] For Tombragel and some in his cohort, the added work of pitching and producing was distracting to their job; others found this new proposition thrilling. Writers now had a better chance at gaining an authorial position and, perhaps, wresting back creative control of their scripts. Moreover, any form of ownership tends to take the form of profit participation and residual rights, where writers can receive a percentage of profits divvied up by the studios or networks.

The lack of copyright and authorial control continues to exasperate writers, but ultimately leaves many with feelings of resignation. In moments of crisis, questions of copyright, control, and authorship inevitably seem to enter into the Guild's debates and sometimes even into its negotiations. It is not just the writers who are haunted by notions of authorship; the concept of the auteur has been a point of fascination for other media makers and media studies scholars. With artistic and creative control also come prestige and recognition within the industry. These attainments lead, in many ways, to another recurring theme: the importance of a writer's name.

The Name

The power and prominence of a writer's name is significant to both the writer and the Writers Guild. One of the terms written into the first Guild contract regulated control over and determination of writing credits, assuring that they were correct and valid. Though writers may not have been fairly compensated at the time, they demanded that their work be properly credited. Screenwriter William Ludwig noted how in the 1930s it was sometimes a gamble whether a film would be credited to the script writer: "You never knew until you saw the picture at the preview what the credit was going to be. You could work on the script all by yourself, you'd go out to see it and there was another name on it. Maybe not your name at all. Maybe your name with somebody else's. Sometimes the other writer's name was also your producer or somebody you never knew. [Studios] determined credits."[40] Credits, as well as rights and residuals, are now non-negotiable and are determined by the Guild's minimum basic agreement (MBA). As legal scholar Catherine Fisk notes, "even hiring contracts for writers on projects not covered by the MBA stipulate 'credit per WGA.'"[41]

While prestige is a legitimate reason for wanting credit, for most writers a more significant concern is that pay scales are based on the success of their pictures. If a writer's name is not on a film, not only does he or she not get credit on that project, but the person might subsequently be out hundreds, perhaps even thousands, of dollars during the next contract negotiation. Howard A. Rodman, screenwriter of *Savage Grace*, vice president of the WGAw, and son of Howard Rodman, creator of the series *Harry O*, explained the complexities of credit. Although the Guild was created in part to protect writers' right to have their names on what they wrote, oftentimes writers worked on projects that paid the bills. And sometimes those projects did not represent the kind of work a writer wanted to have associated with his or her name. "The issue of credits is as fraught as anything we do. It was believed that the fewer the number of writers' names on a project, the more dignity it had. . . . It was part of the dignity of writing, but very quickly there are all kinds of thorny problems. I grew up in a house where my dad used a pseudonym far more often than he used his real name. Our family motto was, 'The script isn't finished until the name comes off.'"[42]

The rules for credits are complex, and only a certain number of writers' names can be attached to a particular script. Given how common rewrites are, many writers are not credited for work they perform. Elaine May, who wrote *Heaven Can Wait* and *Primary Colors*, also worked on the scripts for *Reds* and *Tootsie*; yet her name is mentioned nowhere in the credits for those films. "You can make a deal if you're going to do the original writing," she said. "But if you're going to do the original re-writing, you can't. . . . No matter how much you write, what you write, you're still a hired gun, and you have no control."[43] Those who excel at rewrites are known as script doctors. Robert Towne doctored *Bonnie and Clyde* and *The Godfather*. He thought that these "could have been arbitrated," but if he "had been on the arbitration committee, I don't think I would have given myself screenplay credit. I did a lot of work on the script, but the conception, the characters, the tone—I was simply enhancing them."[44] Since the Guild's earliest days, members have called upon it to negotiate difficult credit arbitration cases.

Starting in the late 1940s, the issue of names and the naming of names during the blacklist tore apart the professional community of Hollywood and severely damaged the careers of many Writers Guild members. The Hollywood Ten were just the beginning: the blacklist destroyed the careers of hundreds of film and television workers and damaged the ability of many others to work in the United States for a decade or more. During this time, one's name became a vulnerability. Veterans agree that the era of the blacklist is easily the most deplorable in the Guild's history, as the Guild failed to protect its members and most members failed to stand up for one another.

Years later, in the late 1980s, the Guild finally, fully, and shamefully claimed responsibility for abandoning its members during the blacklist. Since then, the Guild's leadership has always put policies regarding First Amendment rights front and center in the union's political agenda, seeing issues of individual credit and of creative authorship as critical to its membership. In 2010, the Guild refused to sign on with the Motion Picture Association of America (MPAA), the DGA, IATSE, SAG, and AFTRA to a joint filing in the Senate and with the White House's Office of the US Intellectual Property Enforcement Coordinator that endorsed reduced regulation of media transmission.[45] The Writers Guild is emphatically opposed to piracy and copyright infringement, and yet support of independent production and openness in content production is of equal importance to the union. In the opinion of some WGA members, studio-endorsed websites with sanctioned content have better access to consumers, a backdoor that threatens to destroy net neutrality under the guise of anti-piracy. For writers, free speech is paramount—a stance that to the media industry community sometimes seems laudable and at other times aggressively contemptible.

Credits and the credibility of writers have been central to individual contract agreements. While much of the Guild's litigation work is over credits, there is little doubt that not just past erasures of writers' names but also the continued diminishment of members' work has compelled many screenwriters to action. Media scholar Mark Deuze speaks of the precariousness of labor as a recent phenomenon, but I would argue that screen and television writers—like many film and television producers—have had their names challenged, their contributions diminished, and their careers held in the balance for enough years that they could be considered experts in tracking the vicissitudes of labor.[46] *Identity Thief* screenwriter Craig Mazin explains how screenwriters' lack of legal control over the fate of their scripts—and thereby over their names and reputations—can lead to bitter disputes. And that distinction is ingrained in the meaning of authorship: "The rest of the world has *droit morale*: the moral right of the author. We don't. The United States is unique. Our unique approach to copyright, to allow work-for-hire . . . [has] created easily the most economically viable climate for writers in the world. . . . You are so much better off financially as a writer in the United States than you are anywhere else. But artistically? There are deep, deep challenges. The things that make the marketplace so rich are also the things that create that state of discontent that occasionally erupts, riot-style, into strikes."[47] The significance of a writer's name and credits continues to be a critical issue, a struggle that can be seen most clearly in the Writers Guild's forty-plus-year battle with the DGA regarding possessory credit. When a film is promoted as "by" a particular director, writers' hackles go up: all collaboration is erased, the labor is denied, and writers are moved to action.

Identity: Outsiders on the Inside

Unlike the days when writers hammered away at typewriters in studio bungalows between trips to the commissary, the majority of writers today spend their working hours outside studio walls.[48] Some have found ways to exist comfortably outside the industry while participating from afar. Sooni Taraporevala, who wrote *Mississippi Masala*, embraces her role on the margin, living in India while writing for the American screen. These sites of solitary production challenge traditional notions of media work as collaborative and, at least geographically, the work of insiders. This position as an outsider is one that writers connect with, given that they perform the majority of their work before the cast and crew appear. This outsider status is often made symbolic as well.

All of the writers I interviewed are established working or retired media professionals. Though some writers said issues of identity do not weigh heavily on them, virtually all recognized the patterns of inclusion and exclusion that serve as evaluators of a writer's professional self. These distinctions play out in varying ways: in a conflicted position straddling roles as both artist and employee, in changing notions of allies and adversaries, and within marginalized communities of writers, in particular, women and minorities.

Screenwriters are not in a comfortable position; both inside and outside of media production, the creation of commercial art is often seen as a conjoining of irreconcilable goals, or at best antithetical ones. Some scholars have pointed to the nature of screenwriters' labor: they are artisans work-ing within a capitalist, bureaucratic system. This paradox is what Joan and Burton Moore call the myth of the "bureaucrat artist."[49] Unlike laborers in blue-collar industries, writers have more regular access to management, both at work and socially, a situation that has led to strange working relationships. Even with this proximity, their pleas for better compensation or public acknowledgment of their work are rarely heard. During the formation of the Screen Writers Guild (SWG), Howard Green, writer of *I Am a Fugitive from a Chain Gang* and one of the organization's early members, was out dancing at the Cocoanut Grove. There MGM studio head Louis B. Mayer walked up to him, irate upon hearing of Green's union membership, and told him, "You'll never work in Hollywood again. Never." Green could not find work for four-teen months.[50] When writer William Ludwig did not comply with Mayer's suggestion that he stay out of labor politics, Mayer called him an "ungrateful son of a bitch" and threw Ludwig out of his office. Ludwig laughed as he said that he was sure all the writers' phones were tapped and that during his entire career at MGM he was regularly dismissed from Mayer's office and told he was "stupid and would never amount to anything."[51]

Though they were essential to the process and were fairly well paid during the studio era, writers were regularly abused for the privilege. Circumstances have changed for writers since then, and the fact that writers often travel in the same socioeconomic circles as management makes for awkward moments. A few writers told me how uncomfortable it was to run into studio bosses at parties or at their children's schools during the 2007–2008 strike and to have to act cordial and friendly, only to confront the same executive hours later driving a car across the picket line at the studio. Los Angeles and New York are big cities, but they are small company towns. Many writers speak with bitter wit about "high-class victimization": in other words, they feel mistreated while in a position of status. A desire for social justice per-vades not only some of their scripts but also the narrative they see playing out within their profession.[52] The financial success of some can be so immense that these bureaucrat artists must struggle with the uncomfortable position of being cast as outsiders within the inner circle of the media industries.

As the industry has grown, the studio and network apparatuses for handling labor disputes have evolved into a highly structured, tightly moni-tored group of businesspeople and lawyers who manage negotiations with unions and guilds. On the other side of the bargaining table, the Writers

Guild and other trade groups do hire executives, but working artists and craftspeople sit on their negotiating committees. And few of them have experience with labor negotiations or contract law. In dialogue about the 1960 strike, David Harmon explained the uncomfortable process of reintegration from being a disgruntled employee back to being a creative worker: "We thought that management was the enemy. They were not. They were businessmen. When the strike was over every one of those men across the table from us were gentlemen. They all stuck their hands out. . . . They were paid every week. It was their job one way or another to get it over with. There was no enmity. They didn't say, 'We'll get you later.' They could not care less. . . . That is what they do for a living. That is not what we do for a living."[53] There is a residual effect for writers as they readjust from outsider to insider again.

Antagonism and frustration about outsider status can happen within the group as well. For minority communities—most notably women and writers of color—the feelings of outsider status are as exasperating as they are demeaning. In her anthropological analysis of screenwriters in Hollywood in 1994, Jorja Prover argues, "To the extent that motion picture and television writers have been overlooked, the minority writer has not even been mentioned."[54] Women who wanted to write strong female lead characters were often passed over for jobs in writers' rooms on television series. "It's pink and blue, in terms of assignments, as well," said Robin Swicord, who adapted *Memoirs of a Geisha* and *The Curious Case of Benjamin Button* for the screen. "All women who work in the film business are swimming in a soup of gender bias, and it is invisible to many people, unacknowledged by many people."[55] Betty Ulius, who wrote for film and television for more than twenty years, explains that the issue was never about barring women from participating. Rather, there was a disconnect between men and women within the community:

Up until 1971, women were almost totally disregarded in the Writers Guild. . . But there was absolutely no feeling that women were left out of the Writers Guild. This was not a big masculine conspiracy. When I came out from New York in 1959, I would go to the few meetings a year that we would have and see maybe two or three women. Women were absolutely not talked to. This was not, again, because of a conspiracy, but because writers are generally shy people. The men would talk to the men and unless you were built like Farrah Fawcett-Majors you were absolutely ignored. . . . We were not asked to play golf or tennis. We never got jobs the way most men get jobs by knowing other men . . . [who would invite] you to come in and tell a story.[56]

Although some of the difficulty that women experienced in finding work within the industry could be attributed to sexism, data on writers' employment follow documented trends in hiring practices at the time. Writers and producers—like many involved in employment—traditionally tend to feel most comfortable hiring people with backgrounds, interests, and experiences similar to their own. And given that most film and television producers are white and male, the discrepancy in numbers is substantial. In 1973, 13 percent of the Guild's members were women—many of whom were underemployed. Thirty years later, in 2003, the percentage had grown only to an average of 24 percent (27 percent for television, 18 percent for film).[57] That same year, the employment of minority writers hit a low point of 10 percent in television and 6 percent in film.[58] These figures say nothing about the substantial gender and race gaps in median earnings over the decades.

Other writers feel that diversity in script writing can be an advantage. Ronald Bass, screenwriter of *Rain Man* and *The Joy Luck Club*, has found great success partnering with women on writing projects. He believes that women and men often focus on different aspects of a story:

In my experience, there is a big gender difference. Men are result-oriented. Fuck the girl. Win the prize. Beat up the guy. Get the money. Close the deal. Win the game. And they do not want to know, they do not want an inner life. . . . Women are process-oriented. They have to have an inner life. . . . That is why I like to write about women. We did *Rain Man* . . . and I said to Tom [Cruise] at one point, "This is about your character becoming more like a woman." He said, "Thanks very much." I explained . . . "It has nothing to do with the character becoming effeminate. It is with your character learning that he has an inner life . . . Dustin [Hoffman] cannot make that change. He cannot have an inner life. So the access character is you, Tom. You are going to be developing through the course of the movie. You are the person who is going to go on the journey. . . . We are going to focus on Dustin and be obsessed with Dustin but we are going to identify with you."[59]

Bass's comments highlight the necessity not just for male and female writers, but also for male and female characters and for masculinity and femininity to be expressed in creative work. While many women write action and many men write process, this drive to tell compelling stories that lure in wide audiences is part of a push for diversity among writers.

When minority writers, whether women or men, discuss experiences working within the industry, they describe the struggle not just to land a job but also to present an alternative thought or opinion to executives and other creative personnel. Susan Kim told of the surprisingly difficult time she had getting one producer to understand the character of the central boy in "The Princess and the Pea" episode of the HBO animated children's series *Happily Ever After*. Kim wanted the boy to be spacey, but the producer was eager to give him thick glasses, a bad haircut, and a pocket protector. Kim responded that she did not want him to be an Asian geek. The producer fought back: "'But nerds are funny.' I said, 'Yes, but Asian nerds—you don't want to go there, trust me on this.'" *Happily Ever After* has been lauded by the industry and parents' groups alike for its representation of minorities and its forward-thinking, reimagined versions of classic fairy tales, but here was a Korean American writer working with a Caucasian producer who could not conceive that the direction she was suggesting invoked a derogatory stereotype. Kim virtually had to plead with her producer: "'Please. You have to believe me when I say that it's an offensive stereotype. Trust me. It is. Trust me. Trust me. That's why you hire diverse writers, so we can bring some of our experience to it. My experience is that it's a really offensive stereotype.' So I like to think that it was an informative discussion for this executive. She didn't press it. I did manage to do what I wanted with the character, but it was eye-opening. Thinking: why do I have to keep repeating this?"[60] The amount of back-and-forth discussion of what was considered a stereotype provides a compelling example of the difficulties minority writers have often faced when trying to put stories on the screen.

As both a showrunner (*Soul Food*) and a media scholar, Felicia Henderson is a uniquely astute analyst of the industry. In her scholarly article on race and gender in the television comedy writers' room, Henderson provides ample evidence of the difficult role women and minority writers play as they try to negotiate the sixty-year-old traditions of a private and highly protected workspace. Even as much has changed (there are more women and minorities than before), much has stayed the same (the rules of engagement and the impulse toward homogeneity). Henderson writes, "Humor is generated within this space through a process of inclusion and exclusion, familiarity and othering, and humor is derived from social categories such as race, gender, ethnicity, and sexuality, which become the means by which the performative space is homogenized."[61] This desire for sameness—in humor, in creative abilities, in background—marginalizes women and minorities within the writers' room.

The creative crafts of the entertainment industry have historically been less difficult environments for LGBTQ (lesbian, gay, bisexual, transgender, queer) workers than other professions. That said, integration has not been easy. Jasmine Love, writer on *The District*, opted for the term *heterosexism* rather than *homophobia* when describing her experiences working in television. She saw institutional bias play out when producers assumed that she could not write heterosexual stories.[62] Dava Savel, who was showrunner on *Ellen* when the character and actor came out, was fired just before receiving an Emmy for writing on the series. Soon after coming out, the star decided to let go of the whole writers' room and repopulate it with gay and lesbian writers.[63] As Henderson deftly argues, homogenization is of primary import for many in positions of power in the industry.

Some minorities arguably have an upper hand in the industry, most notably Jewish writers, especially in the comedy genre. As Neal Gabler details in *An Empire of Their Own*, every studio head in Hollywood during the studio system was Jewish,[64] and even today the number of Jews in the entertainment industry is disproportionately larger than national figures. Ring Lardner Jr. remembers being asked by Paul Jarrico whether the close ties between Lardner, Hugo Butler, Dalton Trumbo, Ian McClellan Hunter, and Michael Wilson resulted because they were all gentiles in a largely Jewish community. Hunter replied that in fact their friendship was based on their proclivity toward hard drinking.[65] Although some of my interviewees discussed the usefulness of being conversant in cultural Judaism, race and gender were much more significant markers in defining writers' experiences of identity within the industry and their feelings of insider or outsider status.

The Story Begins

In 1978, the Writers Guild established a committee to preserve the memories of its members as part of a vast oral history project.[66] A bulletin in the monthly newsletter encouraged writers from the East and West branches of the organization to be interviewed at the WGAw branch headquarters about salient moments in Guild history they remembered. Had they witnessed the Guild's formation? How did they feel about the blacklist? The notice beckoned: "However memory serves you, rightly or wrongly, the object is to capture, not the dry recounting of absolute fact or dates, but the vibrancy and texture of the times as lived by the membership through the various period of the Guild. . . . This is *your* history as *you* lived it. The brickbats and bouquets."[67] Erna Lazarus, writer on *The Donna Reed Show*, was one of the ninety-four professionals who answered this call. Her recollections of her adventures as a founding member of the SWG and one of the first women to build a steady career in the Hollywood studios bridged more than three decades of turbulence and triumph. At the end of her interview, Lazarus struggled to find words to express her gratitude for the Writers Guild. Not surprisingly, this veteran screenwriter conjured a film that could tell the tale of the writers:

> I just wish that all the new writers could have a complete motion picture to view of what it was like from the 1930s until [the] present time, and I think then they would really appreciate what they have got. Our kids do not know what it means to [have] electric light. We do not know what it means. Our mothers, perhaps our grandmothers, knew what it was like to turn on a gaslight. So we take it all for granted. Do not take the Writers Guild of America for granted. It is a very important part of our lives and of the industry.[68]

Few historians or screenwriters today know Lazarus's name. She is one of hundreds of extraordinary writers—some legendary, others mostly forgotten—who enrich the remarkable history of an industry. So, as Margo Channing warned in razor-sharp words by Joseph Mankiewicz in *All About Eve*, "Fasten your seatbelts . . ."

IMAGE 5 Illustrated script and storyboard for the film that would become *Alice in Wonderland*, c. 1933. Screenplay by Joseph L. Mankiewicz.

Writers Guild Foundation Archive, Shavelson-Webb Library, Los Angeles

1

The Artist Employee

INTERVIEWER: Now we look back at . . . the 1930s, as the Golden Age of Hollywood–

JULIUS EPSTEIN, writer of *Casablanca*: We didn't think so at the time. We did not think it was Golden at all. Maybe a little Bronze here and there, but far from Gold [laughs].

> –*The Writer Speaks: Julius Epstein*, 1994

[David O. Selznick] even gave me a screen test, which, after he saw it, he said I was definitely going to be a writer.

> –Ring Lardner Jr., interview by the Writers Guild Oral History Project, 1978

In the winter of 1933, the steady foundation under Hollywood began to crack. Quite literally, the walls started to shake when the Long Beach earthquake rumbled its way across the Southern California landscape on March 10. But it was not the first seismic shift noted that year. In the weeks preceding it, the film studios were facing the rapidly falling box office sales. Although the wild success of sound film and audiences' desire for escapism during the dark economic times of the Depression had ensured big box office numbers for a few years, the cost of sound conversion along with a decrease in box office sales finally forced the moguls to reexamine their spending habits. This belt tightening, in turn, pushed Hollywood's creative talent to open their eyes to the potential power of unionization.

Across the United States, the situation for working and unemployed Americans was dire. In the richest country in the world, more than fifteen million workers were unemployed and looking for jobs that did not exist.[1] In the middle of this national devastation, an American president came to power who used popular media as a central means to communicate with his suffering citizens. In the first of his "fireside chats" on March 12, 1933, Franklin

Delano Roosevelt took to the radio airwaves to calm the public regarding the banking crisis, explaining clearly and in lay terms the notions of value, credit, and capitalism, and declaring a bank holiday. Roosevelt emphasized his confidence in the American people and American workers, whom he valued as "more important than gold."[2] Citizens were scared, and they were looking to their leaders for inspiration and for a clear path out of financial ruin.

The same was true for individual businesses and industries, including the Hollywood studios. The studios were indebted to stockholders and to personnel and feared that it would be impossible to pay off both debts with funds so tight. In January 1933, RKO and Paramount had gone into receivership, declaring their theater chains bankrupt.[3] Studios were unable to meet payroll. MGM cobbled together the funds to pay its employees in cash, but Universal suspended contracts, and Fox told its employees outright that they would not be paid. Across the eight major studios, the outlook was grim, and a shutdown looked likely.[4] Employees were anxious and concerned. On February 3, 1933, ten screenwriters met informally at the Knickerbocker Hotel in Hollywood to discuss a growing number of concerns. Writers working within studio walls had previously gathered under the moniker "Screen Writers Guild," or "The Writers," as a social organization. Now they gave the name "Screen Writers Guild" (SWG) new meaning and a heightened sense of urgency.[5] As stirrings of unionization began among screenwriters, the studio heads were anxious to deter any talk of the Hollywood workforce organizing. Louis B. Mayer, the MGM studio boss, stood in front of his employees with a plan to counteract the effects of the Depression.

The preceding months had been difficult for Mayer. Irving Thalberg, his vice president in charge of production, had suffered yet another heart attack—though the press reported it as only a bout of influenza. Even when Thalberg was available, tension between the two executives was on the rise.[6] The studio had barely made its payment to employees during the bank closure. At the last-minute the studio sold its lucrative Treasury bonds and in a dramatic—arguably cinematic—move, hired a private airplane on the East Coast to airdrop the cash to a line of grateful employees. Still, the studio's cash flow was drying up, and selling more bonds was not possible. MGM needed bold action and got it: Mayer called an emergency meeting and gave the performance of a lifetime. Even though the SWG's first meeting had occurred weeks before, screenwriters and historians have often seized upon this event as the moment of the Guild's formation—a narrative that makes for a grander origin story for a union of people who tell stories. Inevitably, the event's details may be embellished, but the actions have been documented in a wide array of memoirs, press reports, and oral histories. The story goes like this:

In early March 1933, Mayer called all of MGM's directors, actors, department heads, and writers to the executive studio projection room. After letting the crowd wait for more than twenty minutes, Mayer entered, unshaven—perhaps, as many have noted, for the only time in his life.[7] He was exhausted and red-eyed. In front of a massive crowd of creative personnel, Mayer declared that the studio was broke. As producer and legendary MGM story editor Samuel Marx describes: "He began with a soft utterance. 'My friends . . .' Then he broke down. Stricken, he held out his hands, supplicating, bereft of words."[8] The only way to save MGM, he implored, was for everyone to take a 50 percent pay cut. Philip Dunne tells the story as he heard it: "At the time I remember [fellow writer] Donald Ogden Stewart describing to some of us what had happened at MGM. He said Louis B. Mayer got up and pointed a finger at all the people who were listening to him saying, '*We've got to take a salary cut.*'"[9] The emphasis was on the community sharing the weight of the studio's future on their collective shoulders. Employees were given the impression that if everyone worked together, the crisis would be averted. After a pause, actor Lionel Barrymore proclaimed in his commanding, avuncular baritone, "Don't worry, L.B. We're with you."[10] But they were not. Fellow actor Wallace Beery rose from his seat and stormed out.[11] Ernest Vajda, screenwriter of *The Merry Widow*, questioned the economics of Mayer's declaration. The pay cuts, he believed, were premature: "I read the company statements, Mr. Mayer. I know our films are doing well. Maybe the other companies must do this, but our company should not."[12] Barrymore boomed back: "Mr. Vajda is like a man who stops for a manicure on his way to the guillotine." At this point, according to some accounts, the entire room went into peals of laughter and applause; others suggest that the chuckles were more dutiful.[13] The drama continued.

May Robson, an Australian-born actress who began her career as a Vitagraph star in 1916, rose from her chair and declared with great aplomb, "As the oldest person in the room, I will take the cut." As if working from a script, eight-year-old child star Freddie Bartholomew took his cue and piped up, "As the youngest person in the room, I'll take the cut."[14] It was then, when Mayer had the full attention of his audience, that he called for a vote to show a declaration of allegiance and a willingness to accept the salary reduction. Frances Goodrich, screenwriter for *The Thin Man, It's a Wonderful Life*, and *Father of the Bride*, remembered, "Everyone got pious and scared." The vote was cast with tears of solidarity, and the employees agreed to accept the loss in pay. Mayer promised that he would personally see to it that every penny was reimbursed someday. The tone was solemn as the room was rocked by the new reality of Hollywood economics. But walking back across the iron bridge to the front office buildings, Samuel Marx overheard Mayer gloating to his right-hand man and talent expert Benny Thau, "So! How did I do?"[15] Albert Hackett, Goodrich's husband and writing partner, said of the meeting, "Oh, that L. B. Mayer, he created more Communists that day than Karl Marx."[16]

As at other studios, there was economic necessity behind Mayer's appeal to his talent for retrenchment. Across Hollywood, creative workers took pay cuts and ensured their studios' safe financial grounding. Lester Cole, writer of *Objective, Burma!*, remembers how forty employees of Paramount Pictures were invited into a projection room to hear that the Depression gave the studio no choice but to cut the salaries of actors, directors, and writers by 50 percent.[17] The dramatic slashing of incomes was later cited in part as a pretense, a subterfuge play-acted by moguls in front of employees to foster fidelity in a time of economic crisis. After six weeks, Mayer and other executives restored workers' pay to their full salaries. But the deducted sums for those six weeks were never reimbursed. And there was more to this story than Mayer let on.

While teary-eyed directors, actors, and writers voted to give back half their salaries to save the company, not everyone working at MGM or other studios was forced to make this financial sacrifice. What became apparent to the creative workers over the ensuing weeks was that two groups of personnel were never asked to cut back: the studio executives and the below-the-line (craft) employees who were covered under the International Alliance of Theatrical Stage Employees (IATSE) union contract. That the studio executives did not dock their own salaries came as little surprise; but the durability of the IATSE's contract, even in the face of budget cuts, provided insight and inspiration to embryonic creative talent unions.

Only a few weeks before the MGM meeting, IATSE workers, angered at the possibility of pay cuts, considered a strike across the studios and flatly refused the reductions. The union argued that its members were not paid well enough to be able to afford the cuts and still feed their families. At

MGM, Thalberg's biographer wrote, most employees were performing "back-breaking work with few guarantees, little protection, and no rights."[18] Though they were paid little, their jobs were vital. Studio heads Jack Warner of Warner Bros., Harry Cohn of Columbia, Carl Laemmle of Universal, Winfield Sheehan of Fox, and Mayer gathered and ultimately agreed not to cut the earnings of those who made fifty dollars or less a week. Cognizant of the critical role these workers played in the daily functioning of the production machinery, the moguls bent to this massive union. For the first time, a union held its ground against the industry. Although word of this victory did not reach the talent in time, writers, directors, and actors agreed that from this point forward they would never be swindled by the studios again. As Philip Dunne remembers, Mayer's cuts and the creatives' realization of their mistreatment were "what kicked off all of the so-called talent guilds."[19] It was clear to Hollywood talent that the best way to ensure their power was to stand up to the studios as unions. For many writers, the newly formed Screen Writers Guild now looked like a necessity if they wanted to protect their wages and basic labor rights.

Although altercations between studios and employees had been common earlier, a revolution in the employment structure of the American film industry truly began in the 1930s. The below-the-line craft union's successful stand against the studio heads catalyzed the above-the-line creative talent to organize across the studios. Writers recognized that although individual contracts and salaries were manageable, protection by a union contract was more secure. The studio heads used every trick at their disposal to prevent the talent guilds—in particular the Writers Guild—from unionizing. But the transformation of the Screen Writers Guild from a social group to a trade organization was already happening, starting with a substantial increase in its membership. Two months after its first meeting in February 1933, the Guild had 173 charter members. By April, studios began to pay full salaries again and, apart from MGM, even offered retroactive pay. Guild membership had climbed to 343 active members by February 1934, far exceeding total membership during its days as a social club. In July 1934, with 640 members, the Guild started publication of the *Screen Guilds' Magazine*, a joint venture with the Screen Actors Guild (SAG). At this point, 90 percent of all screenwriters working in the industry were members of the Guild.[20] But by the end of 1936, only two years after membership reached 750, the Guild was nearing extinction. A bitter three-year jurisdictional battle ensued, ending with the US Supreme Court interceding to name the Screen Writers Guild the sole organization sanctioned to negotiate with the studios on behalf of the writers. It took another two years, until 1941, before the Guild started its first negotiations with the studios. Finally, after many twists and turns, the Guild secured its first contract with the Hollywood studios in 1942, nine years after the creation of Screen Writers Guild as a union.

This chapter reviews the state of labor for Hollywood writers in the late 1920s and early 1930s, and traces the evolution of the Screen Writers Guild from a social club into the critical era when writers battled bitterly with studio heads for jurisdiction over a screenwriters' union and for a minimum basic agreement (MBA). During this period, writers gained significantly more power within the industry, as the new technology of sound made their services markedly more critical to the success of Hollywood films. The Hollywood studios used a series of tactics to subvert the Guild's efforts to gain recognition as the sole entity allowed to represent writers in collective bargaining, that is, a system of negotiations between the studios and the writers regarding wages, terms of employment, rights, and so on. The studios' initial strategies included the formation of the Motion Picture Academy and then support of an ersatz guild, the Screen Playwrights. The battle for an MBA played out not only on studio lots but also in the US Supreme Court. Studios stalled contract talks until an MBA—and World War II—seemed inevitable. Although individual writers' contracts can exceed the provisions established in the MBA, this first agreement set the precedent for standards of treatment and payment for screenwriters and provided a foundation for the system of contract negotiations still used today. The final achievement for the Guild out of this battle, namely, jurisdiction over screenwriters and a Guild contract with signatories, forever redefined the relationship between studios and writers.

Professionalization and the Status of Writers and Writing in Early Hollywood

> In those thoughtless days, none of us ever associated movies with art; such "easy money" placed them in the category of striking oil.
>
> —Anita Loos (writer of *Intolerance* and *The Women*),
> *Kiss Hollywood Goodbye* (1974)

In the early days of Hollywood, writers—or, as they were known at the time, film scenarists—were in a bind. Those who found success, like Anita Loos, were paid well for their labor. But recognition, by way of screen credits, control of authorship, and respect on the set, was decidedly harder to come by. A standard clause in writers' contracts appeared some time in the 1910s, stipulating that all literary material composed, submitted, or produced by a writer during the terms of an agreement with a particular studio "shall automatically become the property of the producer who, for this purpose, shall be deemed the author thereof."[21] In other words, during the term of the contract any work written by a screenwriter, even though it *may* be credited to that person, is held under corporate authorship by the studio. Since companies began adopting this language over a century ago, producers have controlled copyright. But the clause takes possession one step further: studios are legally defined not just as the owners but also as the authors of a writer's work. In 1916, the *New York Times* quoted an Authors League statement that the "conditions in the motion picture industry are more unsatisfactory than in any other field in which an author is active. The author is practically at the mercy of irresponsible and dishonest producers. Piracy is rampant and redress uncertain, copyright questions are obscure and contract matters are chaotic."[22] The article listed long and varied complaints by screenwriters, including underpayment, outrageous delays in returning scripts, butchering of scripts, plagiarism of stories, and ambiguous contracts.

It was in this environment in the fall of 1920 that the Screen Writers Guild established an affiliation with the Authors League of America (itself a part of the Dramatists Guild), with a short-lived eastern branch of the SWG appearing the following June. In the spring of 1921, members of the Guild bought a building on Las Palmas and Sunset Boulevard, thereby launching "the first motion picture professional club to be established in the capitol of the industry."[23] The clubhouse became a shared space for the Guild to hold its professional meetings and for the launching of a social group, "The Writers," that summer.[24] The Writers held parties, plays, and other events for members and industry insiders. But the series of goals that members laid out for themselves defined this new group as an organization dedicated to protecting the work and livelihood of writers and as a precursor to an organized union.[25] Their mission was to defend the rights of screenwriters, to elevate their status, and to redefine the relationship between writer and producer. Concerns focused on ensuring copyright protection of manuscripts and film scenarios, establishing freedom from censorship, securing credits for both original author and screen author for adaptations, safeguarding fair compensation, and insisting

IMAGE 6 The Writers, the first home of the social club known as the Screen Writers Guild, from *Blue Book of the Screen*, 1923.

Writers Guild Foundation Archive, Shavelson-Webb Library, Los Angeles

on increased cooperation between writers and producers.[26] One of the young club's successful endeavors was the establishment of a grievance committee that provided basic arbitration between producers and writers.

Guild membership grew quickly for a few years, but the prosperity of the film industry, and the exorbitant salaries of many writers in Hollywood in the 1920s, ultimately made the need for membership less critical. In fact, national prosperity prevented any growth in labor groups during this period: union membership across the country declined from over five million in 1920 to three and a half million in 1924.[27] The organization relaxed its dues policies, and as Ring Lardner Jr. remembers, it never even had a consistent method for questioning a member's standing.[28] Increasingly, the Guild became a social club, and during the 1920s it also became less important to writers as a policy-making organization. The leadership never brought to the fore the central issue of salary minimums. The larger desire was for the elevation of the status of the writer: writers saw their role as essential, and they wanted not just compensation but also acknowledgment of their creative labor. Writers' early demands included equal prominence with the names of other key players (director, producer, star) in the credits as well as in marketing and advertising.[29] Because of the lack of ownership over their material, some writers found themselves in a predicament if they stayed too long at one studio or went on vacation. Frederica Sagor, writer of *The Plastic Age*, pointed to the pressures of working in an industry where rights were minimal: "Whether you were a writer, producer, director, cameraman, actor, or actress—it was very easy to be forgotten in filmland with so much available talent to replace you. Hard work and good credits were often not enough. Even if you were an old pro like Waldemar Young [writer of *The Lives of a Bengal Lancer*], if you stepped too far beyond the men's room, you could return and find someone else in your chair."[30]

The Screen Writers Guild did little to support writers' grievances. Sagor said that credit on a script usually went to the last writer brought on to do a rewrite: "Once in a while, there might be a sharing of credit with one of the previous writers, providing he or she had sufficient clout to demand it. Otherwise, the last writer hired snatched the merry-go-round gold ring."[31] Few studios were concerned about writers. A rare exception was Samuel Goldwyn's short-lived Eminent Authors project, which tried to use a writers-as-stars system to sell pictures. (Many of these authors did not transition well to writing for the screen, and the project proved unprofitable.[32]) It was the writers' wish for a bigger role in authorship and status, a stance they would continue to define over time, that angered and exasperated producers in their dealings with these upstart employees.

The studios controlled writers' working conditions and the content of their scripts. Producers limited writers to stories they imagined audiences wanted to see, suggesting to writers that they stick to optimistic or cheerful scenarios. Frances Marion, who wrote *The Champ* and adapted *Camille* and *Rebecca of Sunnybrook Farm*, explained: "We writers were fed to the teeth with Love and Happy Endings. But what could we do? The bosses told us that if we wanted to write bleak, realistic stories which ended unhappily we could spin our yarns for magazines or publishers of books. The movies must be heart-lifting, not eyebrow-lifting."[33] Marion's description hints at the threats of film censorship that began in the late 1920s and continued for the next two decades.

With the coming of sound in 1928, Hollywood needed not just stories but also spoken words. Suddenly there was a desperate call for scribes who were facile with dialogue. "It was the era where the word became the most important thing in the picture business," said Bernard Schubert, writer of *Mark of the Vampire* and *The Mummy's Curse*, who was under contract at RKO during this flurry of hiring for writers. "This was the era—definitely the era of the written word—the spoken word."[34] The excitement over the pleasures and the promise of the talkies was not just for audiences—or the moguls who saw dollar signs attached to every song sung or bon mot quipped by a star on the screen. Producers demanded that writers carefully develop scripts and build detail into the action. The days of vague plot outlines were over. Now, the emphasis was on the specifics of each character's language. Dudley Nichols, who in the coming years would write *Bringing Up Baby*, *Stagecoach*, and *Scarlet Street*, delighted in these new creative opportunities: "In spite of its complicated mechanics, the motion picture is, in the present writer's opinion, the most flexible and exciting storytelling medium in the world. Its possibilities are enthralling. It is a continual challenge to the writer. With talk has come *character*, the one phase of human existence that never palls in interest. When people talk, they reveal themselves. And once you have character, and its endless diversity and interest, you will never run out of 'stories.' Character itself is the best of all stories."[35] With the coming of sound, Nichols argued, cinema had become a more plastic, even a more captivating medium. This transformation was the result not simply of the technology or the inclusion of sound and words, but rather depended on how sound brought depth into character and story.

Writers who specialized in dialogue and incorporated words and language into their work were suddenly in high demand. Screenwriters who got their start during this time included Nichols, Ring Lardner Jr., John Bright (who wrote *The Public Enemy* and *She Done Him Wrong*), Herman Mankiewicz (writer of *Dinner at Eight* and *Citizen Kane*), Laurence Stallings (writer of *The Big Parade* and *She Wore a Yellow Ribbon*), Nunnally Johnson (who wrote *The Grapes of Wrath* and *The Woman in the Window*), and Alvah Bessie (who wrote *Objective, Burma!*). After Mankiewicz arrived in Hollywood in 1925, his unofficial and ironically titled "Fresh Air Fund" lured a dozen more East Coast writers out to the Los Angeles sunshine.[36] He famously sent a telegram to his friend Ben Hecht: "WILL YOU ACCEPT THREE HUNDRED PER WEEK TO WORK FOR PARAMOUNT PICTURES. ALL EXPENSES PAID. THE THREE HUNDRED IS PEANUTS. MILLIONS ARE TO BE GRABBED OUT HERE AND YOUR ONLY COMPETITION IS IDIOTS. DON'T LET THIS GET AROUND."[37] Julius Epstein also received a telegram from writer friends in Hollywood: "OFFER YOU A JOB AS OUR SECRETARY. $25 A WEEK. ROOM AND BOARD. HOP A BUS." He arrived on a Friday evening in October 1933, and by midnight he was writing a scene that was due on Monday. "On Sunday they took me to the Paramount Theatre and the picture was *College Humor*, with Bing Crosby and Mary Carlisle. And they said to me, 'That's a close-up, that's a fade-out.' They gave me what was later to be a four-year college film school education in one afternoon."[38] By 1935, Epstein and his brother Philip were writing dozens of pictures.

Threats of film censorship during this time were of increasing concern, for studios as well as for writers. Debates about censorship started in the 1910s with city and state film boards; demands for new laws controlling content appeared throughout the 1910s and 1920s.[39] To circumvent censorship at the state and local levels, the studios created the Motion Picture Producers and Distributors of America (MPPDA), which directed that all films conform to its "Don'ts and Be Carefuls" rules starting in 1927. These rules were replaced by a stricter Production Code in 1930, monitored by the newly formed Production Code Administration starting in 1934. Writers felt that these idiosyncratic mandates, though not officially censorship, were similarly oppressive. No divorces, no affairs, no representations of homosexuality.[40] Ben Hecht, who scripted *Scarface, Spellbound*, and *Notorious* and was regularly called in as a script doctor, recounted the advice his friend and fellow scenarist Herman Mankiewicz gave him about writing characters according to Hollywood logic.

> "I want to point out to you," said Manky, "that in a novel a hero can lay ten girls and marry a virgin for a finish. In a movie this is not allowed. The hero, as well as the heroine, has to be a virgin. The villain can lay anybody he wants, have as much fun as he wants, cheating and stealing, getting rich and whipping the servants, but you have to shoot him in the end. When he falls with the bullet in his forehead, it is advisable that he clutch at the Gobelin tapestry on the library wall and bring it down over his head like a symbolic shroud. Also covered by such tapestry, the actor does not have to hold his breath while he is being photographed as a dead man."[41]

Some writers would try to add a few risqué scenes, hoping that one might survive the MPPDA's vetting process and make it onto the screen.[42] Writers were deeply frustrated by the limitations of censorship, as were producers: on this they could agree. But they could do little in the face of protests from organizations such as the Catholic Legion of Decency. Overall, writers had to give producers what they wanted, no questions asked. And if they did not produce what was expected of them, producers would threaten to start pulling scripts from the more than 40,000 that arrived in Los Angeles annually from aspiring writers.[43]

With each studio churning out fifty to sixty films a year, studios were desperate for material. Novelists and dramatists were lured to Hollywood for their talent—and for their names. Aldous Huxley adapted *Pride and Prejudice* and *Jane Eyre*, P. G. Wodehouse reworked one of his short stories for *A Damsel in Distress*, Lillian Hellman wrote *Dead End* and adapted her play *The Little Foxes*, Nathanael West scripted *It Could Happen to You!* and *Five Came Back*, Dashiell Hammett wrote *Watch on the Rhine*, Dorothy Parker worked on the original *A Star Is Born* and *Saboteur*, George S. Kaufman wrote *A Night at the Opera*, Moss Hart adapted his play *Winged Victory* and wrote *Hans Christian Andersen*, and F. Scott Fitzgerald wrote *Three Comrades*. Many arrived on the Santa Fe Railway's Chief during the 1920s. However, it is worth noting that the first substantial wave left New York only *after* the literary market started to collapse. The migration was instigated by neither the coming of sound nor the stock market crash. Richard Fine estimates that 138 writers working in the Los Angeles film industry between 1927 and 1938 were eastern transplants, most from theater, newspapers, magazines, publishing houses, and literary agencies.[44] Of these, about 30 percent came before 1930; the percentage would increase to 50 percent by 1933. The rest came over the next few years. As John Schultheiss has documented, there was also a regular stream of British authors moving through Los Angeles during those years.[45] Expatriate writers arrived from Europe in the mid-1930s, many of them fleeing the Nazis. Distinguished writers descended upon Los Angeles, renting out bungalows, basking in the sunshine, and trying to harness their skills for a new medium. Many considered screenwriting a sideline occupation secondary to their true profession. Some were quite successful; others found the pay and the parties more alluring than trying to work for boorish producers and studio heads.

The famous novelists courted by producers and invited to their parties often struggled in this new industry. One of those notoriously unmoored was F. Scott Fitzgerald, who was shocked when he came to Los Angeles and realized, "This is no art. This is an industry."[46] Thinking back on his first difficulties, Fitzgerald explained that he was not so much above the industry

IMAGE 7 Members of the social club The Writers. c. 1930.

Screen Writers' Guild Records, 1921–1954, Writers Guild Foundation Archive, Shavelson-Webb Library, Los Angeles

as baffled by it. "The truth is that I got scared. I was scared by the hullaballoo over my arrival, and when they took me into a projection room to see a picture and kept assuring me it was all going to be very, very easy, I got flustered."[47] While he perfectly captured the characters of Hollywood in his novel *The Last Tycoon*, Fitzgerald, like many other writers, could not adapt his novelistic skills to script form. Billy Wilder, who wrote *Ninotchka, Double Indemnity, Sunset Blvd.*, and *Some Like it Hot*, described the irony of Fitzgerald's failure in Hollywood: "He made me think of a great sculptor who is hired to do a plumbing job. He did not know how to connect the pipes so that the water would flow."[48] Wilder's comment speaks to a sense of hierarchy of the two writing forms: novel writing as art, screenwriting as skilled labor. And yet no single group of writers entering Hollywood succeeded more than another in terms of their ability to translate their talent to scriptwriting. Some playwrights had great success, as their knowledge of dialogue was invaluable, and journalists had the ability to write at great speed. Virtually all of them, though, had to adjust to the rules of Hollywood, where producers controlled not just the script but also the writers themselves through a legal contrivance known as the long-term contract.

Studio heads and producers were shrewd showmen and often ruthless overseers. Writers were expected to write every day on the job, as Jack Warner reminded his stable with a memo. One of their key instruments of control was the seven-year contract, which stipulated that the studio had no obligation to hold on to a writer as an employee for more than six months at a time, but that the writer was obligated to remain with the studio under the terms of the original contract if the studio chose to exercise its semi-annual options, which it had the right to do for seven years. Some successful writers, like Philip and Julius Epstein, were quite prolific; the pair wrote seven scripts in 1935, all of which were made into films. But their success did not guarantee a pay raise.[49] For young writers, this was a "kind of indentured servitude,"[50] because the contract also transferred to the studio all rights to a writer's material.

Studios even looked ahead, adding into contracts new technologies that were still in the development phase but might prove profitable down the road. For example, when the first television sets appeared in the late 1920s, even though telecommunication would not be a viable delivery system on a popular level until the late 1940s, the studios included clauses regarding television in writers' contracts. Devery Freeman, who wrote *Ziegfeld Follies* and for *The Loretta Young Show*, remembered:

> This was a time when . . . studios took the philosophy that when they hired a writer they were buying his ideas, they owned them forever in perpetuity. . . . My first contract . . . you would see that they would throw in everything but the kitchen sink in terms of the future. The future that they didn't know about. They were tying up television rights. . . . Now [when I signed that contract,] television didn't exist. . . . Perhaps a picture was being sent experimentally, but television didn't exist. It was just a remote long-range billion-to-one shot theatrically to most of our way of thinking, yet, just on the off chance, it was put into contracts. I know it was in my contracts.[51]

With control of content and of contracts, studio heads monitored writers, their writing, and, in many ways, writers' ability to move up in status in Hollywood. Producers could change scripts at will without the writer's agreement or even knowledge. Thalberg regularly had a series of writers working on the same script, not only to ensure that he could get the story he wanted, but also to guarantee that his stars would not be idled by a script delay.

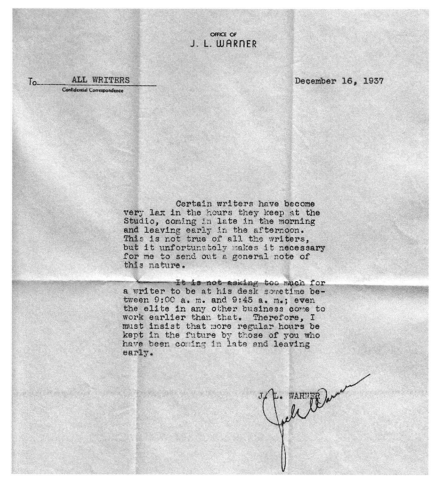

IMAGE 8 After getting this letter from Jack Warner, writers Julius and Philip Epstein called a meeting with Warner to tell him they finally found the perfect ending to *Casablanca*. They came up with it at 8:30 A.M.

Screen Writers Guild Records, 1921–1954, Writers Guild Foundation Archive, Shavelson-Webb Library, Los Angeles

Thalberg's biographer explained: "In a deadline situation, he often sought the inspiration of two or more writers. He reasoned that he couldn't afford to wait for one writer to come up with a solution he so sorely needed."[52] William Ludwig described the frustrations attached to this common practice: "You never knew who else was working on your material. There could be six, eight, ten, twelve [writers] working on the same thing. You didn't know whose script was eventually going to be used or if any one script was going to be used. They might say they wanted my first scene and your second scene and somebody would patch it together and you had no way of determining it."[53]

For this reason, writers had great difficulty in securing credits, even when they were deserved. Sometimes one writer would redraft another's script entirely. Others became experts on endings, on love scenes, or in punching up comedy. Still, producers often assigned writers because they were available rather than because they were good at a particular type of script.[54] Carey Wilson, who wrote *Ben-Hur: A Tale of the Christ* and *Mutiny on the Bounty*, was one of those writers Thalberg depended upon for last-minute rewrites. Whether Wilson's changes were substantive or not, Thalberg always compensated him not just with pay but also with his name in the credits. Donald Ogden Stewart, who adapted *The Philadelphia Story* and *Holiday* for the screen, argued, much like Frederica Sagor, that the best way to ensure credit was to be the last writer before the start of production: "It became a game to be the last one before they started shooting so that you would not be eased out of screen credit."[55] Those writers who learned to work the system used their success to demand solo credits, to affiliate with a particular producer or director who appreciated their skills and respected their writing, or to become directors or producers themselves.[56] Preston Sturges wrote and directed *Sullivan's Travels* and *The Lady Eve*; Nunnally Johnson wrote and directed *The Man in the Gray Flannel Suit* and *The Three Faces of Eve*; Ernst Lubitsch wrote or co-wrote many of his films before coming to the United States and continued the tradition when he arrived in Hollywood; and Billy Wilder co-wrote and directed *The Lost Weekend, Sunset Blvd.*, and *The Apartment.* Among those who became producers were Charles Brackett, who co-wrote and produced *The Lost Weekend* and *Sunset Blvd.*; Joan Harrison, who wrote *Rebecca* and *Foreign Correspondent* and produced *Alfred Hitchcock Presents*; and Dore Schary, who wrote *Boys Town* and later worked for many years as head of production at MGM and was eventually made president of the studio.

It was in this environment that the Academy of Motion Picture Arts and Sciences was formed in May 1927, with a dinner party for thirty-six in the Crystal Ballroom of the Biltmore Hotel as its first event. The Academy was Louis B. Mayer's brainchild: he intended it to be a mediating agency that ideally could curb any talk of further creative or craft organizing. The Academy would bring together prominent producers, directors, actors, writers, and technicians. Potentially anyone "who had contributed in a distinguished way to the arts and sciences of Motion Picture Production" was eligible to be voted in as a member.[57] This vague terminology was precisely what the studio heads liked best: it allowed them to exclude possible troublemakers. Officially, the Academy was designed to arbitrate between concerned parties, but in actuality it was a mock company union intended to repress further unionization. For five years, by rallying around the Academy, the studios were able to keep talent from mobilizing through the start of the Depression.

Even though the Guild and the Academy offered some arbitration, there was no codified method to adjudicate credits when a dispute arose about whose name should appear on a film. Attribution is critical to a writer's ability to build a reputation, and a writer with a good reputation could garner better writing assignments and better wages. Under the seven-year contract, writers struggled to make a name for themselves within the profession, whether or not they came to Hollywood with previous success. Many writers were ultimately just cogs in the wheel of the studio system—or, as Aldous Huxley remarked, prisoners to it. At every studio, he wrote, there were "rows and rows of hutches, each containing an author on a long contract at a weekly salary. You see their anxious little faces peering through the bars. . . . There are authors on some lots whom nobody has seen for years. It's like the Bastille."[58] The cultural myth of Hollywood as a place that ruined literary and theatrical writers is a common one. As Richard Fine argues in his study of 138 writers who came to Hollywood, "The members of this group . . . lie at the heart of the Hollywood-as-destroyer legend, for it is their experience which initially provoked complaint about the studios' treatment of its imported writing talent. . . . Not all writers came to sad ends in Hollywood, then, but virtually *every* writer was disquieted or unnerved by the experience."[59]

Many writers came to Hollywood in the 1920s and 1930s for the money and not for the status or for the recognition. However, once they became a part of the industry, they realized the tremendous injustices toward workers within the studio system. Edmund North, who wrote *In a Lonely Place, The Day the Earth Stood Still*, and *Patton*, described their treatment: "I don't want to suggest here that the life of a screenwriter in those days resembled that of a galley slave. What I am trying to say is that management treated writers with a high-handed disdain that made possible, if not inevitable, the creation of a Writers Guild."[60] Still, some groups in Hollywood had succeeded in coming to terms with the studios. In 1929, the American Society of Cinematographers negotiated a five-year contract guaranteeing a minimum wage of $50 a day or $200 a week, along with basic working conditions, such as a fifty-four hour maximum work week, and a closed shop agreement, meaning that the studios would hire only union members in good standing. But the cinematographers were the anomaly within the industry, and they also settled their negotiations the summer before the stock market crashed.[61] As writers soon learned after Louis B. Mayer's performance in the spring of 1933, most employees were without recourse. The position of Hollywood workers was clear: those with unions and collective bargaining agreements behind them refused the cuts; those without negotiated contracts had little, if any, choice. After the lies they were told by their bosses about the state of the studios, writers decided to reestablish their former social club and create a labor union under the same name.

Formation of the Guild and the Academy Battle

In April 1933, the Screen Writers Guild drafted its first contract for the studios to sign. The intention of the document was basic: to establish uniform working conditions for all writers within the motion picture industry. Salary cuts like those instituted by Mayer had strengthened writers' determination to fight back against this manipulation of compensation. They also considered other demands, such as control over the allocation of screen credits and restoring some authorial control to writers, but decided against them. As Christopher Wheaton explains, part of what made the Hollywood unions unique at this moment was that they were not fighting for better wages or better working conditions; rather, their primary goal was to keep the status quo in the face of studio rollbacks during the Depression. Above all, the Hollywood talent guilds were defensive entities.[62]

The first Screen Writers Guild union meetings crackled with excitement as writers debated plans for unionization. John Howard Lawson, who had come to Los Angeles five years earlier after a successful career as a playwright on Broadway, became the Guild's first president. Frances Marion was elected vice president, and Joseph Mankiewicz was voted in as secretary. Marion's position among the elected officials was no surprise. At the time, many women had successful careers as screenwriters, including prolific veterans like June Mathis (writer of *The Four Horsemen of the Apocalypse*), Jeanie Macpherson (*Male and Female*), and Sonya Levien (*The Hunchback of Notre*

Dame). In the early days of the Guild as a labor organization, female screenwriters played a fundamental role in ensuring its success. Lizzie Francke argues that female screenwriters volunteered for the Guild in its earliest days as a way to channel their varied frustrations with their profession. The organization rewarded some for this hard work, and these women rose to positions of power within the union.[63]

Each new member promised to bring other writers as guests to the meetings, with hopes that these visitors would soon join the Guild. Membership was available based on a merit system. Active membership required meeting one of three criteria: three months of studio employment as a staff writer, a screen credit for a feature film, or three screen credits on film shorts. Writers who had not yet received credit on a film but were being paid by a studio were given junior status. Working with fellow writers, members courted new members, explaining their plan to end the tyranny of the long-term contract. Frances Marion remembers tackling this task with Anita Loos and Bess Meredyth, writer of *The Mark of Zorro*: "Anita, Bess, and I drew into these meetings other writers who had long-term contracts like ours [who] felt as we did toward the newcomers who had been fighting for credits on movies to which they had contributed, and for protection against being dismissed without cause. The contracts given to these potential scenarists abounded in clauses, and many [writers] had been let go before they had had an opportunity to prove their worth."[64] That desire to support younger, less experienced, or lower-paid employees was something writers continually mentioned in these conversations about the establishment of the Guild as a trade union. Lawson contacted Louise Silcox, head of the Dramatists Guild, to tell her of the screenwriters' newfound success, mentioning how writers on top were looking out for writers at the bottom of the pay scale: "You will be glad to hear that the re-birth of the Screen Writers Guild is being accomplished with tremendous success and enthusiasm: in fact, a more immediate response than we had even dared to hope . . . the rush to sign and pay at last night's meeting, and the solid support of the Screen Writers Guild was so heartening that I have not quite recovered from the excitement: many people spontaneously offered two and three hundred dollars [to cover dues] for those writers who could not afford the payment."[65] Writers were not as keen on unionization as they were on opening up lines of communication and negotiation between themselves and studio heads. The reorganized structure of the Screen Writers Guild became the model for the formation of both the Screen Actors Guild and the Directors Guild of America. With President Roosevelt in the White House and labor leader John L. Lewis spearheading the new Congress of Industrial Organizations (CIO), it was a time of increased interest in unionization. Labor was on the rise across the country, and the climate in Hollywood was such that its creative workers were interested.

The SWG's immediate priorities were to stop imminent pay cuts and to gain control of the allocation of screen credits. Writers wanted a standardized system that would ensure that a writer deserving attribution would get it. As it was, the studios had control. Only when they saw their films in a theater would writers know whether they would be credited for their work or whether they would have to share attribution with a producer or his pet employee of the moment. As Nancy Lynn Schwartz explains:

> For writers in Hollywood, then as now, a screen credit is the only form of identity he has. Faceless, and generally three pictures down the road by the time a film is finally made, the screen credit, whether it reads "Screenplay By," "Original Screenplay By," "Screenplay Based on the Novel By," "Story By," or "Additional Dialogue By," tells the world the writer was there. A writer can work for years and make an exceedingly respectable living without ever seeing his name on the screen. . . . The level of income rises in direct proportion to screen credits, which prove a writer to be a good risk, and the writer with the longest and best list of credits has the safest berth.[66]

Stopping the capricious allocation of credits was critical to writers and to their new guild. It was not simply recognition or acclaim that writers sought. Rather, with more film titles to their names, especially more substantial films, writers might be able to renegotiate their contracts and leverage a pay increase.

Some writers whose personal contracts were up around this time began putting clauses into their new contracts to ensure that whatever terms they agreed to as individuals would not hurt the Guild's collective bargaining agreement. Sonya Levien informed her studio that she was unable to sign a new contract pending the preparation of the Code of Practice and Procedure.[67] In response, the studio's lawyers suggested that if the contract met Levien's approval, she sign it and leave it with her lawyer, to be released only after the Guild had resolved its negotiations.[68] She agreed, but her lawyer sent on the contract before negotiations were completed. Sadly, she had allowed the studio to get exactly what it wanted: a signed contract that went behind the back of the Guild. Not surprisingly, this example was only the beginning. Studio heads fought the Guild with a degree of viciousness that few writers saw coming.

Many of these writers were young, in their mid-twenties and early thirties, and were going up against the paternalistic structure of the industry. Fay Kanin, writer of *Tell Me Where It Hurts*, explained how many young and ambitious writers were not taken seriously: "Today a young person is very much welcomed into the industry, as you know, because they [producers] feel the audience is young and the young people have a kind of way to communicate with their contemporaries. But in that day and age, young was a dirty word in terms of getting a job in the movie industry."[69] A young writer was also much easier for a producer to push around. Although some studio heads like Harry Cohn at Columbia were willing to play along with the SWG at first, Louis B. Mayer threatened to throw out any writers under contract with MGM who joined the union.

When the SWG suggested that writers withdraw as members from the Motion Picture Academy of Arts and Sciences, the studio heads took notice. Thalberg regarded his writers' unionization as a personal affront: "How can you do this to me?" he bellyached. He could not understand why they would ever want to organize: "Those writers are living like kings. Why on earth would they want to join a union, like coal miners or plumbers?"[70] The comparison of creative workers with blue-collar employees was part of a larger strategy that the studio heads had been using for years and would continue to employ against writers. Writers would have to go up against their own egos and discard the notion that they were "artists" if they were to accept their position in the way the SWG needed to define it—as employees.

When Upton Sinclair won the Democratic nomination for the governorship of California in 1934, a group of writers set up an "authors committee" to raise funds for his election. In response, the studio heads did everything in their power to stop Sinclair and undermine writers' support for his candidacy. As Ian Hamilton observes, the nascent SWG adopted a resolution that condemned the studios for their tactics and "implied coercion and intimidation."[71] This early political action is significant as the Guild's first step in speaking out on issues external to the realm of creative work, as well as in taking a position on national- and state-level politics that countered the voice of the studios. As Allen Rivkin, a founding member of the SWG and writer of *Dancing Lady*, remembered, "We rebelled, because we felt the man had the right to a fair campaign and that we had the right to speak for ourselves. It was democracy in action and a rebellion against the control of the studios over our non-studio lives."[72]

The national movement toward unionization was a part of this difficult era. President Roosevelt's National Industrial Recovery Act (NIRA) affected not just blue-collar workers but white-collar workers as well. Under the NIRA and the authority of the National Recovery Administration (NRA), which created a Motion Picture Code, the government suggested that Hollywood's newly formed creative guilds all coalesce under the auspices of the Academy. The government's plan for cooperative action seemed acceptable at first, and SWG and SAG were eager to garner national support.[73] But the Academy pushed back with so many provisions that it lost this opportunity for negotiation and created an angrier and more determined union movement. "Instead of gaining power by cozying up to the NRA regulators," Tom Kemper argues, "the Academy managed to mobilize and strengthen the opposition, inspiring stronger pushes for unions by writers, directors, and actors."[74]

It quickly became clear to the two guilds that the code openly favored studio employers. As Larry Ceplair and Steven Englund note, the guilds "soon discovered, along with other newly formed unions around the country, that the NIRA was not a silver platter, but a brass bell opening round one of a violent struggle over union recognition and industrial reform in America."[75] Ceplair and Englund detail how the NIRA failed to recognize the authority of the newly founded guilds and lacked a mechanism to improve the status of writers and actors. The guilds quickly went to work to stop the NIRA. SWG president Lawson said, "We're going to fight. We won't allow them to place the burden for all their waste and inefficiency on the creative talent which is responsible for every dollar brought into the box office."[76] Using every social tie they had in Washington, the two guilds held off the controversial provisions of the Motion Picture Code of the NIRA. In May 1935 the NIRA itself was declared unconstitutional by the US Supreme Court, which at the time was extremely hostile to Roosevelt's New Deal legislation. Rather than place power in the hands of the Academy, Roosevelt's administration suggested five-by-five committees (five writers paired with five producers, or five actors paired with five producers), which would oversee disputes regarding wages and hours for their respective constituencies. *Variety* prematurely reported that the Academy was "about to fold up completely and fall into the ash-can of oblivion," but the moguls would not give up so easily.[77]

Intimidation and control were the moguls' first line of defense. The studio heads countered writers' efforts by instituting a series of measures that restricted their rights. Writers were allowed to work only with particular producers on specific projects; as a result, the total number of writers employed at any time by the studios declined.[78] As Ceplair and Englund detail, MGM dropped ten writers in one week, and more writers were finding themselves on week-to-week contracts or per-picture deals. They also document how some blacklisting occurred at the major studios against a few of the more active heads of the SWG. These acts did not amount to much, as most of the writers were quickly scooped up by competing studios, but it was "a taste of what was to come."[79] Everyone observing these changes in the behavior of the front office was on edge. Frances Marion recalls in her autobiography, "We would not have blinked had L.B. [Mayer] roared out a threat to close the studio unless we gave up the [Guild] idea, but when Irving Thalberg made this threat in chilling tones we were shocked into a dread silence which revealed his enormous power over us."[80]

The moguls' second line of defense, the Academy, was still the organization through which they tried to wield their power. First they stalled the five-by-five committees for as long as possible. Then, when Academy negotiators finally did show up for meetings, they rejected every proposal the writers and actors placed on the table. When the NIRA was declared unconstitutional in May 1935, the five-by-five committees dissolved.[81] The moguls argued that the Academy was the only trade organization that was needed. But Guild writers and the actors who had joined SAG knew that the Academy was really a sweetheart organization for the studios disguised as a mediatory union. The SWG and SAG thus banded together in these early years, sharing legal counsel as they worked against the Motion Picture Code and the constraints of the Motion Pictures Producers Association. As Harry Tugend, writer of *Pocketful of Miracles*, remembered, "The membership meetings were more frequent, louder, until they woke up the news media."[82]

The crisis between the Guilds and the Academy peaked on Oscar night in 1936 with the national news media in attendance.[83] Outside the Roosevelt Hotel on Hollywood Boulevard, members of the SAG and the SWG protested the event, insisting that the Academy Awards did not fairly represent all members of the motion picture community. Inside the hotel, when Dudley Nichols won for his adaptation of Liam O'Flaherty's novel *The Informer*, he stood up and declared that he refused to accept the award. Nichols's shaming of the studio heads on their most self-congratulatory night made clear to the studios that any guise of the Academy as a mediating unit between management and employees had disappeared. The curtain had lifted on their union-busting scheme.

Though the NIRA was lost, the Wagner Act of 1935 brought new hope for the SWG. This piece of legislation guaranteed collective bargaining for trade unions with jurisdiction over a particular industry. It outlawed company unions and prohibited coercion and blacklisting. The act established the National Labor Relations Board (NLRB), which adjudicated disputes regarding which union might represent a group of workers as well as union violations. The key for mobilized writers was to establish the Screen Writers Guild

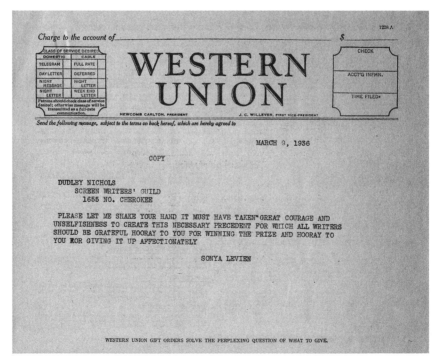

IMAGE 9 Telegram from Sonya Levien to Dudley Nichols, after Nichols refused the Academy Award for *The Informer* in 1936.

Screen Writers Guild Records, 1921–1954, Writers Guild Foundation Archive, Shavelson-Webb Library, Los Angeles

as the one-and-only trade organization with jurisdiction over all screenwriters. But studio heads had other plans. First, the moguls spent almost two years challenging the constitutionality of the Wagner Act; second, when that tactic failed in 1937, they argued that the motion picture industry was outside of the jurisdiction of the Wagner Act because the vast majority of its work took place in California and should not be considered by the US government as interstate commerce.[84]

Despite these actions, the SWG kept fighting, and writers became hopeful not just about jurisdiction within the industry but also about the possibility of increased power through amalgamation with the more established Authors League of America. Here was the chance to become a professional organization that would carry weight with other forms of writing outside Hollywood. The SWG executive board listed for its members thirteen potential benefits of amalgamation, including control of credits, fair arbitration, a prohibition on blacklists, a prohibition on general salary cuts, a prohibition on speculative screenplay writing for any producer, a requirement that producers purchase rights before adaptation, and notification to writers when others are hired to write on the same project for the same producer.[85] Sound made great writers invaluable to producers, since tight scripts ensured speedy production. But with so many people eager for good work, a strike, though it might affect the quality of work, would have little effect on production schedules. Amalgamation promised to give the Guild power in a strike: if all writers were unified in a syndicate, no dramatists or novelists would be available as strikebreakers if Hollywood writers went on strike. Joining a national federation was a bold endeavor that would propel the industry into a direct confrontation between producers and talent. But the writers did not stop there. They had an ace in the hole.

The leaders of the SWG proposed an addition to the amalgamated guild's bylaws. Article XII called for prohibiting contracts or options for services or the sale of any material to a studio after May 2, 1938, unless the studio was a signatory of a Guild contract. Under this provision, long-term contracts would be null and void without a Guild contract for all writers working at the studios. Producers were quick to remind writers that these acts of defiance—amalgamation, Article XII, or a possible strike—would lead to dire consequences. Thalberg reportedly told his writers, "If you wish to put all these people out of work, it is your responsibility. For, if you proceed with this strike, I shall close down the entire plant, without a single exception.

Make no mistake. I mean precisely what I say. I shall close this studio, lock the gates, and there will be an end to Metro-Goldwyn-Mayer productions. And it will be you—all you writers—who will have done it."[86] As early as 1938, Charles Brackett, in his role as president of the SWG, asked the NLRB to ensure that the Guild's membership list would remain private. If producers got hold of lists, Brackett argued, they could strong-arm or, worse, fire writers who belonged to the Guild.[87] Studio lawyers declared that amalgamation would destroy the studios and make them vulnerable to federal antitrust law as well as California's antitrust legislation, the Cartwright Act.[88] Though they accepted plenty of Wall Street money, the moguls refused to imagine making deals with a trade union of writers that was "being governed from New York."[89] This accusation, of course, made some writers bristle: they feared losing their negotiating power to playwrights and novelists.

Some highly successful screenwriters who were politically more conservative and also sympathetic to the producers—people like John Lee Mahin (*Captains Courageous*), Howard Emmett Rogers (*Libeled Lady* and *For Me and My Gal*), and James K. McGuinness (*A Girl in Every Port, A Night at the Opera*, and *Rio Grande*)—started to express distaste for the Guild's agenda. They declared that the leadership was going too far and might put the Guild in the hands of eastern Reds, a prospect they found intolerable.[90] Others found themselves wavering, wary of amalgamation but not willing to walk away from the Guild.

The primary targets of the producers' attacks were Article XII and the writers' proposal for a closed shop. The newspapers came at the Guild at full throttle, most notably William Randolph Hearst's papers and the conservative trade journal *The Hollywood Reporter*. An April 1936 editorial in Hearst's *Los Angeles Examiner* described the SWG as a self-serving group that was threatening the heart of the industry: "The beneficiaries of the industry generally should not allow greedy and selfish cliques to kill the prolific geese which have laid such marvelous golden eggs for all. There are no such other golden eggs to be found in the world."[91] A few days later an editorial in the *Los Angeles Times* asked, "Why do you want to turn over your independence to a group of men who have continuously expressed nothing but contempt for you as artists and to whose dictation the producers would never and could never submit?"[92] The public attacks were unrelenting. On May 2, the producers issued a statement: "There is not the slightest change in the position of the motion picture producers with regard to proposals to establish a closed shop for screenwriters. Any attempt to cripple the industry by invoking Article XII will be fought to the limit; any effort to curb the free and independent relationship between producer and writer will be resisted at any cost."[93]

The SWG chose to respond to its own constituency through the *Screen Guilds' Magazine.* To the question posed by W. R. Wilkerson, owner and editor of *The Hollywood Reporter*, as to why writers would want a closed shop, Dudley Nichols replied with a list of benefits: "Fairness. Honesty. Genuine friendship with producers. A more courageous stand against foolish censorship. More integrity as craftsmen. Abolish fear. A stronger industry and a better art. Pride and self respect. In fact they are too many to enumerate. Better just to ask, 'What have producers to fear?' Nothing. 'What has the dishonest producer or writer (assuming that the human race is fallible) to fear?' Everything!"[94]

Even as the SWG battled with the press and the producers, there was cause for concern within the Guild. Devery Freeman called it a time of tremendous polarization among writers.[95] Some writers expressed frustration with the liberal leadership of the SWG. Samson Raphaelson, writer of *The Jazz Singer, Trouble in Paradise*, and *Suspicion*, recalled feeling that SWG president Ernest Pascal was overly combative in his tone against the producers:

> I got a letter saying we were going to organize, we were going to have a big meeting and it was a letter full of defiance terminology. "We will defy the producers." It had a kind of class war inflection that I felt was not needed. I felt this is . . . going to unduly create a fear that we're Communists, that we are going to destroy the system instead of organizing. . . . I called him and I said, "God almighty, why did you have to use inflammatory language? The battle has not started. You know, you're sounding as if you are waving a flag and saying, 'Let's all come girded to the loins.' . . . You just scared the hell out of the studios when all you want to do is have a stronger Guild."[96]

At the same time, Raphaelson felt pressured by producer Bernie Hyman to show more allegiance to the studio than he felt at the time.[97] Raphaelson and many others were looking for some kind of balance between declaring war against the studio moguls and kowtowing to their demands. But there was no middle ground. Moreover, time was running out.

In May 1936 the membership gathered to vote on amalgamation. Many writers were bracing for fireworks at the meeting; the Hollywood police department was even summoned in case things got out of hand. Instead, the event turned into what many described as a lovefest. A number of the conservative members called for a vote, not about amalgamation but rather for the principle of amalgamation with the Authors League of America. This resolution, they declared, would allow the Guild to maintain some autonomy as members hammered out the details. The process seemed reasonable, and the membership voted overwhelmingly in favor. Then, in a good faith effort, three liberals on the board stepped down so that the membership could vote in three conservatives.[98] The conservatives then explained to the assembled writers that everyone would be released from the prohibition on signing contracts that extended beyond 1938, and with this surprising turn of events, the membership voted to rescind Article XII. Writers were happy, the meeting was declared an overwhelming success, and the membership adjourned to the bar at the Hollywood Athletic Club to celebrate.

But three days later, two of the newly elected conservative members of the board, film lyricist Bert Kalmar and Morrie Ryskind (writer of *Animal Crackers* and *Stage Door*), resigned.[99] Within days, the staunchly conservative Rupert Hughes, writer of *Souls for Sale*, declared secession. Within the week, 125 members of the SWG—about a quarter of its membership—swayed by the fears of the conservative writers, walked away. The rug had been pulled out from under the Guild, and within the month, all 125 ex-members had joined the newly formed rival association, the Screen Playwrights.

Screen Playwrights: Artists or Employees?

[I was] not only soliciting members, but fighting off this company union that was springing up in all the studios, which sprang full-armed from the brow of Louis B. Mayer one night. Like Pallas Athena.

—Philip Dunne interviewed by Thomas Stemple,
Oral History Collection, American Film Institute,
Louis B. Mayer Library, Los Angeles

The exact origin of the Screen Playwrights (SP) is disputed. Some say it was conceived by a group of conservative writers disgruntled with the SWG, namely Mahin, Rogers, McGuinness, and Patterson McNutt, writer of *Curly Top*. Others say the idea was hatched in Irving Thalberg's office at MGM.[100] Either way, the association's allegiance was to management. The professional success and plum writing assignments that were awarded to its core members during those ensuing months, as well as the new opportunities that arose for writer-producer or writer-director contracts for the SP members, reinforced the argument that theirs was a sweetheart deal. Ceplair and Englund detail how MGM gave the SP free access to office space, meeting rooms, secretaries, and lawyers. The founding of the SP, they argue, "may not have been a conspiracy, merely a set of coincidences," but its leaders "acted conspiratorially from the outset."[101] As Dunne said when asked about the SP's origins: "You say by MGM and we thought by MGM, but we can't be sure. That's the way it smelled to us."[102] As became clear over time, the SP had formed well before the May vote on amalgamation and had plotted to gut the union and lure away writers.

The bylaws of this new association clarified its leaders' intention to attract top storytellers. Membership was by invitation only, and additional requirements defined the group as Hollywood elites. Members had to have worked at one of the major studios for at least two years, or, if they were freelancers, they had to have had at least three pictures produced in the prior two years. Studio heads and members of the SP played off the ambivalence of writers torn between staying with the SWG or joining the SP. As Dore Schary explained, "Contracts were offered. And raises were offered. And suggestions were made that they would lose jobs. There was real coercion. Quite a few fellows caved in under pressure. Quite a few were signed to contracts—new contracts. Some took raises and sold out. Some quit the Guild. A lot of them quit the Guild."[103] Erwin Gelsey, who scripted *Flying Down to Rio* and *Swing Time*, called the SP a company union, implying that it was devised by the studios to destroy the SWG. Gelsey remembered that he was regularly pushed to join SP, although he never did.[104] The pressure on successful writers to join was intense—and the rewards were great. Among those who joined were P. G. Wodehouse, Grover Jones (writer of *Lady and Gent*), Howard Green, Howard Estabrook (writer of *Cimarron*), and Herman Mankiewicz. Declaring the Screen Playwrights the more sensible organization, the studios acted immediately to recognize the legitimacy of the SP. Together, the studio heads and the SP campaigned to destroy the Guild, declaring its remaining members to be leftist radicals.

At the heart of the argument against the SWG was the definition of writers' labor: were they artists or workers? The SP appealed to the egos of its brethren by declaring all writers working for the studios to be creative artists. The SP regarded with contempt the idea that writers were simply employees. The argument here was not just theoretical, but legal. If writers were creative writers—not employees—then they would not be covered by the Wagner Act, which applied only to workers. The SP leaders thought they still might hold sway and the writers might find it undignified to be part of a union, even if they used the more rarefied term "guild." The SP was the studios' best chance to break the Guild. The SP and the producers argued that screenwriters were independent, professional artists in contract with producers as individuals, and, as such, they were ineligible for the protection of collective bargaining as defined by the Wagner Act.[105] Wage cuts soon appeared in SWG writers' contracts when they came up for renewal. There was talk in *Variety* that studios were considering paychecks of no more than $1,000 a week for the top scribes.[106]

Paradoxically, the idea of declaring their writers to be artists was the best legal option available to the studios. By elevating their scribes to a seemingly sublime status, the studios also managed to deprive writers of their bargaining power. Previously, producers had been threatened by the notion of a writer as an artist. As Ben Hecht said, "In the court of the movie Owner, none criticized, none doubted. And none dared speak of art. In the Owner's mind art was a synonym for bankruptcy. An artist was a saboteur to be uprooted as quickly from the company's pay roll as a Communist with a pamphlet."[107] But now the situation for "artists" was turned completely on its head. Suddenly, the use of the term "artist" became an opportunity for the producers to define themselves as something other than employers of traditional workers. Consequently, a trade union like the Guild would be unnecessary. The SP began ratting out to producers any writers they deemed possible communists; the association even claimed that the Guild was a communist organization. Dudley Nichols said of the SP, "They imagine any writer bold enough to stand up for his reasonable rights must be a radical."[108]

Tensions grew between the two groups. As historian Nancy Lynn Schwartz observes, the issue centered not just on unionism but also involved paternalism. To lure writers into the SP, studio heads used words like "betrayal," "loyalty," "obligation," and "family." Schwartz notes that producers not much older than their writers would patronize them "with claims of,

'You're like a son to me,' [with] their salutations of, 'Hello, boys,' and [with] the [shows of] devotion that benevolent father figures like Louis B. Mayer extracted from his darling daughters Anita Loos, Bess Meredyth, and Frances Marion. . . . The susceptibility to and need for paternalism by the young migrants in Hollywood cannot be underestimated."[109] This paternalism had been part of the fabric of the studio system for more than a decade, and its power over writers was significant. Through these tactics and the work of the SP, the Guild's numbers dwindled to a precious few. Those who stayed in the SWG were angry and prepared for battle against the group that Frances Goodrich called the "Screen Playrats" and Sam Ornitz, writer of *Little Orphan Annie*, referred to as "the company-suck cabal."[110] The SWG ceased holding public meetings, its few holdouts driven underground for almost a year. Those who stuck around were among the faithful: Lillian Hellman, John Howard Lawson, and Donald Ogden Stewart. Producers were particularly paranoid about these renegade writers. One of Thalberg's biographers said of this group: "Seen from the producers' perspective, what had started out as an attempt to form a writers' union now seemed more like a communist attempt to infiltrate, subvert, and perhaps ultimately control the motion picture industry."[111] Members of the SWG had their phones tapped (they were never sure by whom), and their employers considered them leftist, communists, and Reds.[112] Still, they held on—in part because they believed in the Guild, but also because they were all successful writers. And producers, no matter how much they hated them as Guild members, needed their scripts.

On April 12, 1937, the US Supreme Court upheld the Wagner Act by a vote of five to four. Within a week of the ruling, the Screen Playwrights and the Producers' Association signed a five-year contract. Producers also signed a contract with the Screen Actors Guild guaranteeing a ten-year closed shop. These contracts amounted to a shrewd attempt to cut the SWG out of the conversation once and for all. If there was going to be a union, then the studios would put their own in place, but it would be difficult for the SWG to prove that the SP was a company union. Instead, the SWG petitioned the National Labor Relations Board to recognize it as the sole organization authorized to represent writers as workers in negotiations with their employers, the studios. As part of this plan, the SWG asked the Authors League for autonomy, which the League granted. The Guild then began working with the Screen Actors Guild and the Screen Directors Guild (later the Directors Guild of

America) to form the Inter-Talent Council, which encouraged mutual recognition and promised mutual protection from a rumored idea in Hollywood that studios wanted to place all workers under the jurisdiction of IATSE.[113] At the time, only the SAG had been recognized by the studios, which made it somewhat wary of the partnership. But the guilds all saw that there was power in affiliation with other like-minded, above-the-line creatives in Hollywood. In a special election, Dudley Nichols was elected president of the SWG and promptly headed off to Washington to encourage the NLRB to resolve the dispute over which organization should be the legal bargaining agent for Hollywood writers.

In June, the SWG held a public meeting, and members planned a vocal counteroffensive to the SP.[114] Slowly, members lured colleagues back to the SWG, until it had a near-complete majority again. The NLRB hearings—held to study whether Hollywood's writers were considered employees under the Wagner Act—took the better part of a year. It was a tough and bitter battle. The lawyer for the SWG was Leonard S. Janofsky, who had previously served as an attorney for the NLRB.[115] In turn, the studios came to the table with nineteen attorneys.[116] Screenwriter Julius Epstein remembered being called to the hearing. The trial lawyers asked him, "How did they coerce you? How did they try to get you to vote against—not to join the Guild?" Epstein recalled, "They had the biggest lawyer in California, Leo McCarthy, and he was doing the cross-examination. I had seventy zingers prepared to wow them. I get on the trial. I said 'Walter MacEwen [executive assistant to Warner Bros. producer Hal B. Wallis] called me into his office and said, 'You don't want to join the Guild.' He said, 'Witness is excused.' And I was left with seventy zingers."[117]

According to the findings released by the NLRB in June 1938, 70 percent of all motion pictures shown globally at the time were produced in the United States, and 90 percent of these were made in Los Angeles County. Writers were workers with no control of the final product made by their industry—and their industry engaged in interstate commerce. For these reasons, screenwriters were entitled to protection under the Wagner Act. The NLRB declared that the five-year contract between the SP and the producers could not preclude collective bargaining and that the collective bargaining agent for Hollywood writers still needed to be decided. Writers had three choices: they could to be represented by the Screen Playwrights, by the Screen Writers Guild, or by no official organization whatsoever. The Labor Board directed that an election be held within twenty-five days.[118]

The NLRB decision resonated beyond the writers' right to unionize. The board set a precedent by laying out policy for all labor guilds yet to be recognized by the studios. Leo Rosten, an academic who also wrote *Sleep, My Love*, affirmed the importance of the NLRB hearing and its findings: "The obstinacy and indiscretion with which the producers opposed Hollywood writers in their fight for recognition, basic working conditions, and a code of fair practices, is one of the less flattering commentaries on the men who control movie production. The National Labor Relations Board changed that. . . . In their dealings with the writers . . . the producers demonstrated that they had no workable concept of employee relations."[119] Rosten's scathing report made clear to all who read it that writers, though often well paid for their work, were treated appallingly when they dared to negotiate in good faith with the studios. It was clear to the NLRB that screenwriters were workers and thus employees under federal law. Now the writers had to choose a bargaining agent.

The NLRB invited all professional screenwriters in Hollywood to cast their votes. The Guild had 615 members and the SP had 158, but the producers did everything they could to sabotage the voting process.[120] Studio heads issued an edict: writers could not vote on studio property. With strict rules and anti-union sentiment high on the lots, social events and drinking parties became the best places where writers sympathetic to the union could hold conversations with undecided writers over the course of the month leading up to the election. Frances Goodrich tells the story of luring writers up to Dashiell Hammett's room at the Beverly Wilshire Hotel with the promise of cocktails:

> Everyone was coming up there and ordering a drink, getting people to come in there and talk, getting them to join the SWG. Lillian Hellman came out of a room where she'd been talking to a writer named Talbot Jennings . . . and said, "Well if I get Talbot Jennings to join this thing, somebody's got to pay for the abortion." Albert [Hackett] added, "Dottie Parker was in another room talking to a writer named Everett Freeman, trying to get him to join the guild, and he said he didn't think any creative writer should belong to a union. . . . And Dottie simply could not stand that and she lost her patience. "That sonofobitch, telling me that *he's* a creative writer! If he's a creative writer, then I'm [Queen] Marie of Romania."[121]

Studios refused to provide lists of their employed writers, making it difficult to assess a potential member's eligibility. Writers sympathetic to the SWG petitioned their fellow writers at each of the studios to vote for the Guild. They even appealed for support from the Inter-Talent Council. As announced in *Variety*, Robert Montgomery, president of SAG, called on writers to vote in favor of the SWG: "It is time for every writer to choose his side. We have no sympathy for fence-sitters. The issue is clear. No vote at all is just as bad as a vote for the Screen Playwrights. Either is a stab in the back, not only to writers but all creative talent. The Screen Actors Guild expects the great body of writers to do its simple duty—vote overwhelmingly for the Screen Writers Guild."[122] Montgomery's position might seem strange, given the actor's enthusiastic support of the investigations of the House Un-American Activities Committee only nine years later; but at the time, Montgomery and his union stood behind the more liberal-minded SWG. Finally, in the last days of June 1938, by a vote of 267 to 57 and with a majority of votes at every studio, the SWG won the election. The NLRB certified the election in August, and the vote was official. The SWG had won the right to bargain collectively for American screenwriters. Now the Guild had to secure a contract.

The Long Road to a First Contract

[Louis B. Mayer said,] "It needs more comedy. I want you to inject comedy in the comedy scenes." For the Lion, the Strawman, and the Tin Man. Which I did. A week or so did it, adding laughs. As he told me then, I would get no screen credit, because I was not writing enough footage. But it didn't matter. I was getting paid, that was the main thing.

—*The Writer Speaks: Irving Brecher* (writer of *Go West* and
Meet Me in St. Louis; script doctor for
The Wizard of Oz), 2007

Two years after the screenwriters voted in favor of it, the studios finally declared Hollywood a closed shop for them. The SWG wanted to guarantee that at least 80 percent of writing jobs would be given to its members, but producers demanded consideration for the SP members.[123] By September 1938, the SWG had drafted a contract. It asked for a prohibition on switching a writer off a project midstream, an assurance that writing credits ("screen-play by" and "original story by") would be determined by the Guild, a three-year limit on contracts between writers and producers, and Guild control of contract dispute arbitration.

The producers flatly refused this proposal. The writers walked out and petitioned the NLRB for help. They soon realized that they would never get a fair contract until all ties between the studios and the now virtually defunct SP (officially disbanded in September 1939) were severed. By this time, Hollywood was a union town, from the above-the-line creative workers all the way to the below-the-line craftspeople. The Guild and the studios knew it was only a matter of time before a contract would be signed with the SWG. The contract with the Screen Playwrights was finally canceled in 1940.[124] When regular bargaining began, the primary goal—beyond simple recognition of the SWG as the writers' bargaining agent—was to set working conditions, wages, and the reservation of rights on material for independent writers (the minimum basic agreement). The Guild was fighting for long-term employees as well as independent contractors, many of whom felt disenfranchised.[125] The Guild believed a two-tiered contract for employees and independent writers was essential to securing the rights of all professional screenwriters.

By 1940, the writers were virtually the only employees at the studios working without the protection of a contract or bargaining rights. The Guild made some concessions in the MBA negotiations and gave producers the first right of refusal, whether or not a writer was working for the studio at the time of creating a particular script. In addition, the Guild waived rights to material from members who wrote during periods of unemployment—so long as the writer was paid for the time if the script was eventually purchased.[126] In turn, producers agreed to a 90 percent closed shop after three years at an 85 percent closed shop. This six-month agreement was voted on and ratified in June 1941 as the first Screen Writers Guild contract.

This working agreement would be structured as a seven-year contract open for negotiation after three years and then every two years thereafter. It included Guild control over the determination of screen credits, with an arbitration committee to handle any disputes, a minimum wage of $125 per week, and a mandatory termination notice for independent writers after eight weeks of employment (or status as employees after eight weeks).

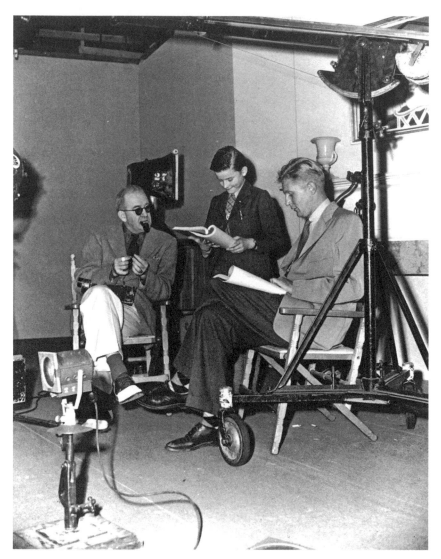

IMAGE 10 Philip Dunne (right) was a founder of the SWG and later served as vice president from 1938 to 1940. Here he reads through the script for *How Green Was My Valley* with director John Ford (left) and actor Roddy McDowall, c. 1941.

Writers Guild Foundation Archive, Shavelson-Webb Library, Los Angeles

The contract prohibited flat fees for scripts under $1,500 ($1,000 for Westerns and action-adventure films). Also, writers had the right to find out whether other writers had been assigned to the same project. Some expenses were allowed for out-of-town writing work, and writers were required to be notified of sneak previews.[127] Another issue on the table was speculative writing. Sheridan Gibney, president of the SWG from 1939 to 1941 and from 1947 to 1948, remembered:

> The one thing that we did stress in our initial contract with the producers was that there would be no writing on speculation. This became a hard and fast Guild rule. But as we know now this rule has been subverted and everybody writes on speculation for television and it is one of the basic things in any contract with the producers that the Screen Writers Guild fought for and won and now it has been abandoned.[128]

Even though speculative writing would not become an issue for several decades, the clarity of the rule at that time—and the level of import placed on it—is worth noting. While negotiating the details of a contract with the studios, the Guild membership also voted to start collecting money to save toward a strike fund. The studios had previously required at least some of their employees to show a viable strike threat in order to be moved to agree to a final contract. The writers, therefore, had to be ready for another showdown.

While writers prepared for a strike, the producers started to listen. They were paying attention not just to the growing power of the writers' labor force, but also to the sounds of war. This was not a time for internal battles. Once the Nazis invaded, Europe rapidly shut down studio productions. Hollywood moguls saw a unique opportunity to make films for audiences craving information and entertainment, not just in the United States but also overseas. Sheridan Gibney posited, "I think that if Pearl Harbor hadn't occurred we probably would not have gotten any kind of contract at all unless we'd actually gone on strike."[129]

When the United States entered the war, the writers convened to discuss their upcoming meeting with the producers. Many in the room felt the war effort was paramount and voted to cease negotiations toward a contract until peace was declared. Harry Tugend, shocked at the idea that all that had been gained by the union could be lost in a moment, urged the writers to let the producers speak first at the meeting, hoping perhaps that the studios would see the need for solidarity within the industry in service toward the country. A few days later at the Brown Derby, the producers committee, the negotiating committee of the SWG, and their respective lawyers gathered. Tugend remembered,

Eddie Mannix, the head of their committee, took the floor. "Okay, you guys. There's a war on. We don't know what's ahead of us. But we do know this. We ain't got time for any more screwing around. . . . Let's get this goddamn thing settled. We'll give the writers a contract. We'll give 'em as little as we can get away with, but whatever we have to give 'em, let's get it done!" . . . That's how we got our contract. It still took months. Factions within the Guild heckling each other, producers whittling down our demands for reasonable minimums. But we finally had a signed contract.[130]

The fractious contract negotiations were resolved in the early months of 1942. The Guild signed its first contract, the Producer–Screen Writers Guild Inc. Minimum Basic Agreement (MBA) of 1942 with the eight major studios— MGM, Paramount, Warner Bros., Columbia, RKO, Twentieth Century–Fox, Universal, and Loew's Inc.—that controlled 95 percent of first-run exhibition in the United States. Three independent producers also signed: Republic Pictures, Hal E. Roach Studios, and Samuel Goldwyn.

In the end, after this exhausting nine-year battle, what the writers had gained was the formation of a union, jurisdiction over all screenwriters, and the determination of credits. As one of Rosten's subjects described it, "This was a battle for self-respect."[131] It was as much about recognition as it was about dignity. Yet, in order to get the contract signed, the Guild had to sacrifice two issues that had been critical for writers during this battle. The first was copyright control; writers had to accept that they had lost it to the studios and would never get it back. As John Bright said, "It's a wistful problem that the screenwriters have always been concerned with and nothing important has ever been done about. It has always been a niggling problem with the Guild because in other fields writers do have that control."[132] The NLRB had determined that the SWG lacked control of copyrights, and it certainly seemed that the writers acquiesced on this point. Their choice not to amalgamate had virtually ended all chance of fighting for authorship—at least for the time being. In 1940, they tried to bar anyone but writers from having the possessory credit ("a film by"), but they were unable to include such a provision in the MBA.[133] The power and dignity of authorship that the SWG had fought for in those early days was set aside in exchange for something more tangible: writers' names established clearly and correctly in credits. That was enough for a first step, they thought.

The second sacrifice was that the new MBA did little to assure salaries beyond minimums. For the Guild's screenwriters, it had become clear that salaries were determined less by seniority and more by a writer's credits. Strong credits, and a number of them, would garner more job assignments and a significantly higher salary. Ultimately, having one's name in a film's credits was the most powerful gain in this first contract. Writers who had had their names on films had the most powerful weapon for front office salary negotiations. But as writers would soon see, a film credit was also something that could be used against them.

personalities in order to get the headlines in the newspapers. I stated that if there was to be a fair and impartial investigation of Communism and Fascism, I and many others in the industry would be glad to cooperate — and that many of us know the names of the comparatively few Communist party members in the industry as well as the names of some persons who to all intents and purpose are Fascists.

The Screen Actors Guild has certainly enjoyed the very friendly relations which we have with the Screen Writers Guild and I hope that we do not let intolerance and deliberate inaccuracy in some sections of the press come between us.

Sincerely,

s/ RONALD REAGAN, President, Screen Actors Guild.

Hollywood Jabberwocky

I. A. L. DIAMOND

'T *WAS ciros, and the cinelords*
Were lollyparsing with their babes:
All goldwyns were acadawards
But demille ruled the nabes.

"Beware the Jarthurank, my lad!
The lion's claw, the eagle's wing!
And when U-I his pix, be glad
That DOS dos everything!"

He took his johnston code in hand:
Long time the ranksome foe he sought —
So rested he by the schary tree,
And stood awhile in thought.

And as in quota-quotes he stood,
The Jarthurank, of happy breed,
Came boulting through the korda wood
And caroled on his reed!

For sin! For shame! On cleavaged dame
The censor shears went flicker-flack!
He scarred the Bard, and coward marred
Went gallupolling back.

"And hast thou haysed the Jarthurank?
Come to my arms, my greenish boy!
O date and day! Elate! L.A.!"
He xenophobed with joy.

'Twas ciros, and the cinelords
Were lollyparsing with their babes:
All goldwyns were acadawards
But demille ruled the nabes.

IMAGE 11 "Hollywood Jabberwocky" by I.A.L. Diamond, from the June 1947 issue of *The Screen Writer.*

Writers Guild Foundation Archive, Shavelson-Webb Library, Los Angeles

2

Two Front Lines

I was a member of the Communist Party . . . and as far as I was concerned there was never, I would say, any discrepancy of any kind between what seemed to me the best interest of the Guild and what those of us in the Party felt . . . should be done in the Guild.

–Ring Lardner Jr., interview by the
Writers Guild Oral History Project, 1978

The real-life spectacle and legal theatrics of the House Committee on Un-American Activities, filmed in the hallowed halls of Congress in October 1947, read like an A-lister's screenplay. But the ending would prove too depressing a scenario for a Hollywood silver screen drama. In the late 1940s and early 1950s, American conservatives on the political right attacked Hollywood Reds, studios fired scores of writers (among other employees), and—perhaps most painful of all—writers betrayed other writers. Without question, this era was the most damaging in the history of the writers and their union, and the story of faithlessness and shame continues to haunt the Guild to this day.

First, Washington politicians placed Hollywood at the center of a campaign to rid American cultural institutions of any hint of communism. Then ten individuals—eight of them writers—were tried, convicted, and jailed for contempt of court. Studio moguls and Guild members crusaded against their peers as fear-mongering and anxiety over reprisal forced Hollywood's practitioners to take sides. Thus began a long, drawn-out period of studio executives and employees naming names and destroying hundreds of their fellow employees' careers. Larry Ceplair and Steven Englund consider the period from 1947 to 1953 the most shameful time in the SWG's history: "The Guild had been weak in the past, but the price of its weakness was never so high nor exacted so completely from its own membership."[1]

In May 1947, key members of House Committee on Un-American Activities (HUAC or "the Committee") boarded a plane to Los Angeles, bound for a strategy session with studio heads. Eric Johnston, then president of the Motion Picture Association of American (MPAA), greeted HUAC's new chairman, J. Parnell Thomas (Republican of New Jersey), and promised full cooperation. Johnston even went so far as to suggest to studio heads that MPAA members terminate employment for any worker "proven" to be a communist, but the executives, though willing to work with the Committee, struck down this proposal. Still, members of HUAC visited each of the studio heads, leaning on them to assist the Committee. Just before the hearings began, Ronald Reagan, then president of SAG, declared his organization's full willingness to cooperate with HUAC.[2] He would subsequently be revealed to have been an informant for the FBI since 1943.

The Committee chair called one big-name witness after another as a phalanx of newsreel cameras captured the Hollywood pageant—produced and directed on this occasion by Washington politicians on location in opulent hotel rooms. Appearing in this drama were studio heads Jack Warner, Louis B. Mayer, and Walt Disney, actors Ronald Reagan, Robert Montgomery (the past head of SAG), Adolphe Menjou, Robert Taylor, and Gary Cooper. Their testimony helped the Committee members narrow the focus of their attack. Assessing the inquiry in Los Angeles, Thomas flatly declared to the press: "Ninety percent of Communist infiltration in Hollywood is to be found among screenwriters."[3] Two screenwriters, James K. McGuinness and Rupert Hughes, gladly volunteered information as so-called friendly witnesses. Notably, both men a decade earlier had served as leaders of the reactionary Screen Playwrights group. These two, along with screenwriter Howard Emmett Rogers, were members of the Motion Picture Alliance for the Preservation of American Ideals (MPAPAI), a right-wing organization of high-profile film industry conservatives based, like the Screen Playwrights, at MGM. Philip Dunne later argued, "In a way . . . the Committee hearings were offshoots of the battle between the Screen Writers Guild and the Screen Playwrights. . . . It was being fought on a new field now. They called in the Congress of the United States on their side."[4] Hughes declared that the Guild he had once helped create (meaning the social group from the 1920s) was now "lousy with Communists." "They began to take over the Guild in 1937," he claimed. "They've been powerful in Hollywood for years, both secretly and openly. They've attacked me and anyone else that ever opposed them."[5]

Anti-left vitriol, which had quieted during the war years, returned with a vengeance. The publicity HUAC achieved beginning in May assured its members that the campaign against so-called Reds in Hollywood was a powerful vehicle for spreading their anticommunist message. By June, Congress had overcome President Harry S. Truman's veto and enacted the Taft-Hartley Act to limit the power of and monitor the activities of hundreds of labor unions within the United States, retracting much of the protection the unions had gained with the Depression-era Wagner Act. Taft-Hartley added a special clause that required affidavits of non-communist affiliations from all officers of a union before they could request an NLRB hearing or certification election.[6] In September, HUAC demanded that the storymakers of Hollywood come to Washington and essentially stand trial.

HUAC issued forty-five subpoenas, this time not to "friendly" witnesses, but instead to Hollywood practitioners who were suspected of having communist affiliations or sympathies.[7] Witnesses were not briefed on what they were alleged to have done wrong or what evidence was to be presented against them, as required in a typical courtroom trial. A good number of the witnesses were young and just starting out in Hollywood. Ring Lardner Jr., thirty-two at the time, recalled that his bright pink subpoena arrived just a week after he had signed a $2,000-a-week deal with Fox Studios and purchased a home on the beach in Santa Monica.[8] Of those called, nineteen publically denounced the Committee's agenda; the *Hollywood Reporter* referred to them as the "Unfriendly Nineteen."

Ceplair and Englund explain that four dozen other names could have been added to the list if it had been based solely on long-term dedication to the Communist Party, to the guilds, or to other Communist-controlled or -influenced organizations. But several characteristics of the Nineteen were particularly relevant to HUAC's agenda: all of them lived in Los Angeles and were employed in the film industry; all were actively involved in pro-Soviet activities; and sixteen were or had been screenwriters.[9] Only one was a veteran of World War II, all of them were men, and ten of them were Jewish. The Committee's first eleven targets were John Howard Lawson, Dalton Trumbo (writer of *Kitty Foyle* and *Tender Comrade*), Albert Maltz (writer of *Pride of the Marines*), Alvah Bessie, Samuel Ornitz, writer and director Herbert Biberman (who had written *The Master Race*), director Edward Dmytryk, producer and writer Adrian Scott (who had written *Mr. Lucky*), Ring Lardner Jr., Lester Cole, and playwright Bertolt Brecht, who had adapted *Hangmen Also Die!*

(Brecht denied he had ever been in the party and then fled the country only hours after his congressional testimony.) Waldo Salt, who later wrote *Midnight Cowboy*, *Serpico*, and *Coming Home*, was to be next in line.

In October 1947, HUAC reconvened in Washington to hear again from "friendly" witnesses Ronald Reagan, Walt Disney, and several others. Their testimony served as confirmation of a premise the Committee already believed to be true: that there were "communist infiltrators" in Hollywood who were systematically taking over the unions. As the proceedings began, Chairman Thomas declared: "It is only to be expected that Communists would strive desperately to gain entry to the motion picture industry simply because the industry offers such a tremendous weapon for education and propaganda."[10] Reagan testified about his experiences in SAG, and Disney told stories of his battles with the Screen Cartoonists Guild. The Committee then called the men now known as the "Hollywood Ten," one by one. Chairman Thomas sat balanced atop two phone books and a cushion, lording over the witnesses, an oversized gavel at the ready. John Howard Lawson was the first to come to the table. Though Lawson tried to make a speech, Parnell interrupted him with two questions: "Are you a member of the Screen Writers Guild?" and "Are you now or have you ever been a member of the Communist Party of the United States?" The juxtaposition of the questions was designed to imply that membership in the SWG was just as sinister as membership in the Communist Party.

Although no Committee member offered a chance to do so, each man attempted to speak, only to be immediately silenced by Parnell's gavel. From their extensive reading of the records, Ceplair and Englund report that "the words 'pounding gavel' stud the transcripts of the hearings and indicate the frequency and relish with which a contumacious witness' words were drowned out."[11] Only Albert Maltz was able to read his statement in full. When asked about his membership in the SWG, Maltz replied, "Next are you going to ask me what religious group I belong to?"—thereby tying the treatment of the Hollywood Left to the persecution of Jews.[12] Trumbo brought copies of his screenplays and challenged the Committee to locate subversive material in their pages. But not one of the Ten was allowed to introduce evidence or ask questions of the Committee members.

Parnell's treatment of the Ten was so contemptuous that some mainstream newspapers, even ones that had toed a patriotic line thus far, briefly expressed some sympathy. An editorial in the *Washington Post* charged that

Thomas "may pretend that his supercolossal Hollywood investigation is aimed not at interference but merely exposure. Its effect, nevertheless, is to intimidate and coerce the industry into an even more rigid acceptance of Mr. Thomas' concepts of Americanism."[13] The *New York Times* was equally repelled by Thomas's behavior: "The Thomas committee and others may do well to remember that respect for individual rights and constitutional processes of law is one of the marks which distinguish a democracy from a totalitarian state; and that one of the best ways to fight communism is to show such respect at all times and places—even on Capitol Hill."[14] As Ceplair notes, the radical difference in the treatment of the unfriendly witnesses in comparison to the earlier treatment of the friendly witnesses by a purportedly neutral legislative body amounted to a blatant violation of due process.[15]

A month later, on November 24, Eric Johnston, as head of the MPAA, chaired a private meeting at the Waldorf Astoria Hotel in New York. He included all eight major studio heads as well as the independents and a few of the studios' East Coast financiers. The next day, in Washington, the House of Representatives cited the Hollywood Ten for contempt of Congress for refusing to say on record whether they were members of the Communist Party. The Ten, who had already been suspended without pay by the studios, were now ordered by the government to serve jail time.

Later that day in New York, the Association of Motion Picture Producers, the Motion Picture Association of America, and the Society of Independent Motion Picture Producers released a statement from their closed-door meeting. The studios called the behavior of the Ten deplorable and promised not to rehire any of them until the Committee cleared them of culpability or wrongdoing. The document, known thereafter as the Waldorf Declaration, read in part: "We will not knowingly employ a Communist or a member of any party or group [that] advocates the overthrow of the Government of the United States by force or by any illegal or unconstitutional methods. In pursuing this policy, we are not going to be swayed by hysteria or intimidation from any source. . . . [We] will invite the Hollywood talent guilds to work with us to eliminate any subversives, to protect the innocent; and to safeguard free speech and a free screen wherever threatened."[16]

A third event that November demonstrated that even Guild members had changed their attitudes about what it meant to be a member: the SWG elected a new "All Guild" slate of candidates to its board. This new, all-but-leftist board was more concerned with saving the Guild's reputation than protecting the rights of individual members. For example, hardboiled novelist and Guild member James M. Cain, who had scripted *Stand Up and Fight*, wrote to the executive board to demand that the Guild not spend money helping the Ten. If they were communists, which he believed they were, then "they are a job for the Communist Party"; if they were not, the writers should simply say so, and they would need no legal support. But "in neither event," Cain wrote, "as this now stands, is Guild action necessary, or desirable."[17]

The underlying question in much of this drama was whether the SWG was, at its core, a political organization. Should the Guild as a whole express a political agenda, and if so, what should that agenda be? Had it formerly been run by a leftist leadership that was furthering a series of unknown political schemes? Of course, the debate about the meaning and purpose of the Guild had begun at its very inception. World War II put a hold on many of these disputes, but in the final year of the war through the aftermath of the Waldorf Declaration, the debate became heated and heightened to a level never seen before in the industry. SWG members were vigorously disputing the purpose and political power of their Guild—both within the industry and beyond. Much of this rancor spilled out on the pages of *The Screen Writer*.

During these critical years, from the end of World War II to the HUAC hearings, the board of directors of the SWG undertook an extraordinary creative, intellectual, and political endeavor: the publication of its own professional journal. The first issue of *The Screen Writer* (*TSW*) appeared in June 1945 and the last in October 1948. This short-lived monthly publication presented a diversity of pieces by screenwriters across genres, across media (radio, television, theater), and even across oceans. *The Screen Writer* also offered space for directors, cinematographers, animators, and critics to expound on their ideas regarding narrative and story. In the journal's editorials, articles, and letters to the editor, a range of members debated key issues, which at their core questioned the overarching purpose and mission of the Guild. Here, writers wrote for one another. But quickly, an audience of Hollywood insiders—as well as creative writers (novelists, critics, journalists, playwrights, and composers)—began to take notice and sometimes to contributed their thoughts. The journal's articles, commentary, and creative writing were celebrated by some in the industry and loathed by others.

At the beginning of the 1940s, writers mobilized as part of the war effort. However, when they returned from fulfilling their patriotic duty, many faced a tough battle getting their jobs back. Further complicating matters was the great turmoil stirring in Hollywood: the Conference of Studio Unions strikes. *The Screen Writer* provided a space for the discussion of labor issues, the rising tide of international cinema production, creative labor in and beyond Hollywood, questions of authorship, and the growing anticommunist sentiment. In the shadow of the Waldorf Declaration, however, writers were far less willing to speak out, and the journal ended its run in 1948.

The Screen Writer was a prestigious enterprise, but also a threatening one. It gave screenwriters a platform within the industry heretofore unavailable to them; by publishing their own journal, they controlled one voice in the larger industry discourse. The articles and essays offered not just thoughtful accounts of the contemporary state of the industry, but also suggestions for radical reforms, unpleasant pictures of the studios and their leaders, and rallying cries to other creative professionals to consider the screenwriters' point of view. The pages presented screenwriters as intelligent, professional, and creative. But they could also appear to be proud, demanding, ambitious, and dangerous. Because these ideas were put forth in print, they proved particularly damning to many contributors who were later blacklisted, including two of its editors, Dalton Trumbo and Gordon Kahn (writer of *Song of Nevada*). While contemporary accounts of the blacklist era tend to focus on the HUAC hearings, those proceedings are only part of the story. To understand the Hollywood blacklist, it is critical first to see how writers landed at the center of the controversy. The residual effect of this period redefined the nature of media authorship and the role of the Writers Guild.

This chapter explores the demise of *The Screen Writer* and the choices the Guild made about how to respond to the attacks against its members. It will track the story through the end of the blacklist to explore what writers and the Guild learned from the ordeal, as well as how the memory of the blacklist is evident in some of the actions and initiatives of the Guild as it exists today.

World War II and the Mobilization of Screenwriters

With a minimum basic agreement (MBA) in place between the Screen Writers Guild and the studios, writers felt some sense of professional security even when the nation was going to war. Decades later, William Ludwig recalled how the studio heads' treatment of writers began to change: "I think they matured a little in their approach to writers. They still referred to us—regardless of age or number of credits or anything of that sort—as 'the boys.' There was no way you could avoid that. As a matter of fact they still do. But they had begun to treat us a little differently."[18] Generally during the mid-1940s, if contract writers asked not to be put on a particular assignment, producers simply offered up another assignment—their contracts were still secure. It seemed as if the terrible days of anti-union attacks had receded, at least for a while.

Throughout Hollywood, as in the rest of the United States, conversations about the war and the nature of the enemy were increasingly common. While right-wing organizations warned about the threat of communism before the war began, concerns about the rise of Nazism took center stage for most Americans. By the time of the Nazi-Soviet Non-Aggression Pact in 1939, socialist-minded workers in Hollywood were seen as particularly threatening; in reality, many Hollywood artists with liberal leanings were equally distressed by this accord between communists and fascists. It was only after Pearl Harbor, when Germany declared war on the United States, that Americans, including reactionaries in Hollywood, settled on Germany as the nation's worst enemy. Nazism, rather than communism, was now the focus of their attention.[19] Director John Ford decried the investigation into communist subversion and suggested the bigger threat was Nazism: "May I express my whole-hearted desire to cooperate to the utmost of my ability with the Hollywood anti-Nazi League? If this be Communism, count me in."[20] Only the most conservative of politicians and citizens were still more concerned about Reds. Still, the thought of any enemy who could operate undetected continued to unsettle many American citizens.

Once the United States entered World War II, many Hollywood employees went straight into action, joining the ranks of the armed services or making films to aid the war effort. The transition was almost fluid. As Nancy Lynn Schwartz contends, "There was probably no place in the country as overwhelmingly affected by the war as Hollywood, and as little inconvenienced by it."[21] After the prosperity of 1939 that peaked with *Gone with the Wind*, the industry had fallen into a slump. Box office sales were down by a third, foreign markets were weak, and the practice of block booking (selling films to theaters only in groups) was starting to be banned.[22] Many of the studios already had war films in production, and now they were set to be released. Even better for Hollywood, film attendance rose at local movie houses around the nation as gas rationing made leisure travel difficult. Everyone still at home was going to the movies.

Classical Hollywood filmmaking was at its finest in 1941: the studios premiered *How Green Was My Valley*, *The Lady Eve*, *The Maltese Falcon*, *Dumbo*,

Sullivan's Travels, and *Citizen Kane*. Many people went to the theaters not just to escape but also to get in touch; civilians were eager to see footage from the front lines, which was accessible to them only through newsreels. The American film industry was still producing movies at an impressive rate, especially in relation to countries where the war had crippled or entirely suspended production of features. Oddly, as screenwriter Marc Norman points out in his history of screenwriting, World War II brought a cease-fire to some of Hollywood's infighting.[23] From the moguls to the above-the-line creatives and the below-the-line craftspeople, virtually everyone in Hollywood was ready and willing to participate in the war effort.

SWG members were active both as soldiers overseas—almost 300 deployed to active service during the war years—and as participants in the Hollywood Writers Mobilization (HWM).[24] The HWM, like its East Coast counterpart, the Writers War Board, served the American government by writing informational materials, public service documentation, advertising, and agit-prop for the Office of War Information (OWI) and the Office of Civilian Defense.[25] Many celebrated writers, including Samson Raphaelson, Pearl S. Buck (author of *The Good Earth*), Howard Estabrook, Arch Oboler (writer of *Escape*), Budd Schulberg (writer of *On the Waterfront* and *A Face in the Crowd*), and Talbot Jennings (writer of *Mutiny on the Bounty*), participated in the Free World Radio, a series of nineteen half-hour radio plays written in conjunction with the OWI. Over the course of the war years, 3,500 writers—novelists, radio writers, cartoonists, publicists, journalists, and screenwriters—joined the HWM.[26] In 1943, the SWG calculated that it had packaged 9,507 programs—each of which included one feature, one or two short subjects, and a newsreel—to be screened on the front lines. The shorts alone tallied 13,027.[27] By October 1944, the HWM had written scripts for 143 shorts, trailers, and documentaries for various federal agencies, as well as 839 radio scripts and spot announcements. Participants crafted 784 sketches for live United Service Organization (USO) shows and staged Department of Defense entertainment events. By 1944, as the SWG's records indicate, its members had provided the OWI, the US armed forces, government agencies (such as the Treasury Department), and American branches of charities like the Red Cross with 861 speeches, 19 brochures, 96 feature articles, 52 songs, and 315 posters and slogans.[28] Guild members even offered creative writing workshops to returning veterans (something the Writers Guild Foundation still offers today).[29]

In order to provide a consistent voice for these materials, writers were instructed on best practices through a *Manual for Writers* that was created by the SWG and the OWI. The goal, particularly for screenwriters speaking to international audiences, was to clarify for viewers "those ideas and ideals we are fighting for" and also to present those American values in such a way "that they are kept continually fresh and interesting to the public."[30] In the chapter entitled "Aspects of the Enemy Which Need Dramatization," the manual instructs writers to keep in mind that the enemy may be lurking at home as well as abroad, and that both battlefronts are crucial to winning the support of Americans and their allies. The enemy at home might be someone who "seeks to shortchange the American people so that they fail to receive their full rights as guaranteed by the Constitution."[31] Consequently, any form of racial discrimination or religious intolerance should be treated as—and should be exposed to the public as—a manifestation of fascism.

Because films were a primary form of entertainment for the troops, the *Manual* reminds writers of their responsibility to serve and to represent the soldier as "a plain guy with a terrific problem": "You can't talk at him; you must talk with him."[32] Didactic language would fail. Writers should strive both to educate and to entertain. The *Manual* encourages writers to know and to explore as characters the soldier, the enemy, and the family at home. It also speaks to the way that women are portrayed in films: "Show women on the job . . . their lives readjusted to the war. American women are finding new expression in jobs they have assumed. Ways and means must be found of interpreting this new role and what it means to the American people. Women are not going to return 'en masse' to the kitchen, as soon as the war is over; many of them are going to remain on their jobs. These new attitudes must be articulated in order that they be understood."[33]

The goal for the OWI was to provide viewers with enough information to decide for themselves who the villains and the heroes were—or rather, to decide that the heroes were Americans and their allies and that the enemies were the Axis and anyone who supported fascism. The Chinese and the Russians were to be treated as new neighbors.[34] Alvah Bessie observed that the quality of Hollywood films improved during this period precisely because multiple voices had to be included in the narrative. "For the first time, Negroes were presented in a responsible and decent light, trade unions were shown for the first time in John Howard Lawson's *Action in the North Atlantic*, films began portraying women with some decency, not just as sexual objects, because women were working in war factories."[35]

The idea behind the mobilization was to pool writers to support the war effort, and the values upheld in the *Manual* are a combination of those

Too many of us have misunderstood the assurance of victory. Any complacency now endangers the winning of the peace which is within our grasp. We must harvest the fruits of victory with the same vigor and determination as we are showing the winning of the military war.

(3) Farms, mines, oil fields and factories throughout the world have been destroyed by the enemy. But our vast natural and production resources have not only been spared the devastation of warfare but have been developed to new levels by the war needs of the fighting democracies. It will be many years before the world can rebuild its productive resources, and during these years the United States will continue its role as a producer nation supplying the food, clothing and household goods -- the tractors, locomotives and mining equipment. -- All the materials needed for the building of the new world society.

Aspects of Production and Home Fronts Which Need Dramatization

A Without government coercion, driven only by devotion to a common cause, management and labor have united their forces against the enemy. Show how efficiency and cooperation in production have provided means for military victories.

B Personalize the worker. He's a human being. So is the boss. Neither is perfect, but, by and large, both are doing the best they can. Don't overstress the importance of either, but give credit where it's due.

C Dramatize the farmer's role. Food literally is just as important for victory as ammunition and weapons and is far more important in the reconstruction period which lies ahead. But the farmer is usually overlooked on the screen. Show how he, too, is playing a vital part in the fight.

D Show women on the job, in training, taking the place of men at the front, their children in nursery schools, their lives readjusted to the war. American women are finding new expression in jobs they have assumed. Ways and means must be found of interpreting this new role and what it means to the American people. Women are not going to return "en masse" to the kitchen, as soon as the war is over; many of them are going to remain on their jobs. These new attitudes must be articulated in order that they be understood.

E Show how little factories as well as big play their part. Show how lives have been readjusted to the 24-hour day. Stress physical fitness for all.

F At every opportunity show people making small sacrifices for war. Show them buying bonds, serving as Air Raid Wardens, donating blood, working for the Red Cross or at Canteens, accepting food and mileage rationing cheerfully, carrying their own parcels while shopping, travelling with light luggage. Show that they do this because they realize the nature of their role in the war. Don't drag such scenes in by the heels, but use them as often as possible when stories permit.

G When pictures are laid in war-time America show service flags in windows, war posters, ceiling prices posted in stores. Show women driving taxis and as streetcar conductors. In crowd scenes scatter a few women around in uniform. Show women alone, without husbands or sweethearts. Show fewer men in civilian clothes in crowd shots. Show homes prepared for dim-outs and air raids, and displaying the V-Home symbol. Show men and women participating in civilian defense, Red Cross, A.W.V.S. and other voluntary services as a part of their normal routine. Above all never ridicule or belittle such work.

IMAGE 12 Draft of the *Manual for Writers*, sent to Robert Riskin, chief of the Bureau of Motion Pictures, Office of War Information, Overseas Division, 1944.

Screen Writers Guild Records, 1921–1954, Writers Guild Foundation Archive, Shavelson-Webb Library, Los Angeles

enumerated by government offices and President Roosevelt's Four Freedoms.[36] The focus should always be on Americans taking actions that will
help win the war overseas. Harold Medford, writer of *Berlin Express*, listed
some of the opportunities for writers: for example, they could work on films
such as Frank Capra's *Why We Fight* series, or they could collaborate with
editors to create documentaries from a mass of unedited raw material. The
writer, according to Medford, "works with celluloid as much as with pencil
and paper. The frames of stock film are his dialogue, his descriptive words,
his phrases. . . . That is the break war film writers get. Their basic material
being life itself, it is at once unimpeachable and matchless."[37]

For some observers like Medford, writing was a process of interpretation
and translation of reality to reflect the human experience onscreen. Looking
back at this era from 2002, blacklisted writer Bernard Gordon, who scripted
Earth vs. the Flying Saucers, defended the screenplays created by more liberal
writers during this period. Rather than being influenced by communism, they
promoted humanist values and followed some of the ideals set out by the HWM:

> Whatever our mistakes and shortcomings, we were people who had a
> keen sense of what was wrong in the world in terms of racism, poverty,
> and war. We quite naturally brought this kind of concern for the human
> condition to our writing and filmmaking. Of course, speaking up for the
> rights of the oppressed, for the right of workers to organize, against the
> evils of unnecessary poverty and for peace and for a world not organized
> solely in the interests of multinational corporations was considered
> then, and is considered now, a threat to domestic security. . . . This may
> be the role of troublemaking dissenters.[38]

Central to these conversations about best practices during the war effort
was a demand for verisimilitude and heartfelt storytelling that captured the
real-life drama in a way that spoke to soldiers, the American people, and even
global audiences. Paul Jarrico said of films like *Song of Russia*, a tribute to
the Russian war effort that he co-wrote, "All the studios made movies like
that. . . . [W]e were writing under orders of the Office of Wartime Propaganda
[the OWI]. Louis B. Mayer never let anything he thought was Russian propaganda into his movies. We even had to take out the word 'community,' because
he felt it sounded too much like 'Communism.'"[39] Created as propaganda for
the American war effort, *Song of Russia* was later condemned by HUAC as

communist propaganda. Michael Kanin, writer of *Woman of the Year*, recalled that "those who were suspected of being Communists were among the hardest and most dedicated workers in all war effort causes."[40] Philip Dunne suggested that perhaps the term "mobilization" came back to haunt some writers as having a sinister, communist ring to it.[41]

Writers' interest in defining their role and supporting the liberal causes of freedom and democracy did at times go beyond their studio work and into the realm of education and outreach. Writers were eager to discuss what they had learned and to share information. Following the first American Writers Congress in 1941 on the craft of writing and the social function of writers, those involved in the Hollywood Writers Mobilization suggested a second congress to bridge the gap between writers and educators and to examine the possibilities of writing in the postwar era. In 1943, 1,500 writers and scholars gathered on the Los Angeles campus of the University of California to hear one hundred papers on the war effort and the ways that writers could provide guidance to audiences, clarifying the stakes of World War II and setting the terms for a future peace. Topics ranged from a talk on "The Responsibility of the Industry" by Darryl Zanuck, to "The Exiled Writer in Relation to His Homeland" by novelist Thomas Mann, to "The Director's Point of View" by Edward Dmytryk, to "The Function of the Radio Dramatist" by Arch Oboler.[42] The event and the discussions it generated were progressive; the writers involved saw it as an opportunity to galvanize support for the war.

But for some in the studio front offices and for politicians like Jack Tenney, a Republican state senator from California who already saw Red whenever he looked at Hollywood writers, the conference came to represent an example of dangerous political behavior and provided evidence of communist infiltration in the motion picture industry.[43] Tenney and his California Senate Factfinding Subcommittee on Un-American Activities (known as the Tenney Committee) had been ready to attack Hollywood liberals for a number of years. Once the war was over, the time seemed ripe to investigate the industry's war efforts and, specifically, the Hollywood Writers Mobilization.

Labor Strife in Hollywood: Screen Cartoonists and the CSU

As detailed in chapter 1, studio moguls fiercely opposed unionization in Hollywood. Two events help to illuminate how anti-union, anti-left sentiment within the industry had been building in the decade leading up to the trial of the Hollywood Ten. The first was the Disney animators' strike in 1941; the second was the Conference of Studio Unions (CSU) strike in 1945. It is important to note that this anti-labor rancor seethed among the independents as well as the eight major studios, and that the managerial attack was aimed not just at above-the-line creatives but also at below-the-line craftspeople.

The Screen Cartoonists Guild formed in 1938 under the leadership of Herbert Sorrell. The union quickly secured contracts with some of the major companies: MGM, Leon Schlesinger Productions (creator of *Looney Tunes* and *Merrie Melodies* for Warner Bros.), Screen Gems, Walter Lanz, and Terrytoons. In the spring of 1941, many artists at Walt Disney Studios, fed up by salary cuts and layoffs, decided to join the Screen Cartoonists Guild. Art Babbitt, who was an animator on such films as *Snow White and the Seven Dwarfs* and *Fantasia* and who created the character Goofy, joined the Screen Cartoonists Guild leadership. Studio head Walt Disney saw Babbitt's action as a personal betrayal and fired him, calling Babbitt a Bolshevik.[44] The following day, in the midst of their work on *Dumbo*, the Disney animators went out on strike.

The Screen Writers Guild officially expressed its sympathy for the striking animators, but the SWG leadership did not go so far as to recommend a boycott of Disney pictures.[45] The tone at Disney Studios changed completely because of the strike; almost half of the employees left or were laid off within months of the walkout. Walt Disney himself declared the Screen Cartoonists Guild communistic and even offered his assistance if the Tenney Committee should want to investigate the possibility of communists infiltrating Hollywood. The strike lasted five weeks. Ultimately, with the assistance of a federal mediator, negotiations took place that ended in favor of the animators, and Disney, grudgingly, signed a union contract.

Skirmishes involving below-the-line unions were not a new phenomenon in Hollywood. For years, craftspeople in IATSE had struggled with their union leadership. In the 1930s, organized crime syndicates and mafia bosses strategically positioned George Browne and William "Willie" Bioff in leadership positions of IATSE, and in 1936 IATSE secured from the studios closed-shop status. Attempts at forming a progressive branch of IATSE met with little success. When Browne and Bioff were sent to jail for extortion, a number of independent labor groups took advantage of this vacuum in IATSE leadership to form a new joint labor union, the Conference of Studio Unions (CSU), that covered a number of below-the-line technicians officially still under the jurisdiction of IATSE. Film producers far preferred the more conservative

IATSE over the CSU, which they viewed as a more threatening and potentially more demanding union in negotiations.[46] As historian Reynold Humphries states, "The IATSE . . . was the producers' union: a threat to it was a threat to themselves."[47] The studio executives still felt they had an advantage, though, because the CSU could not call a strike since most Hollywood unions had agreed to a no-strike pledge during the war.

In late spring 1944, members of thirty-eight guilds and unions gathered to discuss how to respond to attacks against labor by the MPAPAI, which was branding unions and their leaders as communists. As a result of these meetings, the unions released a statement that declared, "The unity of the war effort and the unity of the industry are inseparable at this time."[48] In April, the board of the SWG officially condemned the Alliance for its statement that "the industry is dominated by Communists, radicals and crackpots," and asked the other Hollywood guilds and unions, as well as the MPAA, to "discuss and find ways and means of combating such harmful and irresponsible statements."[49] As a whole, SWG members were ready and willing to support the war effort and to fight what they saw as outrageous and unfair vilification.

At issue was whether workers had the right to be represented by the union of their choosing. Their livelihoods and their basic rights as workers were at stake. The tension escalated to the point of crisis with the CSU strike in 1945. Under the umbrella of the CSU, the Painters Union local was the first of the below-the-line unions to face the producers and ask for a pay raise. Herb Sorrell, then the Painters Union's business agent, had some success lobbying for this cause; consequently, he rose to the top ranks of the newly formed CSU. Other locals from IATSE were eager to join the CSU's collective bargaining units and to renegotiate their contracts, and thus affiliations and local charters were granted for Story Analysts, Screen Set Designers, the Screen Office Employees Guild, and the Screen Publicists Guild.

In January 1945, seventy-seven members of the Screen Set Designers asked to go into labor negotiations with the producers, but the producers refused to meet, declaring that they could not talk to the members without IASTE leadership present. This jurisdictional issue left the Screen Set Designers no easy choice: they could acquiesce and accept the status quo of being represented by IATSE, or they could walk out in protest. One local paper specifically questioned whether a work stoppage by the Screen Set Designers would be a strike or a lockout.[50] What was clear was that others in the CSU would soon face a similar conundrum, and so the CSU unions together made the decision to strike. Producers declared that the strikers were "lawfully discharged and ceased to be employees because they struck in violation of the War Labor Disputes Act."[51] After a cooling-off period, the painters called a strike in March 1945, and soon other locals within the CSU joined. Bearing down on the strikers were not just the studio heads but also Roy Brewer, the new head of IATSE, and his anticommunist enforcers. The first few months on the picket lines were relatively peaceful; but as time went on, threats against CSU workers became more frequent, and by autumn 1945, the picket line had become a dangerous place.

Writers were conflicted, both as a unit and individually, about how to respond to this below-the-line walkout. They had a number of concerns to weigh: their contractual obligations to the studios, their agreement not to strike during wartime, and their strong desire for solidarity with other film workers and their unions. Officially, a sympathy strike was not an option; contractually, writers were obliged to cross other employees' picket lines. The only circumstance under which they could avoid crossing the lines would be threat of bodily harm. In the early days of the strike, the possibility of physical injury seemed absurd. As John Bright recalled, with dance directors, story readers, and publicists pacing the picket lines, the fight was far from a bloody battle.[52] Many sympathetic writers felt caught between their desire to support their fellow workers and their position as "essential employees" in the war effort. Erna Lazarus remembered: "We were at war and we were considered an essential industry and, as such, we had certain privileges. But one of the things that we could not partake in was a jurisdictional strike. And I happened to be the SWG representative at Columbia at the time that this happened, and it was a very difficult thing because writers wanted to go out on strike."[53] Many writers hated the idea of turning a blind eye to their fellow workers' struggles when they themselves had suffered so much at the hands of the producers.

Few studio heads supported their writers, although there were some exceptions. Daniel Taradash, writer of *From Here to Eternity*, was at Columbia Pictures at the time. He described Harry Cohn as "much more a writer's man. In fact, he liked to taunt his producers. In a meeting with a producer, a director, and a writer in his office, Cohn would almost always direct his questions first to the writer. The director he paid a lot of respect to. And if he wanted to make a nasty crack he would direct it at the producer."[54] But other moguls, like Zanuck, sided with their producers in any dispute. As tensions rose in Hollywood, more executives—and unions—jockeyed to take sides.

Writers at the time were doing fairly well for themselves, and many writers were apathetic to the concerns of the CSU and hostile toward the idea of engaging in labor actions, given that their long struggles for unionization had ended only four years earlier. With the MBA in place, they had a sense of security. And business was booming. The studios needed new products for their movie houses every week. Mel Shavelson, who wrote for Bob Hope for many years, saw the mid-1940s as a great era for writers, especially those who were tied to a popular star: "The day you started working on a screenplay, you'd know when it was going to appear in the theaters because the studios were like factories. Everything was done to schedule."[55]

SWG meetings were heated, with different constituencies declaring very distinct allegiances. The more conservative members asserted that, on principle and in keeping with the terms of their contract, Guild members could not and should not support the CSU. The more liberal-leaning writers demanded that the Guild take a stand in solidarity with fellow film workers. John Bright remembered Mary McCall Jr., writer of *Craig's Wife*, announcing that she could not join the picket line; instead, she proposed that the SWG contribute $25,000 to the CSU strike fund. Bright found this idea disconcerting at best, the equivalent of "buying our way with money" and "putting a price tag on our conscience."[56] This kind of conflicted behavior manifested itself collectively in Guild decisions and also in the stances taken by individual writers. As William Ludwig explained, some writers played for both sides:

A few of those people who maintained publicly that they would never walk through a picket line and got great kudos for the nobility of their principles—they wrote at home and they sent their stuff in by studio car. I never felt that this was too much of an adherence to principle because Metro never minded if you worked at home. They didn't get off payroll. They never announced to the studio that they were not working because there was a picket line around. But they got great public acceptance for their extremely liberal positions and I always felt that was kind of shabby.[57]

A handful of writers did support the strike both in word and in deed—but the punishment for this choice was severe. Bright, in good conscience, decided he could not cross the picket line and refused to continue working on a project with Arthur Freed. Though MGM's general manager Eddie Mannix tried to strong-arm him and then to shame him by making an example of him, Bright refused to budge. As he remembered, with a laugh, "I was blacklisted before the blacklist."[58]

No matter which side each writer supported, virtually every writer experienced conflicting emotions and serious concerns about the rising temperature in Hollywood. Ring Lardner Jr. remembers that writers were worried about being associated with militant trade unionism, given that producers and the press were branding the CSU as a Red-influenced organization.[59] And while the Communist Party was still active in Hollywood, the MPAPAI was drumming up recruits, too. William Ludwig recalled:

> I remember one morning . . . two writers came into my office—[they] shall be nameless. After a little fussing around they said that they had been watching me and they thought I was good material and they invited me to join the Communist Party and they left. That afternoon King Vidor came into my office and after the same kind of fussing around he invited me to join [laughs] the Association for the Preservation of American Ideals. It was one of my more baffling days. And I said to King, "What are you people *for?*" And he said, "Well, we are against so and so and so and so." And I said, "King, I have decided I am not going to join anything anymore that is *against.* What are you *for?*" And he thought for a while and he said "I'll have to ask Sam Wood." And he left the office and I never heard about that again. And I never heard from the communist invitation again either. It was the inevitable position of the liberal—the middle.[60]

The SWG itself tried to remain nonpartisan. Philip Dunne described the teetering, anxious stance the Guild leadership took as a "plague on both your houses" position.[61] But as the strike continued through spring and summer and into autumn, individual writers called upon the MPAA to end the strike. Three hundred and fifty Guild members signed a petition in support of the CSU, but the Guild itself stayed neutral. Within the next five years, HUAC or the MPAPAI declared 10 percent of those who had signed the petition to be communist subversives.[62]

The struggles for power during the CSU strike are critical to understanding the conservative turn in Hollywood at the close of World War II. The shifting of allegiances and coalitions would ultimately become a defining feature of the postwar era. Looking back objectively, the below-the-line workers' cause was liberal, perhaps even marginal. The Guild position was to try to stay neutral. The CSU strike became progressively contentious and, ultimately, violent. Roy Brewer's thugs attacked striking workers. Ceplair claims that Brewer, head of the IATSE, had brokered a backroom arrangement with the MPAA to keep the CSU's president, Herbert Sorrell, so bogged down by strike turmoil that he had little time to focus on the jurisdictional fight against IATSE.[63] Brewer's and the trade press's ceaseless attacks on Sorrell also helped to keep the CSU marginalized.

In his history of labor and culture in the 1940s, George Lipsitz explains that the trouble with striking workers was exacerbated by the vast numbers of returning servicemen looking for work. "By the winter of 1945–6," he writes, "one-quarter of all war workers had lost their jobs. Nearly two million workers found themselves unemployed by October 1, and real income for workers fell by an average of 15 percent in three months. Prospects for the future offered little hope for improvement, as 10 million servicemen and women returned to civilian life to join the competition for jobs."[64] Like any other workers on strike, writers could be replaced by returning servicemen, which only increased the pressure to conform.

Officially, the SWG stuck its neck out only far enough to join the other guilds in requesting that studios find common ground with the striking workers and settle labor disputes. In October the SWG declared, "It is a prerequisite to renewed peace in Hollywood that all employees and union contracts be reinstated without prejudice."[65] In the end, the studios locked out 7,000 workers from fourteen Hollywood trade unions for eight months.[66] For thirty-three weeks workers were intimidated on the picket line, harassed, and, on occasion, even arrested. Abraham Polonsky, who wrote *Body and Soul* and *Force of Evil*, remembers: "It was a very devastating strike, because it destroyed almost all the good unions in Hollywood. . . . The Screen Writers Guild, in effect, sided somewhat with the Conference of Studio Unions. And when the strike was lost, the leadership in the Screen Writers Guild changed, too."[67] While the Guild as a whole failed to take a strong stance in relation to the producers, and as the CSU strike built momentum, writers found a new venue for expression and their call to action.

The Screen Writer

In June 1945, a month after victory had been declared in Europe, the Screen Writers Guild published the first issue of its monthly journal, *The Screen*

Writer (*TSW*). Although the Guild had issued publications before, both independently and jointly with the Screen Actors Guild, *TSW* had a decidedly different approach. It was literary in tone, it encouraged a multiplicity of voices, and it aspired to an audience broader than just the Guild member-ship.[68] Dalton Trumbo, a novelist, screenwriter, cultural critic, and chair-man of Writers for Roosevelt, was the journal's founding editor. The editorial board included Lamar Trotti (who scripted *Young Mr. Lincoln* and *The Ox-Bow Incident*) and Ring Lardner Jr.

One fascinating characteristic of the journal is the seriousness with which the editors undertook the task of writing about the film industry. Their passion for the craft is tangible in every issue, and their prime direc-tives, clearly, were to elevate the profession in the eyes of fellow writers and other industry professionals and to address the role of writers within the industry. In its premiere issue, the editorial column posed to its readership the potential for the journal and explained the editorial board's desire to use *TSW* as a site for conversation, discussion, and debate among writers.

> This magazine can develop in either of two directions. It can become the personal organ of a small clique consisting of particular Guild members whom the executive board happened to appoint as its editorial staff. If that happens, it will only be a question of time until it withers and dies an unlamented death. Or it can become the actual voice of the Screen Writers Guild, in which case it will assume an ever-increasing stature, not only in Hollywood but among people with a serious interest in motion pictures all over the world.
>
> To achieve that latter and desirable goal, the pages of *The Screen Writer* must be wide open to all shades of opinion within the Guild, limited only by considerations of space and the judgment of its editors as to the relative value of contributions and the proper proportion of content.[69]

In the early issues, there were high expectations for *TSW* and a sense of hope that journal could create a roundtable for conversation, instruction, and debate. Seven general categories of articles persisted throughout *TSW*'s three-year run: commentary on the experiences of writers, studies on the making of films, reports on global film production and the global marketplace, essays on particular genres and emerging media, debates on the subject of authorship, and editorials on the rise of anticommunist sentiment in Hollywood. The discussions and debates in the pages of *TSW* illuminate the central concerns that screenwriters faced during this transformational time from the end of the war through the first few years of the blacklist.

The first four issues of *TSW* offered three articles by writers who were in the armed services or who had recently completed their service. The editors believed it was central to the Guild's mandate to support writers returning from service and to help them secure employment in the industry as soon as possible upon their return. In editorial columns, they argued that "the returning screen writer has no one but the Guild to intercede for him if intercession becomes necessary."[70] Although data on the number of SWG members who served in the armed forces vary, veterans made up between 275 and 301 of the Guild's approximately 1,275 members.[71] A call rose among these writers for producers to consider writing during wartime as part of a veteran's overall body of work. In the pages of *TSW*, screenwriter Robert R. Presnell Sr., who worked in the Signal Corps during the war, criticized the studio heads for their looking at a writer's war record of film writing as a parenthesis (or, perhaps a better analogy, an ellipsis). Rather, the returning writer represents an untapped asset for the studios: "Have any story editors or producers considered my army credits? There are no press agents or screen credits to say, 'This man wrote a film that trained five million men to use weapons in half the estimated time. That one wrote a film that made the landing in Normandy possible. Joe Doakes saved countless lives by his dramatization of malaria prevention. Another trained pilots for the B-29s.'"[72] Veterans like Presnell asserted that they should get their jobs back, but not out of sentimentality or patriotic duty on the part of the industry. Instead, he argued that many writers in active duty had developed new talents and gained experiences that could enrich their screenwriting, guaranteeing new angles and plots for cinema audiences.

As the war came to an end, articles in *TSW* outlined work available to writers in varied genres, in other media, and in different fields of writing. Lester Koenig, who wrote the acclaimed documentary shorts *Thunderbolt* and *The Memphis Belle*, pressed the studios to support writers' adjustment back to Hollywood modes of writing. He also encouraged the studios to produce documentaries by writers who had experienced the war firsthand.[73] Koenig believed that feature film creators could benefit from the honesty presented in this most recent influx of wartime documentaries.

A number of novelists also wrote in *TSW* about their impressions of writers and writing in Hollywood. For example, novelist-turned-screenwriter James Hilton, who wrote *Mrs. Miniver*, opined that Hollywood was a good place for novelists to expand their reading audiences. "The average successful picture of 1945 has qualities of dignity and integrity" that might also make for good reading, he wrote.[74] Other articles suggested commercial film companies as another venue to consider in order to achieve an economic security unavailable to many writers in feature films. Writing-as-persuasion already came naturally to seasoned writers, and this genre harnessed those skills. Audrey Wood, a literary agent, offered guidance to writers who might be interested in playwriting.[75] Writers who specialized in genres like action-adventure, animation and fantasy, or the Western contributed articles that examined and explained the particulars of their craft. There were practical articles as well, as Guild lawyers expounded on authors' rights, tax considerations, and ownership of story ideas. Still other articles covered the economics of the new medium of television. In 1948, George Corey, writer of *Mr. Winkle Goes to War*, predicted that television might be the best place for screenwriters to claim ownership of their writing in a way heretofore unavailable in film.[76]

Beyond analyses of the art and craft of the American screenwriter, *TSW* presented opportunities for rich conversations among constituents in the film and media community. Film artists and craftspeople examined the process of filmmaking in the broader scope of global film writing and reception from their unique vantage points. This kind of communication between groups had not been a common occurrence in the Hollywood studio system. Looking back on this era, George Seaton, who wrote *A Day at the Races* and *Miracle on 34th Street*, explained that "the director and the writer very seldom worked together—practically never. Either the writer would finish the script and would go on to something else or they would hire the director a couple of weeks later and you didn't meet each other until the picture was all over."[77] Writers usually collaborated only with producers and almost never stepped onto the film set. *TSW* was doing something innovative by inviting all the collaborators in a film's creation into the discussion.

The celebrated cinematographer of *The Thin Man* and *Body and Soul*, James Wong Howe, wrote an essay in response to an earlier article about the role of the cameraman and his relationship to the writer. As he pointed out, "There are many studio workers behind the scenes whose contributions toward the excellence of a motion picture never receive credit because outsiders have no way of discovering where one leaves off and another begins."[78] Howe offered a gentle reminder that other craftspeople in Hollywood, and not only writers, can be dismissed, misunderstood, neglected, or utterly forgotten in credits, but he also presented writers with ideas for creative collaboration. In another article, playwright and screenwriter Arch Oboler provided a thoughtful assessment of film sound and how writers can best incorporate the power of sound in their scripts.[79] Similar pieces looked at opportunities for collaboration between writers and composers, and others examined independent production and assessed the advantages and disadvantages of paring down—or even eliminating—the studio's chain of command. In 1947, out of conversations that began in the pages of *TSW*, the SWG made a deal with Fox's Darryl Zanuck and MGM's Dore Schary to bring writers onto films sets so that they could learn and internalize the nuts and bolts of film practices. David Bordwell, Janet Staiger, and Kristin Thompson argue that the presence of screenwriters on set presaged the burgeoning trend of writers taking on multiple roles, such as the hyphenate writer-director in cinema and the writer-producer in television.[80]

What began in *TSW* as a global perspective on the war evolved into a deepened interest in international perspectives on cinema. During World War II and in the early months of peacetime, writers filled the pages of *TSW* with reports on war and postwar conditions in various theaters of operation. Charles Grayson, who scripted *One Night in the Tropics*, described running into members of his "ink-stained fraternity" everywhere he was deployed.[81] Budd Schulberg wrote about searching for archival, lost, or abandoned Nazi film footage as evidence to help the prosecution in the Nuremberg Trials. As Schulberg explained, "Motion pictures had gone to war. Now they were helping to win the peace."[82] In many ways, the *TSW* articles published toward the last days of the war and articles about international cinema became de facto studies of the lives of writers on the frontlines around the globe.

The most common studies were of the state of British and French cinema. Editorials commented on the attempts of British film producer J. Arthur Rank to create parity between British and American film exports.[83] Legendary French writer-director Jean Renoir (*Grand Illusion* and *The Rules of the Game*), who was a member of the SWG, celebrated writer-producer-director-actor Charles Chaplin's work in *Monsieur Verdoux*.[84] Two articles (including one from MPAA president Eric Johnston) debated the possibility of renegotiating the screen quota system with France.[85] There were articles about cinema trends in the Soviet Union, Mexico, and Argentina, as well as dispatches from Venice and from the first Cannes Film Festival. One article offered an overview of contemporary West German film production. A number of articles by Chinese writers examined and explained the reception of Hollywood films in China. In a 1945 editorial, *TSW* predicted that "in the years to come, it is not inconceivable that the film industries in India and China may further encroach upon areas which we once held almost exclusively."[86] The scope and depth of this global lens is striking. Writers were actively engaged and eager to understand international cinema, the issues affecting writers in other countries, and how to write American films that would appeal to global audiences.

One of the most vibrant debates that played out on the pages of *TSW* involved the rights of authorship, which peaked in a series of articles calling for the creation of the American Authors Authority. As discussed in chapter 1, screenwriters had been frustrated for years because they did not own the copyright to their works. They debated whether it was feasible or even proper for them to seek ownership from the studios. Not owning their work made writers feel vulnerable—especially those who came to Hollywood from long-established professions like literature and the theater where authorship and ownership were one and the same. Novelist Raymond Chandler, who wrote the screenplays for *Double Indemnity* and *The Blue Dahlia*, furnished a sharp critique of his experiences in the film industry in *The Atlantic* in 1945:

> The impulse to perfection cannot exist where the definition of perfection is the arbitrary decision of authority. That which is born in loneliness and from the heart cannot be defended against the judgment of a committee of sycophants. The volatile essences which make literature cannot survive the clichés of a long series of story conferences. There is little magic of word or emotion or situation which can remain alive after the incessant bone-scraping revisions imposed on the Hollywood writer by the process of rule by decree. That these magics do somehow, here and there, by another and even rarer magic, survive and reach the screen more or less intact is the infrequent miracle which keeps Hollywood's handful of fine writers from cutting their throats.[87]

Philip Dunne reviewed Chandler's essay in *TSW*, celebrating his rapier wit and declaring that "he gives Hollywood—and particularly its writers—a bloodier beating than any he has ever allowed his Philip Marlowe to suffer at the hands of corrupt police. He rips the skin whole off the Hollywood system. He disembowels it and has its bones hot from its carcass."[88] But Dunne takes the argument one step further, linking Chandler's frustrations to the Wagner Act and the role of writers as employees. As Dunne explains, copyright was not guaranteed, under a union contract, as a condition of employment: "That word 'employment' is the key to Mr. Chandler's argument. As long as the writer accepts a salary, as long as he does not share the producer's financial risk, just so long, thinks Mr. Chandler, will he be a lackey, a creator constrained from creating, a second-class citizen in the Hollywood community."[89] Dunne makes clear that the notions of freedom, integrity, and independence are all secondary to employment and earning a living. He reminds readers that a writer's sense of dignity and self-respect are not guaranteed in one's job description; however, they are essential goals that writers must strive toward enshrining in future contracts as basic rights. As Hollywood reporter Thomas M. Pryor put it, "until such time as script writers do something to assert individual effort, the best they can hope for is reflected glory."[90] Writers, the editors of *TSW* knew, were living in the shadow of directors, producers, and actors. But, as they had to admit, it was a golden shadow.[91]

These concerns and others prompted novelist James M. Cain to propose the establishment of an American Authors Authority (AAA) in 1946. Cain had written a few screenplays and contributed to others (notably *Blockade* and *Algiers*), and he was not always pleased with the adaptation of some of his most famous novels (*The Postman Always Rings Twice*, *Mildred Pierce*, and *Double Indemnity*) into major Hollywood films. The frustrations he experienced led him to champion an organization that would serve the Authors Guild, the Dramatists Guild, the Radio Writers Guild, and the Screen Writers Guild as a repository, recordkeeper, and legal enforcer of writers' copyrights in all formats. Accessing information about the financial accounting of the studios was extremely difficult, if not impossible, for creatives and craftspeople. In relation to novels and adapted works, where royalties were sometimes paid, producers often modified their bookkeeping methods to create a royalty structure that best suited the studios' needs.

Cain brought his proposal to the board of directors of the SWG, which in many ways saw the AAA as a parallel organization to the American Society of Composers, Authors, and Publishers (ASCAP), but designed for writers. Ring Lardner Jr. was appointed chairman of a committee to study the plan and report back to the board and the SWG membership. On the whole, the committee was supportive of Cain's proposal. Lardner argued that the plan would essentially provide writers 1 percent of the gross of films they wrote.[92] More than four hundred writers gathered in July 1946 to discuss the plan, the largest attendance at any Guild meeting to date. At the night's end, the members voted 343 to 7 in favor of establishing the AAA.[93] The editors of *TSW* explained this landslide vote by saying that writers wished to control secondary rights on their writing, to control remakes of their work, and to have recourse against producers who shelved their scripts for indefinite periods.

Though Cain did not bring the issue directly to the journal, the editors of *TSW* staked out a role in this discussion of authorship by using its pages for debate and opinion pieces about the purpose and the proper purview of the AAA. For the better part of a year, *TSW* featured articles and collected statements from Hollywood insiders and selected clips from national newspapers and journals about the idea. They even devoted an entire special issue to it. As Cain explained it, the AAA as an organization would regard the writer as "the creator of properties."[94] In some ways, this re-envisioning of ownership was a simple act: it ensured that writers would be compensated every time their work was used. But in other ways, the AAA meant a radical redefinition of film authorship and therefore was perceived by the studios as a fundamental and significant threat to their power as the legally recognized creators of media properties. Perhaps more disturbing, if writers could secure this level of control over their work, might directors and actors soon demand their fair share?

Writers could predict that the studios would be hostile to the notion of returning copyright to them and that producers would dismiss their demands as "outlandish."[95] But many studio heads, Hollywood executives, and media insiders chose a different tack. They declared the AAA proposal to be a leftist plot. William Wilkerson, founder and publisher of the *Hollywood Reporter*, addressed the Hollywood community in the summer of 1946 with an editorial equating a vote for the AAA to the title of his tirade, "A Vote for Joe Stalin."[96] In this fateful screed, Wilkerson named a number of screenwriters who would later turn up on the blacklist: Dalton Trumbo, Maurice Rapf (*Song of the South*), Lester Cole, Howard Koch (*Casablanca* and *Sergeant York*), Ring Lardner Jr., and John Howard Lawson. It was the first of a long series of Red-baiting editorials that ran in the *Hollywood Reporter*. Wilkerson went on to attack Cole in particular, posing to him the two questions that would later become the core queries in HUAC's interrogation: Are you a member of the Writers Guild?

Are you a member of the Communist Party of the United States? Trade journals held power in the Hollywood community, and these words burned. As columnist Ezra Goodman well knew, "Hollywood is narcissistically sensitive about the printed word. . . . As a result, the Hollywood press has become something more than a press corps. It is an integral part of the social and business life of the community. The Hollywood press does not merely chronicle the show. It is part of the show itself."[97]

The vehement opposition of the *Hollywood Reporter* toward the writers and the AAA turned public opinion, ultimately on a national level. The *Los Angeles Examiner* called the proposal "Stalinist." The *Chicago Tribune* described the AAA as a "sly scheme," "communist inspired," and "certainly totalitarian," and it cautioned "real writers" like former Screen Playwrights members John Lee Mahin, Howard Emmett Rogers, and James K. McGuiness, as well as Fred Niblo Jr. (who wrote *The Fighting 69th*) and Ayn Rand (who wrote and adapted *The Fountainhead*), that they must fight this despicable attack on their livelihood, their community, and their country.[98] A group of nine writers, including Marguerite Roberts (*True Grit*), David Hertz (*The Devil Is a Woman*), Howard Estabrook, and Waldo Salt, wrote to SWG members to remind them that an attack on writers at this moment was, in many ways, an implicit attempt to shut down the AAA and to foment disunity within the SWG: "Remember that the French authors have for decades controlled the French stage, and the French authors were moving in the direction of royalties on motion pictures when the war intervened and demolished the French picture industry. Remember that British writers long ago instituted the leasing of literary properties instead of outright sale. Remember that the American dramatists control the American stage. Remember that American film writers, through their Guild, have been moving steadily toward a greater protection for writers and their work."[99] These SWG board members hoped to impress upon the membership that the movement toward authorial control for writers was a universal concern in democratic nations and that opposition to this idea amounted to an attack on unionization in Hollywood.

TSW welcomed readers to decide for themselves how to respond, and the amount of space devoted to the AAA debate illustrates how important the editors thought the topic was to their community. The majority of *TSW* readers, most of whom were writers, were sympathetic to the plan. Soon, the plan itself—and the writers who backed it—were increasingly the targets of right-wing attacks. Studios and legislative committees like HUAC saw conversations about the AAA and anyone who wished to debate this issue as leftist and liberal and, therefore, dangerous. Ring Lardner Jr. saw several reasons behind this guilt by association: "Partly, perhaps, through my identification with it, [the AAA] became thought of as kind of a left-wing plan. Although Jim Cain who had started it was anything but left wing. But the same people in the Guild who had originally worried about the Guild being under the domination of Eastern writers in the Author's League . . . became concerned about this 1 percent of the gross. [Some], I don't know quite how, saw a very sinister implication through all this that it was somehow going beyond our status as salaried employees, or independent contractors, to demand a share of the take."[100] As Lardner explained, many of the writers on the SWG board were interested in getting the AAA approved; however, some saw the AAA as an important cause that, while worth supporting, would never win. As allegations of communist infiltration in Hollywood intensified, the writers used their journal as a site for political expression and public outrage.

In its first two years, *TSW* built an impressive reputation. Many pieces originally written for the journal were picked up by mainstream newspapers and magazines. The National Board of Review praised *TSW* and the journal *Hollywood Quarterly*, declaring that they provided readers with a more complete portrait of Hollywood and its denizens: "These magazines leave a double impression: of the high competence of contemporary filmmakers, and of the magnitude of their problems. Also they leave in mind a notion that the modern inhabitants of Hollywood are citizens of the world. The journals will gain more respect for the industry among leaders of American opinion than a million dollars worth of 'public relations.'"[101] Even amid the politics, there was always a place in *TSW* for wit and great writing. Howard Koch, a master of sophisticated screenplays like *Casablanca* and *Sergeant York*, reimagined his daily exploits in light of the news that Congressman John Rankin (Republican of Mississippi) had declared writers to be workers and Reds: "Once accepting my class status of worker, and I don't quite know how I can avoid it, I find myself in the company of labor unions, guilds, and, in fact, people in general."[102]

By the end of 1945, as the tone in Hollywood shifted and the SWG board increasingly criticized HUAC and its "friendly" witnesses, some more right-wing writers began attacks against both *TSW* and left-leaning SWG members, not only to provoke pro-AAA writers but also to stop what they believed was leftist infiltration of the industry. Some even used the pages of *TSW* to vilify the journal and its editors. Lewis R. Foster (*Mr. Smith Goes to Washington*) wrote in a letter to the editor, "It is being said that *The Screen Writer* has at last appeared in its true colors—red and yellow."[103] Foster called the journal communistic (red) and cowardly (yellow) and claimed that *TSW* represented only the subsection of writers on the extreme Left. In the same issue, the editors replied, "It is to be hoped the time will never come when writers are obliged in their work to express the 'collective viewpoint' of any group."[104]

Frustrations about the tone and temperature of Guild meetings made their way into *TSW* as well. Garrett Graham (*The Noose*) dismissed the possibility of communist infiltration, given the structure of Hollywood film production: "In all this time, I have never seen the slightest crevasse through which any Communist propaganda could possibly trickle to the screen. Motion pictures are big business, controlled from Wall Street. Even the most autocratic studio head in Hollywood is a mere chore boy for the financial powers that direct the major companies and the theater chains." Having shown that writers had no chance to infuse films with their own political agendas, Graham issued a "plea for urbanity" at Guild meetings and an end to infighting.[105]

Philip Dunne, as a member of the editorial committee of *TSW* but writing as an individual Guild member, posed the question directly in his article "SWG—Trade Union or Writers' Protective Association?" Dunne argued that the Guild should be both: it should serve as a workers' syndicate that protects writers as employees and also as a trade association that protects writers as the authors of original material.[106] Dunne became a board member of the SWG at the end of 1946 in hopes that he could keep pertinent political issues front and center for writers—which he did, but not at all with the outcome he hoped.

The Hollywood Ten and the Waldorf Declaration

The battle to define the Guild's politics—from within and by outsiders—was reaching a climax as 1946 came to a close. The Red-baiting in Hollywood was merely an echo of the panic that had taken hold in the public discourse on a national level. Republicans had been voted into the majority in both the US Senate and the House of Representatives; from then on, as Nancy Lynn Schwartz notes, any official opposition to HUAC or to its investigations was minimal. By December 1946, the newly elected SWG board faced a number of inherited crises: the effects of the pending anti-union Taft-Hartley Act and the heightened public Red-baiting of Hollywood writers. Cries for an AAA had petered out. Everyone in Hollywood seemed to be bracing for a storm of attacks from the East Coast. Even as the politicians focused on left-leaning writers, studio heads came under the microscope as well. In January 1947 the *Chicago Tribune* published a series of articles claiming that Hollywood was overly friendly to the Soviet Union because of familial legacies. It noted "three Hollywood dynasties"—the Schencks, the Mayers, and the Warners—thereby implicitly aligning Jews with communism.[107] Emmett Lavery, president of the SWG at the time, was also under attack. Lavery, who had written *Behind the Rising Sun* (directed by Edward Dmytryk) and had run for the 16th US Congressional District in Los Angeles, seemed unimpeachable, given that he was a staunch Catholic, a blue-blooded Democrat, and the author of a play and screenplay based on the life of Supreme Court Justice Oliver Wendell Holmes. In discussing his own convictions, he declared, "I take my social conscience from the Gospels of the Apostles, not from the essays of Karl Marx."[108] Yet conservatives argued that he was sure to be a Red, since he was president of the SWG, the former chair of the Hollywood Writers Mobilization, and a member of the Hollywood Independent Citizens Committee of the Arts, Sciences, and Professions. In February 1947, IATSE leader Roy Brewer boldly asserted in *TSW* that the SWG was a "Fellow Traveler organization" colluding with the Conference of Studio Unions.[109]

When Representative J. Parnell Thomas became head of HUAC in May 1947, the offensive against the Hollywood left truly began, first with the testimony of friendly witnesses and then, in September, with the delivery of subpoenas to nineteen above-the-line creatives. HUAC claimed that Communist Party members who were Hollywood insiders had been inserting dangerous anti-American material into mainstream films. Hollywood moguls narrowed the targets of this attack, pointing specifically at the writers. Though he claimed he "wouldn't know one if I saw one," Jack Warner told the Thomas Committee that "Communists injected 95 percent of their propaganda into films through the medium of writers."[110] The list of HUAC's nineteen suspected infiltrators included mostly writers and actors, but also a few directors. Ivan Goff, who wrote *White Heat* and later created *Charlie's Angels*, mused about the committee's rationale in formulating this list: "Writers and actors are fair game. They make headlines, quick headlines, because you're talking about Hollywood, which reaches the world and [with] a Writers Guild or an Actors Guild you have headlines all over the world."[111] Of the witnesses, both

Lester Cole and Ring Lardner Jr. were serving on the Guild's executive board. And it was certainly true that the board had become involved in some minor social and political action. In 1945, the SWG had sent a telegram to President Harry S. Truman urging him to request that General Francisco Franco of Spain commute the death sentences of two leaders of the short-lived social-ist Spanish Republic.[112] In 1946, the Guild demanded that the management of the Ambassador Hotel in Los Angeles apologize to Carlton Moss, writer of *The Negro Soldier*, who was refused service in the hotel elevator.[113] Maurice Rapf, the Guild's secretary, threatened to publish an account of the affront in the Guild journal if an apology was not forthcoming. (Rapf had just penned *Song of the South*, which depicts a joyful, "idyllic" relationship between a slave and his master.)

Arthur A. Ross, who wrote *Creature from the Black Lagoon* and episodes of *The Alfred Hitchcock Hour*, believed that the goal of HUAC was in fact "the weakening of the democratic and militant trade union movement in the United States and the suppression of the radicalized American intellectual. I suppose that [an] intellectual was anybody who read books other than those that came out of the Book of the Month Club."[114] Emmet Lavery, in a depar-ture from his previous stance and in an attempt to curb the damage to the SWG by the inclusion of so many writers among the Nineteen, demanded, upon threat of termination, that all board members sign an affidavit of non-communist affiliation. Philip Dunne refused to sign and reprimanded Lavery for believing that such a request would be necessary for writers who wished to serve on the Guild's executive board.[115]

In this atmosphere, the group since known as the Hollywood Ten was called to testify in Washington in October 1947. The men had agreed upon a strategy: they would assert their right to free speech under the First Amendment. Although the obvious defense might have been to invoke the Fifth Amendment, legal counsel for the Ten wanted to avoid any correlation between their clients and the notorious gangsters who were appealing to the protection against self-incrimination during criminal testimony around that same time. More important, the Ten wanted to speak their minds and defend themselves. But they faced an obvious conundrum: they could not answer the questions put before them. In his book about these events, Dalton Trumbo explains that a witness who was a communist and denied it when asked would be committing perjury. If he were to acknowledge his affiliation, then the next question would be to name others—relatives, friends, and acquaintances—in the party.[116] The initial affirmative response would also virtually guarantee that the witness would lose his studio job and that he would be investigated by the FBI and the American Legion and doubtlessly shunned by his friends and neighbors. But beyond all these personal tribulations attached to a positive answer was the certainty that everyone he knew would be exposed to speculation and attack. "His compulsory confession will not affect his own destiny alone," Trumbo asserted. "It will touch twenty, fifty, a hundred lives, baring each of them the ugly, discriminatory climate of the age."[117] Trumbo would refuse to be an informant, whereas fellow witness Albert Maltz felt that invoking the First was a straightforward way to question the authority of the Committee.[118]

Rather than answer the Committee's questions, the Ten planned to read prepared statements. But the Committee began its inquiry with a question none of the writers had foreseen: "Are you a member of the Screen Writers Guild?" It was followed by: "Are you now or have you ever been a member of the Communist Party of the United States?" Ben Margolis, one of the lawyers for the Ten, believed that a witness's refusal to answer either question made it seem that the SWG and the party were synonymous.[119] A better strategy, he proposed, would be to respond by expressing their right to First Amendment protection. This tactic angered writer Sheridan Gibney: "[The Ten] acted as if they were the Guild's representatives, which they were not. . . . This, of course, lumped the two organizations and the implication was that they did not want to admit they were members of the Writer's Guild because it might incriminate them in some way."[120] Only the third of the Ten called to testify, screenwriter Albert Maltz, read his entire statement; the fourth witness, Alvah Bessie, managed to deliver about a half of his statement before Committee members cut him off.[121] This concession, he believed, was a response to public censure for HUAC's blatantly hostile treatment of Lawson and Trumbo in comparison with its friendly attitude toward the witnesses who preceded them: Lela Rogers, a former assistant at RKO and founding member of the Motion Picture Alliance for the Preservation of American Ideals, and Walt Disney.[122]

Of course, not everyone in Hollywood sat passively watching these scenes broadcast from Washington. The Committee for the First Amendment (CFA) mobilized supporters of the Ten and organized a trip to Washington in late October 1947 to protest what it viewed as baseless attacks. Philip Dunne remembers calling Darryl F. Zanuck at his home in Palm Springs to tell him about the formation of the CFA and its plan to save the industry. "There was

Twentieth Century-Fox Film Corporation

STUDIOS
BEVERLY HILLS. CALIFORNIA

November 24th, 1947

To the Executive Board
Screen Writers' Guild
1655 No. Cherokee
Hollywood, California

Gentlemen:

This is to offer my services for committee work. I think
I could be most useful on the two committees to be set up
on the resolutions offered by George Seaton and myself
on blacklist and censorship. Parenthetically, it occurs
to me that one committee might well be able to handle both
jobs, since the censorship function requires little more
than the inspection and appraisal of documentary evidence.
The blacklist function, I am very much afraid, will involve
a great deal more work.

In a series of informal talks with studio executives,
William Wyler and I, representing the Committee for the
First Amendment, have been advocating an industry-wide
producer-guild-union organization to counteract the propaganda of the Thomas Committee and the Motion Picture
Alliance against the industry. We have found the producers
receptive to the idea. We feel that if the industry thus
becomes officially involved, the Committee for the First
Amendment can gladly relieve itself of a great part of its
burden. If such an organization is set up, I should very
much appreciate the opportunity to serve as a delegate of
the Screen Writers' Guild.

I think that we have a fine board; it will be a privilege
to serve it in any capacity it designates.

With good luck to you all,

Sincerely,

Philip Dunne

PD/:

IMAGE 13 Letter from Philip Dunne to the executive board of the SWG regarding
participation on the Committee for the First Amendment. His letter was sent one
day before the Waldorf Declaration was announced.

Screen Writers Guild Records, 1921–1954, Writers Guild Foundation Archive, Shavelson-
Webb Library, Los Angeles

quiet for about ten seconds. Then he said, 'Well, if you've got to go, you've got to go.' . . . [Even] Eric Johnston was making the same noises we were at the beginning, before the whip cracked and they all turned around."[123]

All fifty members of the CFA were elite Hollywood talents, including Lauren Bacall, Danny Kaye, Gene Kelly, Groucho Marx, Frank Sinatra, Ira Gershwin, John Huston (writer and director of *The Maltese Falcon*), William Wyler, and the group's chair, Humphrey Bogart. Their intention was solely to demand due process and express distaste for the structure of the hearings.[124] But HUAC's attack on communism was only a slightly masked version of anti-Semitism. Congressman Rankin declared he served on the Committee to protect "the Christian people of America." In a public reading of the names of CFA members, he made sure to point out that "another one was Danny Kaye, [but] we found out his real name was David Daniel Kaminsky. . . . One . . . calls himself Edward G. Robinson. His real name is Emanuel Goldenberg."[125] Philip Dunne returned from the CFA trip to Washington and joined Huston and Wyler in closed-door sessions with all of the studio heads—all except for Jack Warner, who was doggedly against the Ten. They asked the moguls to hold their ground, remain firm against HUAC's allegations, and protect their employees.[126] As time would soon show, the moguls had other plans.

On November 25, 1947 HUAC cited the Ten for contempt of Congress. On the same day, the studio heads announced what would be known as the Waldorf Declaration. Philip Dunne remembered going to Darryl Zanuck's office soon afterward, where Zanuck told him that denouncing and firing the Ten was a financial decision. The moguls were anxious to avert any possibility of an audience boycott of Hollywood films. "[Zanuck] intimated at the time what I believed to be true, that it was pressure from the banks that led to the Waldorf Declaration. The bankers had said, 'Look there's too much trouble. Get rid of those guys and go on.'"[127] The MPAA reasoned that the only way to stop HUAC's meddling into the inner workings of Hollywood was to sacrifice the Ten. But the studios actually went one step further. Any individual under contract with a major studio who was found by the Committee to be a communist sympathizer would be discharged without compensation and would not be allowed to return to studio work until swearing under oath to have ended all communist ties. All of the Ten were terminated. MGM suspended Trumbo and denied him $60,000 in back pay. The statement released by the studios in conjunction with the dismissals did say that as yet nothing subversive or un-American had ever been seen or portrayed in a Hollywood picture—and yet inclusion on a blacklist inferred that these writers had committed or been party to nefarious acts.

The MPAA called upon all of the trade unions to help in its mission to root out subversives, essentially asking the organizations that were designed to protect employees to turn against their members. The MPAA's November 1947 statement read: "Creative work at its best cannot be carried on in an atmosphere of fear. We will guard against this danger, this risk, this fear. To this end, we will invite the Hollywood talent guilds to work with us to eliminate any subversives."[128] The MPAA called for all guilds to pass a resolution stating that employees could be denied credit on a picture and compensation for their work if they were suspected of communist sympathies and had not formally cleared their names. Ultimately, the MPAA was pressuring the guilds to require loyalty oaths. Although the MPAA did not officially hold power over the guilds, this was a case of an employers' organization compelling employees' associations to act. In light of the citations against the Ten, it was clear that the stakes were high. In short order, the guilds acquiesced, and SWG members began vociferous, contentious debates over whether loyalty oaths should, could, or would become a fixed part of contract language.[129]

By that time, the SWG was in the throes of reorganizing from the top down. The election held in November 1947 offered two slates. The "Progressive Slate" supported Sheridan Gibney for president and included I.A.L. Diamond (writer of *Some Like It Hot*, *The Apartment*, and *Irma la Douce*), Arthur Kober (writer of *Me and My Gal*), Frances Goodrich, Albert Hackett, and Lester Cole, a current SWG board member and one of the Hollywood Ten. They campaigned under a platform of upholding a "unified, progressive, and militant Guild" that would support the AAA, oppose the Taft-Hartley Act, and repudiate the actions of HUAC.[130]

The alternate candidates, the self-proclaimed "All-Guild Slate," was, as Leonard Spigelgass (*Gypsy*) described it, "a merger of innocent liberals like myself and some very right-wing people, but more non- than anti-Communist." The All-Guild Slate promised to "restore control to the people who would use it for the purposes for which it was intended, the protection of writers' economic interests."[131] Rather than focus on political discussions, HUAC, or Red-baiting, the candidates argued that the key issues facing the Guild were salary raises and improvements to the minimum basic agreement. They believed that the current, more left-leaning board was using the Guild as an "organ for political propaganda" and had to be stopped.[132] But they described themselves as committed to restoration, and they promoted the idea of a Guild serving solely an economic purpose. It was a campaign intended to create an image of a sanitized Guild and to absolve the SWG of all charges or hints of communist affiliation.

The All-Guild slate won handily, and in the process the Guild redefined itself as a trade association designed to help working writers rather than a union mandated to defend all of its members, not just A-listers or Red-baiters. As described by a *TSW* editorial a year after the change in leadership, this iteration of the board was elected "primarily on the platform of restricting Guild activities to Guild affairs" and "pledged to do all in its power to drive politics out of the Guild."[133] In fact, the push was not so much to drive out politics as it was to drive out radical politics within the Guild. From a historical standpoint, scholars could argue that it was an utterly political move to sacrifice the Ten and turn a blind eye to the threats soon to come for other left-leaning liberals who remained in the Guild.

Victor Navasky argues that A-list writers had a higher stake in the economic structure of Hollywood production. Thus, those at the top were most vulnerable to the pressures of HUAC.[134] The voices of some A-list writers swayed a few on the Guild leadership who wavered about turning away from the Ten. That is not to say that the Guild did nothing to support members who were targeted by the Committee; however, the new leadership had simply decided to focus on protecting the majority rather than risking controversy to rescue the minority.

The Guild did offer some assistance in the form of legal aid for the Ten. Thurman Arnold, an iconoclastic antitrust lawyer and friend of screenwriter Charles Brackett, was hired to represent the Guild in an *amicus curiae* brief less in support of the Ten than a call for an injunction against the blacklist, which Arnold called a conspiracy. Charging the industry with collusion against employees seemed one of few options for a legal counterattack.[135] And while *TSW* quickly changed its tone and pulled back from its liberal stance, other small publications attempted to raise their voices on behalf of the blacklisted writers. *Hollywood Review* and *California Quarterly* provided some commentary and opinion pieces critiquing the blacklist, but these journals did not have the clout or the reach of *TSW*, let alone the audience of an industry trade paper or big-city newspaper.

The right-wing press berated the left-leaning writers mercilessly. In particular, William Wilkerson, the owner and publisher of the *Hollywood*

Reporter, seized the opportunity to declare that the film industry was in crisis: theater attendance had dropped precipitously, and foreign films were threatening the livelihood of Hollywood's industry. According to Wilkerson, everyone—except the writers—was uniting to support the cause of preserving Hollywood. His outrage toward writers was unbridled:

> SOMETHING MUST BE DONE ABOUT THESE PEOPLE! IT MUST BE DONE IMMEDIATELY! . . . Producers, directors, actors, technicians, labor—all have agreed, WITH BUT ONE DISSENTING VOTE: THE WRITER! The Molotov of our industry! . . . Either the SWG is still dominated and controlled by a Communist bloc that will gladly destroy the industry to protect the Unholy Ten and their fellow travelers since it can't be captured for the Soviets, OR the sentiments expressed at the meeting Monday night ARE the sentiments of the Guild majority, whether that be left or right. In either case the SWG is rotten to the core.[136]

The Taft-Hartley Act also placed unions and guilds in a new and increasingly more defensive position. Members of the CFA began backtracking from their earlier statements of support for the Ten. Humphrey Bogart was pressured by his studio and publicists to write an article for *Photoplay* called "I'm No Communist." Fellow A-list actor John Garfield also wrote a *mea culpa* to fans, "I'm a Sucker for a Left Hook," declaring that he had been duped. And then in September 1948, the editors of *TSW* announced that the journal would henceforth be published on a "voluntary basis," a vague term that seemed to imply that it would continue, but perhaps not for a while. The editors claimed the reason was purely financial: they could reduce the normal cost of $2,000 per issue to $419 by employing a volunteer staff and adding advertisements and paid subscriptions. But that amount still seemed exorbitant if *TSW* was not to be a "live and dynamic publication."[137] The editors made an appeal to readers to contribute toward the future of the journal. Looking back, it is clear that *TWS* was far too progressive for its time and that many writers could not or would not support it. The next issue of *TSW* was its last.

Out of a concern for diminishing funds and lost time, the Ten agreed that only two among them, Lawson and Trumbo, would stand trial in the US District Court in Washington, DC. Whatever verdict was decided in those trials would be accepted by the other eight in their cases. The trials began in April 1949, and the judge soon found Lawson and Trumbo guilty of contempt of Congress for refusing to answer the questions posed by the Committee. The remaining eight defendants went before a judge and a jury and were convicted as well. Each hearing took less than an hour. After an appellate ruling in 1949 in the Court of Appeals for the DC Circuit, Lawson and Trumbo began serving one-year sentences in a federal prison in Kentucky in early June 1950. The eight began serving their same year-long sentences soon after.[138] In a strange twist, J. Parnell Thomas, the HUAC chairman, joined Lardner and Cole in a federal prison in Danbury, Connecticut, where he served nearly nine months of an eighteen-month sentence for conspiring to defraud the US Treasury by padding his staff payroll.

Around this time, the executive board of the SWG passed a resolution to support a loyalty oath. Some members of the board wanted every Guild member to sign a statement of non-communist affiliation, but others pushed back. Carl Foreman, who wrote *High Noon* and *Bridge on the River Kwai*, remembered that "the fights were so bitter, and I stood out against that loyalty oath. And Spigelgass, who had been my commander when I was in his regiment during the war, begged me, crying, not to vote against the loyalty oath. 'It'll ruin you,' he said to me; 'you're throwing your career away.'"[139] Ultimately, all of the members of the board signed the oath, which stated:

> BE IT RESOLVED that we, members of the Board of the Screen Writers Guild, affirm our anti-Communist position and voluntarily have signed the following oath:
>
> > "I AM NOT A MEMBER OF THE COMMUNIST PARTY NOR AFFIL-IATED WITH SUCH PARTY, AND I DO NOT BELIEVE IN, AND I AM NOT A MEMBER OF, NOR DO I SUPPORT ANY ORGANIZATION THAT BELIEVES OR TEACHES THE OVERTHROW OF THE UNITED STATES GOVERNMENT BY FORCE."
>
> AND BE IT FURTHER RESOLVED that, deep in the conviction that the Guild is nonpolitical and a professional organization, we will resist any motion or efforts to impose on the Guild's general membership any loyalty oaths not required by law.[140]

The odd language of this statement reveals the conflicted opinions of the board members. Though they describe the Guild as a "nonpolitical" organization, the statement is political. They signed it voluntarily, and yet there is a clear sense that they were concerned about outside persuasion or force that might impose a loyalty oath on SWG members. This resolution became part of the Guild's constitution in 1951 and remained in effect until 1973. Thus, by agreeing to the MPAA's loyalty requests, the Guild effectively aided in the institution and enforcement of the blacklist.

During the court challenge to HUAC, there was a reprieve in Committee hearings for others in Hollywood who had been labeled radicals or subversives. The studios turned their attention to the new realities of vertical deregulation under the Supreme Court's Paramount Consent Decree, which called for the divestment of theater chains from studios' holdings. Then, in 1951, with the Ten still imprisoned, HUAC initiated a second wave of hearings in Hollywood and later subpoenaed Hollywood writers to testify before the Committee in Washington. This time, more than a hundred Hollywood professionals (writers, actors, and directors, among others) were called. The Red-baiting began anew and with even greater fervor. At the SWG, the All-Guild board members were inclined to duck and ignore loudmouthed members on the right and the left.

In fact, both election slates had endorsed Sheridan Gibney for president, believing him to be nonpartisan and a figure who might unite the organization. However, Gibney detested the subpoenaed writers. Nearly thirty years

IMAGE 14 Carl Foreman at HUAC hearings, c. 1951. *High Noon* was in the midst of production when Foreman was called to testify.

Writers Guild Foundation Archive, Shavelson-Webb Library, Los Angeles

later, he was still incensed: "The Guild almost was destroyed by the Communist-minded members. . . . [T]hey had done the Guild a tremendous disservice by bringing about this situation where the Guild and the Communist Party were identified in the form of dual membership and there was never any attempt on the part of these people to preserve or protect the Guild as an organization for representing writers with a nonpolitical base."[141] Gibney and others felt that some of the Guild's left-leaning members had misused their organization as an instrument for political causes. To Gibney, this selfish activity seemed like a betrayal of the organization he had been elected to lead.

The blacklist proper consisted of individuals whom the government deemed to be under suspicion, disfavor, or attack, and who the studios, in turn, unofficially dictated should not be allowed to work in Hollywood. A HUAC subpoena alone could mean the end of studio employment. Paul Jarrico knew that he had been blacklisted the morning he arrived at RKO and studio security stopped him from passing through the studio gates. The previous day Jarrico had received a subpoena at his home, delivered by a US marshal who happened to be accompanied by a throng of news reporters.[142] His writing partner and friend Richard Collins, who wrote *Song of Russia* and had been a member of the Communist Party, had named Jarrico among twenty-six individuals he alleged were communists.

Individuals who were blacklisted had no idea how long their exile might last, nor could they guess the extent to which a HUAC subpoena would destroy their careers.[143] While there was no official list of names, several organizations cropped up offering Hollywood and Congress their "assistance" in rooting out the enemy. With America's entrance into the Korean War in 1950 and Wisconsin Senator Joseph McCarthy's declaration that 205 communists were currently working in the State Department, the scourge of communism weighed heavily on Americans' hearts and minds.

By 1950, the talent guilds had suspended any remaining objections to the existence of the blacklist, and the guilds' leaders were fully cooperating with HUAC's agenda. The blustery air of the Cold War became the new reality, not just in Hollywood but throughout the country. The talent guilds began to insist that all members provide a statement of non-communist affiliation.[144] The SWG agreed that studios could, without awaiting trial, remove any blacklisted writer's name from the credits of a film. Writers had worked tirelessly in the previous decade to secure the power to determine their credits in films but now relinquished this right without much resistance. Even having one's name attached to a project that was retroactively deemed suspect—most notably, films such as *Mission to Moscow* and *Crossfire*—could end a career. Walter Bernstein, who was blacklisted during the 1950s, explains the significance of a writer's reputation: "It was all about your name. . . . They wanted your name. When they were asking you to give the names of people who were in the Communist Party, they already had all those names, they didn't need it from you particularly. They wanted to be able to say, look he gave his name to us. Essentially, you were collaborating. And they could say, look [Elia] Kazan is one of us. Budd Schulberg is one of us. They cooperated."[145] It was now a liability for a writer even to be in the membership ranks of a suspect labor organization.

Having one's name exposed and ending up on the blacklist was a cataclysmic event in people's lives. In an interview with historian Howard Suber, Joan Scott sadly recalled what it felt like to work in Hollywood during this time: "This is a subpoena commanding me to appear before the Committee. It's pink and still gives me chills to look at it. When Adrian and I were married, we talked about having our subpoenas framed. We grew up in a time when a very appropriate wedding gift was his and hers bath towels and we thought that we'd have our subpoenas framed side by side saying his and hers. Unfortunately, we were never in that kind of freewheeling position to do that."[146] Adrian and Joan Scott would otherwise have been at the prime of their careers—a young, talented couple, newly married—but instead struggled to make a life for themselves and worked under pseudonyms (both wrote a number of episodes of *Lassie*). Some writers, like Schulberg and Kazan, felt it was their patriotic duty to expose others. Schulberg concluded that he had no choice: "It's not easy to do. My own feeling was that while I didn't like the Committee being so right-wing, I didn't think it was healthy having a secret organization trying to control the Writers Guild. I felt it was wrong and undermining [to] democracy."[147] Schulberg, like Gibney, felt that leftist partisans within the Guild were destroying their community and, on a larger level, jeopardizing America's democracy.

There was another incentive to name names. Guild members who acknowledged previous communist affiliation and gave the Committee the names of other writers were permitted by HUAC to continue to work. In 1952, soon after his success with *A Streetcar Named Desire*, director Elia Kazan, a previous member of the American Communist Party in New York, identified Lillian Hellman, Dashiell Hammett, Clifford Odets (a playwright and screenwriter of *Sweet Smell of Success*), and others to the Committee. Hammett had already served time in federal prison for contempt of court in connection with his leadership of a "subversive" civil rights organization; he testified about his own activities before HUAC in 1953 but refused to cooperate with his interrogators and was blacklisted. Hammett never published again. Hellman, a celebrated playwright and screenwriter, refused to testify before HUAC in 1952, declaring, "I cannot and will not cut my conscience to fit this year's fashions." It took her eight years to resurrect her career; she returned to writing plays, but never again wrote for film.

The list of celebrated writers who were censured is staggering. Sidney Buchman, who wrote *Mr. Smith Goes to Washington* with conservative anticommunist writer Lewis R. Foster, was cited for contempt of Congress after he refused to supply HUAC with names of communists. The Committee fined him $150 and gave him a year's suspended sentence, and he found his career halted by the blacklist for ten years. In 1952, Gibney was removed from his office and blacklisted for suspected subversive writing.[148] Some members of the SWG, like Borden Chase, who scripted *Red River* and *Winchester '73*, called on the Guild board to demand that individuals who agreed to testify before HUAC be cleared from all past deeds.[149] Nevertheless, access to the industry was blocked for all blacklisted employees, and it would remain so for over a decade.

In *Naming Names*, Victor Navasky assessed the wider damage: "Ultimately it was the informer's contribution to spoil the possibility of trust and thereby the sense of community. People in Hollywood lost not only their myths (of the happy ending, among others), their careers, possessions, place, status, and space, but also their sense of self. . . . And for many the trauma came as much in reaction to being disconnected from a familiar network of unspoken understandings as from any job or other loss suffered directly as a result of being called a Communist or being up on a list."[150] This period of inquisition, stigmatization, and exile devastated Hollywood artisans, craftspeople, and their families' sense of trust in the industry and in their community. The collective memory of the industry, the guilds, and their members would be forever scarred by the choices people made during these years.

Beyond the blacklist, so-called graylists captured the names of another three hundred individuals, who were smeared in publications and pamphlets like *Red Channels*, *Alert*, and *Counterattack*. *Red Channels* was a privately distributed pamphlet that focused on suspected communists within American broadcasting. Larry Markes, who later wrote for *The Dean Martin Comedy Hour*, explained why some Americans found the idea of communist-affiliated radio and television writers more insidious than film writers with checkered pasts: "The networks were very pure and upstanding guys who said, 'Look, it's one thing to have a commie write a movie because you don't have to go and see that movie. . . . But we're coming into these people's houses with these communistic viewpoints and that's why they were blacklisted, because we're coming right into their living rooms, we're mind-washing the children.'"[151]

The adoption of signed anticommunist oaths became the industry standard not only in film but also in the newly devised television contracts. Producers would deny screen credit to all subpoened writers who refused to testify before HUAC, or to any writer who falsely signed an oath denying communist affiliations. And, in keeping with the decisions of other talent guilds' leadership, the SWG board authorized its president to disclose private union records to HUAC.[152]

In 1952, Ring Lardner Jr. resigned his membership after what he called the Jarrico Resolution, when the SWG board agreed to permit the staunchly right-wing Howard Hughes to remove Paul Jarrico's name from the film *The Las Vegas Story*. Mary McCall Jr., then president of the SWG, tried to prevent the erasure and consequently endured an admonishment by HUAC herself. Lardner accused the board of assisting in the blacklisting of writers. Consequently, he declared, the SWG no longer represented him, and he had no reason to pay dues. Though he continued writing under various pseudonyms and ultimately under his own name again, Lardner did not rejoin the Guild until the early 1960s.[153]

By 1954, when HUAC finally ceased its long inquiry into the entertainment industry, more than 320 film and television professionals had been censured. Many writers who had been blacklisted resigned from the SWG or were removed from Guild membership for nonpayment of dues. A vast number of other writers just kept their heads down and tried to stay out of the crossfire. Many of them years later said in interviews that they wished they had done more—or even done something at all.

Writing Under the Blacklist

The public is not to be protected from my work, however beguiling and subversive it may be. The public is only to be protected from my name.

–Paul Jarrico, quoted in Dick Vosburgh, "Paul Jarrico: Obituary,"
The Independent [UK], 5 November 1997

By the early 1950s, the entire American film industry was undergoing a radical metamorphosis. The studio system was dying. On a global scale, currency freezes in all of the major European markets (Great Britain, France, Germany, and Italy) locked up American finances, and the studios had to search for new ways not only to make money internationally but also to spend it. On a national scale, the Supreme Court's Paramount Consent Decree forced the studios to divest their theater chains; consequently, they were no longer assured distribution for all the films they produced. At the same time, the staggering success of early commercial television was keeping more viewers at home.

With the marketplace for cinema shrinking, the blacklist became a means for the studios to downsize. Jon Lewis argues that the blacklist bailed out the studios at a moment of crisis:

> The blacklist was a first step in a larger transformation of the film industry from its roots in entrepreneurial capital to a more corporatist, conglomerate mode. Impending deregulation—and what can only be characterized as industry-wide panic in response—prompted change that the Red Scare made not only possible but easy. In the final analysis, the blacklist did not save America from films promoting Communism, liberalism, or humanitarianism. Instead, it encouraged studio owners to develop and adopt a corporate model more suited to a future new Hollywood, one in which, despite market deregulation and stricter self-regulation of film content, studio owners would maintain profitability and control.[154]

The swiftness with which the studios accepted and incorporated the blacklist into the industry's new modus operandi is, in retrospect, quite striking. That so little pushback occurred or is documented among studio heads seems to affirm Lewis's argument. The studios' collusion with HUAC provided an easy means to terminate a number of longstanding employees' contracts, to phase out the first-generation Jewish studio moguls, to attack the unions, and to move toward a more corporatized, conglomerate model.

Writers bore the brunt of the blacklist in Hollywood, especially at the beginning. As Nancy Lynn Schwartz explains, the censorship of writers was taking place on two fronts.[155] First came the stifling of creativity through Hollywood's Production Code and criticism from national and local organizations and media outlets on the watch for subversion. Second, self-censorship for career preservation became the norm: writers chose lighter, less controversial topics to avoid questions about their political leanings. As the number of blacklisted writers grew through the early 1950s, other types of creative and craft workers suffered as well. But unlike other industry employees, writers could work anonymously. That writers never stepped on the set was suddenly a saving grace, and they devised tactics to avoid being seen at all by the individuals signing their paychecks.

Two expedients enabled blacklisted writers to get and keep work: using pseudonyms and asking another writer to serve as a front (signing his or her name to a script written by a blacklisted writer). Starting in 1948, the SWG allowed members to work under pseudonyms unless they were contractually obligated to use their real names. However, the Guild demanded registration of pseudonyms to ensure payment and to preclude the use of offensive names.[156] Blacklisted writers were not allowed to use pseudonyms, but many disregarded the rule. Television was a slightly safer place for blacklisted writers to work: producers were desperate for content, and many new writers were getting a chance to write for series, even if they had little experience. Thus, unknown names (and the writers behind them) had a good shot of getting work, especially if someone on the set was willing to vouch for them.

While blacklisted, Walter Bernstein, Abraham Polonsky, and Arnold Manott (who previously scripted *Man from Frisco*) wrote under pseudonyms for the CBS series *You Are There*, with the sympathetic Sidney Lumet directing their episodes. They wrote about heroic rebellions against angry vigilantes, the Salem witch trials, and persecuted heroes like Socrates, Galileo, and Joan of Arc. Polonsky recalled: "This was a very good show on television and it was probably the only place where any guerrilla warfare was conducted against McCarthy in a public medium. . . . Every once in a while the pseudonym would be revealed, so we would just use another one, because they would blacklist even a non-existent writer."[157] Joan Scott remembered, "We did a lot of *Lassies.* . . . I fronted for [her husband, Adrian] on the TV show from 1955 on until 1961. I wrote some and he wrote some, but they were all under my pen name—Joanne Court. I got to be known as 'the woman who writes like a man.'"[158]

The fight to get blacklisted creatives and craft workers back to work, and for them to use their real names again, was long and hard. In 1952, Trumbo and Cole sued MGM for $350,000 in unpaid wages and canceled contracts.[159] Lardner sued Twentieth Century–Fox, and Adrian and Joan Scott filed suit against RKO. Altogether, the Hollywood Ten sued the studios for $61 million in back pay.[160] They were not alone in demanding compensation for the lost the opportunity to work. In 1960, Nedrick Young, who wrote *Jailhouse Rock*, became a plaintiff in a twelve-person class action lawsuit that claimed the MPAA had violated the Sherman Antitrust Act in its authorization of the blacklist. Young testified, "We've counted our losses, waited, and fought for the day when we would have not only jobs but names."[161] In a supporting affidavit John Howard Lawson explained to the court the significance of a writer's name: "A writer's name is his most cherished possession. It is the basis of his economic life, and the 'trademark' which establishes his competence and craftsmanship. It is more than the means by which he earns his bread. It is his creative personality, the symbol of the whole body of his ideas and experience."[162]

Young's case was settled out of court for $100,000, far less than the $7.65 million demanded by the plaintiffs. But in many ways, the lawsuits had a more fundamental, far-reaching impact: they forced the studios to face the blacklisted writers in the courtroom. Around this time, a number of writers started getting work in Hollywood again. Still, the return to work was slow and not at all certain. The blacklist had started in 1947, but for some it did not fully end until the middle of the 1960s. For a small group, blacklisting stretched well into the 1970s.[163]

Writers often took extraordinary steps to continue writing or to help friends and colleagues who wanted to keep writing. Some screenwriters were lucky enough to find advocates who fronted for them, and some of the films written under these conditions became box office hits and are among the most celebrated of the 1950s. Young was a front for Alvah Bessie on *Passage West* before being blacklisted and writing *The Defiant Ones* and *Inherit the Wind* under the pseudonym Nathan E. Douglas. Michael Blankfort fronted for Albert Maltz on *Broken Arrow*. Dalton Trumbo sold scripts for *Gun Crazy*, *Roman Holiday*, *The Brave One*, and *Spartacus* using fronts and pseudonyms. In 1957, Hollywood had to face the absurdity of this blacklist in a most embarrassing way. At the Academy Awards that year, Robert Rich won Best Motion Picture Story for *The Brave One*. Not only was Rich not in the audience, he did not exist. Jesse Lasky Jr. rushed onto the stage to accept the award from actress Deborah Kerr, telling the audience that his good friend Rich was in the maternity ward with his wife, who was about to deliver. In reality, Rich was Trumbo's pseudonym. At that same ceremony, the screenplay for *Friendly Persuasion*, by blacklisted writer Michael Wilson, was nominated for Best Adapted Screenplay, although no writer had been listed in the film's credits. Wilson did win the SWG award for Best American Drama that year.

Groucho Marx told guests at the awards dinner that although Moses was originally given credit for *The Ten Commandments*, the producers had removed his name when they found out he had crossed the Red Sea.

After these incidents, the Academy's board of governors passed a bylaw prohibiting the presentation of Academy Awards to witnesses who had been "unfriendly" before HUAC. (Strangely, such individuals could still be nominated.) Trumbo began a letter-writing campaign, declaring that he was

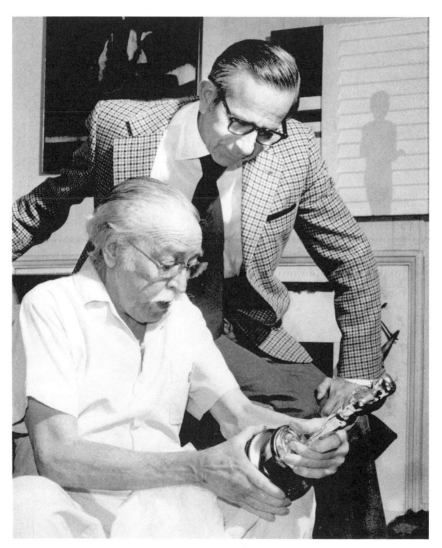

IMAGE 15 Dalton Trumbo finally getting his 1957 Academy Award for *The Brave One* in 1975, delivered to him by the then Academy president, producer Walter Mirisch.

Writers Guild Foundation Archive, Shavelson-Webb Library, Los Angeles

"Robert Rich" and demanding that the studios end the blacklist. The Academy agreed to rescind the 1957 bylaw against blacklisted writers so long as they agreed not to embarrass the Academy publicly. A year later, the script written by Wilson and fellow blacklisted writer Carl Foreman for *The Bridge on the River Kwai* won the Oscar for Best Adapted Screenplay. However, at the ceremony the statuette was handed to the French author of the novel, Pierre Boulle, who could not speak or write English. After Ned Young agreed in 1959 not to embarrass the Academy by revealing his identity as the writer of the Oscar-winning screenplay for *The Defiant Ones*, the board of governors rescinded the bylaw. In 1960, Otto Preminger publicly announced that he had asked Trumbo to write the screenplay for *Exodus.* Soon afterward, Kirk Douglas declared that Trumbo had authored the script for *Spartacus.* By 1968, the Guild had slowly begun to reinstate credits. However, to this day, many blacklisted writers remain uncredited or miscredited.

The Legacy of the Blacklist

> The blacklist was a time of evil, and no one on either side who survived it came through untouched by evil. . . . It will do no good to search for villains or heroes or saints or devils because there were none; there were only victims. Some suffered less than others, some grew and some diminished, but in the final tally we were all victims because almost without exception each of us felt compelled to say things he did not want to say, to do things that he did not want to do, to deliver and receive wounds he truly did not want to exchange. That is why none of us–right, left, or center–emerged from that long nightmare without sin.
>
> –Dalton Trumbo, Laurel Award acceptance speech, 1970

Looking back on the blacklist era, Devery Freeman, one of the founders of the SWG, believed that Hollywood learned a lesson in going against its writers: "I think that what Hollywood has learned through that is that good writers are not replaceable. Certainly not that easily because . . . so many of them that were blacklisted continued to be needed by Hollywood—wrote a lot of the product and surfaced after the tension and became some of our proudest boasts—our greatest writers."[164] It took until 1970—the year that Ring Lardner Jr. wrote *M*A*S*H* (and a year later won an Oscar for it)—for the SWG to repeal its bylaw barring admitted communists from membership.

In 1976, when Carl Foreman introduced Michael Wilson as the winner of the Writers Guild Laurel Award, he reminded the audience, "our bloody Oscar has been sitting in Pierre Boulle's living room, and I suppose that by now he's given up wondering how the hell it ever got there."[165] Wilson, in his acceptance speech, implored the younger generation of writers never to forget the story of the blacklist and reminded the Guild of its responsibility to defend mavericks and dissenters.[166] In 1985, nine years after this event, Foreman and Wilson were awarded posthumous Oscars for *Bridge on the River Kwai.*

The legacy of the blacklist, for writers, Guild members, and the Guild as an institution is something individuals still grapple with. In many ways, the blacklist battles continued to define the politics and the policies of the Guild as it matured, a topic to be explored in the following chapters. Since the 1970s, but particularly since the fiftieth anniversary of the blacklist in 1997, the Guild has trained its focus on authors' First Amendment rights and authors' rights overall. In 1982, Al and Helen Levitt, both of whom had been blacklisted in the 1950s and then wrote for *That Girl* in the 1960s, convinced the Guild leadership to issue supplementary benefits to writers who were unable to contribute to their pension funds as a result of their forced unemployment. In the 1990s, persuaded by Paul Jarrico, the Guild created an official Credit Restoration Committee. In 1997, at an enormous star-studded event, the AMPTP and the presidents of SAG, WGA, DGA, and AFTRA officially apologized for their organizations' complicity in the blacklist. [167]

For the individual writers, survivor status came at a complicated cost. Are these individuals first and foremost writers—or blacklisted writers? Joan Scott questioned how much she should hold on to her name and thus the identity and memory of her past experiences: "[T]here is something romantic about dead Reds, but not necessarily about the live ones who are trying to get writing assignments. . . . The whole question of the blacklist, the whole question of identity. Should I have kept my maiden name—should I have taken another name? Do I have [three] lives: one as Adrian Scott's widow, another as a writer, another as a woman who tries to work for what I believe in. It's very confusing . . . even trusting [people] today. Wondering what the neighbors know. Wondering if there are more phone tappings and more FBI stakeouts."[168] The next chapters will explore the transformations in the industry that Scott pointed out here and will examine how these shifts, in turn, altered the work of writing.

229   EXT. OPEN COUNTRY - MOVING SHOT - ETHAN

        as Martin runs and grabs hold of his stirrup, trying to
        fight the horse to a stop. Ethan swings on him -- once,
        twice -- and Martin is knocked sprawling. Ethan rides
        on, relentlessly. *MARTIN JUMPS ON AFTER HIM.*

230   EXT. OPEN COUNTRY - FULL SHOT - DEBBIE AND ETHAN

        She is running and dodging trying to escape the horseman.
        Ethan has his gun drawn. She ducks to one side and the
        horse goes past. Both figures are almost obscured in the
        dust. Ethan spins his mount and charges after her. She
        runs and then falls -- and he is off his horse, and striding
        toward her. ~~ETHAN ... DEBBIE!~~ *{MARTIN: NO, ETHAN, NO!}*

231   EXT. OPEN COUNTRY - ETHAN AND DEBBIE

        Ethan is at the left of CAMERA and slightly closer to the
        foreground, with Debbie at the right, supine on the ground
        and the dust swirling around her. Ethan draws and raises
        his gun. The hammer goes back. *IN B.G. MARTIN HAS SCRAMBLED*
        TO HIS FEET AND IS RUNNIN FORWARD.
                            ETHAN — *DEBBIE!*
                      ~~(quietly)~~   *{MARTIN: NO, ETHAN, NO!}*
                 ~~I'm sorry, girl. Shut your eyes...~~

        The dust clears. The CAMERA MOVES slightly forward along
        the gun-arm and HOLDS on Debbie's face -- the eyes gazing
        fearlessly, innocently into Ethan's. We HOLD for a long
        moment and then the gun lowers. Ethan slowly holsters it
        and walks over to her. ~~fast~~

232   EXT. OPEN COUNTRY - CLOSE SHOT - ETHAN

        He looks down at her.

                            ETHAN *LET'S GO HOME!*
                      (softly) →
                 ~~You sure favor your mother...~~

233   EXT. OPEN COUNTRY - MED. CLOSE SHOT - THE TWO *HER UP IN*
                                                    PICKS HIS ARMS.

        He extends his hand to her. She takes it and he helps her
        to her feet. And then she is against his chest and his
        arm goes protectingly about her. They are standing that
        way when Martin stumbles up -- and stares.

                                                    WIPE TO:

233-A   EXT. COMANCHE CAMP - WIDE ANGLE - DAY

        The line of Rangers is afoot now, each man near his horse,
        each man with rifle out, pumping shot after shot at the
        fleeting remnant of Comanches riding down the long valley

IMAGE 16 Frank S. Nugent's notes on a draft of *The Searchers*, c. 1955.
Writers Guild Foundation Shavelson-Webb Library, Los Angeles

3

The Infant Prodigy

BANKS: Did you think about the potential for reruns when you created *The Dick Van Dyke Show*? It still feels fresh. It is a series with longevity.

CARL REINER: I'm so happy you say that, because I was aware that it could be. I realized I was writing about human relationships, and I was very aware . . . that it could be a classic. I was not saying it to people—they would think you were crazy. But I assiduously told every writer . . . no slang of the day . . . a gun is a gun, not a gat or a rod. Use words. . . . And I get letters from people who are kids seeing it for the first time and they are digging it.

—Interview, 29 August 2013

By the late 1940s, television sets were quickly becoming the most coveted accessory for the modern American home. Media historian Lynn Spigel has masterly documented the installation of television into American families' daily lives.[1] The simultaneous process of integrating television writers into professional writing communities provides an important lens for viewing the evolving nature of screenwriting and of labor's voice within the media industries. Television was new territory for professional writers, and, during the early 1950s, three of the four writing branches of the Authors League of America—the Dramatists Guild, the Radio Writers Guild (RWG), and the Screen Writers Guild (SWG)—were eager to claim jurisdiction over television in labor negotiations.

While each guild made its case for jurisdiction, television writers themselves were not convinced that affiliation with any of these organizations would help them to gain better pay and solid benefits.[2] Many of the writers were already dues-paying members of either the RWG or the SWG, or both. The SWG represented approximately 70 percent of the 375 writers on contract to write for television shows at this time—but many of those writers were members of the SWG based on their filmed works.[3] The SWG claimed that only 11 percent of television writers were in the RWG.[4] But the newest entertainment labor group, the Television Writers Association (TWA), claimed sole jurisdiction over all television writers, given that only a handful of series were even being recorded on film.[5]

In August 1952 some of the biggest names in television writing came together to express their concerns about how the production studios and agencies creating live-action series were treating them. This group, made up of approximately thirty-five men and women who were writing the bulk of all scripted series on television at the time, united to form the TWA. In a press release, the new organization announced its purpose and declared itself necessary because no existing union was capable of supporting the unique needs of this group. The SWG and RWG, it claimed, "are concerned with other media, radio and pictures, and working television writers believe that the only answer to their problems is a union which will be concerned solely with television."[6] The TWA established itself under the umbrella of the Authors League of America and set up headquarters in New York. It filed for certification with the National Labor Relations Board, requesting that TWA serve as the bargaining agent for all labor negotiations involving professional television writers, whether they worked for live or filmed series. The group appointed Charles Isaacs, writer on *The Colgate Comedy Hour*, president; Jess Oppenheimer, the creator of *I Love Lucy*, became vice president, and Richard Powell, later a writer on *Hogan's Heroes*, publicity director.

Many television writers were justifiably concerned about joining any guild that could, and did, turn against its own during the blacklist era. Nate Monaster, a writer on *The George Burns and Gracie Allen Show*, was among those who were uncomfortable with the SWG: "The Screen Writer's Guild had entered into this NLRB election and wanted to be the union for television writers. Now we resisted this because a lot of us felt, I know I felt, that the role of the Guild in the entire Blacklist was not a noble one."[7] Despite these concerns, the SWG was determined to win jurisdiction. It continued to add members from the television world over the next few months and demanded that the TWA withdraw its application for NLRB certification.[8] But the TWA kept signing new writers, and by the end of August 1952, it had 125 members.[9]

In October 1952, SWG leaders hosted an informal meeting with the heads of the TWA and the RWG, hoping yet again to persuade the TWA to withdraw its application to the NLRB. It didn't work. The television writers instead used the occasion to issue a list of non-negotiable conditions. Oppenheimer, as the head of the committee on objectives, presented the following principles:

- No blacklist for reasons of race, creed, color, sex, or political beliefs or associations.
- All negotiations for television writers to be conducted by a representative committee, elected by and responsible to a majority vote.
- Complete ownership of material by the television writer.
- Payment [by producers] for first-use of material. Payment for each re-use.
- Ownership-participation in series by writer who has contributed all or part of the format of characters used.
- No speculative writing.
- Full payment for audition or pilot film scripts.
- Limitation on re-writes. Original author shall have exclusive right to revise his own material.
- Limitation on time for consideration of freelance scripts.
- Credits for writers on a show on a guild-established procedure.
- Arbitration machinery for the settlement of disputes.[10]

With this list, television writers identified outstanding issues on which the SWG had failed film writers, most notably blacklisting and ownership, and they expected the TWA to do better by them.

Two years after the premiere of *I Love Lucy*, with his show garnering the top television ratings, Jess Oppenheimer was called to testify before the NLRB at the instigation of the SWG. Testimony that day related to Oppenheimer's disparate roles as a producer working for Desilu Productions, as vice president of the TWA, and as head writer of *Lucy*. The attorney for the SWG insisted that Oppenheimer, as a prestigious producer and an employer of writers, had exercised unfair influence in recruiting his two writers, Madeline Pugh and Bob Carroll Jr., to join the TWA.[11] That Oppenheimer was also a dues-paying member of the SWG was of no consequence. His privilege as a producer and employer overshadowed his claim as a writer.

It seems difficult today to understand why this brilliant and talented writer on a meteoric rise to the top of this newly formed media industry posed such a threat to his fellow screenwriters. One reason is that Oppenheimer had created a television series so popular that it kept audiences at home

IMAGE 17 Madeline Pugh, writer for *I Love Lucy*, with producers and stars of the series, Lucille Ball and Desi Arnaz, c. 1953.
Writers Guild Foundation Archive, Shavelson-Webb Library, Los Angeles

watching *Lucy* instead of heading out to the movies. In 1953, the big studios faced significant obstacles: the 1948 Paramount Decree was forcing the studios to divest themselves of their theater chains; the seven-year contracts for all above-the-line talent were tying up key financial resources; and film audiences were dwindling at the larger city movie houses. The studios, and their employees, were anxious to stop this financial hemorrhaging. Oppenheimer and the TWA were easier to attack than the more diffuse troubles the film industry faced.

But something else about Oppenheimer that made him a concern for screenwriters: he was both a writer *and* a producer. The SWG was in the business of representing writers in negotiations and disputes with the studios, and their chief opponents were producers. Screenwriters had battled fake, studio-backed unions before, including the Screen Playwrights, and they were wary of any representative that could be aligned with management. It is not surprising, then, that after twenty years of battling with studio producers, the Screen Writers Guild leaders could not fathom the notion that an upstart writer-producer forming a new union could be good for their constituents.

While Oppenheimer was among the first writer-producers in the industry, there had been other kinds of hyphenates that had not provoked the ire of the Guild, including Ernst Lubitsch and John Huston. Writer-producer-director Billy Wilder ruled a rowdy writers table in the studio lunchroom. Dore Schary and Phillip Dunne, among others, were active members of the SWG and became producers without having to renounce their membership. Schary even rose to the stature of studio head at MGM. When Dunne became a producer at Twentieth Century–Fox, he contacted the SWG to say that he would rarely, if ever, supervise the work of other writers in his role as a producer, but he did ask for clarification: "Does my new status in any way affect my membership in the Guild? Are there any special dues and obligations I incur in this situation? Must I, for instance, grow a mustache like [former SWG and current AMPAS president] Charlie Brackett's?" The SWG assured him that being a writer-producer did not affect an individual's membership.[12] Dunne struggled with this hyphenated role: "even the writer-producer is not completely free. He is still, however glorified, an employee, subject to the directions, and, in some cases, the apparent lunacies, of the studio executives. His chain may have become a mere web of gossamer, but he is still caught."[13] What was unique about hyphenates in television was that this new position was quickly becoming the rule rather than the exception.

A writer-producer of a television series, especially in the early days of television, would also quite often be the creator of the series. A creator provides the original story, builds a story world that the show's cast inhabits, and often has a continuing role as head writer-producer.

This head writer is, at best, a benevolent dictator who oversees the consistency of voice from episode to episode, runs the writers' room, works on set with the director, actors, cinematographer, and designers to ensure that the words on the page translate to the screen, and often sits in the editing room. Stanley Rubin, writer and producer on *Your Show Time*, explains: "In television, the power lies not in the field of direction but in the field of producing. The producer or the writer-producer in television is the strongest individual on a show. He's the one who's there from start to finish. He provides the continuity to a show. Not the actors and not the director. Not even the individual writer on an individual episode but the writer-producer or producer on a series. He's the one that the network wants to know about first. When it buys a series, the network says who's going to produce it."[14]

In both film and television, the writer-producer hyphenate straddles territory that is difficult to define in terms of labor rules. While a hyphenated writer-producer for film might work in different capacities from film to film, the hyphenated role for television usually remains consistent for many years, as in the case of serialized television series. Gertrude Berg embodied the hyphenate as a true television pioneer: she was a writer, producer, and actor on *The Goldbergs*. Unquestionably, she was a showrunner forty years before the term was conceived.

The SWG desperately wanted to control this new medium, but the Guild's leaders did not yet understand what television was, what its writers' needs were, or how television writers as members could expand the reach of the Guild. They focused narrowly on the danger of producers becoming writers, overlooking the fact that the vast majority of these hyphenates saw themselves as writers first. But in just a few years, the Guild's perceived threat—the television writer-producer—became its most powerful asset. By 1960, film and television writers were walking the picket lines together, a display of unity and determination that, arguably, has never manifested itself so purely again. And the Guild negotiated its biggest wins. Writers gained the right to a fixed percentage from the studios' royalties and, later, won residuals on television reruns and on the broadcasting of cinematic films on television. They also secured health and pension benefits for writers working for signatory companies.

This chapter traces this critical era of transition, from the earliest days of television, to the battle over the jurisdiction of television writing, to the formation of the Writers Guild of America, East and West branches, and to the 1960 WGA strike and its aftermath. Though at first this brokered writers union was an uncomfortable marriage of convenience, by the mid-1960s, the members' alliance—and their solidarity—emerged as a powerful labor force and defined the Writers Guild of America as the strongest voice for creative workers within American media industries. And by the end of this era, the voices of television writers dominated the Writers Guild.

The Coming of Television

I said, "How much will you pay me?" [And Paramount producer Y. Frank Freeman] said, "Oh, nobody has ever written a television show before. We have no idea what to pay you. . . . Maybe three years from now when the salaries are established, we will pay you the highest salary going for that kind of writing." I said, "Fine, you will get the script in exactly three years."

—*The Writer Speaks: Mel Shavelson*
(three-time president of the WGAw), 1996

In 1944 the appeal of the little screen was simply its novelty. When Michael Kanin first saw a television set that year, he wasn't exactly clear about what it was or what it would become, but he was sure that he had see something significant:

One day a friend took me to someone's house. . . . They took us into the back room where in a corner was a box. On the box was a picture. That was the first time I had ever seen a television set. The programming at that time was all very experimental and cursory. There were no regular programs of any kind. But I stared at this damned thing and it fascinated me because there it was: the future before my eyes. And it was so obvious that it had to be an important thing. The following night there was a Screen Writers Guild board meeting. . . . When the subject of New Business arose, I raised my hand and I told them of this experience . . . and I said, "You know, I don't claim to be a prophet but obviously anybody can see that this is going to be a new development of great importance to all of us and I suggest that we investigate it." And I don't know why that touched the funny-bone, but there was a big, big laugh. But at any rate, as a kind of half-joke, I suppose, I was appointed a committee of one to investigate television.[15]

While its aesthetics were inchoate, Kanin and others saw the possibility of a medium that would broadcast image and sound into homes as professionally and economically exciting. Realizing that other guilds were interested in studying television, Kanin began talking with them. What emerged was the Affiliated Committee for Television, a coalition of fifteen guilds and unions in Hollywood—including writers, directors, cartoonists, and cameramen—all working together to "investigate television."[16] The committee also collaborated with professors at UCLA to develop a curriculum for teaching the technical aspects of television to students who wanted to master the new trade.

These film workers were not altruistic in their pursuit of information about television. They were hoping, as one journalist reported, to harness television to the needs of the motion picture industry. They claimed that "the coming of television has reduced the unemployment problem to a remnant of what it was. . . . Television film production affords a picture professional work of the kind he knows how to do when he can't find it in the studios; for less money, to be sure, but work. . . . Bit by bit, evidence piles up to indicate . . . that television's ultimate place . . . will be one of an advertising medium and training school, maybe a proving ground, experimental laboratory. Could be a pretty good thing."[17] But much to Hollywood's dismay, television was not going to slow its pace in order for film practitioners— never mind the film studios—to keep the medium under its control. Soon this device moved beyond the experimental stage to become a legitimate commercial medium. It beamed its mercurial pictures into American homes with tinny jingles as exuberant actors peddled products to anyone listening. The small screen was rapidly becoming a big medium, and with such wealthy corporations behind it, from radio networks to national product sponsors, television was a powerful new force in entertainment. The question not yet answered for writers was how television would transform their craft.

Even in its earliest iterations, television desperately needed writers. Young hopefuls flocked to television writing positions, and television studios and their deep-pocketed sponsors attracted some exceptional talent from the New York stage and vaudeville. Among the new challenges for the guilds in organizing television writers, first and foremost was basic geography.

Television writers were scattered across studios, agencies, networks, and independent production houses primarily in, but not restricted to, New York and Los Angeles. In an age of telegrams and postal mail, any attempt to organize this group would not be easy.

In addition, there were significant differences between television production on the East Coast and production on the West Coast. Ernest Kinoy, who was president of WGA East from 1967 to 1969, saw greater polarization in television than in film production.[18] Los Angeles production was an outgrowth of the film industry, and there producers controlled decision making. Most series were filmed, only a few of them in front of live audiences. In contrast, New York television programs were produced live and were simultaneously recorded on kinescope (a film capture of a television monitor) for later airings. There the industry was rooted in the work of playwrights, radio writers, and news writers, who already understood the speed, structure, needs, and peculiarities of live production.

There were other differences, as well. Writers in New York had more control of talent. David Dortort, creator of *Bonanza*, took part in the casting process for the projects he wrote in New York. The actors who came to audition were all theatrically trained. Coming out of a theater model, where the playwright is celebrated as the author of the text, writers were expected—or allowed, depending on one's perspective—to play a more active role in television production. As Dortort simply put it, "Writers were held in more respect in New York."[19]

The issue of authorial identity and reputation became a problem in television, particularly for writers on anthology series (the leading exemplars of which included *Playhouse 90* and *Philco Playhouse*). Certain writers began gaining acclaim in this milieu. Erna Lazarus highlighted what this kind of recognition meant to television writers: "Television brought the writer's name into prominence. Suddenly people spoke of the Rod Serlings and the Paddy Chayefskys.... Prior to this nobody ever knew who wrote the screenplay. Never [knew] who wrote the picture.... But television did bring importance to the writer, and I don't think we would have it today if there had never been television."[20] But as Jon Kraszewski explains, the networks and advertising agencies were disinclined to promote the names of writers or highlight their identities because television writers at that time were not under exclusive contracts with the studios.[21] Writers were employees, and the studios, as the owners of their writers' words, vied for copyright control, redefining themselves as the authors of the television text.

Television was not as profitable for writers as film had been, but the probability of getting hired for repeat business was much greater. In 1952, the federal Wage Stabilization Board set the minimum salary for writers working for independent producers at $250 a week, which was made retroactive to work starting in April 1951.[22] The board also set prices for first use, exclusive use, and reuse (via kinescope recordings) of live television stories.[23] Signatories to the Wage Stabilization Board had exclusive use of content for up to sixteen years, as long as they used it originally and continued to reuse it. Writers would also get paid if a character they created for one series became a central character in another series. Mary McCall Jr., president of the SWG, declared to the membership in a memo, "We are determined that writers in this new medium shall retain the creators' rights in the work of their brains and shall continue to profit from the continuing use of those works in all media forever."[24]

It is difficult to compare salaries for film and television writers at the time, since a television script may be two to four times shorter than a film script. But to get some sense of the numbers, pay for live television writing was noted as approximately one-sixth of theatrical scale, with minimum compensation for a television script set at $500, and minimum for a motion picture at $3,000. Two rewrites of any script were expected as gratis unless a writer had been contractually guaranteed a better deal.[25] The Independent Motion Picture Producers Association had flat fees for film writers: $2,000 (up from $1,500) for pictures budgeted under $100,000, and $3,000 (up from $2,250) for pictures over $100,000.[26] Producers paid writers of telefilms (filmed television series) between $650 and $750, but writers complained that they were often spending up to three weeks in script conferences and hammering out rewrites without any additional payment. In comparison, top radio writers at the time, who often worked freelance, were paid between $400 and $450 per radio script.[27]

The SWG saw television's potential for profit, but many members were more focused on the medium's impact on film writers, the film industry, and writers' profits. Karl Tunberg, who adapted *Ben-Hur* and who was president of the WGAw from 1950 to 1951, remembered that a number of elite film writers wished to reject any sort of professional alliance with their small-screen brethren. He and his fellow film writers suggested a calculated compromise: "We felt we had to adopt this monster; otherwise it would come in and murder us. . . . [Although it] would not raise the standards of the craft, nor our intelligence, nor education; we needed them for two reasons: one, because we've got to have access into their business and two, each one of them is a potential strikebreaker."[28]

The Battle for Jurisdiction

Television was viewed by many screenwriters, playwrights, and radio writers as an inviting and lucrative new space for their creative labor. The popular genres and commercial structure used in early television derived almost wholesale from the radio program model. The live audiences reminded playwrights of the stage. The combination of sound with illuminated images on a screen made television an obvious counterpart to film. Furthermore, television was desperate for stories—and writers. Historian William Boddy quotes the manager of NBC's script department in 1948: "Television's primary need is for material, and the one who provides that material in a suitable form may be said to be one of the most important, if not *the* most important, person in the television picture—the writer."[29]

Writers who worked in live television during its first decade speak of accidents, the brutality of the work schedule, the slapdash style of writing in groups, and the pleasures of crafting material to be performed in front of a live audience. Robert Schiller, writer on *I Love Lucy, All in the Family*, and *Maude*, embraced the actors' occasional slips and falls: "It was immediate. No turning back. I liked that. Thrilling."[30] For Leonard Stern, who wrote on *The Honeymooners* and *Get Smart*, "Live television was exhilarating. There's nothing comparable. *The Gleason Show* was opening night every week and 3,500 people [were] in the audience. So you have got to realize, when you got a laugh, you got a *laugh*. And all of us there knew each other. There were only about twenty comedy writers. And if we didn't personally know each other, we certainly knew of each other."[31] Writers were feeding on the energy, but they were also living an untenable lifestyle. Norman Lear, who worked on *The Colgate Comedy Hour* and *The Martha Raye Show* during those early years, remembered the impossible pace: "We were all last-minute writers. . . . [We wrote] a book musical every two weeks, and I'd work until two o'clock in the morning, sleep for three hours, get up at five, be at the mimeograph—a word you may not know—at seven, page by page coming off the machine, for rehearsal that started at ten, and I was directing. So there was a pharmacy . . . where we used to get our Seconal to sleep and our Dexedrine to stay awake. No prescription or anything. Every writer I knew was taking something to help sleep, something to wake up."[32] Though many memoirs celebrate the storied writers' room on *Your Show of Shows*, Carl Reiner, who acted on the series and later wrote sketches, disputed the term *room*. He remembered a stairwell: "The writers' room in the old days was Max Liebman's office. He used to leave and we used to hang around. Until [the writers] got their own room, they used to go into the landing between the stories. Or into the toilet."[33] This was a medium in its infancy and many writers fell in love with the speed of the production schedule, the exponentially growing audiences, and the inventiveness and adventures of creating a new form of entertainment.

The guilds soon realized that jurisdictional control of the new medium would be critical to their future as stakeholders in the American arts and entertainment industry. An extraordinary potential for revenue and power was at stake. The various guilds that covered writers had had complicated relations before 1950, and television now had the potential either to destroy inter-guild relations or—as luck would finally have it—to bring them together.

The Dramatists Guild argued that motion photography of a live television series was the equivalent of broadcasting a staged production. That argument persuaded some other guild leaders—at least until telefilm took over as the dominant form. At the first National Television Conference in 1951, the Dramatists Guild gained temporary jurisdiction over live and filmed television on the West Coast. Many young writers maintained simultaneous careers in the theater and in television anthology series, including Paddy Chayefsky on the *The Philco-Goodyear Television Playhouse* and Reginald Rose on *Studio One*.

The SWG had viewed television first as a curiosity, then as a potent rival for film audiences; but unlike the major Hollywood moguls, who refused for many years to see television as anything other than a threat, SWG leaders decided it would be better policy to fold in the writers in this new medium. Guild writers knew about story, they knew about moving pictures, and they genuinely believed their union was best positioned to represent television writers. Although very few filmed series existed in 1949 (that year, *Fireside Theater* was the first), the SWG was now, five years after Kanin introduced the medium to the union, determined to control television.

The SWG's resolve was based partly upon an overarching concern for wider control during a historic moment when the Guild and its members were still under attack for leftist leanings. The case of Reuben Ship was only making matters worse. As a radio writer on *The Life of Riley*, he had not yet been granted membership in the SWG, but officially he was a dues-paying member. After HUAC declared Ship an unfriendly witness, US immigration officials had him deported to his native Canada. He had not been declared a communist, just an "undesirable alien."[34] Roy Brewer, president of the Motion Picture Alliance for the Preservation of American Ideals, asked, "If Reuben Ship, identified communist, is not good enough for the USA, why is he good enough for the SWG?"[35] Publisher William Wilkerson used the story as a basis for further attacks against the SWG in the *Hollywood Reporter*: "Many members of the SWG honestly feel the red danger is over. Are they aware of the infiltration into SWG of communists today through television?"[36]

Ronald Reagan, then the head of the Screen Actors Guild, favored the Motion Picture Industry Council's call for a loyalty board. SWG opinion was split on the matter. President Mary McCall Jr. stated that she was "violently opposed to Communists" but that she rejected the loyalty board because it "sets up a blacklist by inference."[37] Among workers in Hollywood, only the art directors and writers were collectively opposed to a loyalty board. Some writers believed that the only way they could improve their lot was to acquiesce to the MPIC's wishes. Virginia Kellogg, who wrote *White Heat* and *Caged*, warned, "If we, out of the twelve guilds, reject this plan, we will, in the public eye, remain red writers."[38]

Whatever the climate among motion picture writers, the Radio Writers Guild was not ready to back down from its belief that it was the ideal guild to represent television writers. In fact, many of the first television writers had been members of the RWG, especially those who were working in television news and comedy and variety shows. They had always written for live broadcast. Moreover, the RWG was accustomed to building contracts with the networks and sponsors that included both staff and freelance writers. It approached the battle for jurisdiction with calculated fervor. The RWG encouraged its membership to learn more about television by providing updates on the market for freelancers in its monthly bulletin, recommending script registration, publishing an annual report of credits for television series, establishing a grievance committee, providing advice on contracts, and offering a series of craft seminars.[39] The RWG told its members, "Since the day it was founded, your Guild has existed purely to serve its member-ship. Whether in Radio or Television, service to writers will continue to be its principal purpose."[40] In a tactical move, the RWG turned to the National Labor Relations Board for certification as the sole bargaining agent for all television writers.

But radio writers were also in turmoil. They were facing scrutiny by political conservatives from without and within, and they were struggling to define the territory of their work, given the speed with which American radio listeners were evolving into television audiences. In 1950, the right-wing journal *Counterattack* published *Red Channels: The Report of Communist Influence in Radio and Television*, which named 151 radio and television writers, journalists, actors, and other creative contributors it suspected were leftist subversives. Two years later, the US Senate Subcommittee on Internal Secu-rity released a 126-page report accusing more than thirty RWG writers, by name, of being "Communists or pro-Communists."[41] Though the number of blacklisted radio writers was few compared with the hundreds under attack in film, writers involved in narrative series were rapidly leaving radio. Sam Moore, who wrote for the radio version of *The Great Gildersleeve* and was founder and vice president of the RWG, recalled: "About 1950, '51, '52 radio began to die and that was the end of it. Nothing could be done. Television was taking over and radio was through. And the Guild situation began to reflect this. The Radio Writers Guild had accomplished most of the major objectives. They had staff contracts all around. They had minimum basic agreements for freelance writers everywhere—in New York, Chicago, Los Angeles. Everything was down to a routine of renegotiation. And [then] television came along."[42] Seeing its imminent defeat, the RWG ultimately withdrew its petition to the NLRB. It would have to join forces with the other guilds to survive.

The jurisdictional fight came to a head in the summer of 1952 over the issue of ownership of television content. When the Authors League of America (ALA) and the SWG called a strike against the Alliance of Television Film Producers in Hollywood, the RWG followed suit. In all, 6,000 profes-sional writers went out on strike to demand ownership of television copyrights in the way that playwrights had control over their material, rather than the way film writers were credited but did not own their work. ALA president Rex Stout explained the significance of this strike: "Television is already a major source of income to many members of the League, and it is quite possible that before many years it may become the largest single source. It is of vital importance to all writers to establish in television practice the principle that a writer owns what he writes and that therefore he may properly claim the profits and privileges of that ownership. If that principle is not established in television now, it may never be, and the resultant loss for writers both of today and tomorrow will be incalculable."[43] Television studios, sponsors, and networks knew the financial stakes as well and were willing to outlast the writers. They argued that the precedent for studio and sponsor ownership of programs had already been set. Many television writers who belonged to the RWG were ready to give in. In August, Richard Powell, then the pro tem head of the television writers within the RWG, advised that "no adequate remedy for the adjudication of TV writers—both live and film—exists within the confines of the ALA."[44]

Television writers were increasingly interested in forming their own labor group. Robert White, who wrote for *The George Burns and Gracie Allen Show* and later *Guiding Light*, did his homework while his new guild, the Television Writers Association, got its bearings. "I started out by getting a hold of every labor constitution I could find, of all the unions—the printers, the teamsters—anybody['s] I could get my hands on and ... if you look at a TWA constitution I think it's the most democratic labor union constitution that's ever been written in the country. It was every, everything—all power went to the membership. The Board simply carried out the wishes of the membership in between very frequent membership meetings."[45] Arguably, this structure was made possible because the TWA was still a very small group.[46]

Although officially the TWA was not required to strike, its members voted as a group to support the strike, in part to respond to the fears of the SWG that they would act as non-union replacements. In explaining their support of the strike, TWA members were careful to note that "neither the Screen Writers Guild nor any other existing union or guild is a true representative of a majority of television writers in the field." Members had "agreed to withhold material from struck producers" because the "idea of violating picket lines, physical or moral, of any writers is abhorrent."[47] Though the TWA walked out, members of the SWG were still concerned that producers would exploit this two-union system.

After fourteen grueling weeks, with little to show for their efforts, the writers broke off their strike. It was at this point that the National Labor Relations Board stepped in to mediate. Between 1952 and 1953, the NLRB oversaw fifty-seven arbitrations between film writers and producers and thirteen arbitrations mediating ownership of telefilms.[48] In the meantime, SWG president Mary McCall Jr. went so far as to call the network pact her guild had signed with live television writers in October 1952 "the most forward-looking contract ever negotiated in the history of writers organizations," while simultaneously declaring that the TWA was a "little group of impatient finks whose loyalties are not to writers but to a fanatic political party."[49] The studios agreed that writers of one-time shows and anthology series would lease their scripts to the producers for television use over a period of seven years. For added compensation, writers could lease radio and sequel rights to a studio for a fixed time period, after which rights would revert to the writer.[50] But with the NLRB case moving forward, the SWG's control was tenuous at best. After a hearing during the spring of 1953, the NLRB presented television writers with an election, asking them to vote by secret ballot for the guild they preferred to join. That summer, the Television Writers of America was declared the winner.

SWG leaders were not willing to back away from the overall battle for television jurisdiction. The Guild published a full-page ad in the trade papers declaring that the NLRB election did not pertain to most television writing because the SWG and ALA already had collective bargaining agreements with 90 percent of active telefilm production companies in Los Angeles and New York, with independent producers of live packaged programs, and with staff writers at all of the networks. The SWG and ALA reminded writers, "*you do not have to be a member of TWA until* TWA negotiates contracts with these employers, *and unless* such contracts contain a Union Shop clause requiring membership in TWA as a condition of employment."[51] In November 1953, the SWG boasted of thirty-six new full members, twenty-four of them from television, and thirty-five new associate members, fourteen from television.[52]

In its twentieth anniversary year, the SWG was anxious to demonstrate its relevance, in part by looking past its struggles with HUAC, right-wing politicians, and industry moguls. A puff piece by SWG president Richard L. Breen interpreted its role during the difficult years of the late 1940s with a breezy tone that placed blame on the studios rather than on the Guild for any communist members among its ranks.

The Guild next turned its attention to a necessary cleaning of its own house. . . . The great majority of SWG members had long been disgusted with the maneuverings of a Communist or Communist-inclined minority. The majority, moreover, was increasingly alarmed at the way the best interests of writers were being shunted aside for the furtherance of the minority's political and ideological purposes. A Guild or Union does not choose its membership, a fact little understood, and sometimes it seems deliberately misunderstood, outside the Industry. A Guild is not a private club with the luxury of the blackball. Under law, it is and must be open to all who meet the working qualifications for membership. Actually, the employers choose the Guild's members.[53]

Despite this attempt to move on, the issue of requiring loyalty oaths was still a contested topic among SWG members. Less than a week before he was elected as the Guild's new president, F. Hugh Herbert, who wrote *The Moon Is Blue*, was reported to have said that "while he will sign all non-Commie pledges required by law he is still philosophically opposed to them" and that "I do not believe that loyalty can be attested by a signature on a dotted line. By the same token, I would resist any attempt to impose on the SWG the function of screening its members for political or other affiliations." Herbert's opponent, Ranald MacDougall, on the other hand, stated that he "favored ratification of a legally feasible non-Commie oath for writers."[54]

The TWA was simultaneously under attack from the right and from its left-leaning members. Actor and producer Dick Powell, who signed the Taft-Hartley anticommunist oath, petitioned the TWA not to bankrupt the union by expelling writers for the sake of pleasing the right. He said that "offering basically the same service as professional blacklisters, unsolicited and free of charge . . . seems to be straining the traditional function of a trade union" and that "attempts to legislate unity of thought are in themselves destructive of true unity."[55] Film and television writers were still trying to understand one another, especially in the midst of the blacklist. Unity was increasingly part of the language the TWA employed, in part because it saw its own membership losing faith in the union's capacity to lead. Even though the TWA had won the election, it was losing the hearts and dues of its members.

Soon after TWA won its certification election, the National Labor Relations Board dismissed a TWA petition to bargain collectively on behalf of the writers at Desilu Productions.[56] Since Jess Oppenheimer was a producer-executive and therefore not qualified to speak for his writer-employees, Desilu did not have to recognize the TWA. The future looked dim for the new union. As Charles Isaacs remembers, "Since we were neither backed by Communists, nor were we backed by anyone else either, we were barely able to pay the rent on our tiny office or even our typewriter, which was also rented. The long fight had taken its toll."[57] Many of the writers who had founded the TWA or had served in its leadership began to defect to the SWG, including Isaacs, Oppenheimer, John Fenton Murray (later a writer on *McHale's Navy*), Benedict Freedman (writer on *The Red Skelton Hour*), regional vice president Irve Tunick (later a writer on *East Side/West Side*), national president Arthur Stander (writer on *Make Room for Daddy*), and ten members of TWA's East Coast office. Robert White mourned, "We ran out of money. We ran out of strength. We couldn't hold on. TWA went out of existence. . . . It simply withered away. TWA was gone."[58]

In 1954, after years of rancor, screenwriters finally came to see what each of the other associations had also come to realize: television was already too big to be simply folded into an existing writers' union. At the same time, there was a great deal of overlap in membership. Of the 1,200 members of the SWG, 503 had written for television.[59] If the SWG wanted television, it would have to agree to a merger that would serve not just film writers but television and radio writers as well. Hy Freedman, writer on *You Bet Your Life*, wanted it on the record that no one union had won out over the others: "TWA didn't collapse. TWA forced screenwriters to come into a guild together. That's what happened. It was an amalgamation actually of the three guilds. While we were in TWA we were also still members of our Radio Writers Guild. So it forced the amalgamation of the Screen Writers, the TWA, and Radio Writers. So we didn't lose any more than screenwriters lost."[60]

The SWG devised a merger that allowed all parties to save face and declare victory. The alliance was announced in the entertainment trades in 1954: writers in the fields of motion pictures, radio, and television—previously represented by separate organizations—would all be under the jurisdictional umbrella of the newly formed Writers Guild of America. The Screen Writers Guild and the Radio Writers Guild would separate from the Authors League as part of the new merger.[61] The writers filed a petition for certification with the NLRB to become the Writers Guild of America, with separate branches for the West and East.

On October 30, the new guild issued its first bulletin under the masthead of the Writers Guild of America.[62] In November 1954, the two branches of the WGA began negotiating on a national scale on behalf of approximately 1,000 screenwriters, 800 television writers (400 on each coast), and 700 radio writers (400 on the East Coast, 300 on the West Coast).[63] Writers saw the advantage of being a part of one guild that had history and experience with negotiations—but they needed a new title.[64] Current contracts that were previously held by the SWG, the RWG, and the TWA were all organized separately but under the umbrella of the WGA. Film and television maintained separate minimum basic agreements with unique boards and officers until the early 1970s.

The resources that each writers group brought to the union varied widely. The Radio Writers Guild was penniless, with $32 in its coffers and a deficit of $2,980.[65] The TWA had exhausted its funds.[66] The SWG leaders were willing to take on these insolvent groups, but they were not altruistic. When the Screen Writers Guild dissolved and became the Writers Guild of America, the SWG's reserves of $135,000 were placed into a newly established Writers Guild Foundation, so that radio and television writers could not profit from screenwriters' previously pooled membership dues.[67] In other words, the SWG had found a way to start off this new guild penniless as well. Its members would hold on to their own funds through the foundation while taking full advantage of their new partners' earning potential.

At the time the new union was formed, it made some logical sense to create two branches. Writers were assigned to the East or West branch according to their location of employment in relation to the Mississippi River; a writer who worked on the other coast for a significant period of time was expected to switch affiliations. East members were primarily radio and television writers working in live broadcasting, whereas West members were primarily film writers and telefilm writers. Tensions between the two branches of the Guild, as well as between film and television writers were evident from the moment the new guild was founded. Regional writers' needs from their union varied greatly. Ernest Kinoy remembers that the tensions "certainly got more obvious as television developed because the difference between what was going on in the East and what was going on in the West in terms of the industry became marked."[68] He argued that writers for comedy variety series—whether they were based in the East or West—had more in common with each other than with the "continuity" scripters on fiction series, who were salaried weekly employees, or with the hourly wage earners who worked in news writing.[69]

Film writers were almost all based in Hollywood, and television writers were almost evenly split between the coasts. But as filmed television became the norm, many television writers based in New York began moving west. Leonard Stern recalled:

> Suddenly, the business had a realization that live television was really limiting profits severely, because if they put it on film, or tape, which had yet to exist, they had something to re-sell and re-sell and re-sell. So within a dramatic one-year period of time, New York closed up. . . . The twenty writers who were working in New York over those years sustaining the *Sid Caesar Show*, the *Bilko* show [aka *The Phil Silvers Show*], the *[Jackie] Gleason Show*, *The Colgate Comedy Hour*, all had to make a decision. What do they do? Do they uproot themselves? Do they move to California? How could they earn a living in New York? And finally seventeen of [the twenty of] us . . . [because] we had families and children to support, said we'd better go to California. Three men decided to stay behind and take a chance at writing a play. If it didn't work, they would come. They figured they had enough money set aside or they were devout New Yorkers or the wife wouldn't move. Whatever the reason, they stayed behind. And the three were Doc [Neil] Simon, Woody Allen, and Tony Webster.[70]

Some writers who were then trying to get into the industry found themselves caught off guard. Writing partners Richard Levinson and William Link, who together created *Columbo* and *Murder, She Wrote*, moved to New York, "only to discover that the migration of television to the West Coast had happened in our absences. The anthology was gone, eclipsed by the series. . . . If we wanted to continue writing for the medium we would have to move, like prime-time television itself, to California. A nice place to live, as Fred Allen said, if you happen to be an orange."[71] The number of writing jobs in New York had also diminished substantially with the introduction of music formats at radio stations. Many series and serials that had been mainstays on radio were transitioning to the small screen—and their writers were moving with them.

In his history of television in the 1950s, William Boddy examines the replacement of the live primetime drama broadcast from New York by the Hollywood telefilm. That transition in formats, he explains was just one of many programming changes, which also included the shift of "anthology programs to continuing-character series, and from the dramatic model of the legitimate theater to that of genre-based Hollywood entertainments."[72] The experience of B movie screenwriter and television writer Maurice Tombragel confirms Boddy's assessment. As live shows were gradually phased out and the East Coast writers came west, the differences between the two branches of the Guild came into relief. "They had, in a sense, a better—maybe a little smaller but more . . . aggressive guild maybe than we had in the television area because, don't forget, we were a kind of a little, poor-relation brother."[73] Television writers—those working on series as well as for news programs and daytime soaps—needed protections for short-term labor. These were issues that screenwriters, during the studio days, had never needed to worry about. The structure, deadlines, and style of writing for these media were vastly different. But while the two branches of the WGA conducted their labor negotiations separately, their collective bargaining agreements would now be published as a single document under the same contract cover.

All writers, no matter their genre, were highly attuned to their roles within the media hierarchy of this new guild. Screenwriter Edmund North described this awkward alliance: "I would not call it a shotgun marriage but I would call it a marriage of convenience and the birth pains were considerable. . . . The birth pains that I refer to are mostly psychological in origin and they sprang from a feeling . . . of the television writers of that period that screenwriters were looking down their noses at them and considering them upstarts rather than fellow craftsmen."[74] Whether or not these sentiments were spoken out loud, and they sometimes were, there was a hierarchy in place that had to do with age, experience, and a clear sense of the importance of film as an artistic medium in relation to television. To try to overcome this inherent tension, WGA members elected a council of eleven film members and eleven television members to discuss questions that emerged about how the Guild would support the disparate needs of its members. Television writers David Harmon and Nate Monaster, who were both on the board at the time, describe this uncomfortable partnership between unequal communities:

HARMON: We were the kid brother, as it were. . . . [T]he screenwriters would list credits that went back to the early '30s. They were noble writers. We would list credits of things that were already off the air.

MONASTER: *Gone with the Wind* was a little more impressive than . . . I wrote *Duffy's Tavern.*

HARMON: I did *Armstrong Circle Theater.* You don't compare that with *Ben-Hur.*

MONASTER: The writing was probably as good but the budget for the chariots was more than the entire season of *Armstrong.* I think, we're not being flip in making these contrasts. . . . In a way, [we were] victimized by our own propaganda. The word "screenwriter" had a ring like All-American Football Player or Nobel Prize. . . . [I] have no great recollection of being upstaged by any screenwriter. We were reading into it and probably were obnoxiously defensive.[75]

Harmon and Monaster exposed the psychological effects of what were, in fact, a number of professional differences. Writing for film and writing for television were decidedly different occupations. The contrast involved not just the length of a script or its format, but also job security. Most screenwriters were working under contracts, whereas television writers were primarily freelancers. Film writers were concerned about salaries, whereas television writers were most concerned about minimums for piecemeal work.[76]

And yet, as the years progressed, television flourished and writing jobs increased. With the rise of the Hollywood telefilm, writers—and the Writers Guild—began to see the substantial monetary and authorial benefits of television writing. Television writers were soon outvoting film writers within the Guild, and many screenwriters, especially those who had written B movies and genre films, were testing the waters of the telefilm.[77] As the popularity of television grew, so did the number of hours stations stayed on the air. Content was desperately needed to satisfy a voracious viewership at just the time when Hollywood was cutting budgets and terminating screenwriters' contracts.

Retrenchment, Reruns, Residuals, Royalties, and the 1960 Strike

BANKS: What do you love about writing?

ROBERT SCHILLER: Adulation.

—Interview, 12 January 2012

Toward the end of the 1950s, the number of writers on contract at the major studios was rapidly diminishing. The number of feature films released by the eight major distribution companies dropped from 263 in 1950 to 184 in 1960—and would sink to 151 by 1970.[78] During the 1950s and into the 1960s screenwriters saw the end of the seven-year contract as the industry norm. The studios claimed that the vast expenses of innovations like 3-D and widescreen systems like CinemaScope were to blame, technologies desperately embraced to distinguish movies from programs aired on the smaller home screen. In hindsight, the film studios shouldered this financial burden not just as a counter to television, but also in response to the end of vertical integration and the beginning of the end of the studio contract system.

Film studios—and therefore film writers—also saw this shift in the workspace as an opportunity to emphasize what made film unique. For a number of years, the film industry had been responding to the threat of television by providing audiences with epic stories, bigger (even deeper) images, and more adult themes. The US Supreme Court's so-called Miracle Decision in 1952 marked the beginning of the end of the Production Code in Hollywood.[79] Writers used the decision's loosening of censorship rules to their advantage. John Michael Hayes, who wrote *Rear Window* and *The Man Who Knew Too Much*, commented on his use of risqué language and on how broaching adult topics played into the challenges and pleasures of writing. "We had censorship in those days. So, if I could do it and make it amusing enough, I could get away with it. I used to do that on radio, on shows like *The Adventures of Sam Spade*, by the time they figured out what I was really saying, it was too late to censor it. I think suggestion is better; I'd rather say things through a literary device . . . than just say it flat out. So much of my dialogue is indirect, with layers of meaning, sub-rosa meanings. It's more challenging to write that way, and people remember the lines."[80] Other film writers used this kind of wit when dealing with serious topics as well, for example, Stanley Kubrick and Terry Southern's transgressive, satiric script for *Dr. Strangelove.* For a number of years, the industry held on to audiences with content that could not play on the small screen.

In the meantime, as Christopher Anderson deftly explains in *Hollywood TV*, television was getting the assembly-line treatment in Hollywood. The major Hollywood studios started producing telefilms as well as selling off their film libraries to networks or production studios.[81] Jon Kraszewski discusses the shift from a focus on the dramatic writer (for example from a particular anthology episode) to the dramatic producer (of a long-running series).[82] Very few writers had the opportunity to create series; most, as Stirling Silliphant noted, worked on a freelance basis. "Back in the fifties and sixties, thirty or so of us were writing eighty-five percent of primetime TV. I don't know if I can explain why—it just WAS. I never stopped freelancing, even while I was writing *Naked City* and *Route 66*. The phones never stopped ringing, and, because once I had a relationship with a given show or a given producer, I was lucky enough to be asked to deliver multiple episodes."[83] Writers who picked up the craft of television writing and excelled were paid well for their labor. By the late 1950s, almost all of filmed television employees in New York had closed shop and moved to Los Angeles.

Slowly, over the course of the 1950s, the power of television writers— both in numbers and in shifting needs—was altering the character of the Guild. For the first time, significant numbers of them were placed in a position of power and authority that few had ever imagined possible for practitioners of their craft. Writers who had hyphenate positions on series had significantly more creative control than screenwriters had ever had on film sets. Screenwriters had more cultural and financial capital, but their loss of rights of authorship gave television writers good reason to appreciate their lot.

While Jess Oppenheimer was originally misunderstood by the Guild, hyphenated writers like Oppenheimer, Gertrude Berg, Jack Webb (showrunner for *Dragnet*), and David Dortort taught screenwriters about new forms of power though dual, even triple roles. In this new, content-heavy medium, writer-producers soon became not just necessary but also valued. At first Lew Wasserman, chairman and CEO of Music Corporation of America (MCA), was sure that Dortort would be a total fiasco in his first role as a writer-producer for *The Restless Gun*: "What does a writer know about budget, what does a writer know about the discipline of coming in on time?"[84] Ultimately, MCA realized who its real star was. The company fired the show's lead actor but held on to Dortort, who was saving them money by filming two episodes a week. From a purely budgetary standpoint, Dortort's next project for MCA in 1959 lived up to its name: *Bonanza*.

With the rise of the Hollywood telefilm, as well as the airing of motion pictures on television networks, screenwriters began to demand that compensation should be extended to cross-media exhibition, global exhibition, and the rerun. Starting in 1958 and into 1959, the studios looked to their vaults for what one reporter called "survival money."[85] Twentieth Century–Fox sold its pre-1948 films for $32 million to National Telefilm Associates, Paramount sold its pre-1948 films (750 in all) to MCA for $50 million, and Universal sold not just its archive of pre-1948 films for $20 million to Screen Gems but also its studio back lot for $10 million to MCA.[86] Approximately 3,700 pre-1948 features films were sold or leased to television for a total of $220 million in revenue.[87] These blanket deals

were a boon to television stations hungry for content, and they created a
windfall of cash for the desperate studios. Without these deals, the trades
asked, "How much worse financial shape might Universal have been
in?"[88] But none of the employees who worked on these films saw any money
for the re-release of their work. With contract negotiations beginning
in 1959, writers saw an opportunity to gain compensation for cross-media
exhibition, not just nationally, but internationally as well. And they were
determined to win rights over the films still to sell; accounts at the time
estimated the value of the studios' post-1948 pictures to be between
$190 million (as calculated by the trades) and $500 million (as the WGA
contended).[89] When rights to these films extended to television, cable,
Betamax, VHS, DVD, streaming, and Blu-ray in subsequent years, $500 million
began to appear the more appropriate, perhaps even conservative, estimate
of these films' worth.

Television writers were also concerned about the re-airing of material
and control of copyright overseas. Although they knew they could not own
their scripts outright, they hoped for some compensation for each use of the
material. This issue was a source of much frustration to writers at the time.
Mel Tolkin, a writer on *Caesar's Hour* and *All in the Family*, remembered seeing his work on television overseas:

> I have no rights. . . . In the summer of 1958 Sid Caesar, myself, and a
> couple of other writers—I think Mel Brooks—went to London that
> summer of '58 and did shows on the British Broadcasting Company. At
> the same time . . . Max Liebman sold the rights to *Your Show of Shows*
> and the sketches appeared re-written on a commercial network in
> London. With horror I watched one of the sketches I wrote being
> shown and I had no credit. As a matter of fact, I recall this was a sketch
> about Sid Caesar climbing towards middle class, getting a maid for the
> first time and in England [it switched] from a maid to a butler. So that
> show was based on *Your Show of Shows* which sabotaged Sid Caesar's
> and other writer's attempt to be fresh in London. [Someone sold]
> these sketches without having to answer to the writers.[90]

It is likely that some of Tolkin's contemporaries experienced similar treatment, whether or not they ever became aware of the fact. Writers had no
method of compensation when their scripts were used for a second time in

the United States or abroad. Some writers were even denied credit if a story was sold rather than a series. Television writers were ready to go into negotiations with a long list of demands.

Both film and television writers started to make plans for negotiations. David Harmon remembered the us-versus-them mentality between his fellow television writers and the film writers. "Nobody really liked us and I don't blame them because they were running a nice little club. And we were trying to run a trade union—and not [doing it] too effectively, because we didn't have power."[91] The needs of film and television writers seemed to be entirely separate. The first contract up for renewal was with independent film producers, most of which were distributing through United Artists. In April 1959, a hopeful WGA West gave film producers a list of twenty demands, including a 70 percent increase in wage minimums, a guarantee that film writers get 6 percent of the first $100,000 of absolute gross receipts for the airing of films they had written on television and pay TV (a tiny segment that writers believed would flourish in time), 4 percent of absolute gross receipts over $100,000, and a detailed renegotiation of separation of rights. Rights, they believed, would recognize film writers' basic proprietary interest in their scripts (something that television writers had been able to work out in 1955).[92] The Screen Actors Guild and Directors Guild of America were eager to get the same deal. But producers refused, claiming in October 1959 that "if we grant the writers' demands, it's possible we would find ourselves giving away all the profits in attempting to meet future demands."[93] Another tactic used by the indie producers was to claim that screenwriters who were hired to write particular scripts could not strike under US law because they were contractors rather than employees. While some agreements were signed by the end of October 1959, a WGA strike against the independents ended in November with a deal set for 4 percent of gross profits after the studio had recouped its costs and deductions were made for distribution fees, prints, and advertising. When the contract was signed, the WGA agreed that the settlement would be reassessed and modified to match the deal it ultimately made with the majors. A *New York Times* reporter commented that the agreement "reveals the theatrical film producers' growing dependence on free television and the dreamed-of golden egg of pay-television."[94]

The writers were able to get a respectable contract with the independent producers regarding minimums, a percentage of post-1948 film sales to television, and compensation for pay television. The Alliance of TV Film Producers (ATFP) and its lawyers were watching closely, and they were determined not to be so generous when it came time for the major studios to negotiate. In October 1959, the law offices of O'Melveny and Myers sent a memo to Alliance members: "In view of the Guild's current strike against certain theatrical producers and our tentative reading of the temperature of the Guild, we thought it appropriate at this time to point to you the expiration date [of the current contract, July 15, 1960] and suggest that any stockpiling of scripts for your production schedule after January 15, which you can achieve between now and then, may be helpful."[95] The Alliance was prepared to refuse residuals or royalties to all three guilds in its negotiations. That lawyers were handling all negotiations for the studio heads was a point of increased frustration for the WGA and its new executive director, Michael Franklin, who would hold the post from 1958 to 1978. "When subordinates are doing the actual negotiating and their superiors are not involved, it becomes very easy for the superior to say, 'Tell 'em no.' . . . But if the company presidents were to sit down across the table from us and become aware of the problems and issues involved, the results could be more fruitful."[96] Contract negotiations were at a near collapse by November. All of the major studios except Warner Bros. publicly announced that they would shoot films abroad if the strike held back their production schedules in the United States.[97]

As 1959 ended and negotiations came to a standstill, film writers realized they would have to go back on strike. David Harmon remembered, "We were not prepared for a strike. We were very ill prepared. We didn't expect it. We figured a compromise would come around. That we would give and they would give. They were like a stone wall."[98]

Writers' income from film and television totaled approximately $30 million in 1959.[99] In a strange turn of events, the WGA realized that it could help fund the film writers' strike against the major studios through a 2 percent assessment on wages from those members still actively working, including members writing for television who were being paid by the same studios that some film writers were striking against. At the time, twenty-seven of the ninety-eight primetime half-hour series were being produced by the majors.[100] And finally, the WGA membership voted to put $47,000 from the Writers Guild Foundation holdings into the WGA's strike fund.

It wasn't long before television writers were ready to strike as well. They wanted extended residuals for reruns and foreign distribution of programs and a ban on speculative writing.[101] The WGA's screen board of directors and television board of directors realized that if they went out on strike together and if they were to respect each other's picket lines, they might find strength in their numbers and a unity in unionism.[102]

On January 16, 1960, 80–90 screenwriters who were working on assignment as well as 425–500 working telefilm writers walked out on their television producers.[103] Two days later the studios laid off a hundred secretaries who had been assigned to writers.[104] The studios seemed to be warning the writers that they had no intention of backing down, or perhaps they hoped the tactic would force the work stoppage to end quickly. And yet that week the WGA and the SAG (whose contract with the major studios would expire at the end of the month) finally met not with the studios' lawyers, but with their presidents, including Spyros Skouras (Twentieth Century–Fox), Barney Balaban (Paramount), Joseph R. Vogel (MGM/Loews), Jack Warner (Warner Bros.), Abe Schneider (Columbia), and Steve Broidy (Allied Artists/ Monogram Pictures).[105] After negotiations over live television broke down in February, approximately 250 additional writers who worked for live series at NBC, CBS, and ABC joined the telefilm writers in their strike.[106]

Early in the strike the Guild drafted written warnings to all television writer-producers, story editors, and writer-directors to clarify what work they were and were not permitted to continue during the strike.[107] None of these hyphenates were allowed to write, provide ideas for lines, or discuss plotting. A special ground rules committee was established to explain to writer-producers the divide between their writing roles and the other aspects of their work, and every hyphenate was asked to come to Guild head-quarters personally to learn the ground rules. Hyphenates were "expected to confine themselves to such non-writing production activities as casting supervision, budget, dailies, editorial, sets, makeup, costumes, etc. They may cut scripts for reasons of budget. They may change a line on set for purposes of bridging. But any basic writing services such as changes in character, plot, motivation [were not allowed. . . . A hyphenate] may diagnose script problems and discuss the same with a studio chief, but he may not prescribe a remedy."[108] This specification of the work of the producer and the writer was a novel idea. Producers could provide language to bridge scenes or actions, and they could cut scripts; writers could not transform, touch up, doctor, rewrite, or do anything that might be considered performing creative labor. What had become a powerful new job in the television profession—writing and producing together—was now being ripped apart for the sake of strike rules.

For individuals, being a part of the managerial ranks and an employee was a particularly difficult position during a work stoppage. Stephen Lord, who was a writer and associate producer on *Johnny Ringo* at the time of the strike, showed his allegiance to writing—and claimed credit for the first use of the term "hyphenate." "I said 'I may be a producer but I'm a writer first and there's a hyphen between those two words.' I said, 'If you noticed I put the writer *before* I put the hyphen and the producer was last.' I said, 'If you want to call me anything call me a *hyphenate*.' And there, I believe, following that meeting there was published a letter in which the word hyphenate was used for the first time in an official missive from this Guild committee."[109] There was much anxiety about whether hyphenates would go out on strike, or, if they did not, whether they would sabotage the strike by writing during the walkout. But most of the hyphenates were committed to the strike, even though many of them, like Rod Serling with *The Twilight Zone*, were paid well enough not to need any of the contractual changes that writers were fighting for.[110] But as the strike went on month after month, some striking freelance writers started to distrust some hyphenates, wondering if they were writing or editing scripts.[111]

The studios did come up with ingenious, if devious, methods for getting new material. Perhaps the most audacious case was that of Warner Bros. Producers. Nonwriters—perhaps secretaries or associate producers—took scripts from one series and switched around characters and locales, thereby turning what might have been a detective series into a Western, and then the company filmed an episode.[112] The credits would read, "Written by: W. Hermanos"—namely, Warner Brothers. Writing credits for W. Hermanos appeared on episodes of *77 Sunset Strip*, *Hawaiian Eye*, *Colt .45*, and *Bourbon Street Beat*, among others.

The SAG had a "no strike" clause in its contract at that time; actors could give as much lip service as they wanted, but they could not go out on a solidarity strike. Rather, SAG continued negotiations for its upcoming contract with the Alliance through the winter. Ultimately, the leadership of SAG settled by conceding revenue on films between 1948 and 1960 in order to assure compensation for films and television series made after 1960. Also as

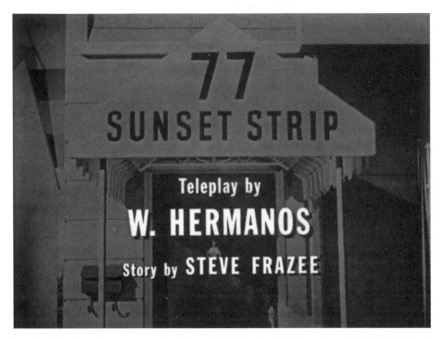

IMAGE 18 Credits sequence for the episode "Sierra" of *77 Sunset Strip* that aired during the 1960 WGA strike, which gives the writing credit to W. Hermanos, or Warner Bros.

Screen grab. *77 Sunset Strip.* Warner Brothers, 1960

part of the settlement, the Alliance established a pension plan for SAG. The DGA agreed to a similar plan: post-1960 compensation and a pension plan in exchange for any rights to residuals for films before 1960.

After months of striking, the writers were eager to find consensus and get back to work. One of the sticking points was the type of compensation structure the studios would create. Many in the WGA were originally interested in a royalty-based plan, which Lew Wasserman was willing to support. The problem was that the writers would receive zero compensation for the first replay.[113] In comparison, the residual plan would allow for pay up front, with gradually diminishing payments for each repeat showing. For a successful film or television series, a royalty plan with continued, steady payment over time would be much more lucrative.

The concept of a royalty plan spoke to old understandings of what it meant to be a writer versus a studio employee. Royalties elevate the level of a writer's authorial control, because royalties are structured on a concept of ownership of written material. With a royalty structure, a screenwriter would become much more like a literary author—something that James M. Cain had petitioned the SWG to fight for fifteen years earlier. Frank Moss, who wrote on *Combat!*, agreed, but "unfortunately Mr. Cain . . . was pretty much booed off the floor for having dared to suggest that writers give up their cushiony salaries at Metro, Universal, and Fox in return for owning their copyrights as members of the Dramatists Guild."[114]

The negotiating committee in 1959 was eager to set up a royalty system, in part because it would ensure that every showing in every country would deliver a payment. Kay Lenard (*The Cimarron Kid, Father Knows Best, Combat!*) lamented the committee's focus on the royalty structure at the expense of a system that could provide income from series that were not long-lived: "The negotiating committee was willing to give up a great deal for the illusion of being paid from every country where American television was shown. And in the three years between 1960 and 1963 we found out that what the producers had given us was a big goose egg."[115] Royalties were ultimately written into the contract in 1960, but by 1966, frustrated writers turned to a residual system of compensation.

As the strike wore on, writers and management realized that they would have to relent on some key issues in order to reach consensus. Screenwriters conceded compensation for their pre-1960 films in order to receive a lump sum to establish a pension plan and a health plan. This sacrifice by older writers to give up their chance at getting royalties in order to guarantee the rights of current writers was an extraordinary act for the greater good of the Guild membership. William Ludwig explained what this provision meant for writers like him. "In 1960, I had thirty-eight feature credits. We threw all of our pictures into the pot in order to get the $600,000 to start the pension plan and that was the grandfather clause. We begged—I remember Jim Webb [writer of *Cape Fear* and *How the West Was Won*] begged the membership to make it a contributory plan because it would have almost doubled their potential pensions and the membership . . . said, 'To hell with it. Why should we put in any of our money? Let the goddamn producers put it in,' and they voted down the contributory plan."[116] John Bright expressed his frustration with the sacrifice: "I have no participation in residuals because all of my pictures were pre-1948 and I feel, and I still feel very strongly, that that contract should have begun—should have been rolled back to the beginning of talking pictures because there isn't a night goes by that one of my pictures is not shown on television and I get nothing."[117] While writers still working would now get percentages of profits, all that former writers could expect was a guaranteed pension and health plan based on their credits and past work in the industry.

Another impasse concerned the role of pay TV. Charles Boren, vice president of the Alliance of Motion Picture Producers, argued that the WGA should accept the same deal agreed to by the SAG, that theatrical exhibition would include any form of distribution on the as yet barely developed model of pay TV. But WGA members held their ground: "The writers' position is that pay-TV may be the biggest thing to hit the industry in years, with single movies bringing in fantastic revenue."[118]

After five months of wrangling and work stoppages, the strike ended. Film writers established a three-and-a-half-year contract, and television writers signed a six-year contract. The independent production houses and producers that had made deals beforehand and were able to continue employing writers during the strike, now had the opportunity to sign on to the same deal the major studio signatories had brokered. Sadly for the writers, the agreement with the majors was worse financially for them.

Film writers saw an increase in salaries through the minimum basic agreement (MBA); 2 percent of proceeds from sales of films to television within the next six years would go to writers; and the signatories set up pension and welfare plans, with producers contributing the equivalent of 5 percent of writers' salaries (up to $100,000) per picture. Producers also agreed to put a one-time sum of $600,000 into the pension and welfare fund in lieu of residuals for pre-1960 films.[119] Foreign box office royalties were established for some countries, including France and Spain, where ticket sales were tracked.[120] The agreement also put in place a system of film credits. The writing credit would have its own card unless a film required additional credit for the source material from which the screenplay was adapted. The writing card would immediately precede the cards of the director and producer; also, a writer's name had to appear in a trailer if the director's and producer's names appeared in it. Finally, the writer owned publication rights three years after the date of contract or six years after general release of the film.[121] Pay TV was left on the table to be picked up again at a later date.

The terms of the television writers' new contract included an increase in salary scales, the signatory's contribution equivalent to 5 percent of a writer's salary toward health and welfare, and a royalty formula for domestic and foreign reruns. The royalty for television was no less than 4 percent of gross, but initial sales of a series in the United States and Canada were excluded.[122] The royalty plan was set to last through 1965, and the writers subsequently negotiated for a residual structure thereafter.[123]

There were differences between the structures and controls set in place in this contract for television writers in the East and television writers in the West, in part because of the differences between live and filmed television. The WGA East retained copyright of live series, such as *Studio One* and *Playhouse 90*. In effect, it leased performance rights to the production company and to the network. In contrast, the WGA West gave up copyright of telefilms, just as film writers had done before them. Frank Pierson, who was WGAw president from 1981 to 1983 and 1993 to 1995, pointed to the 1960 strike as a key moment in defining the relationship between the East and the West branches of the Guild: "Sometimes the members of our board of directors in the West will ask me, 'I don't understand, the East are so impossible. Why are they so damn hard to deal with?' And I have to tell them, 'Because we gave away something which was absolutely, terribly important.'"[124] Writers working in the tradition of New York theater expected copyright control; writers in Los Angeles had long ago given up hope of owning the copyright for screenplays. But as live television became scarce in primetime and many television writers moved west, the easterners realized they could not bring their copyright deal with them into the telefilm medium.

Although neither film nor television writers achieved all that they had hoped for, negotiations had finally established a system of compensation that has since ensured writers will see a profit from the replaying of films and television series, along with guaranteed pension and health benefits. And for all screenwriters, having one's name in the credits ensured not just recognition but also an enduring mode of financial compensation. The card at the beginning or end of a production's credits carried extra weight: writers were now guaranteed a stake in future profits. It was around this same time that Otto Preminger announced that Dalton Trumbo had written the script for his new film *Exodus*. That one of the Hollywood Ten was finally using his own name again and would not only be paid for writing the film but also, according to the new MBA, collect royalties on the film was an extraordinary landmark that demonstrated how many battles the writers had won in the past thirteen years.

Looking Forward into the Unknown

Though at its start the WGA existed as an uncomfortable marriage of convenience between film and television writers, by the 1960s its members had realized that this alliance could serve as a powerful labor force and as a strong voice for creative workers within the American media industries. The screenwriters had been eager to gain jurisdiction over the new medium, though reluctant to embrace its practitioners. Herb Meadow, creator of the series *Have Gun—Will Travel*, pointed out that before the SWG merged to become the WGA, television was a lost opportunity: "The [SWG] had no teeth. It couldn't function in television. . . . I don't mean the television industry but the television writers were the ones who gave it to us. There were no fat cats. There were no elitists among them. They were working stiffs and they knew they had to go out and march."[125]

The merger signaled new challenges in understanding the work of the writer and highlighted critical differences between film and television in terms of prestige and authorial power for individual writers. While the jurisdictional battles had been hard fought, these writers' choice to join ranks in 1954 saved the Guild during troubled times and redefined the power and potential of entertainment writers and of their union. Nate Monaster, who speculated in the early 1950s that it might be thirty years before a television writer became a president of the Guild, became the first for the WGA West in 1963, and Ernest Kinoy was the first for the WGA East in 1967.[126] By the mid- to late 1960s, screenwriters could see change coming. Edmund North said in 1978 that a "preponderance of power both numerical and otherwise in the Guild has shifted towards television now—the screenwriter being in the minority as he was not originally."[127] When asked about how the Guild had changed over time, Michael Kanin, who had introduced television to the SWG and had been charged to investigate it as a committee of one, said, "The most distinct change has been the fact that it has become now a Guild of television writers, with the screenwriters in a minority."[128]

A number of critical issues for writers and the Guild emerged during the 1960s: a call for fair and equal treatment of women writers, the ongoing struggle to define the labor status of the writer-producer hyphenate, the shift from studios owned by individuals to studios run by corporations or conglomerates, and the evolution of new genres in film and television. Women had always been in the Guild, but the situation for female writers had in many ways regressed since the 1920s. Regarding the treatment of

IMAGE 19 The annual WGA television awards show was created when the screen-writers refused to allow television writers to participate in their awards ceremony. According to many who attended the annual events, the television awards were one of best nights of live entertainment in town. They were never televised. Left to right: James Komack, E. Jack Neuman, Ellis Marcus, Rocky Kalish, unidentified, Joel Rapp, Bruce Howard, and two unidentified writers, c. 1963.
Writers Guild Foundation Archive, Shavelson-Webb Library, Los Angeles

women like her during the 1960s, Jay Presson Allen, who scripted *Marnie* and *Cabaret*, remembered: "One, the writer is a lowly thing, and two, a woman writer is a doubly lowly thing, perceived as being so unthreatening that they can say anything in front of you."[129] Starting in the 1970s, a group of concerned writers—women and men—asked the Guild to compile research that would help improve the situation for women within the profession.

The confusion over how to deal with writer-producer hyphenates at the bargaining table and on the picket line continued to grow during the 1960s. Hal Kanter, himself a hyphenate, expressed distrust: "Where are their loyalties? There's always been a hyphenate problem.... [To] paraphrase Napoleon, in every soldier's knapsack there's a field marshal's baton. I think that in every writer's pencil box there's a hyphen. And the whole strange business of hyphenates is one that I doubt is ever going to be solved to everybody's satisfaction. Because a pure writer today can be a writer-story editor tomorrow or a producer-writer. . . . Unfortunately, a lot of writers hate to write. And the moment they become a producer . . . they cease to write. Although they will maintain their Guild activity."[130]

In 1966, a group of writer-producers asked the WGA to represent them in their capacity as producers. Technically, the Guild could not do that, but it did begin to help hyphenates improve their compensation deals.[131] Stanley Rubin expressed his frustration with this attempt by the Guild to represent the parties on both side of the hyphen: "I have never agreed with the WGA position that the WGA has the right to represent what they call the whole man. The Writers Guild has always wanted—and this is certainly no secret—has always wanted the power of representing the whole hyphenate because the hyphenate represents an enormous amount of power in the television industry."[132] Around this time the Producers Guild of America (PGA), formed in 1962 with the merger of the Screen Producers Guild (established in 1950) and the Television Producers Guild (established in 1957), became interested in building an agreement with the newly formed trade association for the studios and networks, the Alliance of Motion Picture and Television Producers and brought up the issue of representing writer-producers. The PGA then focused its efforts not on compensation but on establishing health and welfare for its members.

As Thomas Schatz details, the films of the 1960s stood out from the Hollywood films of the classical era for their oversized budgets, enormous casts, bloated running times, and wider screens.[133] The studios hoped to draw mass audiences away from televisions and into theaters by making films special events. But time and again this formula flopped, and box office failures like *Doctor Doolittle, Hello, Dolly!,* and *Paint Your Wagon,* devastated the Hollywood studios. Television series were Hollywood's butter—though not necessarily its bread—during this era. Many television shows had been designed for mass audiences and were succeeding far better at keeping families entertained with what NBC executive Paul Klein called "least objectionable programming." But other writers began pushing the envelope in shows ranging from Serling's *Twilight Zone* to *The Dick Van Dyke Show.* Carl Reiner's series featured three television writers as central characters. Reiner said that over the years many people told him that the series made them realize that television writing was an actual profession, one that even seemed appealing. "They always thought comedians made up their own material. . . . They saw this show with these writers writing for a comedian [. . . and] they tell me 'I'm a writer because of *The Dick Van Dyke Show.*'"[134] With the rise of film schools and college courses in film and television, writing for film and television increasingly became a craft to be studied and learned. The draw of these writing professions would only become stronger in the 1970s.

Producing television series kept Hollywood's major studios afloat; but as media researcher Justin Wyatt explains, these television successes in the middle of a film downfall made the majors tempting properties for large corporations. In 1966, Gulf+Western purchased Paramount; a year later, TransAmerica purchased United Artists; and then, in 1969, Kinney National Services bought Warner Bros.,[135] and Kirk Kerkorian bought MGM.[136] As Wyatt points out, between 1969 and 1972 the majors lost more than $500 million. Independent films—by focusing on subjects outside the mainstream and testing new distribution models—began to gain traction in the market-place. Many of the majors began to look to the independents for ideas about how best to reach audiences. This shift for the majors was facilitated by changes in the ratings system in 1968. The country was experiencing a cultural revolution. Audiences' tastes were changing, and filmmakers' interests were shifting as well.

By late 1960s, the industry and the profession of writing itself were changing. In the years to come, film and television writers would push the boundaries of preexisting genres and of audience expectations. The union of film and television writers heralded what would become over the next three decades a series of mergers at the very top of the industry, corporate buyouts of the majors in the 1960s, and the dawning of a new era wherein corpora-tions began taking over the film and television industries. The Guild had survived the arrival of a new medium and its first major strike, and over the next twenty years, the diversity of the Guild would prove to be both its greatest asset and the underlying source of its greatest defeats.

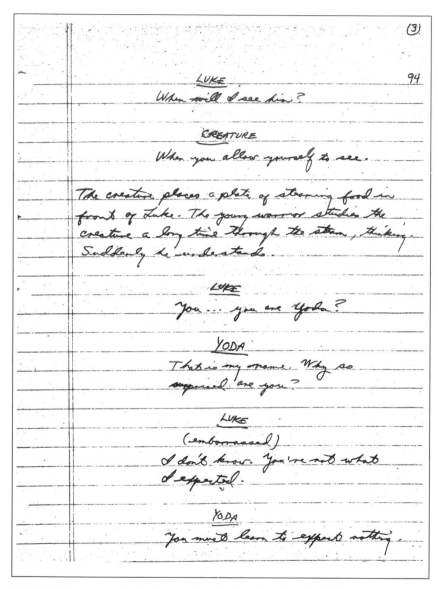

LUKE   94

When will I see him?

CREATURE

When you allow yourself to see.

The creature places a plate of steaming food in front of Luke. The young warrior studies the creature a long time through the steam, thinking. Suddenly he understands.

LUKE

You ... you are Yoda?

YODA

That is my name. Why so surprised are you?

LUKE

(embarrassed)
I don't know. You're not what I expected.

YODA

You must learn to expect nothing.

IMAGE 20 Lawrence Kasdan's notes for the introduction of Yoda in an early draft of *The Empire Strikes Back*, c. 1978.

Lawrence Kasdan Collection, Writers Guild Foundation Archive, Shavelson-Webb Library, Los Angeles

4

Mavericks

I'm a writer by choice, a producer through necessity, and a director in self-defense.

—The Writer Speaks: Mel Shavelson, 1996

We don't have the numbers but we have the strength. We should combine this advantage and work together toward the common goal of bettering the lot of the writer instead of squabbling amongst ourselves. . . . This Guild . . . is a very remarkable organization. It is made up of people who don't particularly like each other very much because half the fellows have rewritten the other half. And nobody likes a good rewrite man. But . . . who ever heard of a *good* rewrite man?

—Sam Rolfe (creator of Have Gun—Will Travel),
WGAw Newsletter, October 1967, 4

In 1950, Billy Wilder and I.A.L. Diamond plotted the grim demise of a screenwriter in *Sunset Blvd.* In 1961, Carl Reiner showcased the endearing adventures of television writers in *The Dick Van Dyke Show*. In the 1970s and 1980s real screenwriters made their first appearance in the popular narrative of financial and critical success in Hollywood. These decades brought tremendous change and upheaval in the entertainment industries: corporate buyouts, mergers and acquisitions, the growth of independents, the rise of ancillary markets of cable and home video, and gradual deregulation during the presidency of Ronald Reagan. An industry that was organized as diverse media companies was evolving into conglomerates with interconnected media holdings in filmed entertainment. This industrial change trickled down, affecting methods of production and of compensation, which in turn shaped the lives and careers of screenwriters. As writers entered the industry in greater numbers than ever before, competition for jobs—as well as for creative control among writers, producers, and directors—generated critical points of conflict.

The era covered in this chapter is bookended by two major spec script sales: William Goldman received $400,000 from Fox in 1967 for *Butch Cassidy and the Sundance Kid*, and Joe Eszterhas got $3 million from Carolco for *Basic Instinct* in 1990. Both events serve as telling examples of a new focus on individual writers—their personal voices, their successes, their personalities, their career trajectories—and on the power of the individual screenplay. Long gone were the days of writers on long-term studio contracts. Though a writer might have a short-term deal with a studio for right of first refusal, agents could shop around writers or spec scripts in search of higher bidders.

Both of these scripts, and ultimately both screenwriters, had name recognition even before the films premiered. The extraordinary bidding war that surrounded the purchase of *Butch Cassidy and the Sundance Kid* and the ultimate success of the film (it became the highest grossing film in 1969 and won four Oscars, including one for Best Original Screenplay) gave aspirants reason to believe that writing was a lucrative profession. Goldman remembers: "It was a shitload of money then but it is really a freakish amount of money now. And it got in all the papers because nobody at this time knew anything about screenwriters because all they knew is that actors made up their lines and directors had all the visual concepts. And the idea of this obscene amount of money going to this asshole who lives in New York who wrote a Western drove them nuts. . . . It was the writing of the screenplay and the money that it went for that basically changed everything in my life."[1] Goldman's wry attitude toward his newfound celebrity, and his simultaneous grouchiness and humility, made him a compelling figure for the media. His continued successes across a variety of genres, including *All the President's Men* and *The Princess Bride*, and his bestselling book *Adventures in the Screen Trade*, put Goldman about as close to being a household name as any screenwriter can hope to get. Around this time, the art and craft of screenwriting started to attract the admiration of people outside of Hollywood.

In television, where the writer-producer had become the norm, these hyphenates were increasingly taking on ownership of their series as well. Smaller production companies produced series for networks. Economically and creatively, this decentralization provided diversity in television production. Norman Lear and Bud Yorkin created Tandem Productions (later known as Tandem Enterprises), which started with variety shows and specials and went on to great success with *All in the Family, Good Times, Maude,* and *Sanford and Son.* Frank Pierson, who twice served as president of the WGA West and started his career in Hollywood writing for television, maintained that the ripple effect of writer ownership spread to film: "It led to a burst of creativity in the industry including the movie business in the 1970s. For a period of the next ten or fifteen years, there was really a creative explosion on all kinds of levels. A swift evolution in television quickly becoming much better than it had been before."[2] The careers of some of the greatest writer-directors in American film peaked in this period: Stanley Kubrick with *Dr. Strangelove, 2001: A Space Odyssey,* and *Full Metal Jacket;* Francis Ford Coppola with *The Godfather, The Conversation,* and *Apocalypse Now;* Woody Allen with *Annie Hall* and *Manhattan;* George Lucas with *American Graffiti* and *Star Wars;* David Lynch with *The Elephant Man* and *Blue Velvet;* and, later, Joel and Ethan Coen with *Raising Arizona* and *Barton Fink* and John Sayles with *The Return of the Secaucus Seven, Passion Fish,* and *Lone Star.* Studio and network executives who were inclined to challenge the status quo in order to back an original idea turned to independent-minded creative talent. This was a time when mavericks had a chance to change American screens—and to change the Writers Guild.

Known for his family-friendly fare, Sherwood Schwartz was a wise observer of his industry. Schwartz owned his series, *Gilligan's Island,* and his next big hit, *The Brady Bunch.* He spoke of the strange role he played in those early days as what he termed a "writer-owner." When he learned of the Guild's oral history project, Schwartz was eager to tell his story because he realized he was one of the first of a new breed: "There was such a thing as the writer and then there was such a thing as a producer. And I was a new animal and I was uncomfortable. I felt I was going to divide the Guild. I'm not making this dramatic . . . I was a precursor of this whole cursed hyphenate problem."[3] In further interviews, a number of hyphenates talked about how there was never a conflict of interest for them on the job, but in the Guild setting their dual roles in the industry made it impossible to ally wholly with either the labor or the management camp.

As this chapter will explore, hyphenate writers both in television and in film struggled to define themselves in a labor environment that regarded groups as either employees or management. The Guild found it difficult to decide whose needs the union should champion in negotiations: hyphenates brought in more money and had more clout within the industry, but they were outnumbered by the steady influx of freelance writers. Sometimes the needs of hyphenates were in absolute opposition to those of television writers. And in the 1985 strike, the concerns of television writers and film writers put them at odds with one another. This lack of cohesion undermined the strike and lead to a quick resolution on VHS residuals that has plagued the Guild ever since.

Weaving through the history of this era are the three motifs that guide this narrative: authorship, the writer's name, and the boundaries of membership. Each motif highlights the changing nature of the business of writing during these two decades and the attempts of the Writers Guild to respond to these transformations. At the center of this chapter is the prominence of individual writers, some of whom gained considerable control over production. This chapter begins with an overview of industrial shifts in the early 1970s and then illuminates a series of issues that were central concerns for writers and the Guild, namely, the possessory credit in film, the role of the hyphenate in television, race and gender representation in the industry, and the strikes of the 1980s. These strikes ruptured trust and solidarity among members. By the end of the 1980s, the prestige of the individual writer superseded the notion of craft solidarity or faith in the WGA's capacity to be a strong representative for its members. One of the paradoxes of this era for the Guild was that, just when it was gaining ground, the role of the writer shifted, the structure of the industry evolved, and the population of writers changed. Its membership—and members' needs—became increasingly diverse.

The variety of career possibilities for writers began to multiply in the 1970s and 1980s. Before, writers had had a diversity of experiences in their careers and professional trajectories based on their primary medium, their skill set, the period in which they entered the industry, and their political affiliations. Gone now was a sense of predictable overlap in their writing experiences, and the WGA could not serve the needs of all of its writers under a single set of provisions. As David Rintels, a writer on *The F.B.I* and president of the WGA West from 1975 to 1977, noted: "When you say writer, you can be talking about a radio writer, a television writer, or a film writer. You can be talking about somebody who has got enough clout to get . . . creative control or a meaningful definition of profits. Or you can be talking about somebody two weeks out of USC film school. . . . We have an infinite number of varieties of writers in this Guild whose interests have to be balanced. You cannot go into a negotiation and have any realistic expectation that you are going to win as much for every classification of writers."[4] Some writers, like Alvin Sargent, experienced ongoing success, and virtually everything they wrote was produced. For others, like Allan Burns, who created *The Mary Tyler Moore Show*, it took years of false starts before they found success. Still others, especially newcomers the industry in the 1970s and 1980s, found it much more difficult to break in. This fracturing of writers' experiences is reflected in the great number of small strikes that occurred through the 1970s, which culminated in a series of three particularly devastating strikes for the Guild in the 1980s. Whereas previous chapters have followed a clear chronology, this chapter and the next one offer a series of chronologies that chart the experiences of different communities of writers while still tracking the story of how their Guild—already divided by its East and West branches—tried to respond to changing times.

The Possessory Credit

In the first minimum basic agreement with studios and producers in 1941, the Screen Writers Guild ensured that writers themselves, via the SWG, would be the ultimate arbiters of writing credits. When screenwriters began working outside the long term contract system and selling scripts directly to studios or producers, credit stood for more than just an acknowledgment of script authorship. If a film was successful, the writer was in a better position to negotiate compensation for subsequent screenplays. Credit determinations have always been critical to verifying a writer's reputation, clout, and pay. In earlier eras successful screenwriters might have forty credits to their names (as contract employees they were constantly churning out scripts that regularly were filmed); it was the rare screenwriter in the 1970s and 1980s who could claim more than thirty film credits over the course of a career.[5]

Most credits have been controlled by clearly defined rules within contractual agreements, both above and below the line. But one credit has caused more battles in arbitration and more inter-Guild hostility than any other. The possessory credit, or "film by" credit, is clear in its attribution, giving credit with a possessive *s*, but is ambiguous because it leaves open questions about what part of the film was made by this particular person and how he or she contributed relative to others. For example, though few may recognize the name of screenwriter John Michael Hayes, he wrote the screenplays for "Alfred Hitchcock's *Rear Window*," "Alfred Hitchcock's *To Catch a Thief*," "Alfred Hitchcock's *The Trouble with Harry*," and the 1956 version of "Alfred Hitchcock's *The Man Who Knew Too Much*." A movie poster or an opening credit in a film may delineate the key contributors by name, but the scope of the job titles is often unclear to the viewer. In contrast, the "film by" credit or apostrophe *s* signals to audiences that the person named has possession or authorship over the final film. The possessory credit, especially when used by a person who did not serve in a hyphenate role, undercuts the notion of film as a collaborative art. The continued use of this credit only further reinforces popular designations of directors as auteurs, the primary authors of the films that they direct. James Crawford argues, "Because the possessory credit's significance circulated within the relatively hermetic confines of the film industry's production culture, it escaped the general public's understanding."[6]

It should be made clear that the possessory credit is in no way tied to issues of ownership and does not legally equate to copyright. As Catherine Fisk lays clear in her work on the possessory credit, neither writers nor directors can lay claim to authorship; rarely, in fact, do producers even hold the copyright under their own names. Fisk explains: "Because of copyright's work for hire doctrine, legal authorship of a motion picture is not factual authorship and is often a legal fiction in every sense of the term."[7] Neither the WGA nor the Directors Guild has cited intellectual property law—or any civil doctrines, for that matter—in their disputes over this credit. There is zero wiggle room under the work-for-hire provision. Other credits help to determine minimums for residuals for the employees on a production, and most challenges to credits revolve around compensation. In contrast, possessory credit is the one designation that does not directly translate to remuneration.

The possessory credit was first appropriated in 1915 by D. W. Griffith for *The Birth of a Nation*, the epic film he directed and co-scripted with Frank E. Woods. In the decades that followed, the possessory credit was used sparingly, sometimes by producers and then by directors. Virginia Wright Wexman contends that the guiding principle of the DGA's creative rights agenda is contained in the "one man, one film" catchphrase; first used by Frank Capra and his publicist in the 1920s, it became an unofficial trademark for films that had a signature aesthetic or style distinct to their director. The idea was that great directors could elevate the caliber of their films from mass entertainment to art.[8] Some producers (independents, in particular) would use a presentation credit; for example, "David O. Selznick Presents" precedes the titles of *Gone with the Wind* and *Spellbound*. Others used the credit outright: "Samuel Goldwyn's *The Best Years of Our Lives*." Daniel Taradash, who was the WGA's president from 1977 to 1979, recalls, "At that point, and I'm talking about the late thirties, forties, into the fifties, the producer was much more important, particularly at some studios, than the director. The writer, of course, except occasionally, was not as important as either of them."[9] The first directors to use the credit regularly were Frank Capra and Alfred Hitchcock. They believed that their names would not only sell a film but also guarantee a level of quality that audiences could trust. Soon, other directors began to see the credit as the best method to improve the quality and cultural stature of their films. This notion was reinforced by the rise of auteur theory, first promoted in France in the 1950s and then in the United States by film critic Andrew Sarris.[10] On the other hand, between 1968 and 2000, by terms negotiated by their guild, film directors could withdraw their names from the credits of any film or series and use the pseudonym "Alan Smithee."

Since 1948, the SWG and the WGA have allowed writers to avoid using their real names on particular films so long as they have registered their pseudonyms and earned less than $200,000 for each script. The $200,000 cap was set with the understanding that a larger payment purchased both the script and the identity of the author. Although many writers used unregistered pseudonyms during the blacklist, writers generally were obligated to comply with rules of attribution. Since 1948, writers have not been allowed to reject outright authorship of a script without a registered pseudonym. The first television credits manual in 1956 stipulated that only when a writer's original material was dramatically altered could that writer remove his or her name, and even in that situation the case would go through arbitration by the Guild. Today, if film or television writers are paid more than three times the contractual minimum, they cannot—under terms agreed to by the WGA—use a pseudonym.[11] One could argue, then, that screenwriters, in particular those who are well paid and cannot remove their names from a film, take on more risk to their names and reputations than directors do. And yet, if a film is a potential success, the director may simply claim primary, and seemingly solitary, credit with "a film by."

In 1963, the WGA secured a critical agreement with the Alliance of Motion Picture and Television Producers (AMPTP). Charles Boren, the

Alliance's executive vice president, agreed that only a director who had also been the writer of a film or of the original source material could procure the possessory credit.[12] In December 1966, the AMPTP ratified the rule in its contract with the WGA. Only weeks later, in January 1967, the DGA sued the WGA, the AMPTP, and its signatories, claiming that the rule violated the rights and traditions of directors.[13] In analyzing this moment, James Crawford claims that, given the precariousness of the film industry at the time, control of authorship was critical to assuring reputation in an industry facing financial turmoil: "In light of this uncertainty, we can see writers and directors attempting to secure their futures through rights to credits, one of the few realms of negotiation they could control."[14] Although the Los Angeles Superior Court denied the DGA's request for a temporary injunction, the guild succeeded in convincing AMPTP members that they did not want to be pitted against directors. Just weeks before the directors were set to strike, the AMPTP reached an agreement with the DGA. The AMPTP saw the DGA as a reliable ally and focused its attention on appeasing directors, even if industry peace came at the expense of writers.

Upon the expiration of the 1967 contract with the WGA, Lew Wasserman, chairman of the Music Corporation of American (MCA) and an experienced negotiator, argued to the Guild that exemplary directors such as Alfred Hitchcock were marquee names that could lure audiences and assure big box office numbers on particular films. The possessory credit was described in these discussions as a vanity credit that would be used primarily in outdoor advertising if the billboard included at least six credits; an individual director would have to negotiate for the credit to be used on screen or in other advertising. The writers acquiesced, knowing that Wasserman was a man of his word and had been a fair negotiator in times past. But in this instance, the promise did not stick. In 1968, the AMPTP sided with the DGA and inserted into its minimum basic agreement a provision that any director could negotiate for the possessory credit regardless of potential box office draw. Soon after, directors began regularly signing contracts with studios that included exclusive rights to the "film by" credit. Wasserman declared that the AMPTP's earlier agreement with the WGA had been a mistaken offer of rights. It was not, in fact, a mistake; rather, the AMPTP realized that the issue was far more complex. In 1970, the AMPTP included in the negotiations a statement that it could no longer provide a guarantee that only writer-directors would get the possessory credit within the rules of collective bargaining.[15]

Whatever trust had developed during the 1960s between writers and the studios began to erode as the now-wary writers returned to the negotiating table. This new friction was only intensified by the fact that the Directors Guild was clearly now an adversary—at least on this issue—and that the AMPTP would never take the side of the writers over the directors. In turn, the directors were eager to work with the companies rather than against them in negotiations. As a result of this moment, the relationship between the WGA and the AMPTP became more strained, and the relationship between writers and directors suffered for many decades to come. Frank Pierson explained how Wasserman's gentleman's agreement had been a terrible blow for the Guild. "Unfortunately we took [Wasserman] at his word. Now . . . we make [an] enormous effort to really pin down what it is that was agreed to. Then afterward Nick Counter and his people—Nick Counter being a negotiator—they sit down and begin to rewrite that. And the next few weeks and months are consumed with arguing over whether or not this was actually agreed to and exactly how it will be applied."[16] Moving forward, the AMPTP would demand in writing all details of negotiations between the studios and the WGA.

Since 1970, the battle over the possessory credit has played out primarily between the writers and directors guilds rather than between the guilds and the AMPTP. In 1977, the writers realized they could not win back what they had lost and prepared for that year's negotiations with the studios and networks with a plan to claim that no party should be allowed the possessory credit on a film. To use a solitary name was misleading, the WGA argued, given that motion picture production was a collaborative enterprise.[17] The DGA replied in the trades with an attack against the WGA that was so vitriolic that the WGA took the possessory credit off the bargaining table during the next round of negotiations. Pierson explained how the studios let the two guilds battle the issue: "The producers finally threw up their hands and said, 'We can't do anything with the directors; you work out a plan with them.' So we tried. But there was nothing forthcoming on their side. It was like Obama and the Republicans. We had nobody to negotiate with."[18] Many writers felt stymied by the weak position they now occupied. A number of them told of the frustrations they felt working with untested directors who demanded the possessory credit. Herb Meadow played up the drama of the situation: "The directors are our sworn enemies. They are the ones who are always demanding the possessory credit."[19] Many writers adopted this defensive position of being misunderstood by collaborators, studios, and fellow unions.

With the rise of independent voices in media production in the late 1960s and 1970s, studios developed a growing interest in filmmakers who offered both a singularity of vision and a willingness to come in under budget. Many more writers than in any era before had the opportunity to steer their own projects to completion, often serving not just as writer and director, but also as producer or actor. Dennis Hopper (*Easy Rider*), Roman Polanski (*Macbeth, The Tenant*, and *Rosemary's Baby*), Martin Scorsese (*Mean Streets* and *Goodfellas*), and later Oliver Stone (*Platoon, Wall Street*, and *JFK*) and David Lynch all found ways to play multiple hyphenate roles. These hyphenates, once lauded by the WGA, were now a source of frustration in the Guild's efforts to limit use of the possessory credit. At the same time, the Guild placed restrictions on credits that aggravated hyphenates who felt that they had played enough roles in the making of a film that they deserved the singular credit. Mel Brooks pointed to the film posters in his office and asked, "Can you see my name? You can't see it. You can only see it as an actor. Right? First billing is as an actor. But right above it, they limited the possessory credit. Now that was crazy. . . . If it's a Mel Brooks film, like a Billy Wilder or Lubitsch, it's going to bring in more money and it's going to mean more to the public and to the studio. And yet, the Writers Guild in their old-fashioned circle-the-building and get up the signs, are still stupid about possessory credits."[20] Whereas, in 1963, the Writers Guild had gone out of its way to ensure the possessory credit for writer-directors, in the 1970s and 1980s the Guild tried in as many ways as possible to limit the possessory credit—even if it ended up hurting some of its members.

While Brooks was incensed by the Guild's choice to abandon the rights of the hyphenate, he was absolutely clear in his belief that a director who is not also a writer should not be given a possessory credit. The hyphenate was someone that both guilds should value.

> The directors, they can't do anything without the script. . . . I'm a direc-
> tor and a member of the Directors Guild, and a big director. Directors
> feel—incorrectly so—that they are the author of the movie or the author
> of the television piece. They're not. . . . And without the writer, they are
> not even the director. They're a guy looking for a job. . . . The writer

gives birth. The writer has always been the true genius of everything that happens in our business. . . . They should bow to hyphenates! . . . The Writers Guild has to bow to it. . . . You're angry about it? Become a hyphenate! Become a director. Become a producer. Just don't stay in your little cocoon and expect the same excitement.[21]

There are far more writers who would love to become hyphenates on successful projects than ever get the chance do so. Not everyone possesses the sheer talent, longevity, and luck that Brooks has had in his career, and competition for such coveted roles within studio productions has only become more difficult. Still, Brooks's point is compelling: by placing writers and directors in adversarial roles, the two guilds have denied rights to some of their most celebrated members. Other hyphenates have either refused the possessory credit or felt ambivalent about it. When asked about his use of this credit, Carl Reiner was easy: "Oh, . . . I guess my agent figured that one out. They just asked me [if I wanted the credit] and I said sure."[22] With the credit, hyphenates can brand themselves and secure a particular level of remuneration, not just for one project but for all subsequent ones.

Feuds about the possessory credit have played out for decades between the two guilds. The DGA states clearly that it has never tried to obtain sole rights to credit and that "everyone involved in a motion picture is eligible" to negotiate for credits above the compulsory minimum.[23] There have even been rare examples of a possessory credit given to novelists—Margaret Mitchell for *Gone with the Wind* or Alex Haley for *Roots*—when their work is adapted. But most seekers of the credit are directors.[24] Ownership is rarely if ever at play, given that legal authorship is always in the hands of a production company. Not even a producer has sole authorial rights.

The history of determining credits is rife with battles over ego, branding, and notions of agency within production. After its failed attempt to control the possessory credit in the 1960s, the WGA has argued that the "film by" credit obscures the collaborative nature of production. Some hyphenates refuse the credit out of support for their fellow WGA members and their antipathy for the auteurist notion of cinema. Woody Allen, for example, has called the credit "pretentious and unnecessary."[25] But if many film hyphenates felt frustrated and abandoned by the Guild during the 1970s, the situation was even more contentious for television hyphenates.

The Television Hyphenate

My dad's joke was always that he used to come into my bedroom when
I was an infant and lean over my crib and say, "Produce! It's the only way
to protect your words!" And he was right.

–Chris Levinson (writer and producer on *Law & Order* and
Those Who Kill) talking about her father, writer-producer
Richard Levinson, interview 14 August 2013

By the 1960s, the writer-producer hyphenate was securely in place as an
essential and unique voice within American television production. Studios
and networks realized that writers who created a series and who became producers were economically desirable because they would have the determination to ensure that the final product was a success.[26] Herb Meadow clarified,
though, that his work as a producer would not give him ownership of series
he created: "This is not really so much a question of control of your material,
because in the end you don't really have control of your material. It's some
jerk executives somewhere up on the fourteenth or fifteenth floor of some
building that have control of your material."[27] Only the rare hyphenate—for
example, Aaron Spelling in his early career, or Stirling Silliphant, or Norman
Lear—would own a series outright. But the power was exciting, as collaborators William Link and Richard Levinson recalled:

> [M]any writers, who would not otherwise commit themselves to the
> brutal treadmill of series production could be seduced by a greater
> salary and the title of 'Producer.' . . . He can write not only with words,
> but with wardrobe, with music, with editing, and especially with cast-
> ing. . . . The television writer has at the very least a chance to become
> the *auteur* of the finished film, be it a segment of a series or a televi-
> sion movie or a mini-series. The terrain is scattered with booby traps,
> and the networks have absolute veto power, but the writer, if he
> is lucky, need no longer be an impotent outsider, provided he's will-
> ing (or able) to move back and forth between the typewriter and the
> producer's desk.[28]

From the 1960s to the 1980s, a television writers' room generally included
a hyphenate writer-producer, who was often also the creator of the series, a
small team of two to four writers, and a story editor. In addition, freelancers

might be hired piecemeal to write a couple of episodes. Freelance writers were a majority in the Guild, and many jumped from series to series for their entire careers. Levinson and Link found freelance work to be drudgery: "Writers were tailors, cutting bolts of cloth to a rigid set of expectations. They would be provided with an existing group of characters and a format, and any flexibility within these parameters was severely limited."[29] David Isaacs, who wrote on *M*A*S*H* and *Frasier*, recalled audio taping an episode of *The Mary Tyler Moore Show* to pick up the rhythms and style of the series before writing a spec script.[30] When freelancers were hired, they would be given access to a show bible and scripts. Cheri Steinkellner explained, "It's very valuable to read [a script], especially if you're creating new work, because that's how your work is first going to be seen. So it's apples to apples. You read it and then you write what you read. As opposed to, you watch it and then you're writing to what you see, it's been through a very different process."[31] Steinkellner said a script is a blueprint for a series episode rather than something final in its own right. Sometimes freelance writers would be hired as staff writers, and sometimes a staff writer would take over for a hyphenate if the hyphenate left the show to work on another series.

Each episode of a series would be assigned to a writer by the hyphenate or the head writer. Once the episode was drafted, the head writer or hyphenate would edit or rework the episode to make sure that the writing was consistent with the series style. Ron Clark, writer on *The Smothers Brothers Comedy Hour* and of *High Anxiety*, described the work of a hyphenate: "You not only wrote, but you got other people's material and rewrote that. Or asked them to rewrite it. Or showed them how to rewrite it."[32] Frank Pierson concurred: "That's true of any really successful television series. And anything that [the hyphenate's] going to be working on, he's going to wind up doing the bulk of the writing himself."[33] Even if they did substantial rewrites, hyphenates would generally leave the original writer's name on an episode and solely take a producer or executive producer credit. Because the writing credit was tied to residuals, sharing credit would mean that only half of any payment would go to the writer. George Eckstein, writer on *The Fugitive* and three *Perry Mason* television movies, described the relationship: "The writer's primary goal in most cases is to preserve his material as he wrote it. The producer's primary goal is to put the best possible show in front of the camera and on the air."[34] In a perfect world, those outcomes would be one in the same; but the reality was that hyphenates regularly reworked scripts, and some were troubled by the Guild tradition that the original writer should receive sole credit. Ernest Kinoy, a hyphenate himself, did not envy the Guild leadership: "The whole problem of the merging of the managerial ranks with writers is a terrible problem."[35]

Much of the tension within the television membership of the Guild was between hyphenates and freelancers. In 1967, Hal Kanter was irritated by the assumption some writers made about the motivations of hyphenates: "It's also a myth that when a writer becomes a hyphenate, he becomes the enemy . . . no longer a fellow writer. Almost every man who gets up to scream about the injustices being done to him as a freelancer would grab at the chance to be a hyphenate—a story editor, producer, whatever would be offered to him. Does this disagreement then boil down to envy? That's hardly a sound basis for good judgment."[36] Some freelancers, many of whom were hired by hyphenates, found it disquieting that their supervisor at work could also be on the board of directors for their rank-and-file union, especially during negotiations. Carey Wilber, a writer on *Rawhide* and *Star Trek*, expressed his outrage at the idea that a union would allow someone in management to decide critical Guild matters. "Listen, for Christ's sake, old man Hearst had cards in half a dozen different types of newspapers unions. He had a card in the typographical union, but they sure as hell weren't asking him to sit around in a decision-making capacity."[37] Writers who were particularly incensed about hyphenates believed that there should be no place for them in the setting of Guild policy. As Ben Roberts, writer on *Mannix* and creator of *Charlie's Angels*, put it, "There is a strike and push comes to shove, the writers are not going to back you simply because they consider you the enemy. Most writers who've worked for us—we consider them our friends. . . . But when it comes to their livelihood, to their families and themselves, I think it becomes a battleground."[38]

Problems came to a head for hyphenates and their relationship with the WGA in early 1973. At stake during negotiations that year were improved health and welfare benefits, salary increases for television writers, and a share in supplemental markets and scales increases for income from these markets (including pay TV and newly introduced videocassettes).[39] As the Guild teetered on the precipice of a strike, the weight of hyphenates on both the labor and the management sides became a crucial factor in seeking a solution to the labor dispute. In anticipation of a strike, the WGA distributed rules to its entire membership, including members who were currently working on series as writer-producers. Among the key provisions was a broad prohibition against any member crossing a WGA picket line, even to perform producing or directing work. In addition, writers could not resign from the Guild during a strike to continue their supervisory roles. Sy Salkowitz, a longtime freelancer on such series as *Naked City* and *Ironside*, remembered, "That night . . . was the first dawning on the hyphenate that he was no longer safe. That he would have to stay out of work. They were aghast. There was an outcry of rage and all kinds of things. However, we held firm."[40] As in the 1960 strike, the studios expected their writer-producers, writer-directors, and writer-story editors to continue their duties on the management side during the walkout. The WGA sent letters to hyphenates who continued to work, threatening them with penalties. The Guild issued disciplinary sanctions for approximately thirty hyphenates and stripped nine additional hyphenates of their union membership, including David Victor, creator of *Marcus Welby, M.D.*, and Jack Webb. The strike lasted sixteen weeks (from 6 March to 24 June), but the feud ignited between the Guild and hyphenate members would blaze for another five years.

Hyphenates were alternately bewildered and outraged by their censure. Virtually all of them considered themselves writers first and foremost; the daily experience of working was not that of wearing two entirely different hats, but rather of one role providing a seamless transition to performing the second role better than anyone else could. Sherwood Schwartz said about being a hyphenate, "I don't believe they're separate. I think that writing and producing—if the same man is involved with both—are a unit. It's not two separate functions [like] . . . a producer with credits. I have been a producer since 1963. I have rewritten every script because you have to."[41]

One group of hyphenates, outraged that their peers had been fined and expelled from the WGA for working as producers during the 1973 strike, created a new organization. It was first called the Hyphenate Committee and then became the Caucus for Producers, Writers & Directors. Leonard Stern, a founding member of the hybrid organization, believed that its role was to protect hyphenates from being exploited or betrayed by any one union.[42] Although the organization never had much legal power, over the years it developed into a lobbying group, becoming the "moral conscience" of the industry and tackling causes such as the Financial Interest and Syndication Rules, ageism, violence on television, and media consolidation.[43] There was also some talk at the time that hyphenates might leave the WGA and join the Producers Guild of America (PGA), which had united the Screen Producers

Guild and the Television Producers Guild in 1962.[44] Ultimately, the WGA was able to hold all of its writers together. As the Guild leadership now understood, hyphenates were some of the most successful working writers within the union and brought the most money into Guild coffers. The WGA could not afford, politically or financially, to cut them off.

Eventually, by action of the membership, the Guild rescinded its penalties against the hyphenates, but by then the hyphenates—with the backing of the studios and later the National Labor Relations Board (NLRB)—had decided to sue the Guild. ABC Television, the NLRB, and the AMPTP argued in their filing that the WGA West had violated the National Labor Relations Act during the strike by barring hyphenates from entering their workplace to perform non-writing tasks. The Guild won the case in the US Court of Appeals in 1977, but the matter was ultimately appealed to the US Supreme Court. Oral arguments took place in 1978, and in June of that year Justice Byron White delivered the Court's five-to-four decision in favor of the hyphenates, the studios, and the NLRB.[45] The ruling centered not on the premise that hyphenates should be able to work in their capacity as producers, but on a technicality. The majority held that the WGA had violated Section 8(b)(1)(B) of the National Labor Relations Act, which states that "it shall be an unfair labor practice for a labor organization . . . to restrain or coerce . . . an employer in the selection of his representatives for the purposes of collective bargaining or the adjustment of grievances." By barring hyphenates from the workplace, the Guild had denied their employers of their right to select representatives and assess employee grievances. The majority noted that "hyphenates who worked were . . . faced not only with threats but also with the actuality of charges, trial, and severe discipline simply because they were working at their normal jobs. And if this were not enough, they were threatened with a union blacklist that might drive them from the industry."[46] The Court's ruling did not clarify the role of the hyphenate. Justice John Paul Stevens expressed serious concern in his dissent. "In reversing the judgment of the Court of Appeals, this Court today forbids a union from disciplining a supervisor-member who crosses its picket line—who clearly gives 'aid and comfort to the enemy' during a strike . . .—solely because that action may have the incidental effect of depriving the employer of the hypothetical grievance-adjustment services of that particular supervisor for the duration of the strike. . . . In short, the Court's decision prevents a union with supervisory members from effectively calling and enforcing a strike."[47]

The situation for hyphenates had been resolved at the highest legal level, but they still needed to define their own principles on a practical level. Sam Rolfe cited the absurdity of these dual roles during a walkout: "We cannot be management when there's no strike . . . and Guild when there is a strike!"[48] Stirling Silliphant asked the Guild leadership if he could picket in front of another studio instead of his own in the event of a strike. Because, he laughed, "it looks foolish for me to be picketing my own show."[49] Hyphenates came to accept that they would always be in a difficult spot during negotiations, but nearly all of them continued to identify themselves as writers. Patricia Falken Smith, a writer on *Guiding Light, Days of Our Lives,* and *General Hospital,* was certain where a writer-producer's loyalties must stand. "The enemy is clearly defined. We are our own enemy. . . . Now we're negotiating with ourselves. Well, that's typical of writers. . . . Basically when the chips are down a writer is a writer is a writer. Any writer who crosses a Guild picket line is not a real writer because no real writer would."[50] And yet, according rules established by the WGA following the Supreme Court decision, hyphenates could not be asked to honor the picket lines as producers. This no-strike rule for hyphenates continued to confound many writers who felt that they were doing a disservice to their union by working. As Saul Turteltaub explained, "I didn't think was fair or right to the writers, to my writer part of my being, because I was now still going into work and making a living, and the writers were not."[51] Through the strikes of the 1980s, hyphenates continued to strike as writers and simultaneously to work as producers. It was only with the mobilization of showrunners during negotiations in 2007 and the ensuing strike of 2007–2008 that the WGA again found a way to leverage the power of the hyphenate.

Independents and Independence

Even as their Guild endured tortured battles over the possessory credit and the role of the hyphenate, writers during this era were creating some of the most innovative and exciting films and television. The productions of the 1970s pushed emotional boundaries, delving deep into grittier, more honest characters. Theatergoers in the 1980s saw the return of the blockbuster film, and primetime television audiences were finding edgier ensemble dramas and independently produced comedy series.

The 1970s were a period of extraordinary freedom for film writers, producers, and directors. Marc Norman describes how "[v]eteran screenwriters look back on the early 1970s as the Happy Time. Almost anybody with a good idea could land a development deal, almost any screenwriter who'd written a few profit-turners stood a good chance to direct."[52] Patrick McGilligan discusses how writers were able to work inside the parameters of a studio with "hitherto unheard-of independence."[53] And those who worked outside the studio system could do so without harming their careers in Hollywood. Many of these writers came from film school backgrounds; others rose up through the Hollywood ranks or came from the world of literature. Novelist William Goldman learned screenwriting in the 1960s from watching films. He found the young writers of the film school generation perplexing. "When I started, there weren't film schools. . . . I never saw a screenplay until I was 33 years old. . . [when] I first heard about film schools I thought it was the stupidest fucking idea I'd ever heard of. . . . Now movies are important, which they never were when I was a kid." In years to come, Goldman's memoir, *Adventures in the Screen Trade*, would be required reading in film schools.[54]

As discussed earlier in this chapter, this new independence allowed writers to get into directing as well. But some writers, like Paul Schrader, realized that directing was not at all what they had imagined. "Being a director is not nearly as rewarding as I thought it would be. Far more tedious. You never get a sense of artistic completion as a director. . . . As a writer you really get a sense of the whole. That is very, very difficult to do as a director, because you are just dealing with pieces, repeated over and over again."[55]

With the further conglomeration of the media industries and the rise of the blockbuster and high-concept films in the 1970s and 1980s, the industry in Hollywood saw a dramatic structural shift. Geoff King argues that these shifts in the workplace brought new challenges and uncertainties for writers: "The freedoms of the Renaissance period were given to filmmakers by the big studios. They could also be taken away. . . . Freedom was a product of uncertainty and transition. It did not last."[56] The radical deregulation of the media industries in the 1980s and 1990s, which remains in effect to the present day, led to a corporatization of the culture of media production at the top. In an interview, Marc Norman tracked the radical shifts in executive personnel and his own sense of alienation from industry insiders. "The 1970s wave was creative people coming out of film school. The 1980s and 1990s wave was business people coming out of business school who saw in the movie business a chance to make a lot of money. . . . It had gone from this domestic, silly-ass little business to this wide kind of megalith. . . . When I started out . . . not only had nobody been to business school, nobody had been to film school. A lot of them had not been to school. What they knew was making movies and exhibition and what the public wanted."[57] This takeover of the executive suite by a business mentality heralded a radical transition: beginning with films such as *Star Wars* and *Jaws*, Hollywood's biggest concern would be to find the next screenplay that would attract mass audiences. The independent filmmakers and small studios still had a critical place in American story-telling, but increasingly into the 1980s, the major studios began to dominate. The rise of Miramax from a small independent producer and distribution company to a studio subsidiary in the 1990s was just one example of how the "independent film" was absorbed into the mainstream.[58]

Although American television in the 1970s did not have the visual aesthetics or the energy of contemporary American cinema, it was ground-breaking in its own way, most notably in its content. The miniseries and the movie of the week were places where many screenwriters found a home in the world of television writing. In 1979, Stanley Rubin explained: "[There used to be] very rigid lines between the television writer and the screenwriter, between the television producer and the screen producer, or the screen writer-producer and the television writer-producer. . . . That rigid line is being erased more every single year starting in the last five years or so. That change has been particularly speeded up by the long form in television. Not only the two-hour movie but, more importantly, the four-hour movie for television. . . . The division is disappearing completely."[59] Some of the most forward-thinking programming in this era came from miniseries and made-for-television movies. If this was the second Golden Age of Television, then the movie of the week was the equivalent of the previous Golden Age's anthology show.

Fay Kanin, who had been a successful screenwriter with her husband, Michael Kanin, talked about her experience with *Tell Me Where It Hurts*, a 1974 made-for-television film she wrote that starred Maureen Stapleton. Until then, she had watched her films only in movie theaters.

I was sitting in my living room and I didn't hear anybody laugh, I didn't hear anybody cry, I didn't hear anybody. And I said to Michael, "I hate this medium. I want to be in a theater with an audience. This is for the birds." And then the next day I went out . . . to the drugstore, I went to the bank—everywhere I went I heard the women talking about this movie. . . . And I suddenly understood the impact of television.

Rather in some movie houses where even if 500 people saw it—that there were going to be hundreds of thousands of people who had seen this. It had a very good rating and just blew my mind. This was a terrific opportunity. . . . I found my medium now—this is it.[60]

Kanin realized that the power of television was in its ability to tell a small story well. The reach of television was thrilling for writers interested in being a part of a conversation with their audiences on cultural and social issues. Kanin went on to win two Emmys for her work in television.

In these television films, writers were able to tackle controversial issues, including racial prejudice (William Link and Richard Levinson with *My Sweet Charlie*, 1970), cancer (William Blinn with *Brian's Song*, 1971), homosexuality (Link and Levinson with *That Certain Summer*, 1972), child abuse (Gerald DiPego with *Born Innocent*, 1974), nuclear war (Edward Hume with *The Day After*, 1983), and domestic violence (Rose Leiman Goldemberg with *The Burning Bed*, 1984). Levinson and Link detailed their frustrations at ABC with the making of *That Certain Summer*, and how the network pushed back out of concern for presenting both sides of the issue. "We countered that the script was neither pro- nor anti-gay and we suggested that a much larger issue was involved: the question of the writer's rights to use the public air for the expression of opinions, popular or otherwise. Was controversy to be denied anyone who wrote for television because of equal time considerations? If a writer dared to take a position, must the countervailing view always be incorporated in the script? What if 'balance' was in conflict with good drama?" Levinson and Link argue that political and social ideas could be challenged and debated within dramatic entertainment.

The most noteworthy entry in the genre by far was *Roots*. Fred Silverman, who was ABC's programming chief at the time, knew that he had something extraordinary: "Every other week, Brandon Stoddard, who ran the movie operation . . . would come in and say, we need another hour. . . . Next thing you know, we have twelve hours of this thing. But it was good. It was really good. We had great writers on it—Bill Blinn and Ernie Kinoy. . . . Sixty percent of the population of the US watched that show. By the time we got to the fourth or fifth night, people were not going out. They were not going to the movies. They were mesmerized."[61] By the end of the week of its first airing in January 1977, approximately eighty million people were tuning in; the final episode had an astonishing Nielsen rating of 51.1 and a 71 share (that is, more than half the households in the United States were watching the series, and 71 percent of all people watching television were tuned into that series during its time slot). In all, 85 percent of American homes with televisions tuned in to least some part of the series.[62] When asked how he was able to write about a black family through the generations, William Blinn, a white man from Toledo, Ohio, explained that he not only had access to Alex Haley (who wrote the book the series was based on), but he also related to the story's family dynamics. "I was writing about Kunta Kinte, I'm writing about a farm kid in a community where the father is the absolute ruler of the roost, outwardly, but everybody knows that momma holds the power. And I do know that world. I know what it's like to say to a kid in stern tones, 'You do it and do it right now.'"[63] The series was a powerful experience for the American people in portraying slavery and African American heritage and generational history, but it also stood out for its lack of representation of minority voices behind the screen.

Blinn lamented the decline of the television film in the 1980s: "We lost a lot when television lost movies of the week. Movies of the week meant two nights a week and sometimes three nights a week there would be a story you hadn't seen before with characters you didn't know about. Some of it was kind of awful and predictable and silly. Some of it, occasionally, was absolutely wonderful and heart-stopping and they were taking risks because they couldn't say, 'Oh, let's do what we did last week.' We didn't do anything last week."[64]

In the realm of comedy, CBS stole Saturday nights in the ratings with season after season of extraordinary series in the 1970s: *All in the Family*, *M*A*S*H*, *The Mary Tyler Moore Show*, *The Bob Newhart Show*, and *The Carol Burnett Show*. Fred Silverman, who was the head of programming at CBS at the time and who, with Bob Wood, scheduled the series in a block, called Saturday "probably the best night of television in the history of television. People didn't go out on Saturday night."[65] Paramount produced *M*A*S*H*, but the rest of these series, like much of primetime in this decade, originated from independent television production companies.

The rise of these production companies—and the reason for their two decades of success—was a direct outcome of the Financial Interest and Syndication Rules (Fin-Syn) established by the Federal Communications Commission in 1970. Fin-Syn prohibited networks from owning equity in the programming they aired, including syndication rights to series. These new

A room. Actually, an entire apartment, but a single large room. There are some -- mostly of the working-girl variety -- who would consider this place a "great find": ten-foot ceilings, pegged wood floors, a wood-burning fireplace, and, most-important, a fantastic ceiling-height corner window. Right now the room is totally empty, but it won't be for long. It will be the main setting for

"THE MARY TYLER MOORE SHOW"

So God Bless It.

IMAGE 21 Opening page of the show bible for Allan Burns and James L. Brooks's *The Mary Tyler Moore Show*, c. 1970.

Allan Burns Collection, Writers Guild Foundation Archive, Shavelson-Webb Library, Los Angeles rules allowed the Hollywood studios to invest more in television programming and encouraged the formation of independent production companies, including Lorimar, Carsey-Werner Productions, Aaron Spelling Productions, Stephen J. Cannell Productions, MTM, and Tandem/TAT.

Great production houses made a programmer's job easier: they had already vetted writers and series—and paid for them. They knew the character of the networks and could assess whether a series might find an audience. Fred Silverman appreciated the simpler corporate structure of the networks at the time, which made the process of greenlighting a series easier and faster. There might be challenges bringing a series to air, but once he had a hit and was working with known hyphenates or established independent production companies, he could make decisions quickly. For example, he told the story of asking Garry Marshall to pull together a test pilot (in fact, just a few scenes) for a possible *Laverne and Shirley* spin-off from *Happy Days*. "It makes a big difference to be able to do something quickly, but also to be able to recognize something that's good. . . . That was probably the best program development."[66]

Easily the most exciting independent players in television production, especially for writers, were Grant Tinker at Mary Tyler Moore's MTM and Norman Lear at Bud Yorkin's Tandem/TAT Productions. John Caldwell argues that many series created under the leadership of Lear and Tinker challenged audiences' opinions on contemporary social issues and intellectual problems but were conservative in terms of their visual aesthetic. "Although the old aesthetic standbys—liveness, character acting, and sensitive writing—increased in programming value and stature during this period, many of television's stylistic capabilities were essentially ignored. . . . For both Tandem and MTM, then, company style was defined entirely as an issue of content, not form."[67] In part, the rationale behind high-content, low-style series was to allow the production companies to create television on a limited budget. If they saved on the aesthetic side, Tandem and MTM could reinvest their profits in more series that they loved and believed would succeed. If the series failed, they were stuck with the bills. Lear described his sense of personal and social responsibility for the programming he created and for the series that his company produced with little to no financial help from the networks. When asked about deficit financing, Lear replied, "Nobody would make *Mary Hartman* so I made *Mary Hartman*. We paid for that. I don't think of it as deficit financing, we just fucking paid for it."[68]

These two independent companies put their money into making intelligent, content-rich, topical programming using extraordinary acting, directing, and writing talent. Pretty much every writer during the era wanted to work on an MTM or Tandem series. Susan Harris, who scripted the abortion episode of *Maude* and later went on to create *Benson* and *The Golden Girls*, expressed her gratitude for working with producers and executives who let her push social and cultural boundaries. "Comedy is a less threatening way to deliver messages to audiences. . . . The first job was to entertain and then I was always looking for something more, something to say, to express myself. And sometimes that comes from a very dark place."[69] Allan Burns described working with Grant Tinker at MTM: "Everybody wanted to work there because of Grant. You knew you would be backed up. The writer came first. . . . That was his *modus operandi* for everything that happened at MTM. He would hire the best people he could find, listen to their ideas, they would work out an idea together, and he would say, 'Go do it.' And, if it was good, he knew it. . . . Look at *St. Elsewhere*, which started with very low ratings. So did *Hill Street Blues.* And then when he went to NBC and started *Cheers* and *Cosby*? He protected everybody."[70]

The two companies had a friendly rivalry. Robert Schiller, who was the head writer for *Maude*, used to joke about *The Mary Tyler Moore Show* as light entertainment: "We have a two-parter on abortion and they're going to counter with a three-parter on mayonnaise."[71] The two programs were arguably the most forward-thinking series about women that had ever been on American television. Norman Lear talked about his relationship with Grant Tinker and how they partnered in picking writers who would best fit their shows: "We actually could talk about what was best for the writer. [If both] of us wanted the same writer, where was the better opportunity? . . . That came up several times. It was easy for us because we cared about the writer."[72] The sense from many writers interviewed was that the system was less paternalistic than it was dedicated to working with writers to craft their skills and to encourage excellence.

David Isaacs and his writing partner Ken Levine mapped three distinct schools of writing in the era: Norman Lear's "socially aware comedy"; MTM's "more sophisticated and smarter and character-based" formula; and "the Garry Marshall school [then Miller-Milikis-Boyett Productions], which was silly and fun and really well written." A comedy writer who could get into one of those companies would be "well-served, you'd learn a lot."[73] Isaacs and Levine were both talented and lucky enough to land sought-after staff writing jobs. Increasingly, during the 1970s and 1980s, there were far more writers looking for work than film and television studios could absorb. And not everyone felt that the playing field for employment was level.

Representation in the Room

Four or five years ago, I was in that woman-writer trap. If it was a show about Army, Navy, business, or war, I had no chance at all. Babies, crying, love, or an ovarian cyst—then I was your writer.

–Lila Garrett (writer on *Bewitched, All in the Family,*
and *The Nanny*), quoted by Martha Humphrey in
Fade In 1 (Summer 1979): 34

Even though women writers had been working in Hollywood since the earliest days of the film industry, their representation in the WGA and among writers of produced films and television series was scant at best in the 1970s and 1980s. Alvin Sargent recalled that in the 1960s and 1970s the number of women writers was so small that they stood out in the room: "What I remember most about meetings was there were mostly men and then little by little women started [appearing]. You'd say, 'There's a woman!' And then more and more women, until now it doesn't make any difference."[74] Sargent is not entirely accurate. The percentages of men and women are still uneven, and the number of minorities is still meager.

The WGA has tracked the employment of women and minorities in television more diligently than in film, both because the overall employment numbers are higher and because the turnover of employees is faster (television writers are sometimes rehired for subsequent seasons). In April 1974, the Guild sent signatory companies a report on how many men and women were writing for television series. Although 13 percent of the Guild's members were women, only 6.5 percent of the current season's television series had hired at least one female writer on staff or as a freelance writer.[75] Of the sixty-two primetime series identified in the survey, twenty-six of them had never hired a female writer. Even more telling, only 1.5 percent of pilots on the air in 1973 were written by women. The Guild emphasized that, "[w]hile we do not favor the employment of one writer over another and we do not and will not recommend any particular writer for employment, we do want all of our members to have an *equal chance* at employment."[76] WGA Executive Director

Michael Franklin signed this letter, but his commitment to the general cause was less than fervent. "I had meetings with several women, four or five women, who had formed a group. And I tried, and we had little gains. We made all kinds of threats to the studios, and we filed suit for the women, and got something, but it was still bad. But with the women writers from the Guild there wasn't anything done. We ignored them [laughs]. There were a number of women that were successful writers, but it was obvious there should have been more."[77] Franklin's letter did some good, at least for a while. Veteran soap opera showrunner Jean Rouverol Butler recalled "a sudden rush of—at least—tokenism on the part of producers."[78]

That is not to say that women were not involved in the production of television series. A good number of women worked as script supervisors (then known as "script girls") and producers. When asked about women and minorities in the writers' room, Norman Lear argued that women were critical to the functioning of the production. "For me, it has nothing to do with color or sex. That was true of everybody in our little club. Most of the people could have been in the writers' room. There was never a show that was produced by men. They were all women. The people who held it together—kept the schedules, kept everybody on time—were women. They carried the script, they knew every word, and they had every schedule, and they had every relationship that mattered, that the director didn't have. They were all women. The glue. The glue was all women."[79] But the "glue" that was holding the production together was not leading it on the set or in post-production.

The statistics had not improved much by the end of the year, when the WGA Women's Committee reported that among 106 production companies it surveyed, sixty-one had posted no writing credits at all for women.[80] Chaired by Noreen Stone (writer on *Amy* and later *Dynasty*), Joyce Perry (writer on *Room 222* and *Land of the Lost*), and Howard Rodman, the group tallied the genders of all writers paid by the networks to write primetime series during the 1973 season. The gender ratios for top-rated series were remarkably skewed (see table 4.1). The report stressed the dismal representation of women writers at the three major networks: 10.8 percent at ABC; 8.2 percent at NBC; and 8.4 percent at CBS.[81] Yet women were scripting some of the most impressive shows on the air. In 1974, Fay Kanin and Treva Silverman (*The Monkees*) were singled out at the Emmy Awards with special awards for Writer of the Year in the categories of Special and Series, Kanin for *Tell Me Where It Hurts* and Silverman for *The Mary Tyler Moore Show.*

TABLE 4.1.

WGA Women's Committee Statistics on
1973 Network Primetime Series

Series	Total no. of episodes	Network	Production company	Teleplays by writer gender	
				M	F
All in the Family	69	CBS	Tandem	65	4
Sanford and Son	49	NBC	Tandem	49	0
The Waltons	40	CBS	Lorimar	37.5	2.5
Hawaii 5-0	133	CBS	CBS T/Freeman	132.5	0.5
Maude	37	CBS	Tandem	26	11
Mary Tyler Moore	75	CBS	MTM	50	25
M*A*S*H	38	CBS	Fox	37	1

Source: WGA Women's Committee, "Women's Committee Statistics Report," 7 November 1974, Archives, Writers Guild Foundation Shavelson-Webb Library, Los Angeles.

Note: Where one-half of a teleplay is noted, a woman was part of a known male-female writing team. Other writing teams may have been mixed, but that information is not clear from the data.

Nevertheless, many women writers were still struggling to land work. Barbara Corday described how she and her writing partner, Barbara Avedon, were treated in the years before their series *Cagney & Lacey* finally made it to air: "Every show we worked on, every producer we worked for, wherever we went, we were 'The Girls.' And Barbara was fifteen years older than me, so I was not only part of 'the Girls,' I was always referred to as 'the Kid.'"[82] Corday noted that rarely would there be more than one woman or a team of women on a writing staff and that often when she and Avedon went out for jobs, they would be in competition with other women. Corday recalled pitching an episode of *Maude* with Avedon to hyphenate Rod Parker. Parker loved the idea, hired them, and walked them out of the office and down the hall. "And as the elevator doors were closing, he said, 'This is great. We've started a lot of secretaries on this show.' He made the immediate assumption that up until 8 o'clock that morning, we had been secretaries and we just happened to come up with that idea."[83]

In the 1980s, there was a concerted effort to end discrimination against women in the writers' room. The way things played out, effectively, access improved for only white women. The Women's Committee of the WGA sponsored events and addressed key issues in its monthly newsletter. Responding to a 1983 article in the *Los Angeles Times* in which WGA West President Frank Pierson stated, "I don't know any good writer *not* hired because she is a woman," Leonora Thuna, who wrote on *Family* and *Lou Grant*, chose a letter to the editor of the *WGAw Newsletter* as her platform. Pierson had missed the point, she observed. When story editors and producers fail to consider women for writing assignments, women writers cannot "build up credits and they remain a minority in the writing world."[84] In 1987, the WGA West commissioned sociologists William Bielby and Denise Bielby to study the Guild's membership. The statistics they gathered were staggering. From 1982 to 1985, males represented almost 80 percent of employed WGA West writers, whereas women constituted just under 20 percent, with minorities of both genders representing approximately 2 percent of employed writers.[85] Among the WGA West's entire membership, minorities made up 2.9 percent of the total. White male writers had an earnings advantage across the board in the industry (at studios, independents, and networks), with women and minorities often making only 60 to 70 cents for every dollar white men earned.[86] Bielby and Bielby continued to conduct regular studies of the Guild, providing detailed numbers and analyses of the representation of women, minorities, and older writers in the Guild until the early 2000s. The Guild attempted to address inequalities in hiring and unequal pay through the MBA, requiring producers to read scripts by women and minorities. But because the Guild was not a hiring agency, members had little power over the signatories.

Despite the skewed gender ratio, some white female writers claim to have experienced no difficulty in getting hired or running a writers' room. Cheri Steinkellner never felt she was treated differently in the writers' room while working on *Cheers.*

> Because I did not know there was a difference, there was no difference—for me. . . . There were times when I was in an authority position . . . with my two male partners where I would be the lightning rod for controversy and I would not understand why. . . . I think if I had

known that there might have been some gender differences, it would have been a lot harder to do the job. . . . I not only went in, I went in with a baby. I was a nursing mother in a room full of men.[87]

Whether other women were fortunate enough to be among those treated fairly or whether they adopted an oblivious attitude toward the institutional sexism that so many other women experienced is impossible to say, but important to consider. Dava Savel had her own take: "Cheri was . . . protected from a lot of that" because she co-wrote and co-ran the *Cheers* writers' room with her husband, Bill Steinkellner. For women working in male-female writing partnerships the situation has historically been different.

Professional opportunities for men of color were limited, and for women of color they were almost nil. Minority writers were an anomaly in Hollywood during the 1970s, and they made up just a tiny percentage of the workforce in the 1980s. In 1969, James Webb, a white writer who scripted *Pork Chop Hill* and *Cape Fear* and who served as WGA West president from 1962 to 1963, categorized all black writers in Hollywood into three factions: (1) writers who saw the industry as the "perpetuation of White Power"; (2) those who were willing to work for the industry "until a black industry can be created"; and (3) "true integrationists."[88] Webb essentially argued that African American writers might be better served as novelists; any success one might have would depend on whether a writer was "basically an integrationist or a separatist."[89] At the time, Webb was writing the script *They Call Me Mr. Tibbs!* for Sidney Poitier. His argument failed to account for the long history of independent African American writer-directors in the United States, from William Foster's *The Railroad Porter* in 1912 to William Greaves's *Symbiopsychotaxiplasm: Take One* in 1968. Webb's naïve assessment probably mirrored the perceptions of many, mostly white, writers within the industry and the Guild at that time.

Others were antagonistic toward the need for equal access within the Guild. Carey Wilber berated the Guild for worrying about the representation of minority writers and issues facing international guilds when other issues, like the hyphenate-freelance debate, were, to him, foremost. "We've had a Board—the same old faces around that Board that were there in 1960 for Chrissakes—that sits around and they come up with equal opportunity for the n****rs? They come up with coffee klatches with the goddamn Russians? . . . Nobody is talking about the fact that maybe two years from now we have got another negotiation."[90]

During the 1970s and into the 1980s, an increasing number of series starred African Americans, including *Julia, Flip, Fat Albert and the Cosby Kids, Sanford and Son, Get Christie Love!, Good Times, The Jeffersons, What's Happening!!, Benson*, and *The Cosby Show*. On many of these series, the writers' rooms rarely mirrored the diversity of the actors on the screen. Bill Boulware, a writer on *Benson* and later *The Fresh Prince of Bel-Air*, described how discrimination behind the scenes changed: "Back in the 50s or 60s, when it was a matter of discriminatory practices, it was easier to define. . . . The majority of the people in the industry [now] are used to seeing colors as definition of some things. Now that may not even be on a conscious level, but their perceptions . . . and how you come across may be colored by the fact that you are colored. . . . When there's not a black subject or subject matter, then it's not that you are not valid, but they just don't tend to even connect you up with it."[91] People of color might sometimes be hired; but if they were not re-hired after a specified period of time, they would lose their voting rights in the Guild. Thus, of the 1,540 writers working in television in 1980, only 4 were black, and of 5,252 members overall, 65 were black (only 15 of whom were eligible to vote).[92] Even though minority families averaged twenty more hours of television viewing per week than white families in the 1980s, representation throughout the industry remained negligible.

Every month, the Black Writers' Caucus and the Women's Caucus published dispatches in the WGA newsletters, but the pace of change was glacial. Although independent studios like MTM, Tandem, and Carsey-Werner made more efforts than most to create inclusive workplaces, minority representation in the writers' room lagged far behind the modest gains for actors. Writers of color were dissatisfied both with their Guild and with its general membership. Hyphenate writer-director-actor Robert Townsend satirized Hollywood typecasting by writers, casting agents, and directors in his 1987 film *Hollywood Shuffle*. But successful African American writers and hyphenates were the exception to the rule. As the 1980s wore on, and as the studios gained a stronger bargaining stance, the WGA struggled to keep its writers unified.

The Alliance and the Strikes of the 1980s

The history of the Guild is a history of interest groups, divided groups.

—Elias Davis, interview, 29 September 2010

1988 is the Guild's Vietnam.

—Marc Norman, interview 9 June 2011

A sweeping trend toward consolidation overtook the media industries during the 1980s. As Jennifer Holt details in her analysis of the structural convergence of the American entertainment industries, the boundaries between formerly distinct media industries were breaking down: film and broadcast merged under Fox; vertical reintegration occurred at Universal, Paramount, and Warner Bros.; and film merged with cable at Warner Bros., MCA/Universal, and Columbia.[93] The phenomenon did not end there; publishing, music, merchandising, and theme parks were part of these corporate empires, as well. The high-concept blockbuster film was Hollywood's focus, leaving room for small independent studios and paving the way at the end of the decade for the rise of Miramax and other corporate independents. Cable was emerging as a significant new competitor to broadcast television at a time when the broadcast audience was in a dramatic decline, with shows' average ratings plunging from 50 in 1981 to 33.9 shares in 1991.[94] For entertainment unions, the progressive consolidation of the media industry meant a decline in the diversity of outlets interested in making or buying content and in the number of signatories at the bargaining table.

The ten-week SAG and AFTRA strike in 1980 delayed the fall season of television as the unions battled with the studios and networks over compensation for original programming on pay TV and home recording devices. At the time, only 5 percent of households with televisions had a home recording device (only 1 percent of which were VCRs), but the unions understood that this market was growing rapidly.[95] In 1981, negotiations between the WGA and the studios and networks broke down over residuals for pay TV exhibition, and the Guild called a strike in April. Independent producers settled quickly on a formula, but the strike continued with the majors for thirteen weeks.

Writers debated the issues among themselves at a series of heated meetings prior to and during the 1981 strike. Some found the gatherings as exasperating as they were entertaining. In describing them, Cheri Steinkellner found an apt analogy: "It was like High Holidays. If there was going to be a strike, that's when everybody shows up to temple. . . . It was hilarious. Heated. Nobody is more political or opinionated than writers. And articulate. [Arguments were] brilliantly stated. Not always eloquently—and not always succinctly—but [it was] fascinating to hear people state their case passionately. . . . Writers are not really equipped for a physical brawl. As a subset of humanity we have not been trained in street fighting. Those aren't the skills that got us to that particular career."[96] That many of the writers were Jewish was a fact never formally documented by surveys, but it was always a part of the collective understanding of writers as a community. David Isaacs picked up on this notion of separateness: "It's not a classic work action because people are pulling up in their Beemers and Mercedes and sports cars and we're going to walk, and we're writers so food is very important, so after two hours . . . [y]ou go off with a bunch of friends to a deli or another restaurant, Italian, and you'd eat."[97] Although the writers' concerns over compensation were completely valid, the presence of mostly privileged, educated, upper-middle-class white males on the picket line made it abundantly clear why questions continued to arise about who in Hollywood was getting writing jobs in the first place.

IMAGE 22 WGA members and Academy Award–winning writers on strike in 1981. Left to right: Robert Carson, Julius Epstein, Daniel Taradash, Sidney Sheldon, and Frank Tarloff.

Writers Guild Foundation Archive, Shavelson-Webb Library, Los Angeles

In July 1981, the Guild and the studios hammered out a deal, a percentage of gross for writers, ending the strike after a brutal forty-week walkout. Soon after, in 1982, the loosely federated Association of Motion Picture and Television Producers changed its name to the Alliance of Motion Picture and Television Producers (AMPTP) and became the single bargaining agent and trade organization representing the signatories in their collective bargaining with the entertainment labor unions: DGA, SAG, AFTRA, IATSE, American Federation of Musicians, International Brotherhood of Electrical Workers, Laborers Local 724, Teamsters Local 399, and the East and West branches of the WGA.[98] The hope for the networks and the studios was in bringing their disparate interests together as one voice. When Nicholas Counter III took over as president of AMPTP, he suggested that perhaps the 1981 WGA strike could have been averted or quashed: "Certainly . . . by having a unified position in the industry, we have less chance of that kind of disruption."[99]

What became clear to WGA negotiators was that creative workers were vastly underpaid based on what they thought the AMPTP was dispersing in residuals. Talent was not receiving 1.2 percent of the worldwide distribution of the gross receipts for video; rather, they were paid 1.2 percent of 20 percent of the gross, a drastically lower percentage.[100] The AMPTP had found a way to inject into the contracts its claim that studio costs ate up 80 percent of the gross, especially the expenses associated with copying and distributing the pricy new medium of VHS. The DGA accepted this new financing structure in its next collective bargaining agreement.[101] With its next round of negotiations, the WGA wanted to renegotiate the 80/20 split, but the AMPTP responded that it could not give the WGA something better than it had given the DGA and, ultimately, the SAG.

When the contract expired in 1985, the AMPTP and WGA struggled over demands on ancillary profits from prerecorded films and television series sold on videocassettes. Writers demanded that their share of residuals come from the total wholesale revenues rather than from the 20 percent defined as the producers' share.[102] At the time the "tape issue," as the press called it, seemed to be a larger concern for screenwriters than for television writers. Home video was the driving new technology, with ancillary revenues rising to over 50 percent of the film industry's income and domestic theatrical revenue dropping to 36 percent.[103] The bulkiness of VHS tapes—and the fact that they could hold only about two hours of programming in standard play mode—made them an illogical choice for a season's worth of hour-long television programming. Given that television production was now outpacing film production in New York and Los Angeles, the WGA membership was more focused on the burgeoning cable market than on screenwriters' percentage of VHS profits.[104]

The Guild voted to strike in 1985, but members were far from united on the matter. A vocal contingent of writers, still angry about the last strike and uninterested in this squabble over tape, was eager to continue working. At an all-membership meeting, this group of anti-strike writers, led by conservative television film writer Lionel Chetwynd (who wrote *Ike*), declared themselves the "Union Blues," took control of the microphones, and called for the Guild to negotiate a resolution immediately. If the WGA would not "bring us back a deal," their blue buttons proclaimed, they would go "financial core," meaning that they would break the strike and not be represented by the WGA. After enduring the 1981 strike, the writers were swayed by this no-strike push, even if some knew that the stakes were incredibly high. In discussing the events years later, Larry Gelbart, writer on *Caesar's Hour* and of *Tootsie*, said to Chetwynd, "You were the Blues, yeah. . . . Well, you made us look like the Reds, which was a very clever ploy."[105]

After a brief two-week strike, the Union Blues swayed the opinion of WGAw Executive Director Naomi Gurian, and the walkout ended. The WGA agreed to an $84 million contract and $1.25 million in pension and health benefits in return for an agreement to withdraw all arbitration regarding percentages over videocassette sales residuals.[106] In a letter to the editor of the *WGAw Newsletter* in May 1985, Edmund Morris, writer on *Lawman*, described the destructive nature of the Union Blues plan.

> Those members of our Guild who believe that we have triumphed are sadly deluded. . . . Management played upon the frets of our internal division with consummate skill, infecting our negotiators with the desolation of defeat. Our negotiators carried back Management's cynical offer and bribe with the pride of a Neville Chamberlain. . . . On the cold and sober morning of March 19, our President told the media that the contract was a lousy one and that "the issue of videocassettes" was "dead for all time." . . .The Union Blues won a Pyrrhic victory. The tidal wave of rollbacks will drown you and the rest of us in 1988.[107]

Though Morris's tone sounds inflated, the Union Blues' victory proved devastating. Television writers who saw videocassettes as an issue only for screenwriters may have had second thoughts. Grace Reiner, who was a lawyer for the WGA at the time, observed, "I find it somewhat telling that Paramount released the entirety of *Star Trek* a month after the Writers Guild strike ended. Coincidence? Maybe."[108]

Few of the writers interviewed could remember which strike in the 1980s was about which issue. Many of them felt that the issues were not entirely clear to them at the time and that perhaps there was a breakdown between the leadership and the membership about what precisely the union wished to accomplish with each successive strike. Later in 1985, outgoing WGAw president Ernest Lehman, writer of *Sabrina, North by Northwest*, and *The Sound of Music*, expressed a hope for closure on this period of Guild history. "These have been a memorable two years which a lot of us would like to forget and never will, and don't ask me how the Guild survived the turmoil and the confusion but it did, and [it] even came up with a new contract that to an overwhelming majority of you had meaningful gains, and to a vocal minority was a big disappointment, and each of us swears that he or she knows exactly what did or did not happen and why, but it's *Rashomon* all over again, with six thousand points of view, all of them equally valid."[109] Lehman's notion of success for the Guild was survival, a low goal given the Guild's accomplishments in the past (residuals, health care, and pensions). Writers were disgruntled with the Guild and confused by how they had been sideswiped by the AMPTP. Moreover, the financial significance of their loss was not yet apparent to them.

In 1987, news writers at CBS and Capital Cities/ABC went on strike for six weeks. They marched in front of Television City and in Century City. Negotiations proved fruitful for the WGA, in that it expanded its jurisdiction further into news and documentary writing. It was a moment of success in the midst of a series of devastating losses. Just one year later, in 1988, the WGA again entered into negotiations with the AMPTP. The central issues were residuals on foreign sales and syndication and expanded creative rights (access to film sets, comments on casting, rights to review the director's cut). Many writers hoped, unrealistically, to regain all that had been lost in the 1985 negotiations, but the AMPTP flatly refused to discuss percentages for residuals on VHS, much less overhaul them. Howard A. Rodman captured the mindset of many writers at the time: "When you believe that you have been screwed out of hundreds of millions of dollars, it's not the best frame of mind to go into negotiations with because you're trying to get reparations for past conduct rather than figure out what you can do going forward."[110] In the spring of 1988, negotiations with the AMPTP broke down, and the WGA went out on strike.

The walkout lasted 155 days (March 7 to August 7), the longest strike in Guild history, and it did not end well for the writers. In May, the WGA signed contracts with sixty-four independent companies, including a number of late-night series. In June, the AMPTP came to negotiations with an offer that acquiesced only on expansion of creative rights—no foreign residual increase, and continued percentage-based domestic residuals. The membership voted by 74.9 percent to refuse the deal, and the strike continued. Cheri Steinkellner remembered the bitterness and deep sense of defeat the membership felt: "Just three years earlier we'd had a big loss that we had not yet recovered from. Those wounds were still so fresh. And so to lose again—it wasn't even a possibility. And yet, there wasn't any winning."[111]

Brandon Tartikoff, president of NBC Entertainment, issued a two-part ultimatum: if the strike did not end by July 1998, the network would refuse to program series from studios that settled independently with the WGA, and it would begin developing "writer-proof" shows, including reality television.[112] In circumventing the requisite costs of unionized laborers—actors, directors, writers, cinematographers, editors—production companies and studios were able to make shows cheaply and hold on to their profits completely.[113] Some shows, like Fox's *COPS*, emerged out of a plan to counter future strikes. Other networks and studios declared their own plans to punish independent studios that negotiated outside the AMPTP.

In July, the WGA pushed back by filing an antitrust suit against eighteen studios and networks. It was at this point that twenty-one writers filed a charge with the NLRB against the WGA. They declared that they would resign from active membership if the strike was not settled by the end of the month. The WGA and AMPTP jockeyed back and forth for another three weeks, with emissaries working behind the scenes. The membership called a stop to strike actions, and the strike finally ended.[114] Not a single writer interviewed who went through the 1988 strike did not feel angry, defeated, and exhausted by the experience.

In the following years, Brian Walton, the WGA West's executive director starting in 1985 and a witness to the worst of the 1988 negotiations, was determined to find an alternative approach. In 1992, he helped establish the Contract Adjustment Committee (CAC). The CAC offered writers, producers, and the companies the opportunity to sit down once or twice a year to discuss contracts and make adjustments to the MBA. As a preemptory bargaining space, the CAC pleased writers and management, neither of whom had any interest in letting negotiations reach a breaking point. In reality, the Guild's agenda during these years was modest; while little was gained, there were no rollbacks. Some members then, and many more members in hindsight, realized that the CAC placed the Guild in a passive position in terms of negotiating power. Existing agreements were extended in 1992 (a four-year contract that was negotiated early) and 1995. That said, almost a decade of labor peace with no rollbacks was perhaps, as WGA Executive Vice President Chuck Slocum stated, the biggest gain of the 1988 strike.[115] For the next ten years, Guild members were not particularly interested in stirring up controversy. This was the case not only in terms of contract negotiations, but also in terms of questions of public policy or conglomeration of the media industries. It would be twenty years before the membership would vote for another strike.

Corporatization and the "Me" Generation of Writers

The WGA's defeats in the 1980s were not just the result of a lack of consensus among different communities of writers or a failure to read industry trends regarding residuals from ancillary markets. The merger mania discussed earlier changed not only the structure of the media industries but also the way that executives were doing business. The new type of executive, Marc Norman said, "basically brought business school ethics into the movie business."[116] George Axelrod agreed: "The producers are no longer colorful. They're lawyers and accountants and business people."[117] The first executives running studios had emerged mostly from the exhibition branch of the industry and understood movie-making as a gut industry. The next generation of studio heads worked their way up through the ranks and learned on the job. The executives emerging out of law schools and business schools had little knowledge of the film industry except at the level of viewership and contract law. Moreover, the concerns of the larger parent company focused entirely on immediate profits. "The confusion over market share with profitability is really enormous," noted writer-producer

Ronald Bass, using a baseball analogy. "So there's no such thing as a single or a double anymore. It has to be a home run because you have to open it in 3,500 theaters, because if you don't, you can't be first."[118] The growing corporatization, in turn, tended to nurture the cult of star power in both films and television. It was the rise of the "Me" generation in America, and writers and their union were both products and perpetrators of that navel-gazing bias. This was the dawning of era of the million-dollar screenplay and the showrunner.

Melissa Mathison's arbitration to secure a share of the marketing revenues (from lunchboxes, dolls, clothing, and toys) generated by the little alien she created in her script for *E.T.* (1982) set a precedent for writers. From then on, writers could negotiate licensing and merchandising. By the end of the decade, Joe Eszterhas had sold his script for *Basic Instinct* for $3 million. The story excited not only the trade papers but even the popular press.[119] The names of A-list screenwriters were beginning to appear in the national entertainment sections of newspapers. But even with these huge paydays, screenwriters felt aggrieved. Ronald Bass explained why: "We feel put down because we never have any control and everybody above us tells us what to do. The public doesn't know who we are. We don't feel we have respect. So we're the least satisfied."[120] Though some apects of that attitude have been characteristic of writers since the 1920s, the volatile, dissatisfied screenwriter became a more familiar stereotype after the strikes of the 1980s.

In television, the networks were turning to auteur filmmakers like Michael Mann (who had written and directed *Thief* and *Manhunter*), David Lynch, and Steven Spielberg (who had written *Close Encounters of the Third Kind* and *Poltergeist*) to create upscale programming, a practice that John Caldwell describes as "boutique programming" to lure audiences bored with the assembly-line production of the average series at the time.[121] Hyphenate writers were paid well beyond scale through their roles as producers on these series. Saul Turteltaub found this trend troubling: "It diminishes the writer's role. On *The Cosby Show*, there were so many people listed as producers, but they don't produce! They just write. . . . I think the pride should be in being a writer. Period."[122]

The proliferation of credits during the 1980s continued through the 1990s. Being a writer was a coveted job, but writers wanted to extend their power as producers as well. Writers began to demand a greater say in the production of their material. If a film or a television series was now a property that could be bought, franchised, and branded multiple times in the marketplace, the value of content continued long after a script was written. Film and television writers had a new role in the corporate landscape of media production as content makers. In the next decades, this concept would lead to the rise of a new model of hyphenate.

ACT ONE

FADE IN.

TITLE CARD "MANHATTAN - 1959"

EXT. MANHATTAN STREET - NIGHT

Stock footage of late 50's Manhattan - night-time shots of
vintage skyscrapers, traffic, and people.

INT. KNICK KNACK BAR

With its vinyl upholstery and mirrored walls. This is a
dive bar of today--but brand new. It's after work, but the
women have their hair done and each man's tie is pushed to
the top of his collar. Highballs and martinis clink under
quiet music and everywhere are the sights and sounds of
smoking.

Alone in a red corner booth is DON DRAPER, early 30's,
handsome, conservative, and despite his third seven and seven,
he is apparently sober. He is doodling on a cocktail napkin.
He crosses something out, puts down his fountain pen, and
taps a cigarette out of a pack of "Old Gold".

The BUSBOY, a middle-aged black man, too old for his tight
uniform, approaches.

                    BUSBOY
          Finished, sir?

                    DON
          Yeah. Got a light?

The busboy pulls out a pack of matches from the back of his
'Lucky Strikes' and lights Don's cigarette.

                    DON (CONT'D)
          Ah, a 'Lucky Strike' man.
               (inhaling)
          'Old Gold', here.

There is an awkward silence. The busboy starts to walk away.

                    DON (CONT'D)
          Can I ask you something? Why do you
          smoke 'Lucky Strikes'?

The busboy seems flustered and looks around nervously. The
burly white BARTENDER approaches.

                    BARTENDER
          I'm sorry sir. Is Sam here bothering
          you? He can be a little chatty.

IMAGE 23 First page of Matthew Weiner's script for the *Mad Men* episode "Smoke Gets in Your Eyes," c. 2007.

Matthew Weiner Collection, Writers Guild Foundation Archive, Shavelson-Webb Library, Los Angeles

5

Confederation

The West is a very exclusive country club. It's for A-list writers, show-runners, movie writers. And the East is truly a Bolshevik cell. They still think it's 1917.

> —Tom Fontana, showrunner of *Homicide: Life on the Street*
> and creator of *Oz*, interview, 23 October 2009

During the first week on the picket line, I started talking to a guy who had been in the Guild for thirty-some-odd years. He said, "Oh this is your first strike?" He said, "This is my fifth one." And then I thought, "Oh my God, I'm going to have to do this *again*?" And here I thought that this was the strike to end all strikes.

> —Courtney Lilly, phone interview, 16 May 2009

"It was bad. It was as bad as it could be," Tom Fontana recalled, thinking back to relations between the Writers Guild of America East and West in 2004.[1] Other feuds had been worse, damaging relations between the Guild and other writers' groups as well as between different factions within the Guild. But this time, the Guild's infighting was between its two official branches, and the two people at the center of the battle were not even writers.

The uncomfortable balance of power between the East and West branches began to topple in the late 1990s.[2] At the crux of the controversy in 2004 were the Guild's two executive directors, John McLean for the West and Mona Mangan for the East, who were refusing to speak to each other. John Auerbach, a Writers Guild East board member and the writer of *Stepfather II*, remembers that the acrimony stemmed from McLean's twenty-three years at CBS, where Mangan, who often oversaw news contracts, challenged him over news writers' negotiations.[3] At the same time that members were growing increasingly uneasy with McLean's ties to CBS, many also faulted Mangan for her negotiating style, which was "long on formality and short on practicality."4 Finally, the writers themselves came together behind the leaders' backs to resolve their differences.

Over a series of phone calls and a weekend-long meeting in San Francisco, a coalition of board members from East and West attempted to untangle union strategy from the melodrama of clashing personalities that had been plaguing Guild negotiations since 1997. The détente focused on issues critical to both branches: dropping formal charges against one another and reorienting the Guild's focus toward negotiations with the studios, improving health coverage, and addressing concerns over the vertical integration of the studios. Fontana recalled: "The people in the room from the West were as determined to make it work as we were. . . . And they realized that when writers talk to writers, there are no major issues. When [Guild] staff members talk to staff members, then it gets complicated."5 But even after the two branches unified on a strategy, more frustrations followed as the Guild entered negotiations with the Alliance of Motion Picture and Television Producers (AMPTP) in 2004.

The Guild's attempts at pattern bargaining in 2004 with the Directors Guild of America (DGA) and Screen Actors Guild (SAG) failed. Writers on the negotiating committee had asked McLean to focus on compensation for DVD sales. McLean recommended that the writers cease their negotiations with the AMPTP, form a strategic alliance with the DGA, and allow the DGA to set the pattern for bargaining that year. The negotiating team accepted the idea, but McLean never attempted establish the alliance he had promised, and the DGA entered negotiations without an opportunity to consider the writers' plan. According to WGA board member Howard A. Rodman, "John McLean negotiated against his own Guild—far more than he was willing to negotiate against his old pals in the conglomerates. Again and again he maintained we'd be 'laughed out of the room' if we asked for the things we asked for—and in many cases won—[in our 2008] contract."6 The WGA emerged from the 2004 negotiations with a few gains in health and pension plans, but also with some rollbacks and no increase in residuals. Writers' exasperation with what they viewed as an autocratic leadership set the stage for a radical change at the top in the West and a transformation in the relationship between the eastern and western branches.

Writers and journalists noted that the Guild was growing increasingly out of touch with its membership. For much of the 1990s, film and television writers and the Guild were staggering from the blows dealt during the strikes of the 1980s. No writer wanted to walk off work, and most wanted peace with the companies, yet tensions ran high across various constituencies: between writers who were exhausted by activist members of the Guild and writers who saw still more battles ahead; between writers of studio films and prime-time scripted television and writers in newer areas of media production; and between the WGA East and the WGA West. Simultaneously, new generations of prospective screenwriters were applying for work in an industry that was busy restructuring itself to reap increasing profits. Many of these writers took positions as flexible contract laborers; as such, their work did not necessarily fall under the jurisdiction of the Writers Guild. Susan Christopherson argued in 2008 that the unions and guilds in Hollywood were failing in their mission: "Because they generally continue to operate as conventional US unions—that is by representing their current membership rather than serving as a *labor* movement—the unions appear to be losing touch with a younger generation that does not perceive union membership as an indicator of 'having arrived' in the media industries. Instead unions are perceived more than ever as gatekeepers for a labor aristocracy whose goals and working style are not relevant to the younger generation of multi-skilled independent contractors."[7] Media companies were developing personal digital technologies that demanded new content. At the same time, questions of what should be considered Guild writing and the appropriate levels of compensation for such writing were under debate.

More than ever, working writers were divided across the financial spectrum. Much like the American economy as a whole, the industry was squeezing out the middle-class writer. There were the A-list screenwriters and television hyphenates who were garnering huge paychecks at the top; there were some people making a good living wage; and there were many who were barely making ends meet. While the million-dollar celebrity film screenwriter was not something new, the television showrunner was. The first appearance of the term in the press occurred in 1995 in reference to John Wells's work on *ER*.[8] "Showrunner" is not an official credit but is used by the industry, the press, scholars, and viewers to describe an individual (or team of individuals) who is responsible for guiding a series over a season or an entire run. The showrunner is the new iteration of the hyphenate: someone who gives a series—and just as important, those who work for the series—a sense of structure and direction. With the development of DVD technology, showrunners are also brand managers.[9] They are made audible through DVD commentaries and podcasts, made visible in behind-the-scenes extras, and, in many cases, made directly available for commentary, conversation, or comment on websites. As this chapter explores, this new role would become particularly important for the Guild in the years to come.

The Guild had to respond to the ever-fracturing state of screenwriting to ensure that all screen entertainment writing fell under its jurisdictional umbrella. The days of companies applying to the unions to become signatories were gone. The rapid process of media consolidation transformed the boundaries between screen entertainment at the levels of production, distribution, and ownership. Given the radical new landscape of the media industries, professional screenwriters had to be courted and their employers coerced. Writers for animation, reality television, video games, and streaming media did not automatically see the benefit of paying dues for union membership. At the same time, not all WGA members were eager to welcome these "lesser" media writers into their ranks. In the process of reassessing the parameters of professional writing, the Guild was transformed from an "inbox" union that waited for new writers and signatories to approach it to one that reached out to professional writers working in new genres, forms, and platforms within American media industries. The core of this chapter explores the internal and external strife that led to moments of unity and hopefulness for coalitions of disparate groups of writers and between writers and other media professionals.

This era began in a moment of disillusionment for writers. Emerging from a series of brutal defeats in the 1980s, writers were licking their wounds just as media mergers and corporate synergies began transforming the economic and technological structures of the entertainment industries. Writers of indie films watched as the studios overtook their genre. The conglomerates hammered away at the Financial Interest and Syndication Rules (Fin-Syn), which barred networks from airing programs to which they had syndication rights and from holding an equity position in the programs they aired (for example, Carsey-Werner Productions and Bill Cosby owned *The Cosby Show*, and NBC bought rights to broadcast the program). The passage of the 1996 Telecommunications Act shifted the broadcast landscape to profit the studios at the expense of independent voices in media production. Speaking seventeen years after the act took effect, Norman Lear lamented deregulation's damage to the entertainment media landscape: "Look at us today. One Comcast. My God. Despite all the channels, the people of the world only listen through three or four megaphones to get news and entertainment and context. There is no context. And this is the country that depends on an informed electorate."[10] Barbara Corday concurred: "The unraveling [of Fin-Syn] could not have been worse for the TV industry, for writers especially, and for producers. . . . There is a reason Fin-Syn existed in the first place, and it has not changed. . . . Literally hundreds of people are being kept from having ownership in their creations. I think it is outrageous."[11] The momentum of deregulation during this era was astonishing, and the talent guilds were not paying close enough attention. At the same time, the rise of the DVD and online websites offered new spaces for writers to express themselves and access audiences. These new venues would become invaluable to writers in mobilizing support for their cause. Ultimately, writers took advantage of digital entertainment—the primary territory they hoped to gain during the 2007 negotiation cycle—to promote the Guild's position.

The conglomeration of independent film and television production, the growth of primetime animation and reality television, the expansion of writing for video games, and the success of ancillary markets of DVD and streaming media were all desirable jurisdictional territories for the WGA. For over a decade, the Guild attempted—but ultimately failed—to react to the growing concerns of its members. But by the time of the 2007–2008 strike, new Guild leadership had devised an argument that appealed widely to its membership: it posited that the gradual interlocking interests of every Guild member in digital media presented an opportunity for a unified action against the companies.

Corporate Power versus Diversity and Independence

Whereas the corporate owners of the 1960s had acquired film divisions within companies that were predominantly not entertainment oriented, the companies merging in the 1980s and 1990s functioned primarily as media conglomerates. By the 1990s, many of these corporations were structured both vertically and horizontally, taking advantage of synergies among television networks, film studios, radio networks, theme parks, video outlets, publishing houses, and, later, Internet holdings. Within this deregulated, conglomerated, multichannel environment, power was in the hands of the majors. The goal was saturation of a variety of demographic markets, where unique divisions could target different segments of an increasingly fragmented audience.

In 1989, the Coalition to Preserve the Financial Interest and Syndication Rules was formed as a new iteration of the Committee for Prudent Deregulation. Two hundred committee members from SAG, the Caucus for Producers Writers and Directors, and the MPAA lobbied various government members and agencies (including the president of the United States, the Federal Communications Commission (FCC), members of Congress, the Department of Justice, and the Department of Commerce), to advocate preservation of the law.[12] With Jack Valenti as its spokesman, the coalition argued that deregulation would shatter the already weakened independent production community in Hollywood. In contrast, the networks pointed to increased competition from the News Corporation's Fox network and the cable industry. The Hollywood studios, they claimed, rather than small independents, were in positions of choice, if not control, about how to capitalize on their productions.

Following an intense lobbying war, the FCC relaxed the Fin-Syn Rules in 1991. A year later, the networks asked a federal appellate court in Chicago to abolish the rules entirely. A three-judge panel unanimously declared the regulations to be not just outdated, but also "arbitrary, unreasonable and capricious."[13] By 1995, virtually all traces of the rules had been eliminated. Within a year of their demise, NBC had become the single largest supplier of its own primetime programming. Jennifer Holt provides dramatic quantitative examples: "In 1995, the networks owned approximately 40 percent of their schedules on average. By the start of the 2000 season, however, CBS, for example, had an interest in or owned outright 68 percent of its prime time schedule, including ten weekly entertainment series. Fox owned 71 percent of its prime time lineup. NBC produced seven shows, all airing on their own network. This trend would continue, and in 2009, twenty-two out of the thirty-two new shows were produced and owned by the network on which they aired."[14] With the rules against network production-distribution mergers dismantled, the Hollywood studios adopted a new strategy. Viacom and Warner Bros. soon joined News Corporation in forming their own studio-based television networks and enlarging their in-house production units. Film and broadcast were now uniting under the auspices of the same corporate entities, which were exploring new opportunities for expansion.

Aside from its vigilance in matters of free speech, the WGA was fairly apolitical when it came to government regulation. The Guild later regretted its failure to foresee the profound impact that the death of Fin-Syn would have on television production and distribution and on its members' income from residuals paid for shows now owned by the networks that aired them. Generally, when a studio sells content internally, it gives itself a discounted rate (a benefit that prompted companies to merge and diversify). Without the competitive pricing made possible by independent producers selling to networks, media workers received lower residuals. Chuck Slocum, executive vice president of WGA West, said, "We weren't involved directly in Fin-Syn. And we should have been. . . . Fin-Syn was a huge loss for the writing community."[15] The only action the Guild leadership took was to present a few papers to the government in defense of the regulation. In written comments to the FCC in 2002, Slocum warned that without Fin-Syn in place, virtually all of the boutique television producers would disappear within a few years.[16]

As the media conglomerates grew stronger, labor's position became more precarious.[17] Most writers saw deregulation as a step backward, a loss of creative control, and a harbinger of what writing would be like in this new conglomerated landscape. Looking back on his own career, Tom Fontana saw a marked effect on his partnership with networks and on the kind of television that could be greenlighted: "A lot has shifted over the last thirty years that I've been doing television—one [part of it] is the corporate structure. The death of the small studios like MTM, Lorimar—that has had an extraordinarily compelling, negative effect on the quality of television. Now there are only six or seven studios, and most of them have a network that they have to feed. So their appetite becomes very narrow."[18]

Like the demise of Fin-Syn, the 1996 Telecommunications Act received little attention in the popular press. In this dramatic overhaul of the Communications Act of 1936, the FCC, under the leadership of Michael Powell (son of future US Secretary of State Colin Powell), pushed for a deregulatory agenda more reminiscent of the Reagan era than that of President Bill Clinton. The act relaxed television station ownership limits and cross-ownership restrictions, revoked regulations on cable ownership established by the Cable Act of 1992, granted the FCC jurisdiction over digital broadcast satellites, and assigned existing television stations digital allotments without charge.[19] Audience fragmentation and the multiplexing of network channels

(NBC, MSNBC, CNBC, and so on) left the cable television landscape looking like a corporate-controlled digital land rush. Digital satellite services, which began in 1990, expanded throughout the decade, improving not just picture and sound quality but also increasing the number of channels available to the average home consumer (even if most of these channels were owned by the same few conglomerates). Although the Guild failed to fight deregulation effectively, its members would take the lessons learned from this period to plot a more forward-thinking approach to regulation in years to come. But the conglomerates were also learning from the gains of the independent industry outside their control.

The astonishing success of *sex, lies and videotape* in 1989, a film that Steven Soderbergh wrote, directed, and edited, heralded a golden age for the "indie film" and the hybrid filmmaker. New work by John Sayles, Joel and Ethan Coen, David Lynch, Jim Jarmusch (*Mystery Train*), and Spike Lee (*Do the Right Thing*) generated increased energy and creative opportunities for writer-directors operating outside the traditional Hollywood studio structure. Other talented hybrids whose first major successes premiered around the same time include Gus Van Sant (*Drugstore Cowboy*), John Singleton (*Boyz n the Hood*), and Quentin Tarantino (*Reservoir Dogs*). A second wave appeared in the mid 1990s, with Alexander Payne (*Citizen Ruth*), Ang Lee (*The Wedding Banquet*), Kevin Smith (*Clerks*), Todd Solondz (*Welcome to the Dollhouse*), Nicole Holofcener (*Walking and Talking*), Wes Anderson (*Rushmore*), and Paul Thomas Anderson (*Boogie Nights*). Emanuel Levy details how Miramax and New Line Cinema were the first companies to establish the independent studio business model, creating mini-major studios with steady financial backing, no ties to established studios, and dynamic personalities at the top who defined the corporate persona.[20]

The success of these mini-majors prompted the major studios to establish specialty branches of their own studios—Focus Features (Universal), Fox Searchlight, and Paramount Vantage—that enabled them to purchase compelling packaged film projects at low prices. These boutique auxiliary units focused on prestige indie films that created subsidiaries of corporate brands for these conglomerates, brands that shrewdly defined themselves as "anti-studio."[21] At the same time, some writers attempted to stay as independent as possible. Gus Van Sant, who made *Drugstore Cowboy* with Miramax and has since worked with specialty studio distributors, compared his experiences working with independent companies versus Hollywood studios: "Hollywood can't eliminate the creative side, the writers and directors and actors, which I think they'd like to do. . . . The studios think you should be able to just take bits of screenplays and have a technical writer restructure the dialogue. Design a screenplay, give it to the guy who knows how the camera works, then eliminate the director, and just let the camera guy set up the shot. Then have the actors do the performance part. But when they do that . . . there's always something missing, like the conductor in the orchestra. Things start to go out of time."[22]

Audiences may not have noticed the slow shift toward incorporating indies into the conglomerate structure. As Alisa Perren explains, the term "independent" is arguably misleading.[23] In this new landscape, "indie" could mean an economic approach, a genre, or both. It can define everything from an independent voice coming from New York but produced by a studio (*Do the Right Thing*), to edgy independent productions picked up on the film festival circuit and distributed by Hollywood (*Slackers, The Blair Witch Project*), to a Miramax-style hybrid indie (*Fargo, Boogie Nights*), or a Hollywood production that only mimics the indie in its genre or style (*Juno*). Levy describes two definitions of the term "independent": one specifically speaks to a structure of film financing, the other to the point of view, aesthetics, or vision of the film or filmmaker.[24]

During the late 1990s, studios began eliminating projects with mid-range budgets; suddenly the majority of films greenlighted were either expensive mass-appeal blockbusters or low-budget indie-like productions. As independent films continued to profit commercially through the 2000s, win prestigious awards, and capture a small but significant share of the audience, studios aimed to package and corporatize independent film as a genre. In 2005, Disney purchased the top distributor of independent films, Miramax.[25] Although writers looking to distribute their films could find other outlets, this takeover signaled a clear end to an era of robust independent production.

Pushing the Boundaries of Jurisdiction

The categories of writing under the jurisdiction of the WGA expanded rapidly during the 1990s and 2000s. New genres and platforms tested the boundaries of what could and should be included under the union umbrella. Many writers working outside Guild's purview were eager for their work to be counted as "insider" labor so they could obtain guarantees on minimum pay, benefits, and pension funds. Television producers experimented with reality television and animated primetime series, both complicated territories for television writers and the Guild to navigate. At the same time, audiences in increasing numbers were plugging in their television sets to video game consoles and DVD players to meet their entertainment needs.

Computer-generated imagery (CGI) was first integrated into popular cinema in the 1970s. By the 1990s, CGI's potential for creating dynamic and innovative film and television cinematography had expanded dramatically. Soon, it transformed the nature of animated film and television. Series such as Fox's *The Simpsons* (which started in 1989) and MTV's *Liquid Television* (the original showcase for *Beavis and Butt-head*) transformed viewers'—and studio executives'—perception of CGI's potential not just for animated entertainment but also for enhancement of the viewer experience.

The overwhelming success of Matt Groening's *The Simpsons* in the 1990s encouraged Fox executives to expand the network's adult-oriented prime-time animation programming.[26] In 1999, with *The Simpsons, King of the Hill, Family Guy, The PJs*, and *Futurama* on Fox's prime time schedule, the campaign for writers of animated television to unionize under the WGA mobilized with relative ease. Peter Chernin, who headed Fox at the time, had already assumed that primetime animation was under a WGA deal. When he found out these writers were not covered and that they had no health insurance, he agreed to put them under a Guild contract. Brian Walton, then the president of the WGA West, said, "It is our hope that this far-sighted agreement will lay the framework for similar contracts in this genre."[27] David A. Goodman, a writer and producer on *Futurama* at the time, detailed the fortuitous nature and timing of this deal: "The fact that the shows . . . got one writer to be the Guild liaison and that they were all unified may have played a big role in Chernin saying yes. At that time there were less union difficulties. It was ten years after the previous strike and everything on television was covered under the WGA contract." Those negotiations came at a moment of relative peace between the union and the studios, that these animated writers were all at one studio, and that the series were successful made it impossible for Chernin to overlook their writers' individual and collective importance to the network. But "once reality [programming] started to take off," Goodman said, "that started to tell the studios and networks that . . . everything doesn't have to be covered under the WGA contract. That was really the chink in the armor."[28] Subsequently, no group of animation writers has ever managed to win such a victory again. And with the increase in primetime reality television, studios had more reason to deny new types of writers Guild privileges.

The effect of reality programming on the media landscape during this twenty-year period rattled television writers to their core. The series *Survivor* and *Big Brother*, both European franchises that premiered on American broadcast television in 2000, altered primetime and set a precedent for reality television's success. Two years later, *American Idol* became an overnight sensation. The genre's colonization of primetime hours was a boon to the networks. These series were cheap to produce, and their potential for ratings soon exceeded the best numbers for scripted programming. Reality was not simply a rising new genre; it began to colonize an older one. Documentary writing also evolved. Television documentarian Sydnye White, who wrote written for *America's Most Wanted* and *NBC Nightly News*, argued, "Reality television is making itself felt in the documentary world. Executives are demanding that documentaries have similar interpersonal conflicts and testy atmospheres. Let's face it, tears pay off. So do fights."[29]

The enormous popularity of reality shows gave executives reasons to consider a radical restructuring of their business practices. In 2003 reporter Bill Carter quoted Leslie Moonves, president of CBS Television, declaring the end of the old model of series television: "The world as we know it is over." Carter spelled out the implications: "Not only will reality shows continue to flood network's schedules next fall, but television executives are also predicting . . . an end to the traditional television season. Instead of the time-honored formula of introducing shows en masse in September and ending them in May, broadcast networks want to stagger the shows' debuts and banish repeats. . . . There could also be fewer orders for dramas and comedies, with a resulting shrinking of jobs for Hollywood writers and actors."[30] The advent of programming that could be produced cheaply, show strong ratings, adapt to a variety of production scheduling structures, be rolled out relatively quickly, and get shelved with little loss gave network executives increasing confidence about delaying negotiations with the guilds.

This is not to say that union workers were not employed on these shows. Rather, they found temporary employment on reality series. As the number of feature films and scripted series being shot in Los Angeles and New York decreased, the ranks of writers looking for work grew. Thus, some union writers—along with new writers—tried to make ends meet by working on these "unscripted" series. Even though shooting scripts for reality television often consist of sketches, monologues for hosts, or stories developed after the fact out of captured footage, reality producers inevitably needed professional writers—often now called story producers or story editors—to craft narrative arcs. As one former sitcom writer, now a story producer, said of his work: "I used to write with all the words in Webster's Dictionary at my disposal; now I write with whatever words Paris Hilton says."[31]

Home video game console sales became robust during the 1980s, and video arcade games began luring some young audiences away from movie theaters and live television. In the following two decades, video games matured in content, technology, and market reach. Some game companies designed content to be played on consoles plugged into a television set; others created content for computers and handheld devices. As games became increasingly complex and their story worlds more advanced, game production houses recognized that they could no longer focus solely on game play and graphics. They now needed skilled writers to build narrative and dialogue. In 1996, writer Del Reisman, who was president of the WGA from 1991 to 1993, described the union's attempts to include new media within its jurisdiction: "We are deeply involved in preparing our members for the exploding interactive media, with frequent seminars, panels, and demonstrations. . . . We are no longer in an institutional industry. New production entities with new sources of financing, new patterns of co-production and new lines of distribution and exhibition are forming and reforming."[32] However, members' comprehension of video games in the 1990s mostly came from their experiences as players or as parents of players rather than as writers interested in new narrative structures, let alone as employees considering professional opportunities.

Compared with steady improvements in visual and gaming technologies, advances in game writing were often slower to emerge. John Zuur Platten, a WGA member and game writer of *Transformers: The Game*, recalled: "When I started writing games, the girl answering the phones at the front desk, who took a creative writing class in junior college, wrote the game's dialogue and didn't get any extra pay for that."[33] As game writers recount, this disjunction led to a kind of reverse engineering of game narratives. Writers were often called in to consult on projects to fill in narrative gaps or to write dialogue after much of the technological structure and design of the game had already been created.

Like everyone else working within video game production, game writers were not necessarily based in New York or Los Angeles, and so the notion of unionization under the WGA was hardly on their radar. The industry's work ethic modeled Silicon Valley far more than Hollywood. Even if some writers of these games were WGA members who also wrote for film or television, it was impossible to push the game companies to agree to Guild rules. Some writers thought they might have a better chance of unionizing once the major media conglomerates began making games. As video game writer and WGA member Christy Marx said in 2004, "The changeover *will* come when more of the big media conglomerates are controlling this stuff. Companies that just come from the game world purely, they're used to abusing people. It's common for managers to work people 80 hours a week and run them into the ground. It's sort of taken for granted in the game world."[34] Because of these attitudes, the unionization of games workers is still in its infancy.

The Digital Versatile Disc, an optical disc storage format, was a revolution for the industry. The combination of cheaper production costs and higher retail value meant that every dollar earned by a VHS was doubled by a DVD sale in the increasingly powerful home video market.[35] For writers, the DVD was not just an ancillary marketing tool; because of DVD extras that often included conversations with cast and crew, many writers' names became more prominent and their faces more recognizable to interested audiences. Writers could be heard in DVD commentaries, could be seen in behind-the-scenes extras, and could communicate directly to the audience via commentary or conversation on websites. In particular, consumers became addicted to DVD box sets of television series, learning along the way about the series' showrunners, who were promoted in the DVD extras as the real-life heroes responsible for creating or shepherding the beloved series. The Guild tried to take advantage of this trend; an internal memo to WGA executive director Brian Walton from members of the WGA staff in 1995 suggested that the "writer is a box of soap": "We have a product to sell, the writer. We need to market our products. We know there is a need for our product. We need to establish the *brand image of the writer.* . . . BENEFIT: establishes writer[s] as superstars in mass media. Also creates economic return for the Guild."[36]

Especially for television, this brand-name recognition defies the nature of collective authorship, and yet the industry and the popular press continue to celebrate the individual writer as a new iteration of the American Dream.[37] Writer-producer David Goodman remarked: "As a career track, most people in the country weren't aware that you could break into it. Now they have heard of these people, they start to identify with them, and they want to be a writer. More people are understanding that there is a man behind the curtain and 'Maybe I want to do that.'"[38] Media studies scholar Denise Mann refers to the persistence of the singular auteur as an obsolete paradigm in a discussion of contemporary quality television production.[39] And yet, the DVD box set promotes the writer-auteur of a television series in ways previously never imagined.

All of these developments show how this period in American media industries was an era of prolonged and profound transition, mergers and acquisitions, centralization and further deregulation, significant technological transformation, and concentration of capital. Media scholar Michael Curtin describes how this dynamic impulse created "interactive exchanges, multiple sites of productivity, and diverse modes of interpretation and use."[40] The rise of digital media, the fragmentation of audiences, and the conglomeration of media corporations in the 1990s set American media on new economic, social, political, and cultural paths as they entered a new millennium.

The State of the Guilds

Homogenization is good for milk, but bad for ideas.

> —Patric Verrone, president of the WGA West, statement read
> before the FCC public hearing on media ownership,
> 3 October 2006[41]

As DVDs grew in popularity, writers realized precisely how much they had lost in their 1988 negotiations. Robin Schiff, who wrote *Romy and Michele's High School Reunion*, explained: "Having been in the Guild . . . since 1980, I've been around not only for strikes, but also [long enough] to have a sense of how the membership views the Guild—which was incompetent, a joke, not worth standing behind, like a litter of puppies that you couldn't get together. And in a way, that's what the companies counted on. There was so much division within our own membership that we could never be effective. You can argue that one guild can't be effective by itself anyway when seven multinational corporations are basically allowed to negotiate together and have a consortium."[42] Schiff's frustrations with the Guild echo many WGA members' concerns that every three years they faced an increasingly powerful force across the table at contract negotiations. To Wall Street's delight, in 1995 Disney purchased Cap Cities/ABC for $19 billion, creating a conglomerate with a combined calculated worth of $48 billion. A year later, Time Warner purchased Turner Broadcasting System, and Viacom picked up Paramount and, later, CBS for $34.8 billion. With little inflationary pressure, media industry expansion in this New Economy increased rapidly.

By 1994, the WGA leaders realized they were gaining little ground in the bargaining space of the Contract Adjustment Committee (CAC), created in 1992 by WGA West executive director Brian Walton, as discussed in Chapter 4. Walton then began to promote pattern bargaining with the DGA and SAG and warned the companies that if the CAC meetings in June 1994 did not yield reasonable increases, the Guild would insist on returning to traditional negotiations—which could, at some point, trigger another strike. This ultimatum worked for a month, but then negotiations with the companies and the other guilds became contentious. At the time, the WGA was in a difficult battle with the DGA over the possessory credits, and pattern bargaining fell apart.

The Guild worked out a collective bargaining agreement with the networks that was signed in December 1994, but an agreement with the AMPTP was not completed until February 1995. Walton's original plan, designed to save time and energy, had turned into an exhausting nine-month-long deliberation that inched forward piecemeal. Grace Reiner, WGA counsel at the time, knew that the membership felt disengaged from the process and that, for them, the ends could not justify the means. "We said, 'This really got you a better deal than you were going to get.' . . . But they just didn't see the value of it because they hadn't lived through it. When you don't see what's behind the curtain, you don't see how much work is being done."[43] The membership preferred traditional negotiations along with membership meetings, opportunities for input and discussion, and last and final offers. For them, more transparent results were better than closed-door meetings.

Walton's idea for the 1998 negotiation cycle was to make sure that industry management followed through across the board on the terms that had been agreed to in earlier cycles and to align Guild members solidly behind their leadership. Walton went into writers' rooms, talked to many major screenwriters, and started meaningful, deliberate negotiations early. He implemented stronger arbitration provisions to protect writers' interests and added more arbitrators. Unfortunately, by then, WGA the West membership had already chosen Walton as the scapegoat for all their frustrations with the union. In 1997, Mona Mangan announced that the East was breaking with the West on a joint contract, and the WGA lost leverage on that round of negotiations. In the end, the WGA returned to traditional arbitration.

In September 1998, after a year of protracted debate regarding the MBA, WGAw president Daniel Petrie Jr. (writer of *Beverly Hills Cop*) and vice president John Wells (showrunner for *ER*) called for a poll among the membership to determine what they wanted from their leadership and for a referendum vote to preserve the early termination clause in Walton's contract.[44] Voter turnout was quite low, only 1,742, with 52.9 percent voting against a poll on strategic goals and against a modification of Walton's employment contract.[45] The matter was taken to the Board of Directors, which reached a fair settlement with Walton and terminated his contract. For six months, an internal three-person committee composed of Paul Nawrocki, Ann Widdifield (both assistant executive directors), and Grace Reiner (director of contract administration) ran the WGA West.

After the 1997 negotiations, ill will between the East and West branches made upcoming negotiations increasingly difficult. Members in the East considered themselves union people, and for almost ten years they had been a part of the AFL-CIO, whereas the West branch had no such affiliation. Elias Davis only part jokingly believed his eastern counterparts considered him and the other members in the West "a bunch of Hollywood dilettantes."[46]

John McLean, a former industrial relations executive at CBS who was well-versed on labor and contract law, was hired to replace Walton in May 1999. Presuming that someone who had worked for management might prove a smarter player in negotiations, Guild leaders thought they would now have a strategic edge with the studios. But members almost uniformly recalled McLean's tenure as disastrous. In 2001, WGA members took a strong stance as they went into negotiations, threatening a strike. But the companies were not convinced of the threat. McLean's focus was entirely on

establishing News Corporation as a signatory, effectively ignoring a chance
for negotiations with cable networks. As one writer recalled, "Basically his
plan backfired and we got nothing, or nothing to speak of. Let's put it this
way: we started out by asking for $225 million over four years for the
improvements in the contract. We got $5 [million]."[47]

Although the contract McLean brokered was helpful in some areas, the
deal was structured around Fox. Grace Reiner saw that choice as personal
rather than tactical. "I said, 'I want to tell you something, John. You're making Fox a network will get $600,000 a year. . . . I want to focus on HBO and
Showtime and get those people more than a million dollars a year.' His was
a personal thing. It was about Fox."[48] McLean's tendency to push his personal goals to the forefront did not end there. He was a central player in the
increasingly tense relationship between the West and the East.

In 2003, under the leadership of Vicki Riskin, the WGA West launched
a billboard campaign in well-trafficked areas of Hollywood and West Los
Angeles in celebration of the Guild's seventieth year, but also with the clear
intention of bringing literal visibility to the Guild among a particular eche-
lon of Hollywood players. The black-and-white billboards showed a close-up
of a writer's face next to a famous line of dialogue from one of his or her
films, with a small WGA West insignia at the bottom. Marc Norman, the
Guild member who devised the campaign, said, "We wanted to change their
minds a bit: Here's a line you know. Here's the face of the writer. You should
know who this is—and if you don't, you oughta make it your business to find
out."[49] William Goldman, one of the first writers picked for the campaign,
expressed his hope for it: "Everybody always thinks that all the directors
have the visual concepts and the actors make up all their lines. There is such
an ignoring of the craft of screenwriting that anything that calls attention to
it is a big help."[50] That the billboards neglected to include the writers'
names was yet another example of the Guild failing its membership. As
noted above, a number of writers on the 2004 negotiating committee were
exasperated by their experience. A group of them, some of whom had been
involved during the San Francisco accords, banded together to run for office.
They had a vision for what they wanted the Guild to become and a plan of
action. They called themselves Writers United.

The three key catalysts for the 2007–2008 Writers Guild of America
strike all appeared in 2005: the introduction of the video iPod, the launch
of YouTube, and the formation of Writers United. To begin, the studios'

astonishing financial success in selling episodes—and whole seasons—of
Desperate Housewives and *Lost* via iTunes commanded the industry's attention. In March 2006, when residuals were due for digital downloads, ABC
chose to pay its writers as if the electronic sell-through (the industry term
for a one-time download of media content for a fee) had the same value as
a DVD sale, that is, a final price that accounted for manufacturing costs. To
writers, this formula made no sense. Chuck Slocum argued, "If on March 1,
2006, they had paid [the equivalent of] the TV rate, there would have been
no strike two years later. Our philosophy in the strike, in the negotiation,
was the Internet ought to act like TV. And it largely does."[51]

YouTube was more than just an overnight sensation. By 2006, the website's traffic was growing at an astonishing rate of 75 percent per week, and
the service reimagined, for producers and consumers of media, the potential for streaming media content.[52] One of the most serious concerns for
writers and media industry executives as they witnessed the switch from traditional film and television media to digital forms was that young people
were becoming so accustomed to using the Internet for entertainment that
industry insiders never knew for sure whether these viewers would miss television were it to disappear. Executives now asked television writers, especially those working on edgy, youth-oriented series, to "make things more
YouTube-able," as *Just Shoot Me!* writer Ross McCall detailed.[53] They wanted
scenes that could be easily excerpted and uploaded into three- or four-
minute streaming videos for use as advertising tools for a series. But as writers witnessed, and studies subsequently quantified, the Internet diverted
many audiences from traditional media. Greg Thomas Garcia, series creator
of *My Name Is Earl* and *Raising Hope*, observed, "Kids today, you take TV away,
they'll say, 'Big deal,' and they'll click on the computer."[54] When writers tried
to calculate appropriate compensation amid the proliferation of new media
outlets, they found the math more nuanced than the numbers that studio
heads put forward to investors and the press about the success of digital
platforms.

The success in 2005 of the Writers United slate in the WGA West
elections—with Patric Verrone as president, David Weiss as vice president,
and Elias Davis as secretary treasurer—proved to be a turning point in the
relationship between East and West. The group's strategy for reorganizing
the Guild had been in the works for a number of years. Mark Gunn, a member of the negotiating committee and writer of *2gether*, described the leaders

as "a shadow government . . . a little revolutionary faction inside the Guild. . . ."[55] In the months leading up to the election, Writers United held meetings to educate the membership on its positions and to request that writers vote for its candidates as a slate, not just as individuals. The plan was to take over the leadership of WGA West, and the strategy involved a three-pronged approach. According to Patric Verrone, "We were campaigning on the concept of organize, organize, organize. We've got to get more members involved internally; we've got to get more people outside the union into the union, expand our jurisdiction; and third we've got to get the other unions—SAG, DGA, IATSE, Teamsters—involved in a coalition that has the power-building mechanisms that the AMPTP already has in place. That was our mantra."[56] On the day after the slate was elected, the newly formed board of directors fired McLean and named David Young interim executive director. A long-time Los Angeles union activist and leader, Young had built a reputation by organizing blue-collar workers, specifically carpenters and textile employees. When asked about his professional transition, Young was unruffled by celebrity: "Here I was doing something that I had become really good at in my second language [Spanish]. I get to do it in English. . . . This is easy, relatively speaking. . . . So now I'm in the big leagues [and] the bats are better. The dining room's better."[57] Young's expertise in mobilizing base membership was critical to the new slate's overall strategy. As he came into the position, he saw a clear point of concern. If the fundamental functions of a union are to organize jurisdiction, negotiate contracts, enforce those contracts, do political work that addresses the broader labor situation, and uphold the craft, the WGA had been working hard on the latter four but had done very little to address the first—hammering out jurisdiction.

In the summer of 2006, the WGA stood in solidarity with the striking writers of *America's Next Top Model* (*ANTM*). Holding picket signs decrying "the ugly side of a beautiful show" were its twelve young, articulate writers, an ideal group to serve as a test case for the WGA in reality television. The series was enormously successful, the writers loved their jobs, and all twelve wanted to become unionized under the WGA. Past modeling contestants on the series were even game to walk the line in solidarity with the writers, making coverage by the press much more likely. The Guild and the reality writers strategically organized a large rally of Hollywood writers to coincide with the launch of *ANTM*'s new parent network, The CW. Knowing that this campaign was as much about public perception as about industry politics, the *ANTM* writers also took their grievances to the forums most visible to fans of the series, MySpace and YouTube. Befriending thousands of fans and posting updates via the Internet and social media, the *ANTM* writers made their case—for health benefits, residuals, regulated wages, and a pension plan—visible not only on the streets of Los Angeles but also in virtual communities.

The reality show's producers removed the striking writers from their payroll in November. In turn, the WGA filed unfair labor practice charges against them with the National Labor Relations Board, alleging that the writers had been fired because of their union activity. Verrone chastised the show's producers in broader terms: "This is illegal strikebreaking, an insult to the Hollywood talent community and an embarrassment to this industry."[58] By focusing on the individual professional craftsperson as the symbol of labor suffering from the effects of corporate greed, the Guild tried to make reality television a central economic issue for the industry. Ultimately, the writers were replaced by peers willing to break the strike, talks ended, and the series went on. Without the unified support of all reality writers under the umbrella of the Guild, each labor struggle carried immense significance. With the *ANTM* writers, the WGA had lost a key battle. And yet, the lessons learned from this campaign helped the WGA leadership prepare for the 2007 negotiations. The following fall, the Writers Guild East and West joined forces across guilds and associations to bring a compelling case to the FCC against further media conglomeration.

Eight representatives from entertainment's creative labor force—a panel that included producers, writers, directors, actors, and composers—faced the FCC commissioners in a large hall on the campus of the University of Southern California in October 2006. Hundreds of concerned citizens, media workers, and independent media company owners looked on. Even though these vastly different organizations representing diverse interests had been at odds about a myriad of issues over decades, on that day the voice of the American entertainment industry spoke as a unified whole against the conglomeration of the media industries. Stephen J. Cannell, creator of *The Rockford Files, The A-Team*, and *21 Jump Street*, representing the Caucus of Television Producers, Writers, and Directors, spoke first. Not surprisingly, he began with the story of an unlikely hero, a thirty-year-old man who tried to sell the character Jim Rockford to ABC. ABC bought the idea but hated the iconoclastic protagonist of the first script. Cannell and Universal Television took that script to NBC, where the series became a five-year Emmy-winning television sensation. Cannell went on to become the third largest supplier of television in Hollywood; but by 1994, after repeal of the Fin-Syn regulations, he could not get a pilot greenlighted by the networks without forfeiting ownership.[59]

Taylor Hackford, screenwriter of *Ray* and third vice president of the Directors Guild of America, presented data that his guild had tracked over the previous decades. In the 1992–1993 television season, independent producers created 66 percent of network primetime programming. Only six years later, the numbers had reversed: the networks and their affiliated producers were responsible for 62 percent of primetime. By 2006, programming by the networks and their affiliates dominated 76 percent of primetime.[60] During that thirteen-year period, the number of independent studios creating scripted programming for networks had decreased from twenty-three to two—and those two so-called independents were actually part of major conglomerates, Warner Bros. and Sony.

Mike Mills, bassist for the rock band R.E.M., representing the Recording Artists Coalition, explained how regionalism had disappeared in radio: "The bond between a local station and its local listening audience has largely evaporated.... Playlists have been corporatized, nationalized, and sanitized."[61] On behalf of actors, John Connolly, president of the American Federation of Television and Radio Artists (AFTRA), spoke of catastrophic job loss, salary compression, a paucity of roles for minority actors, and the loss the of localism in news reporting.[62] Anne-Marie Johnson, first national vice president of the Screen Actors Guild, informed the FCC commissioners about the strain that media conglomeration had placed on her membership: "The days of an independent producer taking his or her creative vision of a series or movie of the week to fruition are a thing of the past." Johnson made her point clear: with increased consolidation of media ownership, viewers could no longer tap into a diversity of viewpoints and a diversity of representation. "As a union, and a vital part of the American labor movement, we are gravely concerned that the continued consolidation of our employers will result in the exclusion of the issues and challenges facing workers."[63]

Mona Mangan, executive director of WGA East, addressed the loss of localism in news, the massive cutbacks in the numbers of news writers, and the retrenchment of news writing.[64] WGA West President Patric Verrone then laid out figures for the commissioners: "Twenty years ago, when I entered this business there were twenty-nine dominant entertainment firms, with $100 billion in annual revenues. Today, there are six, making nearly $400 billion. Fifteen years ago, less than a third of writing employment was controlled by these firms. Today, they control over 80 percent of it. . . . Homogenization is good for milk, but bad for ideas."[65]

Marshall Herskovitz, president of the Producers Guild of America and creator of *thirtysomething* and *My So-Called Life*, echoed the concerns that talent had expressed since the earliest days of unionization:

> Ask any showrunner on any network and they will tell you that the level of control now exerted by network executives—over script, direction, cinematography, costumes, even the color of sets—is unprecedented in the history of the medium. . . . Eccentric choices that went into making *thirtysomething* the groundbreaking show it was would absolutely never be permitted today. . . . The independent producer no longer exists in television. . . . Consolidation of media is turning our artists into employees, and make no mistake, the result will be harmful for our society. I'm of the belief that storytellers matter, that art matters, that art helps a society define itself. The consolidation of media inherently endangers the storyteller, because, to that conglomerate, the story has no inherent value other than as an asset to be exploited.[66]

Following this eloquent and candid testimony about the need to support Hollywood's creative crafts through diversity of media ownership, the PGA, the WGA East and West, the DGA, AFTRA, and SAG had a proposal. They asked the FCC to ensure that 25 percent of television primetime programming would be designated for truly independent production companies and producers who were working outside of the oligarchy.

In this rare moment of cooperation, producers, writers, directors, actors, and composers demanded that federal regulators open their eyes to— and take a stand against—media conglomeration. This time, the voice of the media industry was not that of the owners or the corporations. Rather, Washington was listening to American media workers who described the damage that deregulation had unleashed. In the subsequent months and years, WGA leaders, staff, and members began to testify more frequently before government officials in Sacramento and Washington, DC, in hopes of distinguishing their needs from those of management, developing political clout, and forging political alliances through advocacy, outreach, and the new WGA West Political Action Committee.

If the event had been scripted, this FCC hearing would have been the dramatic turning point when the historic underdogs finally had their chance to speak and where their heroic, united action against the giant beasts gobbling up the media industries would herald a clear shift in the narrative. In reality, after a nationwide, multiyear listening tour, the FCC commissioners released their report on February 4, 2008, three months to the day after the Writers Guild had gone out on strike. The majority opinion determined that limits on television ownership, radio ownership, and radio-television cross-ownership should not change. Commissioner Deborah Taylor Tate wrote for the majority: "Many wanted us to go further in repealing the ownership restrictions, but we have chosen a measured and cautious approach. We recognize the changing dynamics of the media market, but also give due consideration to the weight of the record before us."[67] Two commissioners, Michael J. Copps and Jonathan S. Adelstein, expressed anger with the decision. Copps wrote in his dissent: "So even as it becomes abundantly clear that the real cause of the disenfranchisement of women and minorities is media consolidation, we give the green light to a new round of—yes, you guessed it—media consolidation."[68] Although Washington remained unmoved by the plight of media artists and creators, this moment of unity hinted that changes were underway, as writers and the Writers Guild began to see the advantage of coalitions of talent working together toward a common cause.

In response to the growing number of members who were scripting video games, both branches of the WGA formed divisions to handle gaming contracts, and the Guild created an outreach program designed to assist writers who were working with video game companies and wanted their work to fall under WGA jurisdiction. In 2003, the video game industry was worth $11 billion.[69] Just four years later, the Entertainment Software Association declared that video game sales had reached $18.85 billion, with $9.35 billion spent on consoles and $9.5 billion spent on software.[70] The WGA also began honoring these writers with an annual Game Writing Award. (Unfortunately, only games created by signatory companies were eligible, which left out the vast majority of the most popular games.) Members formed a New Media Writers Caucus, which offered associate membership to any working video game writer. Given the vast potential audience switching their home television sets to auxiliary modes, this film- and television-based media union could no longer ignore the significance of a growing labor force. Furthermore, the video game industry was one of the only media sectors actively hiring a significant number of writers at the time.[71] The industry was changing rapidly, and the Guild, as always, wanted to remain relevant.

Organizing the Membership

I never worked harder, being out of work.

–Bill Scheft, writer on *Late Night with David Letterman*,
interview, 6 April 2012

The WGA's new leadership was particularly astute in crafting a top-down approach to energize their membership base in the lead-up to the 2007 negotiations. Part of this strategy involved the mobilization of key individuals, notably A-list writers, who functioned as ammunition against the AMPTP. Here, notions of hierarchies and authorship were used to the advantage of the entire writing community. These key writers used their celebrity to influence public opinion and to encourage other writers to join the Guild's campaign. The Guild's leadership targeted television showrunners and well-respected feature film writers, inviting them to join the board and the contract negotiation committee. Executive Director David Young understood the unique power of showrunners: "Our television screenwriters operate the most successful franchises in this industry. . . . They are in this quasi-management role and yet, because of the history and culture of this organization they came out of a writing room. . . . We have paid a lot of attention to that. Not because I wanted to be elitist . . . but because I just analyzed the situation and said, these people can almost make or break us in a strike situation."[72] At a dinner hosted by the WGA for 120 writer-producer hyphenate members, these prominent showrunners realized that many among them had been asked to create "promotional" web shorts for the studios without compensation. This gathering galvanized key members, and they agreed that if a strike were to happen, the hyphenates would walk out. Reversing the stance they had taken in previous Guild struggles, most hyphenates now agreed that the two jobs could not be separated.

The WGA used the power that successful writers held in board rooms, writers' rooms, and programming meetings not only to build awareness and visibility but also to remind the AMPTP of the creative labor it would lose in a walkout. David Goodman, a member of the WGA's board and negotiating committee, emphasized that the Guild "made a concerted effort to get A-list people half in TV, half feature [film]. By doing that . . . we were telling the companies that this was something to be taken seriously, not just by Guild activists but by rank-and-file Guild members, and by rank-and-file I mean *important* members, members who have big earnings and who the companies can't not be in business with. Setting that example in the negotiating committee got us a few steps further down the road in terms of organizing both sides, feature and television, than we could have been if we had just gone with Guild activists."[73] The committee included a showrunner from each of the networks as well as Oscar-winning writers from virtually every major studio, including Ronald Bass, John Bowman (writer on *Saturday Night Live* and *Murphy Brown*), Marc Cherry (creator of *Desperate Housewives*), Bill Condon (who adapted *Chicago* and *Dreamgirls* for the screen), Carlton Cuse (showrunner for *Lost*), Stephen Gaghan (who wrote *Traffic*), Carl Gottlieb (writer of *Jaws*), Susannah Grant (who wrote *Erin Brockovich*), Carol Mendelsohn (showrunner for *CSI*), Marc Norman, Shawn Ryan (creator of *The Shield*), Ed Solomon (who wrote *Men in Black*), and Larry Wilmore (creator of *The Bernie Mac Show*), among others. Putting these members in positions of authority was a strategic step in building the membership's trust in the board and the negotiating committee. In years past, some of the most egregious infighting during negotiations and strikes came from high-profile writers who felt their needs were not being served. When these writers defected, others followed, and the AMPTP would take advantage of the weakened Guild to make a deal beneficial to the companies.[74]

The WGA East used a model of strike captains, each of whom was responsible for galvanizing a group of writers.[75] The East also sent veteran writers to the negotiating table, including Terry George, writer of *In the Name of the Father* and *Hotel Rwanda*, Brian Koppelman (*Ocean's Thirteen*), and Raphael Yglesias (*Fearless*). The diversity of well-respected players sitting across the bargaining table from the AMPTP sent a message to both the membership and the studios that the union was mobilizing its community for the fight ahead.

In the months leading up to the strike, the whole industry was hopeful that a walkout could be averted. But from very early on, there were signs that an agreement responsive to the writers' demands would be virtually impossible without a standoff. In mid-July 2007 the AMPTP told a group of national journalists, "We want to make the deals. We want to share in success with both the networks and our creative partners, but we just need some time to figure out what those business models are going to look like."[76] Whatever desire the studios claimed to have "to share in success" was absent at the preliminary contract negotiations later that month. Rather than offering the Guild a point of entry into digital compensation rates, the AMPTP put forward proposals that partially revoked rights to residuals previously won by the WGA. According to Mark Gunn, who was on the WGA negotiating committee, that hard-line tactic ended up helping the writers to unite: "The AMPTP had every opportunity to split us. All they had to do is make us a low-ball offer and a chunk of our membership would have said, 'Take it, we can't afford a strike.' Instead they made us a series of ridiculous offers that no reasonable member of the Writers Guild would say yes to—thus forcing us to go on strike."[77]

As the months allotted for negotiations dwindled down to weeks, the Guild conceded key issues, but the AMPTP held its line. The WGA contract would expire on October 31, 2007, but the Guild's plan was to stay on the job until the following summer so that writers could walk out together with the Screen Actors Guild and possibly the Directors Guild. (AFTRA's MBA was up for renewal in January 2008, and the SAG and DGA MBAs would expire on June 30, 2008.) Then came an idea from the East. At one of the East's negotiating committee meetings in late September, Susan Kim remembered screenwriter Adam Brooks (*French Kiss*) asking, "What if we go out [on strike] now?" meaning when the WGA contract expired rather than waiting until June.[78] The studios were planning to stockpile scripts all winter. Warren Leight, then the showrunner for *Law & Order: Criminal Intent*, told the group that a November strike would instantly end his show's ability to run new episodes. The East talked to the West, and the two boards decided that if the writers were going to have to strike, they would go out when the WGA contract expired. Michael Winship, senior writer of *Moyers & Company*, who had assumed the presidency of the WGA East in September 2007, saw surprise as key to success. The strike "really caught them flat-footed, which will never happen again, but in that instance, they caught them totally off guard."[79]

The strike authorization passed with an astonishing 93 percent of the membership of both branches of the Guild giving approval. With negotiations going nowhere, a walkout suddenly seemed inevitable. On November 5, 2007, the 12,000 members of the WGA began a strike that would last 100 days.

The decision to harness the power of the celebrity writer was crucial to the Guild's strike plan. Television showrunners—not just those on the negotiating committee, but all head writers—became key players in spreading the right message about the strike. This outreach was highly successful: showrunners encouraged their staff writers to join them on the picket line, and those writers then informed others about the action, thus building a network of strikers who felt connected to their picket teams. "It was an absolutely intentional strategy for a number of reasons," David Goodman explained. "There would be people out in the world who may not know Carlton Cuse, but they may know 'Carlton Cuse, executive producer of *Lost*'; you may not know Marc Cherry, but they know 'Marc Cherry, creator of *Desperate Housewives*.' The general public knows those names."[80] The WGA could not indemnify showrunners from the possibility that studios would sue them for breach of contract, but it was unlikely the studios would mount lawsuits. They needed their showrunners back as soon as the strike ended and were disinclined to create ill will with these indispensable employees.

On the first day, 3,000 WGA West picketers circled the sidewalks in front of Fox, CBS, Warner Bros., Sony, Paramount, and Disney. Their red union T-shirts against the blue California sky and white studio buildings created perfect images on the covers of newspapers, on television screens, and on websites. On average, 1,500 WGA West writers walked every weekday for three months.[81] In the East, the Guild coordinated its members to picket at a different corporate headquarters or studio each day. The images of WGA East members picketing the conglomerates in the freezing cold and snow struck a different chord and gave the group an aura of gravitas.

The two branches of the Guild displayed their unique styles on the picket line. Bill Scheft of the East remembers, "The difference between the East and the West? They had Alicia Keys and we had the not-yet-disgraced John Edwards."[82] But getting Edwards was actually a major coup. After standing with the East, Edwards refused to cross a picket line to take part in a presidential debate at CBS on the Wednesday before Thanksgiving. The other candidates, including Hillary Clinton and Barack Obama, quickly sidestepped also, and the debate was canceled. "That was very effective," according to

IMAGE 24 Striking writers in front of the iconic Paramount Studio gates on Melrose Avenue in Los Angeles (2007).

Photo by author

Winship. "It fell on that very slow news day just by accident. So it got this huge amount of coverage."[83]

The AMPTP placed a series of full-page ads in the business trades and national newspapers. In response, the WGA turned to its own membership to assemble a communications campaign for the strike. In addition to using phone banks and traditional press releases, the WGA exploited digital communication to access members, the Hollywood community, the press, and the general public by way of private e-mail and public blogs. Writers recognized, as did the AMPTP, that positive public relations and media attention would help sway professional and public opinion. Roger Wolfson, a television writer for *Saving Grace* and *The Closer*, remembered the third day of the strike, when the WGA realized how tough this war of words would be:

> When all seven media companies responded by consolidating their PR operations under the guidance of Sony's Jim Kennedy, a former White House spokesman—and eventually, Mark Fabiani and Chris Lehane, two of the highest paid and previously most sought-after media consultants in America—Guild members bolstered the Guild's

communications department with a media room of its own. At 4:00 on Thursday, November 8th, we put out a call for writers with PR, political, or journalistic experience. Within an hour, the room was staffed by a rotating group of thirty WGA members, many having worked for national campaigns or major newspapers, and they worked nearly fulltime for the rest of the strike.[84]

The importance of e-mail, especially for a membership dispersed across the country, should not be underestimated. The leadership was able to coordinate with and spread official word to Guild members more cheaply, simply, and efficiently than ever before.[85] Strike captains regularly sent out e-bulletins to update members on the state of negotiations or picketing schedules. The Guild also launched a number of e-mail campaigns to promote government support and public awareness. They asked that writers encourage their friends and family to spread information about the strike and invite them to get involved through support campaigns.

Blogs offered a less structured and more public approach to disseminating strike information and opening lines of communication between writers and the larger community. A variety of websites became popular, two in particular being *United Hollywood*, created by the WGA, and *Deadline Hollywood Daily*, run by a sympathetic media reporter. These sites provided a centralized space for immediate access to information about the strike and about negotiations that was unavailable through traditional print and broadcast media. Blog visitors could access, update, or comment on content instantly, day or night.

To develop *United Hollywood*, a group of WGA strike captains worked with what the site itself describes as "advocates for working people in the entertainment industry facing the digital revolution."[86] Dante Atkins, an Internet outreach adviser for progressive causes and Democratic candidates, helped design the site. Its name, he admits, "may have seemed like an odd choice for a website devoted to protecting the interests of the WGA, but in truth, the name fit right in with one of the principal messages the WGA captains were trying to communicate: that the fate of the WGA in these negotiations over Internet royalties would set the bar for negotiations with other Hollywood unions like the DGA and IATSE."[87] With frequent updates, rapid responses to negative statements by the AMPTP, extensive video links, and blog entries by writers of popular films and television series, *United*

Hollywood quickly gained a large audience of followers and on-site commentators, and it provided an important voice to counter the AMPTP's public relations machine.

Deadline Hollywood Daily was born out of entertainment reporter Nikki Finke's weekly column "Deadline Hollywood" in the free alternative paper *LA Weekly*. A year before the strike, Finke created an online version of her column in which she editorialized on the politics and culture of Hollywood business practices. Finke's access to insiders, her frequent news scoops, and her relentlessly pro-labor attitude toward industry business made her site popular for information and debate among WGA members and supporters in the months before and during the strike. Courtney Lilly remembers walking the picket line during the first week of the strike and checking Finke's blog every twenty minutes on his iPhone to see whether the strike would end.[88] *Los Angeles Times* television reporter Scott Collins derided the unprofessionalism and sensationalism of Finke's blog but admitted that it was a key weapon in the WGA's artillery against the conglomerates. "Blogs are, in fact, the chief difference between [the strikes of] '88 and '08. Blogs replicate, amplify and sometimes distort stories in ways that simply weren't possible 20 years ago. And no blogger left a bigger footprint on strike coverage than Finke."[89] *Deadline Hollywood Daily* reported the latest news from the negotiation tables, picket lines, and backroom meetings and provided a space for labor to discuss and debate the news—even the facts.

The diversity of articulate, witty, and heated discourses within the blogosphere was precisely what made the strike discussion compelling. The WGA offered writers suggested talking points when speaking to the media but never restricted its members from expressing individual opinions. Filmmaker Jennie Chamberlain and scholar Daniel Chamberlain note the multiplicity of voices that emerged: "Unlike the AMPTP, which made its decisions behind closed doors and then paraded its sound bites through the very mainstream media it owned, the WGA membership clamored with a cacophony of voices across a variety of Internet sources. One-way communication was broken—no longer controlled by the media or the Guild, but taken on by the membership."[90]

While the wordy and often boisterous blogs offered useful details for insiders, the WGA realized that part of this message war was about winning the support of the general public. And, not unsurprisingly, entertainment writers knew just how to tell their own story. The crucial lesson they had learned from the failed *America's Next Top Model* walkout was the power of streaming media to speak to the masses. One *New York Times* writer called the WGA's short videos aimed at strike watchers and supporters "creative venting," but these image campaigns were targeted and purposeful.[91] In "Sorry, Internet," writers Frank Lesser and Rob Dubbin of *The Colbert Report* present the cute furry animals that dominate so many online videos, but in this one the pet stars refuse to perform their adorable antics out of solidarity for the striking WGA members.[92] Work is still work, even if that work is just being cute. The reach of these videos was substantial: "*The Office* Is Closed," a streaming video produced by *The Office*, received over 280,000 views in its first week on YouTube.[93] With veteran writers creating content for the Internet, the possibilities of the medium for entertainment—and for political action—became clearer. Strike captain Peter Rader, writer of *Waterworld*, said, "The strike is about the Internet, so we're using the Internet to fight back. . . . We are going to get America to recognize one way or another that the Internet is a democratic space and there need to be unions to protect those who provide its content."[94]

A month into the strike, *United Hollywood* released a series of higher quality videos entitled "Speechless." Produced by Screen Actors Guild members working in solidarity with the WGA, the series celebrated the collaborative nature of media work. Without writers, the videos demonstrated, actors would have no lines. One particular video featured actors Amy Ryan and Patricia Clarkson deep in an emotionally gripping conversation with dialogue provided by the plumbing ads in the Yellow Pages.[95]

Although the battle against the conglomerates—each with its own enormous advertising budget and media connections (most of them owned television stations and newspapers)—was decidedly uphill, the weight of public opinion slanted toward the writers. A Nielsen survey released after the strike reported that 100 percent of 800 respondents were aware of the strike, with 77 percent supporting the writers either strongly (55 percent) or somewhat (22 percent).[96] Michael Winship said of American viewers, "They got it. They understood what the issues were. The public was incredibly supportive."[97] Paradoxically, the AMPTP's singular voice, a result of decades of mergers and acquisitions, was less adept, less nimble, and ill suited for this battle.

In December, the Directors Guild of America went into closed-door sessions with the AMPTP. A group of about forty writer-directors (who campaigned under the name WD-40) published a statement asking the DGA to forgo negotiations until the writers had a contract. Instead, the AMPTP essentially held out to bargain with the less demanding DGA, hoping that the WGA would eventually settle for the same contract.[98] The directors, as they had done in previous strikes in the 1980s, undercut the power of the WGA by continuing negotiations with the AMPTP. Once a deal was settled with the DGA in January for less compensation for digital residuals than the WGA had asked for, the AMPTP began cutting costs by ending expensive, often unproductive long-term development contracts with certain writers. The WGA negotiators, who had already dropped their demands for jurisdiction over animation and reality series, entered into two intensive weeks of bargaining with the media moguls, led by News Corporation's Peter Chernin and Disney CEO Robert Iger.[99] NBC's Jeff Zucker compared the strike to the wildfires that ravaged California in the fall of 2007: "Change isn't easy, and sometimes it requires a catalyst. . . . A strike has devastating consequences for thousands of people who are directly or indirectly dependent on this industry to feed their families. . . . Fires fertilize the soil with new ash and clear the ground, often setting the stage for robust growth."[100] Many writers were tired of the strike and eager to return to work. Some showrunners who had proved a powerful force at the beginning of the strike were considering returning to work as producers. The strong ties among writers that the Guild had worked so hard to foster during the strike were starting to unravel.

Tensions were also building among the various unions. One writer mentioned to a sympathetic friend in the DGA a conversation he had had with a DGA member who objected to directors allying with the writers. The writer's DGA friend said, "I heard something that I didn't think I'd ever hear. . . . It was the disdain of the house slave for the yard slave."[101] This inflammatory conversation highlights a problem the Guild had faced time and again, both internally and externally, with other unions: rather than all workers focusing on bettering their lot, they wasted time quarreling among themselves. The Directors Guild had always acted as an ally of the studios rather than of its sister unions, and this strike was no exception. Arguably, the DGA landed a better deal from the companies than it would have achieved had the writers not been on strike. The executives' fear that the directors might join ranks with the writers gave the DGA a small amount of unearned negotiating power.

Despite cracks in its united front, the WGA membership officially held strong until a deal was reached with the AMPTP on February 12, 2008. Many writers were devastated by the end of the strike and felt it ultimately demoralized the community and split the stalwart Guild faithful from the workaday members. Others believed that the Guild had grown stronger. To some, however, that unity mattered little. Craig Mazin's view represented a faction of writers who felt that the Guild had been too focused on organizing and forgot that, first and foremost, writers want to write. "When they say that it brought writers together and gave them a sense of unity, all I can say is that they value that so much more than they ought to. The union's purpose ultimately is to protect my financial interests, protect my creative rights, and to protect my health and my retirement. I don't need a sense of unity with the people with whom I compete for jobs."[102] On the other hand, Mark Gunn praised the writers' leaders for understanding both the demands and the limits of their membership: "David Young and Patric Verrone had a very good sense of where the membership was in terms of their patience for a deal—and they went up right to the edge of that, but they didn't go past that edge."[103] In the end, as Ross McCall said, "We didn't get a foot in the door so much as we got a toe."[104] Others might argue for a toenail: writers acquired compensation for streaming media and electronic sell-through, but no minimum was set.

During the strike, the Guild leadership had attempted to present a unified front, but it also allowed for a multiplicity of voices. Del Reisman, WGA president from 1991 to 1993, was awestruck by the relative cohesion within the union he once led. As a child, he had roamed the Universal Studios back lot in the 1930s; then he wrote for live television in the 1950s, made telefilms in the 1960s, and saw his work transferred to DVD in the 1990s. The night the negotiating committee presented its final agreement with the AMPTP to the membership, Reisman was there. "I got there early and went down to the first row and turned around and . . . I recognized about ten or twelve people. And I had once been president and extremely active in the Guild. But there was a generational change. . . . Unity, unity, unity. Never experienced it before, never observed it before. . . . It was the complete openness of that meeting. The directness of it. The ability of the negotiating committee to say, 'We tried hard on this and we couldn't get it' without any attempt to cover it over."[105]

Something had changed for the Guild. Out of a fractured group came decisive action at the start of the strike. Even though the divisiveness had not disappeared, there was a movement toward unification between East and West, between film writers and television writers, and between new writers and veterans.

Post-Strike Assessments

That's what I mean about using the Internet as asymmetric warfare. . . . That's part of the reason Andy Stern [former president of Service Employees International Union] said, "It was the first strike of the 21st century." . . . It wasn't about steel workers or car workers. It was about intellectual property.

—Michael Winship, interview, 9 April 2012

The WGA, DGA, AFTRA, and SAG all signed contracts in 2008 allowing for compensation for digital exhibition. Although the direction of future digital media production is impossible to foresee, as Mark Deuze points out, it will involve a "delicate and contested balance between the creative autonomy of culture creators and the scientific management of commercial enterprises."[106] In a multinational conglomerated media landscape eager to downsize, it is easy to see why labor has had such a difficult time getting its voice heard. Finding parity between creative labor and the bottom line within the rapidly evolving, virtually unchartered territory of the digital sphere is a nearly insurmountable challenge. And although the studios had argued during the strike that their streaming of series was solely for promotional purposes, their actions immediately after the strike demonstrated something different.

A month after the strike ended, major conglomerates began announcing their streaming partnerships. Hulu, a joint venture of NBC Universal and Fox Entertainment Group, debuted, and the popularity and accessibility of streaming television and features expanded greatly. One year after the site launched, Hulu's audience reached 40.1 million unique users who viewed 380 million streaming videos in the month of March 2009 alone.[107] Still, individual practitioners' economic woes were heightened by the larger economic crisis within the world markets that started in September 2008.

The DVD slowly started to disappear from the marketplace. People were buying programs online and downloading them, or simply streaming the films and television they wanted to watch, when they wanted to watch them. Streaming series like *Web Therapy*, created by Dan Bucatinsky, Lisa Kudrow, and Don Roos, and *Childrens Hospital*, created by Rob Corddry, made a successful jump from web to television series in 2010. Others, like Felicia Day's *The Guild*, stayed online. A new season of *Arrested Development* in 2012 helped lure audiences to Netflix as an original content provider, and *House of Cards* and *Orange Is the New Black* proved to the industry that series could start on the web, find substantial audiences, and prosper there.

The potential applications of online media became more enticing to creatives in the years right after the strike. Television writer and actor Jason Sklar began pitching television series to media executives using a web series he and his brother Randy Sklar produced. Whether or not a pitch sells, the series could be viewed freely online. The speed and flexibility of production, Sklar says, makes his work for the new medium uniquely satisfying. "The digital platform provides a practical space to execute your vision. . . . Hollywood tends to be a fear-based business. So if anything can be proven as a success on one platform, it increases your chance that another larger platform would take a chance [on you]. In the past, you would make a pilot and it would be seen by the executives at the network and maybe 300–400 people in focus groups across the country. If it did not make it to the air, then no one ever saw it. Now . . . online, you can create something that can entertain people."[108] In 2010, the WGA added to its ranks Ruth Livier, its first member to gain admission based solely on writing a self-financed web series, *Ylse*. Streaming media has propelled careers for some writers: the assignments began flowing in, not just for one medium, but often for two or more formats (though the pay is far from equal). Erica Rothschild, a writer on *Just Shoot Me!* who had sold many scripts but rarely saw them through development, was enthusiastic about developing her first web series in 2009. "For so many years my job has been divorced from actually making content. [Laughs.] Nothing gets made. I'm excited that, even if it's only three minutes long, we're going to *make* something."[109]

With the industrial shifts toward increased conglomeration and digital distribution came another kind of convergence: an overwhelming meeting of the minds between film and television writers in the WGA. Tom Fontana thinks that solidarity developed on the picket lines.

[What] makes the union in the East really special is that we aren't just one kind of writer. We are a union of writers who write for television and film. Nothing brought that home more for me more than the last strike. Unlike previous strikes . . . people really started to talk to other people. So you would see Tony Gilroy [writer of *The Bourne Identity* and *Michael Clayton*] having a conversation with a daytime writer or you would see a news writer talking to an animation writer or episodic writer, or a comedy writer talking to an episodic drama writer. I was very moved by that, to see that all of these people who wrote completely different kinds of things actually came together, because the one thing we love is the writing, to be able to write, to be treated with respect.[110]

Moreover, for the first time in a long time, the Writers Guild East and the Writers Guild West were allied. Howard A. Rodman saw this as the first step in what may be a long process. When asked whether the two branches of the Writers Guild might amalgamate, Rodman said, "If I live long enough in my lifetime I may get to see a Writers Guild of America. That would be the hope. I may not get there. I may be able to see what the top of the mountain would look like but not get there myself."[111]

There are significant issues that make a union between the East and West branches complex—from the size of the respective guilds to disputes over jurisdiction for public radio writers, news writers, and network television writers. Walter Bernstein, a WGA East veteran who survived the blacklist and saw the worst of times for writers and for the Guild, stressed the significance of the unity writers had achieved: "This last strike was very moving because we all came together, East and West, and we'd been fighting each other for several years. And we held tough on things. It was hard for a lot of people. And we won. Much to everybody's surprise."[112]

Only six months after the strike, the 2008 financial crisis hit. Media conglomerates began divesting selected holdings, and it was unclear whether the strike or the economy was to blame and whether this new paradigm was a trend or a correction. Writers, like others in the industry, feared the loss of audiences, an even greater concern of the studios for ensuring the profitability of content. The recession underscored the financial losses to the industry because of the strike. This was only compounded by the collapse of the DVD market. Yet, industrial and technological structures that seemingly created fissures in the labor dynamics of creative production have in fact provided new opportunities for creative workers to change the rules and use new technologies to their advantage—not just onscreen, but behind the scenes, as well. Convergence has never been just about technological change. It is about the definitions of labor shifting, the lines between production and consumption compressing, and divisions between producer, product, and audience breaking down.

BREAKING BAD #516 "FELINA" FINAL 4/3/13 49.

44 CONTINUED: 44

BIRD'S EYE VIEW: we look straight down on Walt as he tumbles into frame, lying flat on his back on the floor. His eyes stare up at us, lifeless. And yet, his final expression is one of faint satisfaction.

We slowly CRANE UP, UP and AWAY from him. Walt shrinks smaller and smaller in frame. POLICE OFFICERS approach him now -- four, six, eight of them. They move in cautiously, their guns aimed.

They're too late. He got away.

We continue SKYWARD, looking down on Walt, rising as high as we can go. Off this image, slowly FADING TO BLACK...

<u>END SERIES</u>

IMAGE 25 Last page of Vince Gilligan's script for "Felina," the final episode of the series *Breaking Bad.*

Writers Guild Foundation Archive, Shavelson-Webb Library, Los Angeles

Conclusion

> Writers will often complain about being poorly treated, and I wonder, where was the book that they read where screenwriters were carried around on velvet pillows?
>
> —Aline Brosh McKenna (screenwriter of *The Devil Wears Prada*), interview, 16 August 2012

> BANKS: I'm so glad I'm not in this industry, but I love studying it.
>
> MICHAEL WINSHIP: You're a China watcher. You're parked on Taipei and you are watching the mainland.
>
> —Interview, 9 April 2012

It should come as little surprise that writers speak about themselves and about their community in lucid, articulate terms; nor is it any wonder that throughout the process of interviewing writers of all generations for this book, I turned to their knack for encapsulating their own history.[1] I found that writers offered much more than a simple vocabulary of agency and professional identity.[2] Writers' memories of the Guild, of their professions, and of themselves were structured more like well-crafted essays. Their self-disclosures provided A and B plotlines. As the interviews came to a close, many of my subjects presented thoughtfully constructed readings of my research, of the story of the Guild, and of themselves as a community. Many have even written their own accounts of this story in some of media studies' most respected journals.[3] I did not see their versions of history as the truth, but as one truth among many I verified and examined with other data points. Rather than trying to theorize about their labor, I decided instead to use their expertise as confirmation of the history I had begun to uncover. My subjects became sources in this cultural history of the American entertainment industry.

Inevitably, innovative screen technologies lure audiences in directions that demand original approaches to storytelling and new structures of compensation. No matter the medium, writing creative content, telling stories, and crafting characters will be central to the work of screenwriters. As this book details, the industry has always been in flux, and the Guild has adapted, whether or not its positions corresponded with writers' individual hopes for their community. While the details have changed, the central demands that emerged in the 1920s are still critical concerns for writers today: their unique role as outsiders on the inside of the production community; questions of authorship, ownership, and control; and the significance of the writer's name.

Insider/Outsider

In my research, I found that most writers articulated with candor and humor their dissatisfactions with studio bosses, network heads, directors, and conglomerates for stifling talent and creativity. These writers were generally grateful for their own lot, but they believed strongly that writers deserve more credit than they get for their contribution to the final media product. As a group, many shared a sense of belonging to an industry of heroes and stars, in which they were typecast in the role of the antihero. There is no question that my sample of writers is skewed in that it includes a great number of acclaimed and successful members of the profession. They are not an average cross-section of Guild members, nor are they necessarily representative of all writers who have come into the industry with hopes of building a career. But each saw his or her career as one story among many in a difficult trajectory for a community of creative laborers. Their worry was less for themselves than for the plight of *the writers.* My subjects talked of unnamed writer-protagonists grappling with industry bottom lines and suffering the indignities of unfair compensation structures, attribution and credit restrictions, and—in comparison with producers, directors, and actors—relative obscurity.

The stories they recalled from their own careers stood in marked contrast to the screen stories that they have crafted about writers more generally. Other characters from the production world may be satirized, but the character of *the writer* is almost always stereotyped. He or she is neurotic, self-centered, or loveless—sometimes all three. A short list of the many films and series featuring writers illuminates this overwhelming trend: *Sunset Blvd.*, by Billy Wilder and Charles Brackett; *The Dick Van Dyke Show*, by Carl Reiner; *My Favorite Year*, by Dennis Palumbo and Norman Steinberg; *Barton*

Fink, by Joel Coen and Ethan Coen; *It's Garry Shandling's Show*, by Garry Shandling and Alan Zweibel; *Adaptation*, by Charlie Kaufman and his fictional brother Donald Kaufman; *30 Rock*, by Tina Fey; *The Comeback*, by Lisa Kudrow and Michael Patrick King; *Studio 60 on the Sunset Strip*, by Aaron Sorkin; and *Episodes*, by David Crane and Jeffrey Klarik. These types of scripts are more often comedies, dramedies, or black comedies. This is not to say that writers do not take themselves seriously. Rather, they understand that they are among the least lucky members of an extremely lucky community and that they are outsiders within a community of insiders.

When writers spoke about their present-day community, they parceled the less fortunate among them into two groups: professional screenwriters who have been barred from organizing because of jurisdictional disputes and minority writers (writers of color, women). Those lucky enough to be under Writers Guild protection said that a critical aspect of the Guild's work is to widen its jurisdictional umbrella to include all writers who are paid by companies to script words for the screen, no matter the genre or platform. As Catherine Fisk notes, under current labor laws, writers who are not on regular staff are defined as independent contractors and consequently denied the right to residuals, health benefits, and pensions, even though "they perform functions that are an essential part of the employer's business."[4] In moving forward, it is critical for writers to consider not only jurisdiction but also the terms of employment and definitions of work within an industry that rarely employs writers in large numbers. The WGA is having more success when it hammers out these terms with companies in the early stages of production development. Its agreements with Netflix and Amazon, for example, were groundbreaking, not because they guaranteed lofty residuals, but rather because they established residual structures in these formats for the first time.

The issue of who gets hired is central to the Guild. And yet, since its inception, the Guild as an organization has never had a voice in determining whom a signatory hires as a writer. Only in extreme cases can the Guild bar people from the union (for example, during the blacklist or, more recently, warnings to individuals who work during a strike). Many of its efforts focus on employment of current members and jurisdiction over potential new members.

As discussed in chapters 4 and 5, the WGA has tried over the years to help more writers of color get work and become members of the union.

Some prestigious diversity and development programs have emerged since 1999, when the networks signed a memorandum of understanding with the National Association for the Advancement of Colored People after the group issued a scathing report on the lack of diversity in front of and behind the camera in Hollywood.[5] These programs were designed to help new or young writers of color hone their skills, meet executives, and start their careers. Nevertheless, the percentage of people of color writing for television is still nowhere near representative of the population, and the statistics in film are even more skewed. Many white writers I interviewed believed that increasing the numbers would solve the imbalance. But the number of minority writers is only part of the problem. While the numbers of writers of color working in the industry has bumped up in recent decades, particularly in television, the extraordinary income gap between white and minority writers, not at entry level work but at mid-career, is of far deeper concern for writers and for their union. This is where the Writers Guild is focusing its attention. Recent studies point to the shockingly low number of minority writers commissioned by networks and studios to write pilots.

Success is not just a matter of producing an exemplary or marketable script but having the access to the critical steps of being commissioned to write a script, selling a script, or having a script produced. In television, if a pilot by a minority writer is not produced, there is no chance that the series will be picked up by a network. As Kimberly Myers, WGA West director of diversity, explained, "You have got three stages to go through and they are not even getting into the first stage."[6] To this end, the WGA has created the Writer Access Project, which is designed to help showrunners identify talented minority writers who have been hired at least once and have at least one credit for writing a television episode. Though many writers think that the issue is initial access to the industry, the Guild is learning that the critical link for minority writers is getting beyond the first job.

Minority women writers have had more of their own new series brought to air with them at the helm than minority men over the last few years, including Shonda Rhimes with *Grey's Anatomy*, *Private Practice*, and *Scandal*, Veena Sud with *The Killing*, which she developed for American television, Mindy Kaling with *The Mindy Project*, Mara Brock Akil with *The Game* and *Being Mary Jane*, and Nahnatchka Khan with *Don't Trust the B—in Apartment 23*. Even a series created by and staring two minority men, Keegan-Michael

Key and Jordan Peele's *Key and Peele*, is currently run by two Caucasian men, Ian Roberts and Jay Martel.

Equal access and frequency of work for women writers is improving, far more swiftly in television than in film, though progress is slow in both. Still, some writers feel a sense of encouragement; with more women in film programs, they reason, more will make it through the entry gate and become career writers. In earlier decades, the names of Ruth Prawer Jhabvala, who adapted *A Room with a View* and *Howards End*, Callie Khouri, scripter of *Thelma and Louise* and creator of *Nashville*, and Diablo Cody, who wrote *Juno* and *Young Adult*, were on the tip of every producer's tongue as new voices in unique genres who succeeded in capturing audiences' attention. More recently, Aline Brosh McKenna pointed to Lena Dunham's meteoric success with her series *Girls*: "It's changing. It's going to change. Lena Dunham has done more for women in film than every Women in Film panel combined."[7]

Authorship/Ownership

Since the end of long-term contracts, writers and studio signatories have agreed to a legal subterfuge regarding authorship that benefits both parties. A writer crafts a script, for which he or she holds copyright. If a signatory buys the script, then the writer and signatory sign paperwork transferring ownership and authorship and retroactively deeming the script a work-for-hire project. The signatory attains ownership, and the writer is protected under a WGA employee contract that assures such rights as minimums for compensation, residuals, and health and pension benefits. Though it is clear why this kind of legal wrangling—relinquishing authorial rights to secure workers' rights—occurs, many of the screenwriters who campaigned in the 1940s for an American Authors Authority would find it counterintuitive, if not downright absurd.

Debates over media ownership are critical at the level of industry, networks, and corporations. As can be seen in the rise and fall of the Financial Interest and Syndication Rules, the effects of ownership trickle down to determine which individual films and series are commissioned and produced. While it once was useful to work with a studio or independent production company, most cable outlets now are interested only in buying series that can be produced entirely in-house—and then controlled vertically as media properties.[8] David Simon, creator of *The Wire*, finds much of television unwatchable because of the industry's narrow focus on maximizing audiences rather than investing resources in telling stories that reflect the real world: "A lot of it is about sustaining the franchise. You know, looking for the hit."[9] Simon experienced the frustrations of trying to appeal to a mass audiences when he wrote for the NBC series *Homicide: Life on the Street*. There are still some smaller outlets where writers can sell stories they believe in, but these companies are increasingly subsidiaries of major conglomerates.

Writers expressed frustrations with the increased corporatizing of the industry and its detrimental effects on the production process. Story notes from an executive are common, but too many layers at the top can weigh heavily on a project. Matthew Weiner, creator of *Mad Men*, recalled a production conference call with forty people on the phone—so many, that the conference telecommunications system broke down in the middle of the production meeting.[10] This corporate conglomerate model changes not just the language of production but ultimately the perspective of an industry that focuses less on content and more on asset management. Aline Brosh McKenna gave an example: "When I started, people would take a flyer on a smaller movie just because they thought it was interesting and thought, 'Well if I think it's interesting, maybe other people will think it's interesting.' Now, movies have to be more justified as a piece of business. You hear that phrase, 'piece of business,' more than you did."[11] And when films or series do not follow conventional models to reach success—whether *Bridesmaids* or *Breaking Bad*—major companies are less likely to gamble on them.

When an atypical script does succeed, it is celebrated as the work of a singular visionary, a situation that raises another common theme. On the one hand, writers demand fair credit, while on the other they refuse notions of authorial exceptionalism. In 1980, Philip Dunne lamented that many people forget that the writer even exists—including critics, whom he calls the worst offenders. "These critics credit the director with the construction, the selection of scenes, the suspense, the dramatic progression, and even, in some cases, the dialogue; in other words, precisely the things a screenwriter does to earn his or her living."[12] Until the 1970s, writers were never considered celebrities and were rarely mentioned in the press, unless they had done something morally reprehensible. Until the 1990s, only a handful of writers had the experience of being recognized in public.

While writers have campaigned for their place of importance as authors of the script, they will downplay the role of the television showrunner or the synergy of a strong writer-director relationship in film production. Lauded for his work as creator and showrunner of *Breaking Bad*, Vince Gilligan said at the end of the show's run, "The worst thing the French ever gave us is the auteur theory. It's a load of horseshit. You don't make a movie by yourself, you certainly don't make a TV show by yourself. You invest in people, in their work. You make people feel comfortable in their jobs; you keep people talking."[13] Writers want to be acknowledged—sometimes even celebrated—for their contributions, but they also recognize that they are part of a collaborative production process.

A recent shift in the role of the film screenwriter follows from the showrunner model in television. The industry has many models of successful hyphenates in television but few examples of cross-discipline work in film. However, the slow economy has made studios less inclined to hire additional writers to rework a script since they can usually keep the original writers for much less money. These writers can assist with the preparation for the film and work with the director, actors, and editors. They can help the marketing division clarify the story and keep a production on track. In their industry podcast *Scriptnotes*, John August, screenwriter of *Charlie's Angels* and *Big Fish*, and Craig Mazin refer to this work as the screenwriter-plus role. "It's a creative partner role," August explained in an interview. "Sometimes it is labeled as a producer role, but it's one of the functions of producing, whether it's labeled a producer or not. . . . Especially as these big movies become 200-day shoots, it's really useful to have a person there to remind you of what that scene is supposed to be about."[14] The success of the television showrunner model has shifted studios' ideas of what the writer's role can be on a film, and some may come to believe that a film will be better served if a writer is a part of the filmmaking collaboration throughout the entire production process.

The Name

Since the merger of the Screen Writers Guild with the Television Writers Association, the bargaining power of the Writers Guild of America has rested on the television side of the equation. In talking about the 2007–2008 WGA strike, screenwriter Craig Mazin said, "The key to thwarting [the studios] . . . is television. Movies take forever to get made. Television is right now."[15] In almost sixty years, the WGA East presidents have always been television writers (including a few news writers). The WGA West leadership, while more balanced, has been dominated by television writers. In July 2013, the WGA West reported that writers' earnings had risen 4 percent the previous year and that the increase for television writers was 10.1 percent.[16] In contrast, the feature film employment numbers had declined, with the major studios concentrating their financial resources on blockbusters rather than middle-budget films.[17]

When asked about the power of television within the Writers Guild, Frank Pierson replied, "Most of the really good writing now is being done in television, and it's interesting to see that as the writing goes to television, so does the directing. So we're increasingly seeing serious directors, established directors in the motion pictures business, going to do series on HBO. . . . The major [film] studios are only doing versions of *Avatar*. We're going to have *Avatar* 1, 2, 3, up your nose."[18] Even one of the most prolific screenwriters in Hollywood, Ronald Bass, agreed: "It's a television union. I think. I mean, that's where all the work is, that's where the money is, that's where the power is."[19] Joan Didion, who adapted her novel *Play It As It Lays* for the screen, once quipped that screenwriters get all the respect and television writers get all the money, but now the narrative has flipped. Not only is television getting respect, but web series like *House of Cards*, adapted for American television by Beau Willimon, and *Orange Is the New Black*, created by Jenji Kohan, have redefined "television" as entertainment that does not require a television set as its primary outlet.

As many scholars have noted, the economic and geographic structures of multiplatform global entertainment conglomerates have made transnational production the norm in what is still considered American media making.[20] The visual effects community provides an example of how creative laborers in the United States are working alongside international organizations to secure the rights of fellow creative workers while also attempting to ensure that production stays local. This anxiety about international industries taking creative labor jobs is nothing new. As discussed in chapter 2, *The Screen Writer* in 1945 had already imagined that the film industries in India and China would challenge American dominance in the global film market.[21] Although some production labor is now regularly outsourced, writing has generally stayed stateside. Still, the WGA has kept a close watch on industry

trends and has started a series of campaigns to help its international counterparts ensure writers' rights, secure jurisdictional control, and bargain
collectively for minimum basic agreements. The WGA's transnational call
for democratic unionization serves the interests of American creative laborers as much, if not more, than the interests of its global partners.

As writers and their Guild look forward into the future—not only for
themselves, but for the American and global media industries—it will be
critical to untangle and debate these questions of outsider and insider status,
authorship, ownership, and credits.

Final Thoughts

Above all, be the heroine of your life, not the victim.

–Nora Ephron (*When Harry Met Sally . . .*), commencement speech,
Wellesley College (Wellesley, MA),
3 June 1996

Most of the writers I interviewed for this book emphasized how important it
was for them to understand their own history as a creative community. They
saw it as their responsibility to guide the next generation of writers entering
the industry and the Guild. Writers spoke about the sacrifices of those who
came before them: those who worked without a contract, those who suffered
through the blacklist, those who gave up their chance for residuals in order
to secure rights for the next generation. Hal Kanter, creator of the series *Julia*,
said he felt proud to be a part of the writing profession. He firmly believed
that new writers should know whose shoulders they stand upon: "People ask
me what I do for a living and I say, 'I'm a writer' and I'm very proud of it. And
I'm proud of the Guild and have supported it right down the line. . . . A lot of
young members who complain about a great many things are completely
unaware of the giant strides this Guild has made on their behalf and . . .
possibly when this history is compiled . . . people might have some of their
anger tempered by reading what we already accomplished."[22]

Fay Kanin stressed that successful writers were often the ones who made
the greatest sacrifices. "The writers who fought and went on strike for minimums were writers who did not need those minimums. They . . . felt that it
was [their] obligation. . . . When I hear new young writers say. . . . 'The Guild
doesn't represent me, really.' I say, 'It doesn't? How do you think you got all the

things that you have that you take for granted? It's because of all the years this Guild fought for it, went on strike for it, and that has been a gift to you.'"[23]

Many writers I met said they first began learning about Guild history during a strike. Pacing the picket lines, they would see generations of writers walking together and understood that they were a part of community of creative laborers. Although many writers bemoaned particular Guild actions, each of them, at some point, expressed gratitude for the commitment and passion of the screenwriting community. As David Dortort said, "What a writer should do is write. But mostly he should help other writers if he can. And that's the greatness of the Writers Guild."[24]

At times the Writers Guild has failed its members and lost sight of its mission. Yet it remains the most passionate, forward-thinking trade union in the American entertainment industry. What these pages offer is a model that can be used to appraise the history of other entertainment labor groups. With each technological, economic, and cultural change, workers must and will respond. As the particulars of their daily tasks change, systems of compensation and rules about labor will need to be renegotiated. Questions about ownership, credit, and status in the creative community will once again be central to these debates.

Writers will never have it easy—and if ever they did, they would surely find the experience woefully dull. Great dramas are rarely born from carefree souls. While they gripe about their lot, screenwriters also feel certain they can craft a satisfying ending. And so they crumple up their last defeat and pitch a better story.

APPENDIX A
SCREENWRITERS AND
SELECTED CREDITS

AA = Academy Award (n = nomination)

EA = Emmy Award (n = nomination)

WGAA = Writers Guild of America Award; pre-1954, Screen Writers Guild Award (n = nomination)

WGA East awards:

  Evelyn F. Burkey (for contributions bringing honor and dignity to writers)

  Ian McClellan Hunter (for a body of work in film and/or television)

  Richard B. Jablow (for devoted service to the Guild)

  Herb Sargent (for commitment, comic genius, and mentoring of new writers)

WGA West awards:

  Animation Writing (for advancing the literature of animation in film and/or television)

  Morgan Cox (for ideas and efforts in service to the Guild)

  Valentine Davies (for contributions bringing honor and dignity to writers)

  Laurel (for advancing the literature of motion pictures or television and contributions to the profession)

  Robert Meltzer (for an act of bravery in defense of freedom of expression)

  Edmund H. North (for creative leadership and professional achievement)

  Paul Selvin (for a script that embodies the spirit of the Constitution and Bill of Rights)

Other awards:

  George Foster Peabody Award: given in recognition of distinguished achievement and meritorious service by broadcasters, cable and webcasters, producing organizations, and individuals (theatrical motion picture releases are not eligible)

  Humanitas Prize: awarded for motion picture and television writing that promotes human dignity, meaning, and freedom

  National Medal of Arts: the highest award to artists and patrons of the arts by the US government

Akil, Mara Brock: *Moesha* (1996–2001), *Girlfriends* (2000–2008), *The Game* (2006–, creator)

Allen, Jay Presson: *Marnie* (1964), *The Prime of Miss Jean Brodie* (1964, WGAAn), *Cabaret* (1972, AAn, WGAA), *Family* (1976–1980, Humanitas Prize 1976), Hunter Award (1997)

Allen, Woody: *Annie Hall* (1977, AA, WGAA), *Manhattan* (1979, AAn, WGAAn), *Hannah and Her Sisters* (1986, AA, WGAA), Laurel Award (1987), *Midnight in Paris* (2011, AA, WGAA)

Anderson, Paul Thomas: *Boogie Nights* (1997, AAn, WGAAn), *Magnolia* (2000, AAn, WGAAn), *There Will Be Blood* (2007, AAn, WGAAn), *The Master* (2013, WGAAn)

Anderson, Wes: *Rushmore* (1998), *The Royal Tenenbaums* (2001, AAn, WGAAn), *Moonrise Kingdom* (2012, AAn, WGAAn)

Auerbach, John: *Stepfather II* (1989, with Carolyn Lefcourt, Brian Garfield, and Donald E. Westlake), Jablow Award (2005)

August, John: *Go* (1999), *Charlie's Angels* (2000), *Big Fish* (2003), *Corpse Bride* (2005), *Frankenweenie* (2012)

Avedon, Barbara: *The Donna Reed Show* (1958–1966), *Bewitched* (1964–1972), *Cagney & Lacey* (1981–1988, creator with Barbara Corday)

Axelrod, George: *The Seven Year Itch* (1955, with Billy Wilder), *Breakfast at Tiffany's* (1961, AAn, WGAA), *The Manchurian Candidate* (1962)

Barbash, Bob: *Zane Grey Theater* (1956–1961), *Alcoa Theatre* (1957–1960), *Starsky & Hutch* (1975–1979)

Barnouw, Erik: *The United States Steel Hour* (1953–1963), RWG president (1947–1949), author of *A History of Broadcasting in the United States* (Oxford UP, 1966–1970), first curator of the Library of Congress's Motion Picture, Broadcasting and Recorded Sound Division

Bass, Ronald: *Rain Man* (1988, with Barry Morrow, AA, WGAAn), *The Joy Luck Club* (1993, WGAAn), *My Best Friend's Wedding* (1997), *How Stella Got Her Groove Back* (1998, with Terry McMillan)

Belkin, Gary: *Caesar's Hour* (1954–1957, EAn), *Car 54, Where Are You?* (1961–1963, with Nat Hiken, WGAA), *The Danny Kaye Show* (1963–1967, EAn), *The Carol Burnett Show* (1967–1978, EAn), *The Tonight Show Starring Johnny Carson* (1962–1992, EAn), *Annie, the Women in the Life of a Man* (1970, EA)

Berg, Gertrude: *The Goldbergs* (1949–1956), *The Gertrude Berg Show* (1961–1962)

Bernstein, Walter: *You Are There* (1953–1957, uncredited), *Fail-Safe* (1964), *The Front* (1976, AAn, WGAAn), *Semi-Tough* (1977, WGAAn), Hunter Award (1994), *Miss Evers' Boys* (1997, EAn, Humanitas Prize), Burkey Award (2008), blacklisted

Bessie, Alvah: *Objective, Burma!* (1945, with Ranald MacDougall and Lester Cole, AAn), *Ruthless* (1948), *Passage West* (1951, Nedrick Young as front, with Lewis R. Foster), blacklisted

Biberman, Herbert: *Action in Arabia* (1944, with Philip MacDonald), *The Master Race* (1944, with Anne Froelick), *Salt of the Earth* (1954, director), blacklisted

Blankfort, Michael: *An Act of Murder* (1948), *Broken Arrow* (1950, as front for Albert Maltz), *The Caine Mutiny* (1954, with Stanley Roberts), WGAw president (1967–1969), Davies Award (1972)

Blinn, William: *Brian's Song* (1971, EA, WGAA, Peabody Award), *Starsky & Hutch* (1975–1979, creator), *Roots* (1977, EA, Humanitas Prize), *The Boys Next Door* (1996, WGA), Laurel Award (2009)

Boulware, Bill: *Benson* (1979–1986), *The Fresh Prince of Bel-Air* (1990–1996), *The Parkers* (1999–2004)

Bowman, John: *Saturday Night Live* (1975–present, EA), *In Living Color* (1990–1994, EAn), *Martin* (1992–1997, creator), *Frank TV* (2007–2008, creator)

Brackett, Charles: SWG president (1938–1939), *Ninotchka* (1939, with Billy Wilder and Walter Reisch, AAn), *The Lost Weekend* (1945, with Billy Wilder, AA), AMPAS president (1949–1955), *Sunset Blvd.* (1950, with Billy Wilder and D. M. Marshman Jr., AA, WGAA), *Titanic* (1953, AA), Honorary AA (1957), Laurel Award (1957), North Award (1967)

Brecher, Irving: *Go West* (1940), *Meet Me in St. Louis* (1944, with Fred F. Finklehoffe, AAn), *The Life of Riley* (1949–1950, creator), *Bye Bye Birdie* (1963)

Brecht, Bertolt: *The Threepenny Opera* (1931, libretto), *Hangmen Also Die!* (1943, with Fritz Lang and John Wexley), blacklisted

Bright, John: *The Public Enemy* (1931, with Kubec Glasmon, AAn), *She Done Him Wrong* (1933, with Harvey F. Thew and Mae West), blacklisted

Brooks, Adam: *French Kiss* (1995), *Beloved* (1998), *Bridget Jones: The Edge of Reason* (2004, with Richard Curtis, Andrew Davies, and Helen Fielding)

Brooks, James L.: *The Mary Tyler Moore Show* (1970–1977, creator with Allan Burns, EA, WGAAn), *Taxi* (1978–1983, creator with Stan Daniels, David Davis, and Ed. Weinberger), *Terms of Endearment* (1983, AA, WGAA), *Broadcast News* (1987, AAn, WGAAn), *The Tracy Ullman Show* (1989, EA), *The Simpsons* (1989–present, developed by, with Matt Groening and Sam Simon), *As Good as It Gets* (1997, with Mark Andrus, AAn, WGAA), Laurel Award (1998, with Allan Burns), Sargent Award (2006)

Brooks, Mel: *Your Show of Shows* (1950–1954), *Get Smart* (1965–1970, creator with Buck Henry, EAn), *Sid Caesar Special* (1967, EA, WGAA), *The Producers* (1968, AA, WGAA), *The Twelve Chairs* (1971, WGAAn), *Young Frankenstein* (1974, with Gene Wilder, AAn, WGAAn), *Blazing Saddles* (1974, with Norman Steinberg, Andrew Bergman, Richard Pryor, and Alan Uger, WGAA), *Silent Movie* (1977, WGAAn), Laurel Award (2003)

Bucatinsky, Dan: *Lipstick Jungle* (2008–2009), *Web Therapy* (2008–present, web series, creator with Lisa Kudrow and Don Roos), *Web Therapy* (2011–present, television series, creator with Lisa Kudrow and Don Roos, EAn)

Buchman, Sidney: *Mr. Smith Goes to Washington* (1939, AAn), SWG president (1941–1942), *Here Comes Mister Jordan* (1941, with Seton I. Miller, AA), *The Talk of the Town* (1942, AAn), *Jolson Sings Again* (1949, AAn, WGAAn), Meltzer Award (1952), Laurel Award (1965), blacklisted

Burns, Allan: *The Bullwinkle Show* (1961–1964), *The Munsters* (1964–1966, creator with Chris Hayward), *The Mary Tyler Moore Show* (1970–1977, creator with James L. Brooks, EA, WGAAn), *Rhoda* (1974–1978, creator with James L. Brooks, EAn), *A Little Romance* (1979, AAn, WGAAn), Davies Award (1992), Laurel Award (1998, with James L. Brooks)

Butler, Hugo: *A Christmas Carol* (1938), *Edison, the Man* (1940, with Dore Schary, AAn), *Lassie Come Home* (1943), *Robinson Crusoe* (1954, with Luis Buñuel, pseudonym Philip Ansell Roll, credit awarded in 1997), blacklisted

Butler, Jean Rouverol: *So Young So Bad* (1950, with Bernard Vorhaus), *Search for Tomorrow* (1951–1986), *Guiding Light* (1952–2009, co-head writer 1975–1976, EAn, WGAA), *Autumn Leaves* (1956, with Hugh Butler [both under pseudonym Jack Jevne],

Lewis Meltzer, and Robert Blees, credit restored 1997), *As the World Turns* (1956–2010), Cox Award (1987), blacklisted

Cain, James M.: *Algiers* (1938, with John Howard Lawson), *Stand Up and Fight* (1939, with Jane Murfin and Harvey Fergusson), *Gypsy Wildcat* (1944, with James P. Hogan and Gene Lewis)

Cannell, Stephen J.: *The Rockford Files* (1974–1980, creator with Roy Huggins, WGAAn), *The Greatest American Hero* (1982, EAn, WGAAn), *The A-Team* (1983–1987, creator with Frank Lupo), *21 Jump Street* (1987–1991, creator with Patrick Hasburgh), *Silk Stalkings* (1991–1999), Laurel Award (2006)

Carroll, Bob, Jr.: *I Love Lucy* (1951–1957, EAn), *The Lucy-Desi Comedy Hour* (1957–1958), *The Lucy Show* (1962–1968), *The Mothers-in-Law* (1967–1969, creator with Madelyn Pugh Davis), *Here's Lucy* (1968–1974, with Madelyn Pugh Davis, EAn), Laurel Award (1992, with Jess Oppenheimer and Madelyn Pugh Davis)

Carson, Robert: *A Star Is Born* (1937, AA [original story, with William A. Wellman], AAn [screenplay, with Dorothy Parker and Alan Campbell]), *Beau Geste* (1939)

Chandler, Raymond: *Double Indemnity* (1944, with Billy Wilder, AAn), *The Blue Dahlia* (1946, AAn), *Strangers on a Train* (1951, with Czenzi Ormonde)

Chaplin, Charles: *The Circus* (1928, Special AA), *The Great Dictator* (1940, AAn), *Monsieur Verdoux* (1947, AAn), Honorary AA (1972)

Chase, Borden: *Red River* (1948, with Charles Schnee, AAn, WGAAn), *Winchester '73* (1950, with Robert L. Richards, WGAAn)

Chayefsky, Paddy: *The Philco-Goodyear Television Playhouse* (1948–1956, EAn), *Marty* (1955, AA, WGAA), *20th Century Fox Hour* (1958, WGAA), *The Hospital* (1971, AA, WGAA), Laurel Award (1974), *Network* (1976, AA, WGAA)

Cherry, Marc: *The Golden Girls* (1985–1992), *Desperate Housewives* (2004–2012, creator, EAn)

Chetwynd, Lionel: *The Apprenticeship of Duddy Kravitz* (1974, with Mordecai Richler, AAn, WGAA), *Color of Justice* (1997, WGAAn), *Ike: Countdown to D-Day* (2004, Humanitas Prize)

Clark, Ron: *The Smothers Brothers Comedy Hour* (1967–1970, EAn), *The Paul Lynde Show* (1972–1973, creator with Sam Bobrick), *Silent Movie* (1976, with Mel Brooks, Rudy De Luca, and Barry Levinson, WGAAn)

Cody, Diablo: *Juno* (2007, AA, WGAA), *The United States of Tara* (2009–2011), *Young Adult* (2011, WGAAn)

Coen, Joel, and Ethan Coen: *Raising Arizona* (1987), *Barton Fink* (1991), *Fargo* (1996, AA, WGAA), *O Brother, Where Art Thou?* (2000, AAn), *The Man Who Wasn't There* (2001, WGAAn), *No Country for Old Men* (2007, AA, WGAA), *Burn After Reading* (2008, WGAAn), *A Serious Man* (2009, AAn, WGAAn), *True Grit* (2010, AAn, WGAAn)

Coffee, Lenore J.: *The Better Wife* (1919), *Street of Chance* (1930, with Howard Estabrook, AAn), *Four Daughters* (1938, with Julius J. Epstein, AAn), *Sudden Fear* (1952, with Robert Smith)

Cole, Lester: *Charlie Chan's Greatest Case* (1933, with Marion Orth), SWG president (1944–1945), *Objective Burma!* (1945, with Alvah Bessie and Ranald MacDougall), *Born Free* (1966, pseudonym Gerald L. C. Copley, credit restored 1997), SWG founding member, blacklisted

Collins, Richard J.: *Song of Russia* (1944, with Paul Jarrico), *Bonanza* (1959–1973), *Matlock* (1986–1995), blacklisted

Condon, Bill: *Gods and Monsters* (1998, AA, WGAAn), *Chicago* (2002, AAn, WGAAn), *Kinsey* (2004, WGAAn), *Dreamgirls* (2006)

Coppola, Francis Ford: *Patton* (1970, with Edmund H. North, AA, WGAA), *The Godfather* (1972, with Mario Puzo, AA, WGAA), *The Conversation* (1974, AAn, WGAAn), *The Godfather, Part II* (1974, AA, WGAA), *Apocalypse Now* (1979, with John Milius, AAn, WGAAn), *The Rainmaker* (1997)

Corday, Barbara: *Wonder Woman* (1975–1979), *Cagney & Lacey* (1981–1988, creator with Barbara Avedon), vice president for Comedy Series Development at ABC (1979–1982), president of Columbia Pictures Television (1984–1987), executive vice president of Primetime Programming at CBS (1988–1990)

Corddry, Rob: *Children's Hospital* (2008–present, creator), *Newsreaders* (2013–present, creator with Jonathan Stern and David Wain)

Corey, George: *Mr. Winkle Goes to War* (1944, with Waldo Salt and Louis Solomon), blacklisted

Cosby, Bill: *The Bill Cosby Show* (1969–1971, creator with Ed. Weinberger and Michael Zagor), *The Cosby Show* (1984–1992, creator with Ed. Weinberger and Michael Leeson, Peabody Award)

Crane, David: *Dream On* (1990–1996, EAn), *Friends* (1994–2004), *Episodes* (2011–present, creator with Jeffrey Klarik, EAn, WGAAn)

Crawford, Oliver: *Rawhide* (1959–1965), *Ben Casey* (1961–1966), *The Fugitive* (1963–1967), *Star Trek* (1966–1969), *The Bionic Woman* (1976–1978), Cox Award (1983, 1997), blacklisted

Cuse, Carlton: *Nash Bridges* (1996–2001, creator), *Lost* (2004–2010, EAn, WGAA), *Bates Motel* (2013–present)

Davies, Valentine: *Miracle on 34th Street* (1947, with George Seaton, AA), *It Happens Every Spring* (1949, with Shirley W. Smith, AAn, WGAAn), SWG president (1949–1950), *The Glenn Miller Story* (1954, with Oscar Brodney, AAn, WGAAn), AMPAS president (1960–1961)

Davis, Elias: *The Carol Burnett Show* (1967–1978, EAn), *The Mary Tyler Moore Show* (1970–1977), *M*A*S*H* (1972–1983, WGAAn, Humanitas Prize), *Frasier* (1993–2004, WGAAn)

Davis, Madelyn Pugh: *I Love Lucy* (1951–1957, EAn), *The Lucy-Desi Comedy Hour* (1957–1960), *The Lucy Show* (1962–1968), *The Mothers-in-Law* (1967–1969, creator with Bob Carroll Jr.), *Here's Lucy* (1968–1974, with Bob Carroll Jr., EAn), Laurel Award (1992, with Jess Oppenheimer and Bob Carroll Jr.)

Day, Felicia: *The Guild* (2007–present), *Table Top* (2012–present, creator with Wil Wheaton)

Diamond, I.A.L.: *Some Like It Hot* (1959, with Billy Wilder, AAn, WGAA), *The Apartment* (1960, with Billy Wilder, AA, WGAA), *The Private Life of Sherlock Holmes* (1970, with Billy Wilder, WGAAn), Laurel Award (1980)

Didion, Joan: *Play It As It Lays* (1972, with John Gregory Dunne), *True Confessions* (1981, with John Gregory Dunne), *Up Close and Personal* (1996, with John Gregory Dunne), Burkey Award (2007)

Di Pego, Gerald: *Born Innocent* (1974), *Phenomenon* (1996), *Instinct* (1999)

Dmytryk, Edward: *Bluebeard* (1972), blacklisted

Dortort, David: *Fireside Theater* (1953–1954), *A Cry in the Night* (1956), *The Restless Gun* (1957–1959), *Bonanza* (1959–1973, creator with Fred Hamilton)

Dubbin, Rob: *The Colbert Report* (2005–present, EA, WGAA)

Dunham, Lena: *Tiny Furniture* (2010), *Girls* (2012–present, EAn, WGAA, WGAAn)

Dunne, Philip: *How Green Was My Valley* (1941, AAn), *The Ghost and Mrs. Muir* (1947), *Pinky* (1949, with Dudley Nichols), Laurel Award (1962), Davies Award (1974)

Eckstein, George: *The Untouchables* (1959–1963), *The Fugitive* (1963–1967, WGAAn), *The Bad Seed* (1985, WGAAn)

Ephron, Nora: *Silkwood* (1983, with Alice Arlen, AAn, WGAAn), *When Harry Met Sally . . .* (1989, AAn, WGAAn), *Sleepless in Seattle* (1993, with David S. Ward and Jeff Arch, AAn, WGAAn), Hunter Award (2003), *Julie & Julia* (2009, WGAAn)

Epstein, Julius J.: *Four Daughters* (1938, with Lenore J. Coffee, AAn), *The Man Who Came to Dinner* (1942, with Philip G. Epstein), *Casablanca* (1942, with Philip G. Epstein and Howard Koch, AA), *Arsenic and Old Lace* (1944, with Philip G. Epstein), Laurel Award (1956), *Reuben, Reuben* (1983, AAn, WGAA)

Estabrook, Howard: *Street of Chance* (1930, with Lenore J. Coffee, AAn), *Cimarron* (1931, AA), *David Copperfield* (1935), *The Bridge of San Luis Rey* (1944)

Eszterhas, Joe: *Flashdance* (1983, with Thomas Hedley Jr.), *Basic Instinct* (1992), *Showgirls* (1995)

Fey, Tina: *Saturday Night Live* (1975–present, head writer 1999–2006, EA, WGAA), *Mean Girls* (2004, WGAAn), *30 Rock* (2006–2013, creator, EA, WGAA)

Fitzgerald, F. Scott: *Three Comrades* (1938, with Edward E. Paramore Jr.)

Fontana, Tom: *St. Elsewhere* (1982–1988, EA, WGAA, Humanitas Prize), *Homicide: Life on the Street* (1993–1999, EA, WGAA), *Oz* (1997–2003, creator, WGAAn), Jablow Award (2009), *Copper* (2013–2013, creator with Will Rokos)

Foreman, Carl: *The Men* (1950, AA, WGAAn, Meltzer Award), *High Noon* (1952, AAn, WGAA), *The Bridge on the River Kwai* (1957, with Michael Wilson, AA, credit and Academy Award restored 1984), *The Guns of Navarone* (1961, AAn), Laurel Award (1969), Davies Award (1977), blacklisted

Foster, Lewis R.: *Mr. Smith Goes to Washington* (1939, with Sidney Buchman, AA), *Manhandled* (1949, with Whitman Chambers), *Walt Disney's Wonderful World of Color* (1954–1992)

Foster, William: *The Railroad Porter* (1912), founder in 1910 of the Foster Photoplay Company

Freedman, Benedict: *The Red Skelton Hour* (1951–1971), *The Andy Griffith Show* (1960–1968), *My Favorite Martian* (1963–1966)

Freedman, Hy: *You Bet Your Life* (1950–1961)

Freeman, Devery: *Francis in the Navy* (1955), *The Loretta Young Show* (1953–1961), *The Girl Most Likely* (1958, with Paul Jarrico, WGAAn), *20th Century Fox Hour* (1958, WGAA), WGA Guild Service Award (1982), SWG founding member

Freeman, Everett: *The Princess and the Pirate* (1944, with Don Hartman and Melville Shavelson), *Bachelor Father* (1957–1962), *Marjorie Morningstar* (1958)

Froelick, Anne: *The Master Race* (1944, with Herbert Biberman), *Harriet Craig* (1950, with James Gunn), blacklisted

Furia, John, Jr.: *Bonanza* (1959–1973), *The Twilight Zone* (1959–1964), *The Singing Nun* (1966), *Hawaii Five-O* (1968–1980), *The Waltons* (1971–1981), WGAw president 1973–1975, Cox Award (1978), Davies Award (1990), North Award (1994), founding trustee Humanitas Prize, founding chair of writing division, USC School of Cinema-Television

Gaghan, Stephen: *NYPD Blue* (1993–2005, with Michael R. Perry and David Milch, EA), *Traffic* (2000, AA, WGAA), *Syriana* (2005, AAn, WGAAn)

Garcia, Greg Thomas: *Yes, Dear* (2000–2006, creator with Alan Kirschenbaum), *My Name Is Earl* (2005–2009, creator, EA, WGAAn, Humanitas Prize), *Raising Hope* (2010–present, creator)

Garrett, Lila: *Bewitched* (1964–1972), *The Other Woman* (1983, with Anne Meara, WGAA), *The Nanny* (1993–1999)

Gelbart, Larry: *Caesar's Hour* (1954–1957, EAn), *M*A*S*H* (1972–1983, EA, WGAA, Humanitas Prize), *Oh, God!* (1977, AAn, WGAA), Laurel Award (1981), *Tootsie* (1982, with Murray Schisgal, AAn, WGAA), *Barbarians at the Gate* (1993, EAn, WGAA), Davies Award (2007)

Gelsey, Erwin: *Flying Down to Rio* (1933), *Gold Diggers of 1933* (1933), *Swing Time* (1936)

George, Terry: *In the Name of the Father* (1993, with Jim Sheridan, AAn, WGAAn), *The District* (2000–2004, creator), *Hotel Rwanda* (2004, with Keir Pearson, AAn, WGAAn, Humanitas Prize)

Gibney, Sheridan: *The Story of Louis Pasteur* (1936, with Pierre Collings, AA), *Anthony Adverse* (1936), SWG president (1939–1941, 1947–1948), *Once Upon a Honeymoon* (1942, with Leo McCarey), *Bachelor Father* (1957–1962), blacklisted

Gilligan, Vince: *The X-Files* (1993–2002, with Chris Carter, John Shiban, and Frank Spotnitz, EAn), *Hancock* (2008, with Vincent Ngo), *Breaking Bad* (2008–2013, creator, EA, WGAA)

Gilroy, Tony: *The Cutting Edge* (1992), *Dolores Claiborne* (1995), *The Bourne Identity* (2002, with William Blake Herron), *Michael Clayton* (2007, AAn, WGAAn)

Goff, Ivan: *White Heat* (1949, with Ben Roberts and Virginia Kellogg), *Man of a Thousand Faces* (1957, with Ralph Wheelwright, R. Wright Campbell, and Ben Roberts, AAn), *Mannix* (1967–1975), *Charlie's Angels* (1976–1981, creator with Ben Roberts)

Goldemberg, Rose Leiman: *The Burning Bed* (1984, EAn WGAA), *Stone Pillow* (1985), *Florence Nightingale* (1985)

Goldman, William: *Harper* (1966, WGAAn), *Butch Cassidy and the Sundance Kid* (1969, AA, WGAA), *All the President's Men* (1976, AA, WGAA), *Marathon Man* (1976, WGAAn), Laurel Award (1985), *The Princess Bride* (1987, WGAAn), *Misery* (1990)

Goodman, David A.: *The Golden Girls* (1985–1992), *Family Guy* (1999–present), *Futurama* (1999–2013), *Star Trek: Enterprise* (2001–2005), Meltzer Award (2004, with Mike Barker, Rob Cohen, Jonathan Groff, Cheryl Holliday, Vanessa McCarthy, Glasgow Phillips, Jon Pollack, Jon Ross, Ron Weiner, Matt Weitzman, and Jean Yu, in recognition of extraordinary courage shown in their efforts to advance animation organizing)

Goodrich, Frances: *The Thin Man* (1934, with Albert Hackett, AAn), *It's a Wonderful Life* (1946, with Albert Hackett and Frank Capra), *Father of the Bride* (1950, with Albert Hackett, AAn, WGAAn), *Seven Brides for Seven Brothers* (1954, with Albert Hackett and Dorothy Kingsley, AAn, WGAA), *The Diary of Anne Frank* (1959, with Albert Hackett, WGAA), Laurel Award (1956)

Gordon, Bernard: *Flesh and Fury* (1952, with William Alland), *Earth vs. the Flying Saucers* (1956, pseudonym Raymond T. Marcus, with George Worthing Yates and Curt Siodmak), *Hellcats of the Navy* (1957, pseudonym Raymond T. Marcus, with David Lang, credit restored 1997), *55 Days at Peking* (1963, pseudonym Philip Yordan, credit restored 1997), blacklisted

Gordon, Ruth: *Adam's Rib* (1949, with Garson Kanin, AAn, WGAAn), *Pat and Mike* (1952, with Garson Kanin, AAn, WGAAn), *The Actress* (1953, WGAAn)

Gottlieb, Carl: *The Smothers Brothers Comedy Hour* (1967–1970, EA), *Jaws* (1975, WGAAn), *The Jerk* (1979, with Steve Martin and Michael Elias), Cox Award (2010)

Graham, Garrett: *A Texas Steer* (1928, with Bernard McConville and Will Rogers), *The Noose* (1928), *Sweetheart of the Navy* (1937, with Carroll Graham and Jay Strauss)

Grant, Susannah: *Pocahontas* (1995), *Erin Brockovich* (2000, AAn, WGAAn), *A Gifted Man* (2011–2012, creator), Davies Award (2011, with Seth Freeman)

Grayson, Charles: *Young Fugitives* (1938, with Ben Grauman Kohn), *One Night in the Tropics* (1940, with Gertrude Purcell), *Battle Hymn* (1957, with Vincent B. Evans)

Greaves, William: *Symbiopsychotaxiplasm: Take One* (1968), *Ralph Bunche: An American Odyssey* (2001), *Symbiopsychotaxiplasm: Take 2½* (2005)

Green, Howard J.: *The Kid Brother* (1927), SWG president (1933), *I Am a Fugitive from a Chain Gang* (1932, with Brown Holmes), *Morning Glory* (1933), *The Gene Autry Show* (1950–1955)

Groening, Matt: *The Tracy Ullman Show* (1986, EAn), *The Simpsons* (1989–present, developed with James L. Brooks and Sam Simon), *Futurama* (1999–2013), *The Simpsons Movie* (2007, with James L. Brooks et al.), WGA Animation Award (2013)

Gunn, Mark: *2gether: The Series* (2000–2001, creator with Brian Gunn), *Bring It On Again* (2004, with Brian Gunn and Claudia Grazioso), *Journey 2: The Mysterious Island* (2012, with Brian Gunn)

Hackett, Albert: *The Thin Man* (1934, with Frances Goodrich, AAn), *It's a Wonderful Life* (1946, with Frances Goodrich and Frank Capra), *Father of the Bride* (1950, with Frances Goodrich, AAn, WGAAn), *Seven Brides for Seven Brothers* (1954, with Frances Goodrich and Dorothy Kingsley, AAn, WGAA), Laurel Award (1956), *The Diary of Anne Frank* (1959, with Frances Goodrich, WGAA)

Hackford, Taylor: *Bukowski* (1973), *Ray* (2004, with James L. White)

Hammett, Dashiell: *Watch on the Rhine* (1943, AAn), blacklisted

Harmon, David P.: *The Man Behind the Badge* (1953–1955), *Walt Disney's Wonderful World of Color* (1954–1992), *Gilligan's Island* (1964–1967), *The Brady Bunch* (1969–1974), Cox Award (1973)

Harris, Susan: *Benson* (1979–1986, creator, Humanitas Prize, 1983), *The Golden Girls* (1985–1992, creator, EAn), *Empty Nest* (1988–1995), Laurel Award (2005)

Harrison, Joan: *Rebecca* (1940, with Robert E. Sherwood, AAn), *Suspicion* (1941, with Samson Raphaelson and Alma Reville), *Saboteur* (1942, with Peter Viertel and Dorothy Parker), *Foreign Correspondent* (1946, AAn)

Hart, Moss: *Winged Victory* (1944), *Gentlemen's Agreement* (1947, AAn), *Hans Christian Andersen* (1952, WGAAn), *A Star Is Born* (1954, WGAAn)

Hayes, John Michael: *Rear Window* (1954, AAn, WGAAn), *To Catch a Thief* (1955, WGAAn), *The Man Who Knew Too Much* (1956), *Peyton Place* (1957, AAn, WGAAn), Laurel Award (2004)

Haynes, Todd: *Safe* (1995), *Velvet Goldmine* (1998), *Far from Heaven* (2002, AAn, WGAAn), *I'm Not There* (2007), *Mildred Pierce* (2011, with Jonathan Raymond, EAn, WGAAn)

Hecht, Ben: *Underworld* (1927, AA), *Scarface* (1932), *The Scoundrel* (1935, with Charles MacArthur, AA), *Wuthering Heights* (1939, with Charles MacArthur, AAn), *Spellbound* (1945), *Notorious* (1946, AAn), Laurel Award (1981)

Hellman, Lillian: *These Three* (1936), *The Little Foxes* (1941, AAn), *Watch on the Rhine* (1943, with Dashiell Hammett), *The Children's Hour* (1961), blacklisted

Henderson, Felicia: *Moesha* (1996–2001), *Sister, Sister* (1994–1999), *Soul Food* (creator, 2000–2004), *Gossip Girl* (2007–2012), *Fringe* (2008–2013)

Herbert, F. Hugh: *Three Faces West* (1940, with Samuel Ornitz and Joseph Moncure March), *Sitting Pretty* (1948, WGAA), *The Moon Is Blue* (1953, WGAAn), SWG president (1953–1954), *Meet Corliss Archer* (1954–1955)

Herskovitz, Marshall: *thirtysomething* (1987–1991, creator with Edward Zwick, EA, WGAA, Humanitas Prize), *My So-Called Life* (1994–1995), *Once and Again* (1999–2002, creator with Edward Zwick, Humanitas Prize), *The Last Samurai* (2003, with John Logan and Edward Zwick), Laurel Award (2012, with Edward Zwick)

Hertz, David: *The Devil Is a Woman* (1935), *Love Crazy* (1941, with Charles Lederer and William Ludwig), *Daisy Kenyon* (1947)

Hilton, James: *Camille* (1936, with Zoe Akins and Francis Marion), *Mrs. Miniver* (1941, with Arthur Wimperis, George Froeschel, and Claudine West, AA)

Holland, Charles: *Murder One* (1995–1997), *Profiler* (1996–2000), *Soul Food* (2000–2004), *JAG* (1995–2005), WGAw president (2004)

Holofcener, Nicole: *Walking and Talking* (1996), *Lovely and Amazing* (2001), *Friends with Money* (2006), *Please Give* (2010, WGAAn), *Enough Said* (2013)

Hopper, Dennis: *Easy Rider* (1969, with Peter Fonda and Terry Southern, AAn, WGAAn), *The Last Movie* (1971, with Stewart Stern)

Howard, Bruce: *The Red Skelton Show* (1951–1971, EAn), *The Beatles* (1965–1967), *The Love Boat* (1977–1987)

Hughes, Rupert: SWG president (1921–1933), *Souls for Sale* (1923), *Tess of the Storm Country* (1932, with Sonya Levien and S. N. Behrman)

Hume, Edward: *The Streets of San Francisco* (1972–1977, creator), *Barnaby Jones* (1973–1980), *The Day After* (1983, EAn, WGAA), Humanitas Prize (1990)

Hunter, Ian McClellan: *The Amazing Dr. X* (1948, with Muriel Roy Bolton), *Roman Holiday* (1953, as front for Dalton Trumbo, with John Dighton, AA, WGAA), *The Adventures of Robin Hood* (1955–1960, pseudonym Samuel B. West), blacklisted

Huston, John: *The Maltese Falcon* (1941, AAn), *The Treasure of the Sierra Madre* (1948, AA, WGAA), *Key Largo* (1948, with Richard Brooks, WGAAn), *The African Queen* (1951, with James Agee, AAn), *Heaven Knows, Mr. Allison* (1957, with John Lee Mahin, AAn, WGAAn), Laurel Award (1964), *The Man Who Would Be King* (1975, with Gladys Hill, AAn, WGAAn)

Huxley, Aldous: *Pride and Prejudice* (1940, with Jane Murfin), *Jane Eyre* (1943, with Robert Stevenson and John Houseman)

Isaacs, Charles: *The Colgate Comedy Hour* (1950–1955), *The Dinah Shore Chevy Show* (1956–1963), *Alice* (1976–1985)

Isaacs, David: *M*A*S*H* (1972–1983, with Ken Levine, EAn, WGAAn), *Cheers* (1982–1993, with Ken Levine, EAn, WGAA), *Frasier* (1993–2004, with Ken Levine, EAn), *Mad Men* (2007–present, WGAA)

Jarmusch, Jim: *Stranger Than Paradise* (1984), *Dead Man* (1995), *Ghost Dog: The Way of the Samurai* (1999), *Broken Flowers* (2005)

Jarrico, Paul: *Tom, Dick and Harry* (1941, AAn), *Thousands Cheer* (1943, with Richard Collins), *Song of Russia* (1944, with Richard Collins), *The Las Vegas Story* (1952, credit restored), *The Girl Most Likely* (1958, with Devery Freeman, credit restored, WGAAn), Meltzer Award (1999), blacklisted

Jennings, Talbot: *Mutiny on the Bounty* (1935, with Jules Furthman and Carey Wilson, AAn), *Anna and the King of Siam* (1946, AAn, with Sally Benson), *Knights of the Round Table* (1953, with Jan Lustig and Noel Langley)

Jhabvala, Ruth Prawer: *A Room with a View* (1985, AA, WGAA), *Howards End* (1992, AA, WGAAn), *The Remains of the Day* (1993, AAn, WGAAn), Hunter Award (1993), Laurel Award (1994), *Le Divorce* (2003, with James Ivory)

Johnson, Nunnally: *The Grapes of Wrath* (1940, AAn), *How to Marry a Millionaire* (1953, WGAAn), *The Man in the Gray Flannel Suit* (1956), *The Three Faces of Eve* (1957), Laurel Award (1959), *The Dirty Dozen* (1967, with Lukas Heller)

Jones, Grover: *Trouble in Paradise* (1932, with Samson Raphaelson), *Lady and Gent* (1932, with William Slavens McNutt, AAn), *The Lives of a Bengal Lancer* (1935, with Achmed Abdullah, John L. Balderston, Waldemar Young, and William Slavens McNutt, AAn)

Kahn, Gordon: *The Death Kiss* (1932, with Barry Barringer), *Song of Nevada* (1944, with Olive Cooper), blacklisted

Kaling, Mindy: *The Office* (2005–2013, with Greg Daniels, EAn, WGAA), *The Mindy Project* (2012–present, creator, WGAAn)

Kalish, Austin "Rocky": *The Colgate Comedy Hour* (1950–1955), *Family Affair* (1966–1971), *All in the Family* (1971–1973), *Good Times* (1974–1979)

Kanin, Fay: *Teacher's Pet* (1958, with Michael Kanin, AAn, WGAAn), *Tell Me Where It Hurts* (1974, EA), Davies Award (1975), *Friendly Fire* (1979, EAn, WGAA, Peabody Award), AMPAS president (1979–1983), Cox Award (1980), North Award (2005)

Kanin, Michael: *Woman of the Year* (1942, with Ring Lardner Jr., AA), *Teacher's Pet* (1958, with Fay Kanin, AAn, WGAAn), Davies Award (1989, with Garson Kanin)

Kanter, Hal: *Road to Bali* (1952, with Frank Butler and William Morrow), *Julia* (1968–1971, creator), *The Annual Academy Awards* (15 shows, 1968–2008, EA, WGAAn), Davies Award (1983), Laurel Award (1989), Cox Award (2005)

Kasdan, Lawrence: *Star Wars: The Empire Strikes Back* (1977, with Leigh Brackett, AAn, WGAAn), *The Big Chill* (1983, AAn, WGAA), Laurel Award (2006)

Kaufman, Charlie: *Being John Malkovich* (1999, AAn, WGAAn), *Adaptation.* (2002, with Donald Kaufman, AAn, WGAAn), *Eternal Sunshine of the Spotless Mind* (2004, with Michel Gondry and Pierre Bismuth, AA, WGAA)

Kaufman, George S.: *Dinner at Eight* (1933, play, with Edna Ferber), *A Night at the Opera* (1935, with Morrie Ryskind), *Stage Door* (1937, play, with Edna Ferber)

Keller, Sheldon: *Caesar's Hour* (1954–1957, EAn), *An Evening with Carol Channing* (1966, with Hal Goldman and Al Gordon, EA) *Buona Sera, Mrs. Campbell* (1969, with Melvin Frank and Denis Norden, WGAAn), *M*A*S*H* (1972–1983, with Laurence Marks, WGAAn), *Movie Movie* (1978, with Larry Gelbart, WGAA)

Kelley, David E.: *L.A. Law* (1986–1994, EA, WGAAn), Selvin Award (1996), *Ally McBeal* (1997–2002, creator, EAn), *The Practice* (1997–2004, creator, EAn, WGAAn, Humanitas Prize), Laurel Award (2003)

Kellogg, Virginia: *T-Men* (1947, with John C. Higgins), *White Heat* (1949, with Ivan Goff and Ben Roberts, AAn), *Caged* (1950, AAn)

Khan, Nahnatchka: *Malcolm in the Middle* (2000–2006), *American Dad!* (2005–present), *Don't Trust the B—in Apartment 23* (2012–2013, creator)

Khouri, Callie: *Thelma & Louise* (1991, AA, WGAA), *Something to Talk About* (1995), *Nashville* (2012–present, WGAAn)

Kim, Susan: *Mystery Files of Shelby Woo* (1996–1999, WGAAn), *Happily Ever After: Fairy Tales for Every Child* (1995–2008), *Dragon Tales* (1999–2005), *Stanley* (2001–2007), *Pocoyo* (2005–2009), Jablow Award (2012)

King, Michael Patrick: *Murphy Brown* (1988–1998), *Sex and the City* (1998–2004, EAn), *The Comeback* (2005–present, creator with Lisa Kudrow), *2 Broke Girls* (2011–present, creator with Whitney Cummings)

Kinoy, Ernest: *Goodyear Playhouse* (1951–1957), *Naked City* (1958–1963, WGAAn), *The Defenders* (1961–1965, EA, WGAAn), WGA East president (1967–1971), *Roots* (1977, with William Blinn, EA, WGAAn), Laurel Award (1978), Jablow Award (1981), Hunter Award (1996)

Klarik, Jeffrey: *Dream On* (1990–1996), *Half & Half* (2002–2006, creator), *Episodes* (2011–present, creator with David Crane, EAn, WGAAn)

Knopf, Christopher: *Zane Grey Theater* (1956–1961, WGAA), *Dr. Kildare* (1961–1966), WGAw president (1965–1967), *Equal Justice* (1990–1991, creator with Thomas Carter and David A. Simons), Cox Award (1991), North Award (2002)

Kober, Arthur: *Me and My Gal* (1932), *The Little Foxes* (1941, with Lillian Hellman), *Leave It to Beaver* (1957–1963)

Koch, Howard: *Sergeant York* (1941, with Harry Chandlee and Abem Finkel, AAn), *Casablanca* (1942, with Julius J. Epstein and Philip G. Epstein, AA), *Mission to Moscow* (1943), *Letter from an Unknown Woman* (1948), blacklisted

Koenig, Lester: *The Memphis Belle* (1944, documentary short), *Thunderbolt* (1947, documentary short), blacklisted

Kohan, Jenji: *Tracey Takes On . . .* (1996–1999, EAn), *Weeds* (2005–2012, creator, WGAA), *Orange Is the New Black* (2013–present, creator, EAn, WGAAn)

Komack, James: *My Favorite Martian* (1963–1966), *The Courtship of Eddie's Father* (1969–1972, EAn), *Welcome Back, Kotter* (1975–1979, with Alan Sacks, George Yanok, and Eric Cohen)

Koppelman, Brian: *Runaway Jury* (2003, with David Levien, Rick Cleveland, and Matthew Chapman), *Tilt* (2005, creator with David Levien), *Ocean's Thirteen* (2007, with David Levien)

Kubrick, Stanley: *Dr. Strangelove* (1964, with Terry Southern and Peter George, AAn, WGAA), *2001: A Space Odyssey* (1968, with Arthur C. Clarke, AAn), *Full Metal Jacket* (1987, with Michael Herr and Gustav Hasford, AAn, WGAAn)

Kudrow, Lisa: *The Comeback* (2005, creator with Michael Patrick King), *Web Therapy* (2008–present, web series, creator with Dan Bucatinski and Don Roos), *Web Therapy* (2011–present, television series, creator with Dan Bucatinsky and Don Roos)

Lardner, Ring, Jr.: *Woman of the Year* (1942, with Michael Kanin, AA), *The Adventures of Robin Hood* (1955–1960), *M*A*S*H* (1970, AA, WGAA), Laurel Award (1989), Hunter Award (1992), blacklisted

Lavery, Emmet: *Behind the Rising Sun* (1943), SWG president (1945–1947), *The Magnificent Yankee* (1950, with Francis Biddle), *The First Legion* (1957, WGAAn), *The Court-Martial of Billy Mitchell* (1955, with Milton Sperling, AAn)

Lawson, John Howard: *Blockade* (1938, AAn), *Algiers* (1938), *Action in the North Atlantic* (1943), *Cry, the Beloved Country* (1951, with Alan Paton, credit restored), SWG founding member, blacklisted

Lazarus, Erna: *The Body Disappears* (1941, with Scott Darling), *The Donna Reed Show* (1958–1966), *Surfside 6* (1960–1962),

Lear, Norman: *Divorce American Style* (1967, with Robert Kaufman, AAn, WGAAn), *All in the Family* (1971–1979, creator, EAn), *Maude* (1972–1978, creator), *The Jeffersons* (1975–1985), Davies Award (1978), Peabody Award (1978), Laurel Award (1993), National Medal of Arts (1999)

Lee, Ang: *The Wedding Banquet* (1993, with Neil Peng and James Schamus), *Eat Drink Man Woman* (1994, with Wang Hui-Ling and James Schamus)

Lee, Spike: *Do the Right Thing* (1989, AAn), *Malcolm X* (1992, with Arnold Perl), *25th Hour* (2002)

Lehman, Ernest: *Sabrina* (1954, with Billy Wilder and Samuel Taylor, AAn, WGAA), *The King and I* (1956, WGAA), *Sweet Smell of Success* (1957, with Clifford Odets), *North by Northwest* (1959, AAn, WGAAn), *West Side Story* (1961, AAn, WGAA), *The Sound of Music* (1965, WGAA), *Who's Afraid of Virginia Woolf?* (1966, AAn, WGAA), Laurel Award (1972), WGAw president (1983–1985)

Leight, Warren: *Law & Order: Criminal Intent* (2001–2011), Jablow Award (2006), *In Treatment* (2008–2011, Humanitas Prize), *Lights Out* (2011)

Lenard, Kay: *Ma and Pa Kettle at Home* (1954), *Father Knows Best* (1954–1960), *Combat!* (1962–1967), *Day of Our Lives* (1965–present, EA, WGAAn)

Lesser, Frank: *The Colbert Report* (2005–present, EA, WGAA)

Levien, Sonya: *State Fair* (1933, with Paul Green, AAn), *The Hunchback of Notre Dame* (1939), *Ziegfeld Girl* (1941, with Marguerite Roberts), Laurel Award (1953), *Oklahoma!* (1953, with William Ludwig, WGAAn), *Interrupted Melody* (1955, with William Ludwig, AA)

Levine, Ken: *M*A*S*H* (1972–1983, with David Isaacs, EAn, WGAAn), *Cheers* (1982–1993, with David Isaacs, EAn, WGAA), *Frasier* (1993–2004, with David Isaacs, EAn)

Levinson, Chris: *Law & Order* (1990–2010), *Dawson's Creek* (1998–2003), *Touch* (2012–2013)

Levinson, Richard: *My Sweet Charlie* (1970, with William Link, EA), *Columbo* (1971–2003, with William Link, EA, WGAAn), *That Certain Summer* (1972, with William Link, EAn, WGAA), *Murder, She Wrote* (1984–1996, creator with William Link and Peter S. Fischer), Laurel Award (1986, with William Link)

Levitt, Alfred L., and Helen Levitt (as Tom and Helen August while blacklisted, credit restored 1997): *The Misadventures of Merlin Jones* (1964), *The Monkey's Uncle* (1965), *That Girl* (1966–1971), Cox Award (1995), blacklisted

Lilly, Courtney: *Arrested Development* (2003–2006, WGAAn), *Everybody Hates Chris* (2005–2009, WGAAn), *My Boys* (2006–2010), *The Cleveland Show* (2009–2013)

Link, William: *My Sweet Charlie* (1970, with Richard Levinson, EA), *Columbo* (1968–2003, with Richard Levinson, EA, WGAAn), *That Certain Summer* (1972, with Richard Levinson, EAn, WGAA), *Murder, She Wrote* (1984–1986, creator with Richard Levinson and Peter S. Fischer), Laurel Award (1986, with Richard Levinson), *The Boys* (1991)

Livier, Ruth: *Ylse* (2008–2010, web series, creator)

Loh, Sandra Tsing: *Clueless* (1996–1999), *Chicken Little* (2005, additional dialogue)

Loos, Anita: *Intolerance* (1916, with D. W. Griffith), *The Women* (1939, with Jane Murfin), *Gentlemen Prefer Blondes* (1953, with Joseph Fields and Charles Lederer)

Lord, Stephen: *Death Valley Days* (1952–1970), *CHiPs* (1977–1983), *Fantasy Island* (1977–1984)

Love, Jasmine: *Moesha* (1996–2001), *The District* (2000–2004), *The Division* (2001–2004)

Lubitsch, Ernst: *Trouble in Paradise* (1932, with Samson Raphaelson and Grover Jones), *To Be or Not to Be* (1942, with Edwin Justus Mayer), Honorary AA (1947)

Lucas, George: *American Graffiti* (1973, with Gloria Katz and William Huyck, AAn, WGAAn), *Star Wars: A New Hope* (1977, AAn, WGAAn), *Raiders of the Lost Ark* (1981, WGAAn)

Ludwig, William: *Love Crazy* (1941, with David Hertz and Charles Lederer), *Oklahoma!* (1954, with Sonya Levien, WGAAn), *Interrupted Melody* (1955, with Sonya Levien, AA), Davies Award (1973), Cox Award (1976), North Award (1992)

Lynch, David: *The Elephant Man* (1980, with Christopher DeVore and Eric Bergren, AAn, WGAAn), *Blue Velvet* (1986, WGAAn), *Twin Peaks* (1990–1991, creator with Mark Frost, EAn), *Mulholland Drive* (2001)

MacDougall, Ranald: *Mildred Pierce* (1945, AAn), *Objective, Burma!* (1945, with Alvah Bessie and Lester Cole), *Westinghouse Playhouse* (1961, creator), WGAw president (1971–1973), North Award (1974)

Macpherson, Jeanie: *The Cheat* (1915, with Hector Turnbull), *Male and Female* (1919), *The Ten Commandments* (1923), AMPAS co-founder

Mahin, John Lee: *Captains Courageous* (1937, with Marc Connelly and Dale Van Every, AAn), *Show Boat* (1951, WGAAn), *Heaven Knows, Mr. Allison* (1957, with John Huston, AAn, WGAAn), Laurel Award (1958)

Maltz, Albert: *The Naked City* (1948, with Malvin Wald, WGAAn), *Broken Arrow* (1950, with Michael Blankfort as front, credit restored 1991, AAn, WGAA), *The Robe* (1953, with Philip Dunne, credit restored 1997), *Two Mules for Sister Sara* (1970), blacklisted

Mankiewicz, Herman J.: *Dinner at Eight* (1933, with Frances Marion), *Citizen Kane* (1941, with Orson Welles, AA), *The Pride of the Yankees* (1942, with Jo Swerling, AAn)

Mankiewicz, Joseph L.: *Alice in Wonderland* (1933), *A Letter to Three Wives* (1949, AA, WGAA), *All About Eve* (1950, AA, WGAA), *The Barefoot Contessa* (1954, AAn, WGAAn), Laurel Award (1963)

Mann, Michael: *Vega$* (1978–1981, creator), *The Jericho Mile* (1979, EA), *Thief* (1981), *Manhunter* (1986), *Heat* (1995), *The Insider* (1999, with Eric Roth, AAn, Selvin Award, WGAAn), Humanitas Prize (2000), *Ali* (2001, with Gregory Allen Howard, Stephen J. Rivele, Christopher Wilkinson, and Eric Roth)

Manoff, Arnold: *Man from Frisco* (1944, with Ethel Hill), *Casbah* (1948, with Leslie Bush-Fekete), *You Are There* (1953–1957, uncredited), *Naked City* (1958–1963, pseudonym Joel Carpenter), blacklisted

Marcus, Ellis: *Lux Video Theatre* (1950–1959), *I Led Three Lives* (1954–1956), *Ben Casey* (1961–1966, WGAAn), *Knots Landing* (1981–1982)

Marion, Frances: *The Son of the Sheik* (1926, with Fred De Gresac), *The Big House* (1930, AA), *The Champ* (1931, AA), *Dinner at Eight* (1933, with Herman J. Mankiewicz), *The Prizefighter and the Lady* (1933, AAn), *Camille* (1936, with Zoe Akins and James Hilton)

Markes, Larry: *McHale's Navy* (1962–1966), *For Love or Money* (1963, with Michael Morris), *The Dean Martin Comedy Hour* (1965–1974)

Marshall, Garry: *The Odd Couple* (1970–1975, creator), *Happy Days* (1974–1984, creator), *Laverne & Shirley* (1976–1983, creator), Davies Award (1995), Laurel Award (2014)

Martel, Jay: *TV Nation* (1994–1995), *The Awful Truth* (1999–2000), *Key & Peele* (2012–present, EAn, WGAAn)

Marx, Christy: *Jem* (1985–1988), *Conquests of Camelot: The Search for the Grail* (1989, video game), *Hypernauts* (1996, creator with Ron Thornton), *The Legend of Alon D'ar* (2001, video game), Animation Award (2000)

Marx, Samuel: *Society Doctor* (1935, with Michael Fessier), *Duel in the Jungle* (1954, with T. J. Morrison), *Naked City* (1958–1963)

Mathis, June: *Four Horsemen of the Apocalypse* (1921), *Blood and Sand* (1922), *Greed* (1924, with Erich von Stroheim), *Ben Hur: A Tale of the Christ* (1925, with Lew Wallace, Carey Wilson, and Bess Meredyth)

Mathison, Melissa: *The Black Stallion* (1979, with Jeanne Rosenberg and William D. Wittliff), *E.T. the Extra-Terrestrial* (1982, AAn, WGAA), *Kundun* (1997)

Maugham, W. Somerset: *Trio* (1950, with Noel Langley), *Somerset Maugham Hour* (1960–1963, stories)

May, Elaine: *A New Leaf* (1971, WGAAn), *Heaven Can Wait* (1978, with Warren Beatty, AAn, WGAA), *The Birdcage* (1996, WGAAn), *Primary Colors* (1998, AAn, WGAAn)

Mazin, Craig: *Scary Movie 4* (2006, with Jim Abrahams and Pat Proft), *The Hangover Part II* (2011, with Scot Armstrong and Todd Phillips), *Identity Thief* (2013)

McCall, Mary C., Jr.: *Craig's Wife* (1936), SWG president (1942–1944 and 1951–1952), *The Fighting Sullivans* (1944, with Edward Doherty and Jules Schermer), *The Millionaire* (1955–1960), Davies Award (1962), *Gilligan's Island* (1964–1967), North Award (1985)

McCall, Ross: *Just Shoot Me!* (1997–2003), *The Andy Dick Show* (2001–2003)

McGuinness, James K.: *A Girl in Every Port* (1928, with Howard Hawks and Seton I. Miller), *A Night at the Opera* (1935), *Rio Grande* (1950, WGAAn)

McKenna, Aline Brosh: *The Devil Wears Prada* (2006, WGAAn), *27 Dresses* (2008), *Annie* (2014, with Will Gluck and Emma Thompson)

McNutt, Patterson: *Curly Top* (1935, with Arthur J. Beckhard), *Come Live with Me* (1941)

Meadow, Herb: *The Lone Ranger* (1949–1957), *Have Gun—Will Travel* (1957–1963, creator with Sam Rolfe), *The Virginian* (1962–1971, WGAAn)

Medford, Harold: *Berlin Express* (1948, WGAAn), *The Damned Don't Cry* (1950, with Jerome Weidman), *Mannix* (1967–1975)

Mendelsohn, Carol: *Melrose Place* (1992–1999), *CSI: Crime Scene Investigation* (2000–present, WGAAn), *CSI: Miami* (2002–2012, creator with Ann Donahue and Anthony E. Zuicker)

Meredyth, Bess: *Ben-Hur: A Tale of the Christ* (1925, with Lew Wallace, June Mathis, and Carey Wilson), *Wonder of Women* (1929, with Marian Ainslee, AAn), *The Mark of Zorro* (1940, with John Taintor Foote and Garrett Fort), AMPAS co-founder

Monaster, Nate: *The George Burns and Gracie Allen Show* (1950–1958), *The Donna Reed Show* (1958–1966), *That Touch of Mink* (1962, with Stanley Shapiro, AAn, WGAA), WGAw president (1963–1965), Cox Award (1984)

Morris, Edmund: *Colt .45* (1957–1960), *Lawman* (1958–1962), *Walk on the Wild Side* (1962, with John Fante)

Moss, Carlton: *The Negro Soldier* (1944, documentary short), *Frederick Douglass: The House on Cedar Hill* (1953, documentary short)

Moss, Frank L.: *Caribbean* (1952, with Edward Ludwig), *Lassie* (1954–1974), *M Squad* (1957–1960), *Combat!* (1962–1967)

Murray, John Fenton: *The Mickey Rooney Show* (1954–1955), *McHale's Navy* (1962–1966), *The Bugaloos* (1970–1972)

Neuman, E. Jack: *Twilight Zone* (1959–1964), *Mr. Novak* (1963–1965, creator), *The Blue Knight* (1973), *Police Story* (1973–1978, developed for television), *Petrocelli* (1974–1976, developed for television), *Voices Within: The Lives of Truddi Chase* (1990)

Niblo, Fred, Jr.: *The Criminal Code* (1931, with Seton I. Miller, AAn), *The Fighting 69th* (1940, with Norman Reilly Raine and Dean Riesner), *Convicted* (1950, with William Bowers and Seton I. Miller)

Nichols, Dudley: *The Informer* (1935, AA), SWG president (1937–1938), *Bringing Up Baby* (1938, with Hagar Wilde), *Stagecoach* (1939), *The Bells of St. Mary's* (1945), *Scarlet Street* (1945), *Pinky* (1949, WGAAn), Laurel Award (1954)

Norman, Marc: *The Killer Elite* (1975, with Stirling Silliphant), *Cutthroat Island* (1995), *Shakespeare in Love* (1998, with Tom Stoppard, AA, WGAA)

North, Edmund H.: *In a Lonely Place* (1950, with Andrew Solt), *The Day the Earth Stood Still* (1951), Davies Award (1967), *Patton* (1970, with Francis Ford Coppola, AA, WGAA), Cox Award (1975)

Nugent, Frank S.: *Fort Apache* (1948, WGAAn), *She Wore a Yellow Ribbon* (1949, with Laurence Stallings, WGAAn), *The Quiet Man* (1952, AAn, WGAA), *Mister Roberts* (1955, with Joshua Logan, WGAA)

Oboler, Arch: *Escape* (1940, with Marguerite Roberts), *Five* (1951, WGAAn), *Bwana Devil* (1952)

Odets, Clifford: *Humoresque* (1946, with Zachary Gold), *The Country Girl* (1954, play, with George Seaton), *Sweet Smell of Success* (1957, with Ernest Lehman)

Oppenheimer, Jess: *I Love Lucy* (1951–1957, creator, EAn), *Get Smart* (1965–1970), Laurel Award (1992, with Bob Carroll and Madelyn Pugh Davis)

Ornitz, Samuel: *It Could Happen to You!* (1937, with Nathanael West), *Little Orphan Annie* (1938, with Budd Schulberg and Endre Boehm), *Three Faces West* (1940, with F. Hugh Herbert and Joseph Moncure March), SWG founding member, blacklisted

Oxenberg, Jan: *Once and Again* (1999–2003), *Cold Case* (2003–2010), *Parenthood* (2010–present), *Pretty Little Liars* (2013–present)

Palmer, Michael Oates: *The West Wing* (1999–2006), *Shark* (2006–2008), *Rubicon* (2010)

Palumbo, Dennis: *Welcome Back, Kotter* (1975–1979), *My Favorite Year* (1982, with Norman Steinberg, WGAAn)

Parker, Dorothy: *A Star Is Born* (1937, with Alan Campbell and Robert Carson, AAn), *Saboteur* (1942, with Peter Viertel and Joan Harrison), *Smash-Up: The Story of a Woman* (1947, with Frank Cavett and John Howard Lawson, AAn), blacklisted

Pascal, Ernest: SWG president (1935–1937), *Lloyd's of London* (1936, with Walter Ferris), *Wee Willie Winkie* (1937, with Julien Josephson), *The Hound of the Baskervilles* (1939)

Perry, Joyce: *Mosquito Squadron* (1969, with Donald S. Sanford), *Search for Tomorrow* (1974, WGAAn), *Land of the Lost* (1974–1977), *Fantasy Island* (1977–1984)

Petrie, Daniel, Jr.: *Beverly Hills Cop* (1984, with Danilo Bach, AAn), *Toy Soldiers* (1991, with David Koepp), WGAw president (1997–1999 and 2004–2005), *Combat Hospital* (2011, creator with Jinder Chalmers and Douglas Steinberg), Cox Award (2013)

Pierson, Frank: *Cool Hand Luke* (1967, with Donn Pearce, AAn), *Dog Day Afternoon* (1975, AA, WGAA), WGAw president (1981–1983 and 1993–1995), *Presumed Innocent* (1990, with Alan J. Pakula), Davies Award (1991), Laurel Award (1992), North Award (1999), AMPAS president (2001–2005), Cox Award (2006), *Mad Men* (2007–present)

Platten, John Zuur: *Fear Effect* (2000, video game), *Venom* (2005, with Flint Dille and Brandon Boyce), *Transformers: The Game* (2007, video game, with Flint Dille)

Polanski, Roman: *Rosemary's Baby* (1968, AAn, WGAAn), *The Tenant* (1976, with Gérard Bach), *Carnage* (2011, with Yasmina Reza)

Polonsky, Abraham: *Body and Soul* (1947, AAn), *Force of Evil* (1948, with Ira Wolfert), *You Are There* (1953–1957, uncredited), *Odds Against Tomorrow* (1959, with Nelson Gidding, with John O. Killens as front, credit restored 1997), *Monsignor* (1982, with Wendell Mayes), blacklisted

Powell, Richard M.: *The Andy Griffith Show* (1960–1968), *Gomer Pyle: USMC* (1964–1969), *Hogan's Heroes* (1965–1971), Cox Award (1994)

Presnell, Robert R., Sr.: *The Real Glory* (1939, with Jo Swirling), *Meet John Doe* (1941, with Robert Riskin and Richard Connell, AAn), *Perry Mason* (1957–1966)

Rabe, David: *I'm Dancing as Fast as I Can* (1982), *Casualties of War* (1989), *The Firm* (1993, with Robert Towne and David Rayfiel)

Rader, Peter: *Waterworld* (1995, with David Twohy)

Rand, Ayn: *Love Letters* (1945), *The Fountainhead* (1949)

Rapf, Maurice: *Song of the South* (1946, with Dalton S. Raymond and Morton Grant), *The Detective* (1954, with Thelma Schnee and Robert Hamer, credit restored 1998), blacklisted

Raphaelson, Samson: *The Jazz Singer* (1927, play), *Trouble in Paradise* (1932, with Grover Jones), *The Merry Widow* (1934, with Ernest Vajda), *The Shop Around the Corner* (1940), *Suspicion* (1941, with Joan Harrison and Alma Reville), *That Lady in Ermine* (1948, WGAAn), Laurel Award (1977), blacklisted

Rapp, Joel: *McHale's Navy* (1964–1966), *The Donna Reed Show* (1964–1965), *Gilligan's Island* (1966–1967)

Reiner, Carl: *Caesar's Hour* (1954–1957), *The Dick Van Dyke Show* (1961–1966, creator, EA, WGAAn), *The 2000-Year-Old Man* (1975, with Mel Brooks), *Dead Men Don't Wear Plaid* (1982, with George Gipe and Steve Martin), Laurel Award (1995), Davies Award (2009)

Reisman, Del: *Playhouse 90* (1956–1961), *Peyton Place* (1964–1969), *Six Million Dollar Man* (1974–1978), WGAw president (1991–1993), Cox Award (1999)

Renoir, Jean: *La Grande Illusion* (1937, with Charles Spaak), *The Rules of the Game* (1939, with Carl Koch), *The Southerner* (1945, with Hugo Butler), Honorary AA (1975)

Rhimes, Shonda: *The Princess Diaries 2: Royal Engagement* (2004, with Gina Wendkos), *Grey's Anatomy* (2005–present, creator, WGAA), *Private Practice* (2007–2013, creator), *Scandal* (2012–present, creator)

Rintels, David W.: *Scorpio* (1973, with Gerald Wilson), WGAw president (1975–1977), *Washington: Behind Closed Doors* (1977, creator), Davies Award (1980), *Andersonville* (1996, WGAAn), Laurel Award (1997), Cox Award (2003)

Riskin, Victoria: *My Antonia* (1995), WGAw president (2001–2004), Davies Award (2009)

Rivera, Jose: *Eerie, Indiana* (1991–1992, creator with Karl Schaefer), *The Motorcycle Diaries* (2004, AAn, WGAAn), *The 33* (2014, with Mikko Alanne, Michael John Bell, and Craig Borten)

Rivkin, Allen: *Dancing Lady* (1933, with P. J. Wolfson), *Dead Reckoning* (1942, with Oliver H. P. Garrett and Steve Fisher), *The Eternal Sea* (1955), Davies Award (1963), Cox Award (1972)

Roberts, Ben: *White Heat* (1949, with Ivan Goff and Virginia Kellogg), *Man of a Thousand Faces* (1957, with Ralph Wheelwright, R. Wright Campbell, and Ivan Goff, AAn), *Mannix* (1967–1975), *Charlie's Angels* (1976–1981, creator with Ivan Goff)

Roberts, Ian: *Upright Citizens Brigade* (1998–2000, creator with Matt Besser, Amy Poehler, and Matt Walsh), *Key & Peele* (2012–present, WGAAn)

Roberts, Marguerite: *Escape* (1940, with Arch Oboler), *Ziegfeld Girl* (1941, with Sonya Levien), *Dragon Seed* (1947, with Jane Murfin), *True Grit* (1969, WGAAn)

Rodman, Howard: *Naked City* (1958–1963, WGAA), *The Man and the City* (1971–1972, creator), *Harry O* (1973–1976, creator), Laurel Award (1980)

Rodman, Howard A.: *Joe Gould's Secret* (2000), *Savage Grace* (2007), *August* (2008)

Rogers, Howard Emmett: *The Mystery of Mr. X* (1934), *For Me and My Gal* (1942, with Richard Sherman, Fred. F. Finklehoffe, and Sid Silvers)

Rolfe, Sam: *The Naked Spur* (1953, with Harold Jack Bloom, AAn), *Have Gun—Will Travel* (1957–1963, creator with Herb Meadow), *The Man from U.N.C.L.E.* (1964–1967, creator)

Roos, Don: *Hart to Hart* (1979–1984), *The Opposite of Sex* (1998, WGAAn), *Marley & Me* (2008), *Web Therapy* (2008–present, web series, creator with Lisa Kudrow and Dan Bucatinsky, EAn), *Web Therapy* (2011–present, television series, creator with Lisa Kudrow and Dan Bucatinsky)

Root, Wells: *The Prisoner of Zenda* (1937, with John L. Balderston and Edward E. Rose), *Magnificent Obsession* (1954, with Robert Blees), *Bat Masterson* (1958–1961), SWG founding member

Rose, Reginald: *Studio One in Hollywood* (1948–1958, EA), *12 Angry Men* (1957, AAn, WGAA), *The Defenders* (1961–1965, creator, EA), Laurel Award (1987)

Ross, Arthur A.: *Creature from the Black Lagoon* (1954, with Harry Essex and Maurice Zimm), *The Alfred Hitchcock Hour* (1962–1965), *The Great Race* (1965, with Blake Edwards, WGAAn), *Brubaker* (1980, with W. D. Richter, AAn)

Rosten, Leo: *The Conspirators* (1944, with Vladimir Pozner), *The Dark Corner* (1946, with Jay Dratler and Bernard C. Schoenfeld), *Sleep, My Love* (1948, with St. Clair McKelway)

Rothschild, Erica: *Just Shoot Me!* (1997–2003), *RoboCop: Alpha Commando* (1998–1999), *Sofia the First* (2012–present, EAn)

Rubin, Stanley: *Your Show Time* (1949), *Macao* (1952, with Bernard C. Schoenfeld)

Ryan, Shawn: *Nash Bridges* (1996–2001), *The Shield* (2002–2008, creator, EAn), *The Chicago Code* (2011, creator)

Ryskind, Morrie: *Animal Crackers* (1930), *A Night at the Opera* (1935, with George S. Kaufman), *My Man Godfrey* (1936, with Eric Hatch, AAn), *Stage Door* (1937, with Anthony Veiller, AAn)

Sagor, Frederica: *The Plastic Age* (1925, with Eve Unsell), *Dance Madness* (1926), *The Shocking Miss Pilgrim* (1947, with George Seaton and Ernest Maas)

Salt, Waldo: *Midnight Cowboy* (1969, AA, WGAA), *Serpico* (1973, with Norman Wexler, AAn, WGAAn), *Coming Home* (1978, with Robert C. Jones and Nancy Dowd, AA, WGAA), Laurel Award (1986), blacklisted

Sargent, Alvin: *Paper Moon* (1973, AAn, WGAA), *Julia* (1977, AA, WGAA), *Ordinary People* (1980, AA, WGAA), Laurel Award (1991), *What About Bob?* (1991, with Tom Schulman and Laura Ziskin), *Spider-Man 2* (2004, with Alfred Gough, Miles Millar, and Michael Chabon)

Savel, Dava: *Dream On* (1990–1996), *Ellen* (1994–1998, EA, WGAAn), *That's So Raven* (2003–2007)

Sayles, John: *Return of the Secaucus Seven* (1979, WGAAn), *Matewan* (1987), *Passion Fish* (1992, AAn, WGAAn), *The Secret of Roan Inish* (1994), *Lone Star* (1996, AAn, WGAAn), Hunter Award (2005)

Schamus, James: *The Wedding Banquet* (1993, with Ang Lee and Neil Peng), *Eat Drink Man Woman* (1994), *The Ice Storm* (1997, WGAAn), *Crouching Tiger, Hidden Dragon* (2000, with Wang-Hui Ling and Tsai Kuo Jung, AAn, WGAAn), Jablow Award (2003), Burkey Award (2014)

Schary, Dore: *Boys Town* (1938, with Eleanore Griffin and John Meehan, AA), *Edison, the Man* (1941, with Hugo Butler, AAn), chief of production at MGM (1951–1956), Davies Award (1969)

Scheft, Bill: *The Late Show with David Letterman* (1993–present, EAn, WGAAn), *The Annual Academy Awards* (2 shows, 1995, 2005)

Schiff, Robin: *Romy and Michele's High School Reunion* (1997), *Grosse Pointe* (2000–2001), *Are You There, Chelsea?* (2012)

Schiller, Robert: *I Love Lucy* (1951–1957, EAn), *The Carol Burnett Show* (1967–1978), *All in the Family* (1971–1979, EA, WGAAn), *Maude* (1972–1978, WGAA), Laurel Award (1988)

Schrader, Paul: *Taxi Driver* (1976, WGAAn), *Raging Bull* (1980, with Mardik Martin), *The Last Temptation of Christ* (1988), *Affliction* (1997), Laurel Award (1999)

Schubert, Bernard: *No Other Woman* (1933, with Wanda Tuchock), *Mark of the Vampire* (1935, with Guy Endore), *The Mummy's Curse* (1944)

Schulberg, Budd: *Winter Carnival* (1939, with Lester Cole and Maurice Rapf), *On the Waterfront* (1954, AA, WGAA), *A Face in the Crowd* (1957), Laurel Award (2008)

Schwartz, Sherwood: *The Red Skelton Show* (1951–1971, EA, WGAA), *Gilligan's Island* (1964–1967, creator), *The Brady Bunch* (1969–1974, creator)

Scorsese, Martin: *Mean Streets* (1973, with Mardik Martin, WGAAn), *Goodfellas* (1990, with Nicholas Pileggi, AAn, WGAAn), *The Age of Innocence* (1993, with Jay Cocks, AAn), *Casino* (1995, with Nicholas Pileggi), Burkey Award (2003)

Scott, Adrian: *Mr. Lucky* (1943, with Milton Holmes), *The Adventures of Robin Hood* (1955–1960, uncredited), *Conspiracy of Hearts* (1960, with Dale Pitt as front, with Robert Presnell Jr.), blacklisted

Scott, Joan LaCour: *Lassie* (1954–1974, pseudonym Joanne Court), *Cairo* (1963, pseudonym Joanne Court), *The Waltons* (1971–1981), blacklisted

Seaton, George: *A Day at the Races* (1937, with Robert Pirosh and George Oppenheimer), *The Song of Bernadette* (1943, AAn), *Miracle on 34th Street* (1947, with Valentine Davies, AA), SWG president (1948–1949), *The Country Girl* (1954, AA, WGAAn), AMPAS president (1955–1958), Laurel Award (1961), Davies Award (1968), *Airport* (1970, AAn, WGAAn), Cox Award (1979)

Serling, Rod: *Playhouse 90* (1956–1961, EA, WGAA), *The Twilight Zone* (1959–1964, creator, EA, WGAAn), *Requiem for a Heavyweight* (1962, EA, WGAA), *The Loner* (1965–1966, creator), *Planet of the Apes* (1968, with Michael Wilson), Laurel Award (1976)

Shandling, Garry: *Sanford & Son* (1972–1977), *It's Garry Shandling's Show* (1986–1990, creator with Alan Zweibel, EAn), *The Larry Sanders Show* (1992–1998, creator with Dennis Klein, EA, WGAAn)

Shavelson, Melville: *The Princess and the Pirate* (1944, with Everett Freeman, and Don Hartman), *Houseboat* (1958, with Jack Rose, AAn, WGAAn), *The Five Pennies* (1959, with Jack Rose and Robert Smith, WGAA), WGAw president (1969–1971, 1979–1981, and 1985–1987), Davies Award (1979), Laurel Award (1984), Cox Award (1998)

Sheldon, Sidney: *The Bachelor and the Bobby-Soxer* (1948), *Easter Parade* (1949, with Frances Goodrich and Albert Hackett, WGAA), *Annie Get Your Gun* (1950, WGAA),

Billy Rose's Jumbo (1962, WGAAn), *The Patty Duke Show* (1963–1966), *I Dream of Jeannie* (1965–1970, creator, EAn), *Hart to Hart* (1979–1984)

Ship, Reuben: *The Life of Riley* (1949–1950, radio program, creator), *The Investigator* (1954, radio play), *Albert and Victoria* (1970–1971)

Silliphant, Stirling: *Route 66* (1960–1964, creator with Herbert B. Leonard), *In the Heat of the Night* (1967, AA, WGAAn), *The Poseidon Adventure* (1972, with Wendell Mayes), *The Towering Inferno* (1974), *The Killer Elite* (1975, with Marc Norman)

Silverman, Treva: *The Monkees* (1966–1968), *The Mary Tyler Moore Show* (1970–1977, EA)

Simon, David: *Homicide: Life on the Street* (1993–1999, WGAA, Humanitas Prize, 1999, with T. J. English and Julie Martin), *The Wire* (2002–2008, creator, EAn, WGAA), *Generation Kill* (2008, creator, EAn, WGAAn), *Treme* (2010–2013, creator, EAn, WGAAn), Hunter Award (2014)

Simon, Neil: *Your Show of Shows* (1950–1954), *Barefoot in the Park* (1967, WGAAn), *The Odd Couple* (1968, AAn, WGAA), *The Out-of-Towners* (1970, WGAA), *Murder by Death* (1976, WGAAn), *The Goodbye Girl* (1977, AAn, WGAAn), Laurel Award (1979)

Singleton, John: *Boyz n the Hood* (1991, AAn, WGAAn), *Higher Learning* (1995)

Sklar, Jason, and Randy Sklar: *Apt. 2F* (1997, creators), *Comedy Central Presents: The Sklar Brothers* (2010–2011), *United Stats of America* (2012)

Smith, Kevin: *Clerks* (1994), *Dogma* (1999), *Zach and Miri Make a Porno* (2008)

Smith, Patricia Falken: *Days of Our Lives* (1965–present, head writer, 1982, EA, WGAAn), *General Hospital* (1963–present, head writer, 1983, WGAAn), *Lone Star Bar & Grill* (1983, co-creator)

Soderbergh, Steven: *sex, lies and videotape* (1989, EAn, WGAAn), *Nightwatch* (1997, with Ole Bornedal), *Solaris* (2002),

Solomon, Ed: *Bill and Ted's Excellent Adventure* (1989, with Chris Matheson), *Men in Black* (1997), *Now You See Me* (2013, with Boaz Yakin and Edward Ricourt)

Solondz, Todd: *Welcome to the Dollhouse* (1995), *Happiness* (1998), *Palindromes* (2004)

Sorkin, Aaron: *A Few Good Men* (1992), *Sports Night* (1998–2000, creator, EAn, WGAAn, Humanitas Prize), *The West Wing* (1999–2006, creator, EA, WGAA, Humanitas Prize), *Studio 60 on the Sunset Strip* (2006–2007, creator, WGAAn), *The Social Network* (2010, AA, WGAA), *The Newsroom* (2012–present, creator, WGAAn)

Southern, Terry: *Dr. Strangelove* (1964, with Stanley Kubrick and Peter George, AAn, WGAA), *Easy Rider* (1969, with Peter Fonda and Dennis Hopper, AAn, WGAAn), *Saturday Night Live* (1975–present)

Spelling, Aaron: *Johnny Ringo* (1959–1960), *The Smothers Brothers Show* (1965–1966, creator with Richard Newton), *The New People* (1969–1970, creator with Larry Gordon)

Spielberg, Steven: *The Sugarland Express* (1974, WGAAn), *Close Encounters of the Third Kind* (1977, WGAAn), *Poltergeist* (1982, with Michael Grais and Mark Victor), *Amazing Stories* (1985–1987, series developer)

Spigelgass, Leonard: *I Was a Male War Bride* (1949, with Charles Lederer and Hagar Wilde, WGAAn), *Mystery Street* (1950, AAn), *Silk Stockings* (1957, with Leonard Gershe), *Gypsy* (1962, WGAAn), Davies Award (1966), Cox Award (1971)

Stallings, Laurence: *The Big Parade* (1925, with Harry Behn), *She Wore a Yellow Ribbon* (1949, with Frank S. Nugent, WGAAn)

Stander, Arthur: *I Married Joan* (1952–1955), *Make Room for Daddy* (1953–1965), *The Andy Griffith Show* (1960–1968)

Steinberg, Norman: *Blazing Saddles* (1974, with Mel Brooks, Andrew Bergman, Richard Pryor, and Alan Uger, WGAA), *My Favorite Year* (1982, with Dennis Palumbo, WGAAn), *Doctor Doctor* (1989–1991, creator)

Steinkellner, Bill, and Cheri Steinkellner: *The Jeffersons* (1975–1985), *Cheers* (1982–1993), *Teacher's Pet* (2000–2002)

Stern, Leonard: *The Honeymooners* (1955–1956, WGAA), *I'm Dickens, He's Fenster* (1962–1963, WGAAn), *Get Smart* (1965–1970, with Buck Henry, EA)

Stewart, Donald Ogden: *Holiday* (1938, with Sidney Buchman), *The Philadelphia Story* (1940, AA), *Life with Father* (1947), *An Affair to Remember* (1957, uncredited, with Delmer Daves and Leo McCarey, credit restored 1997), Laurel Award (1990), blacklisted

Stewart, Mike: *Caesar's Hour* (1954–1957, EAn)

Stone, Noreen: *Amy* (1981), *Dynasty* (1981–1989), *Brenda Starr* (1989, with James D. Buchanan and Jenny Wolkind)

Stone, Oliver: *Midnight Express* (1978, AA, WGAA), *Platoon* (1986, AAn, WGAAn), *Wall Street* (1987, with Stanley Weiser), *Born on the Fourth of July* (1989, with Ron Kovic, AAn, WGAAn), *JFK* (1991, with Zachary Sklar, AAn, WGAAn)

Sturges, Preston: *The Great McGinty* (1940, AA), *The Lady Eve* (1941), *Sullivan's Travels* (1941), Laurel Award (1975)

Sud, Veena: *Cold Case* (2003–2010), *The Killing* (2011–present, developed for US television, EAn, WGAAn)

Sutton, Phoef: *Cheers* (1982–1993), *The Fan* (1996), *Boston Legal* (2004–2008), *Terriers* (2010)

Swicord, Robin: *Little Women* (1994, WGAAn), *Matilda* (1996, with Nicholas Kazan), *Memoirs of a Geisha* (2005), *The Curious Case of Benjamin Button* (2008, with Eric Roth, AAn, WGAAn)

Taradash, Daniel: *Rancho Notorious* (1952, with Silvia Richards), *From Here to Eternity* (1953, AA, WGAA), *Picnic* (1955, WGAAn), AMPAS president (1970–1973), Davies Award (1971), WGAw president (1977–1979), Cox Award (1988), North Award (1991), Laurel Award (1996)

Tarantino, Quentin: *Reservoir Dogs* (1992), *Pulp Fiction* (1994, with Roger Avary, AA), *Django Unchained* (2012, AA, Humanitas Prize)

Taraporevala, Sooni: *Salaam Bombay!* (1988, with Mira Nair), *Mississippi Masala* (1991), *The Namesake* (2006)

Tarloff, Frank: *The Andy Griffith Show* (1960–1968, as David Adler), *The Dick Van Dyke Show* (1961–1962, as David Adler), *Father Goose* (1964, with S. H. Barnett and Peter Stone, AA, WGAAn), *A Guide for the Married Man* (1967, WGAAn)

Thuna, Leonora: *Family* (1976–1980), *Lou Grant* (1977–1982, WGAAn), *I Know Why the Caged Bird Sings* (1979, and Maya Angelou, WGAAn)

Tolkin, Mel: *Your Show of Shows* (1950–1954), *Caesar's Hour* (1954–1957, EAn), *The Danny Kaye Show* (1963–1967, EAn, WGAA), *All in the Family* (1971–1979, EAn, WGAA, Humanitas Prize)

Tombragel, Maurice: *Zanzibar* (1940, with Maurice Wright), *Adventures of Wild Bill Hickok* (1951–1958), *Walt Disney's Wonderful World of Color* (1954–1992)

Towne, Robert: *Chinatown* (1974, AA), *Shampoo* (1975, with Warren Beatty, AAn, WGAA), *The Firm* (1993, with David Rabe and David Rayfiel), *Mission: Impossible* (1996, with David Koepp), Laurel Award (1997)

Townsend, Robert: *Hollywood Shuffle* (1987), *The Parent 'Hood* (1995–1999, creator)

Trotti, Lamar: *Young Mr. Lincoln* (1939, AAn), *The Ox-Bow Incident* (1943), *Wilson* (1944, AA), *There's No Business Like Show Business* (1954, AAn, WGAAn), North Award (1971), Laurel Award (1983)

Trumbo, Dalton: *Kitty Foyle* (1940, AAn), *Tender Comrade* (1943), *Roman Holiday* (1953, with Ian McClellan Hunter as front, AA, WGAA, AA credit restored 1993), *The Brave One* (1956, pseudonym Robert Rich, with Harry S. Franklin and Merrill G. White, AA, credit restored 1975), *Spartacus* (1960, WGAAn), Laurel Award (1970), *Johnny Got His Gun* (1971, WGAAn), *Papillon* (1973, with Lorenzo Semple Jr.), blacklisted

Tugend, Harry: *Poor Little Rich Girl* (1936, with Sam Hellman and Gladys Lehman), *Take Me Out to the Ball Game* (1949, with George Wells, Gene Kelly, and Stanley Donen, WGAAn), *Road to Bali* (1952, with Frank Butler, Hal Kanter, and William Morrow), *Pocketful of Miracles* (1961, with Hal Kanter)

Tunberg, Karl: *Tall, Dark and Handsome* (1941, with Darrell Ware), SWG president (1950–1951), *Ben-Hur* (1959, AAn, WGAAn), *Mannix* (1967–1975)

Tunick, Irve: *Armstrong Circle Theater* (1950–1963), *Lady of Vengeance* (1957), *Murder, Inc.* (1960, with Mel Barr)

Turteltaub, Saul: *Candid Camera* (1960–1967), *The Carol Burnett Show* (1967–1978, EAn, WGAAn), *Sanford and Son* (1972–1977), *Cosby* (1996–2000, Humanitas Prize, 2000)

Ulius, Betty: *Lux Video Theatre* (1950–1959), *Matinee Theatre* (1955–1958), *Psych-Out* (1969, with E. Hunter Willett, WGAAn)

Vajda, Ernest: *The Love Parade* (1929, with Guy Bolton), *The Merry Widow* (1934, with Samson Raphaelson), *Marie Antoinette* (1938, with Claudine West and David Ogden Stewart)

Van Sant, Gus: *Drugstore Cowboy* (1989, with Daniel Yost), *My Own Private Idaho* (1991), *Elephant* (2003)

Verrone, Patric M.: *The Tonight Show Starring Johnny Carson* (1962–1992, EAn), *Muppets Tonight* (1996–1998), *Futurama* (1999–2013, WGAAn), Animation Award (2002), WGAw president (2005–2009), Cox Award (2012)

Victor, David: *Gunsmoke* (1955–1975, WGAAn), *Dr. Kildare* (1961–1966), *Marcus Welby, M.D.* (1969–1976, creator)

Webb, Jack: *Dragnet* (1951–1959, creator), *Adam-12* (1968–1975, creator with Robert A. Cinader), *O'Hara, U.S. Treasury* (1971–1972, creator with James E. Moser)

Webb, James R.: *Cape Fear* (1962), *How the West Was Won* (1962, AA), WGAw president (1962–1963), Davies Award (1965), *They Call Me Mister Tibbs!* (1970, with Alan Trustman), Cox Award (1974), North Award (1975)

Webster, Tony: *The Phil Silvers Show* (1955–1959, EA), *Car 54, Where Are You?* (1961–1963), *The Love Boat* (1977–1987)

Weiner, Matthew: *Becker* (1998–2004), *The Sopranos* (1999–2007, EA, WGAA), *Mad Men* (2007–2015, creator, EA, WGAA)

Wells, John: *ER* (1994–2009, EAn, WGAAn), *China Beach* (1998–2001, EAn, WGAAn), WGAw president (1999–2001 and 2009–2011), *The West Wing* (1999–2006, WGAAn, Humanitas Prize), Laurel Award (2007), *The Company Men* (2010), *Shameless* (2011–present, developed for US television)

West, Nathanael: *It Could Happen to You!* (1937, with Samuel Ornitz), *Five Came Back* (1939, with Jerome Cady and Dalton Trumbo)

White, Phyllis, and Robert White: *The George Burns and Gracie Allen Show* (1950–1958, Robert only), *Death Valley Days* (1952–1970), *Guiding Light* (1952–2009, EA, WGAA), *My Favorite Martian* (1963–1966)

White, Sydnye: *Detroit S.W.A.T.* (2000), *Moneywise with Kevin Boston* (2000)

Wilber, Carey: *Armstrong Circle Theater* (1950–1963), *Bonanza* (1959–1973), *Star Trek* (1966–1969)

Wilder, Billy: *Ninotchka* (1939, with Charles Brackett and Walter Reisch, AAn), *Double Indemnity* (1944, with Raymond Chandler, AAn), *Sunset Blvd.* (1950, with Charles Brackett and D. M. Marshman Jr., AA, WGAA), *Sabrina* (1954, with Ernest Lehman and Samuel Taylor, AAn, WGAA), *The Seven Year Itch* (1955, with George Axelrod, WGAA), Laurel Award (1957, with Charles Brackett, and 1980, with I.A.L. Diamond), *Some Like It Hot* (1959, with I.A.L. Diamond, AAn, WGAA), *The Apartment* (1960, with I.A.L. Diamond, AA, WGAA), National Medal of Arts (1993)

Willimon, Beau: *The Ides of March* (2011, with George Clooney and Grant Heslov, AAn), *House of Cards* (2013–present, creator for US television, EAn, WGAAn)

Wilmore, Larry: *In Living Color* (1990–1994, EAn), *The PJs* (1999–2001, co-creator), *The Bernie Mac Show* (2000–2006, creator, EA, WGAAn, Humanitas Prize, Peabody Award), *The Office* (2005–2013, EAn, WGAAn)

Wilson, Carey: *Ben-Hur: A Tale of the Christ* (1925, with Lew Wallace, June Mathis, and Bess Meredyth), *Faithless* (1932), *Mutiny on the Bounty* (1935, with Talbot Jennings and Jules Furthman, AAn), AMPAS co-founder

Wilson, Michael: *A Place in the Sun* (1951, with Harry Brown, AA, WGAA), *Salt of the Earth* (1954), *Friendly Persuasion* (1956, AAn, WGAA, credit restored 1996), *The Bridge on the River Kwai* (1957, with Carl Foreman, AA, AA credit restored 1984), *Lawrence of Arabia* (1962, uncredited, with Robert Bolt, AAn, credit restored 1995), *Planet of the Apes* (1968, with Rod Serling), Laurel Award (1976), blacklisted

Winship, Michael: *Bill Moyers Journal* (1972–1976, 1979–1981, and 2007–2010, EA, WGAA), Jablow Award (1998), *Nova* (1974–present), WGA East president (2007–present), *Moyers & Company* (2012–present, WGAA)

Wodehouse, P. G.: *The Magic Plus Fours* (1924, short), *The Man in Possession* (1931, with Sarah Y. Mason), *A Damsel in Distress* (1937, with Ernest Pagano and S. K. Lauren)

Wolfson, Roger: *The Closer* (2005–2012), *Saving Grace* (2007–2010)

Woods, Frank E.: *A Corner in Wheat* (1909, with D. W. Griffith), *Judith of Bethulia* (1914, with D. W. Griffith and Grace Pierce), *The Birth of a Nation* (1915, with D. W. Griffith), AMPAS co-founder

Yglesias, Rafael: *Fearless* (1993), *From Hell* (2001, with Terry Hayes), *Dark Water* (2005)

Young, Nedrick: *Passage West* (1951, as front for Alvah Bessie, with Lewis R. Foster), *Jailhouse Rock* (1957, as Ned Young), *The Defiant Ones* (1958, pseudonym Nathan E. Douglas, with Harold Jacob Smith, AA, WGAA, credit restored 1997), *Inherit the Wind* (1960, pseudonym Nathan E. Douglas, with Harold Jacob Smith, AAn, credit restored 1997), blacklisted

Young, Waldemar: *Island of Lost Souls* (1932, with Philip Wylie), *Cleopatra* (1934, with Vincent Lawrence), *The Lives of a Bengal Lancer* (1935, with Achmed Abdullah, John L. Balderston, Grover Jones, and William Slavens McNutt, AAn)

Zweibel, Alan: *Saturday Night Live* (1975–present, EA, WGAA), *It's Garry Shandling's Show* (1986–1990, creator with Garry Shandling, EAn), *North* (1994, with Andrew Scheinman), *The Story of Us* (1999, with Jessie Nelson), Hunter Award (2010)

APPENDIX B
METHODOLOGY

Writing is an emotionally draining thing. It is a psychologically damaging occupation. It is to the soul what asbestos clearing is to the lungs. [*To the waiter:*] I'm fine, thank you.

—Craig Mazin, interview, 12 June 2011

In *The Writers*, I explore the history of the American film and television industry through the lens of a particular group of practitioners. I integrate these industries in ways that mirror not only their common structures but also the career paths of many screenwriters. My decision to examine film, television, and streaming media writers, echoes the work of scholars who have traced connections between the often balkanized areas of film studies and media studies. The practice of moving among media is neither a contemporary nor a rare phenomenon. Though writers have always crossed media boundaries, their labor has rarely been examined in a way that takes the specificity of these migrations or its effects into account.

Studies of distinct communities of American media practitioners afford significant insights into media production, and this scholarship grounds much of my work. This methodology breaks down notions of a monolithic industry, explaining the collaborative nature and complex networks of media production, distribution, and exhibition infrastructures, as well as those of local auxiliary support communities. Hortense Powdermaker's and Leo Rosten's studies of Hollywood in the 1940s and 1950s inform my reading of the classical Hollywood era.[1] The statistical studies of the WGA by William T. Bielby and Denise D. Bielby, as well as scholarship by Todd Gitlin, John Caldwell, and Denise Mann provide guides on how to combine grounded industrial research with subject interviews and data.[2] Collections of detailed interviews with screenwriters were invaluable, in particular

Horace Newcomb and Robert Alley's *The Producer's Medium* and Patrick McGilligan's *Backstory* series.[3] Production studies scholarship would not be as rich without a parallel scholarly trend toward media industry studies. There the scholarship of Thomas Schatz, Jennifer Holt, and Alisa Perrin has been of particular use.[4] Research on the Writers Guild by Nancy Lynn Schwartz, Ian Hamilton, Joan Moore and Burton Moore, Christopher Wheaton, Howard Suber, and Marc Norman was my grounding to understand this rich history.[5]

Although this book pulls from previous film and television histories, trade journals, memoirs, and documentaries, I have focused much of my scholarship around 155 personal interviews with American film and television writers. I conducted 60 formal interviews between 2008 and 2013. I sat down with professional writers for around three hours each to discuss their careers and their experiences in the Guild. (I also recorded five interviews with industry executives and WGA executives and directors about their work with the Guild or with writers.) All but a handful of these conversations were conducted in person.

In the process of doing research at the Writers Guild Foundation Library, I uncovered transcripts compiled for an oral history project carried out under the auspices of the WGA in 1978 and 1979. The Guild History Committee and its two-person staff conducted 104 interviews with prominent WGA members and executives. A copy of each transcript was sent to the interviewee for corrections or amendments, although the committee hoped to preserve "the flavor of conversation" rather than achieve "a pure literary presentation."[6] Transcripts were returned unedited or with a letter that acknowledged approval. They were then stored and forgotten in the Writers Guild Foundation library. Now brought to light, these oral histories provide a personal perspective from which to understand changes in the media industries and cultures of production.

By placing media ethnography in conversation with industry history, *The Writers* provides a qualitative analysis of industry history. As Mark Williams says, "oral history can demonstrate to us and reacquaint us with the fact that the personal is not only political, but historical and dialogical as well."[7] Each writer's story provides the context for my discussion of aesthetics, technology, politics, and individual experience within this cultural and industry history. During our interview, Craig Mazin offered this warning: "Writers are the most dangerous people to try to discern history from, because we're particularly good at lacing together the narrative we want you to hear, and those narratives always flow toward a purpose or a point, the dramatic intent of the narrative."[8] As I wove this history, I parsed the competing narratives presented by subjects who often care passionately about their personal narrative and history.

My research demands an integrated methodology, combining archival research, media industries analysis, and production studies methods in order to understand the fluctuations in the economic, political, and discursive dimensions of this cultural history, and then measuring these factors against the memories and observations of my interviewees. Todd Gitlin states that the language of media practitioners provides "a sense of the ambiance and texture of the industry's life-as-it-is-lived." Anecdotes become a part of industry speech, especially among writers, since it is their job to create stories. Gitlin describes Hollywood as a "place where many of the practitioners are brighter and more engaging than their products, and the story of the making of the show more revealing than the show itself. I think these stories, once scrutinized and interrogated, are the royal road to the industry's workings."[9] Like Gitlin, I found my subjects as compelling as most screen characters. I use these writers' accounts as verification, testimony, or personal insight into a larger history I ground in historical research.

My use of oral history is in part practical: the work of writers lends itself well to conversation rather than observation. I can observe subjects at pitch meetings, in the writers' room, or at Guild meetings, but watching writers actually write proves too distracting to my subjects and less useful to me as a scholar.[10] Oral history is also a particularly rewarding method for studying media practitioners whose central tools are words. In my career as a scholar I have interviewed a number of film, television, and digital media workers. Not surprisingly, writers as a group have been among the most deliberate speakers; they are not just aware of their position and role within the industry but are also uniquely articulate in their analysis of that role. Their facility with words ensures that their observations and their choices of terms withstand exploration and analysis as scholarly data.

American film historian Robert Sklar points in his work to Paul Veyne's concept of "lengthening the questionnaire," and I find this concept apt as well. Because my work has depended so much on interviews and oral history, the analogy is particularly prescient. Veyne notes, "Like the art of design, history is descriptive knowledge: the reader of a history book feels, when he sees the springs of human affairs working, a pleasure of the same order as a Florentine amateur observing the form and the play of each muscle, each tendon. . . . The heartfelt cry of the historian, like that of a designer or of a naturalist, would be, 'It is interesting because it is complicated.'"[11] In deciphering history, one is always searching for the truth, which entails a process of constructing and adding multiple plots. This book is a story of storytellers. And while, in their work, finding satisfying conclusions is part of the trade, as a historian, I look more to the serial and its multiple intertwining plots than the clear and closed narrative.

This book has been a deep collaboration with film and television writers to make sense of their careers and of their community. Some of my subjects are aware of my community as well. Many screenwriters work within colleges and universities, teaching the art and craft of writing as they work on scripts. James Schamus, writer of *The Wedding Banquet* and *Crouching Tiger, Hidden Dragon*, points to parallels between screenwriters and scholars. Both know "full well what it means to work in large institutions whose existences depend on the production and marketing of intellectual properties, and where, as a rule, 'making sense' is a 'collaborative' process—one in which intelligibility requires succumbing to protocols and dictates that are often in great tension with the original thoughts and inspirations that motivate our work."[12] We write intellectual property for a living, we pitch our ideas, and we work within vast organizations.

My interest in screenwriters first emerged as a love of the films and television series they wrote—the great narratives, compelling characters, and crackerjack wordplay of the best of American media. I grew up in Los Angeles, where the stories of the industry were embedded into of the fabric of the city. During the lead-up to what became the 2007–2008 strike, I started to see that, in compelling ways, the history of the screenwriting profession mirrored the larger trajectory of the American film and television industry. It was then and there that my work on this book began.

NOTES

INTRODUCTION

The following chapters are populated with the names of writers, only a few of whom are immediately recognizable. Yet many of them are instantly recognizable by their credits. Thus credits provide a shorthand to identify these writers, providing some landmarks for readers to identify films or series a writer worked on or to note the era when she or he was active in the industry. The first time that I mention any writer, I identify him or her generally with one title, sometimes a few. As the following pages will detail, since their earliest days of organizing as a group, writers have fought for their names to be attached to the films that they scripted. In respect for this primary struggle, I offer an appendix of writers mentioned in this book for reference. I do not make note in the body of the text if a writer has co-written a screenplay or is a co-creator of a series, but these notations are made in the appendix, as are other details, such as whether a writer's career was affected by the Hollywood blacklist of the 1950s or whether he or she served one of the writers' guilds in an official capacity.

1. Nick Counter, long-time president of the Alliance of Motion Picture and Television Producers (AMPTP), frames the issue similarly: "While the past is not necessarily prologue for the future, it is evident that technological advances have fundamentally changed the economic landscape for the survival of the motion picture and television industry." J. Nicholas Counter III, "Foreword: Key Issues Facing Producers and Distributors in the Motion Picture and Television Industry," in *Under the Stars: Essays on Labor Relations in Arts and Entertainment*, ed. Lois S. Gray and Ronald L. Seeber (Ithaca and London: ILR/Cornell University Press, 1996), vii.

2. Elihu Winer, interview by the Writers Guild Oral History Project (Los Angeles: Writers Guild Foundation, 22 June 1978), 20; Larry Markes, interview by the Writers Guild Oral History Project (Los Angeles: Writers Guild Foundation, spring 1978), 18.

3. Quoted in Bob Thomas, *Thalberg: Life and Legend* (New York: Doubleday & Co., 1969), 183.

4. Mel Brooks, interview with the author, 15 August 2013.

5. George Axelrod, interview with Patrick McGilligan in *Backstory 3: Interviews with Screenwriters of the 60s* (Berkeley: University of California Press, 1997), 59.

6. Robert Towne, "On Moving Pictures," in *Chinatown and The Last Detail: 2 Screenplays* (New York: Grove Press, 1997), ix.

7. Cheri Steinkellner, interview with the author, 12 August 2013.

8. Philip Dunne, *Take Two: A Life in Movies and Politics* (New York: McGraw-Hill, 1980), 43. Also see Howard A. Rodman's wonderfully witty character study of the screenplay, "What a Screenplay Isn't," *Cinema Journal* 45, no. 2 (Winter 2006): 86–89.

9. Paul Schrader, quoted in Marc Norman, *What Happens Next: A History of American Screenwriting* (New York: Three Rivers Press/Random House, 2008), 397.

10. Norman Lear, interview with the author, 20 August 2013.

11. Saul Turteltaub, interview with the author, 16 August 2013.

12. Elias Davis, interview with the author, 29 September 2009.

13. William Goldman, *The Writer Speaks: William Goldman*, DVD, 27 May 2010, Writers Guild Foundation Shavelson-Webb Library, Los Angeles.

14. Alvin Sargent, interview with the author, 25 August 2009.

15. Courtney Lilly, interview with the author, 16 May 2009.

16. Sandra Tsing Loh, "Punching Up the Chicken," in *Doing It for Money: The Agony and Ecstasy of Writing and Surviving in Hollywood*, ed. Daryl G. Nickens for the Writers Guild Foundation (Los Angeles: Tallfellow Press, 2006), 95.

17. Michael Oates Palmer, interview with the author, 12 August 2009.

18. Lizzie Francke tells the story of the many successful female screenwriters working in early Hollywood. Francke, *Script Girls: Women Screenwriters in Hollywood* (London: BFI, 1994).

19. I will discuss data on women writers in chapter 4. For some information on contemporary television, see Neely Swanson, "Women Can't Create and White Men Can't Jump," *Baseline Intelligence*, 4 February 2010, http://www.baselineintel .com/research-wrap?detail/C7/women_cant_create_and_white_men_cant_jump.

20. Joan Moore and Burton Moore, "The Hollywood Writer" (unpublished manuscript, c. 1970), 15, Writers Guild Foundation Shavelson-Webb Library Archives, Los Angeles.

21. Andrew Ross, *No Collar: The Humane Workplace and Its Hidden Costs* (Philadelphia: Temple University Press, 2002), 10.

22. This book focuses on the American screenwriting industry. Some scholars concentrate on writers in other countries, in particular, Eva Novrup Redvall on television screen authorship in Denmark and Bridget Conor on British screenwriters. See Redvall, *Writing and Producing Television Drama in Denmark: From "The Kingdom" to "The Killing"* (New York: Palgrave Macmillan, 2013); Conor, "Subjects at Work: Investigating the Creative Labour of British Screenwriters," in *Behind the Screen: Inside European Production Cultures*, ed. Petr Szczepanik and Patrick Vonderau (London: Palgrave Macmillan, 2013); and Conor, *Screenwriting: Creative Labour and Professional Practice* (London: Routledge, 2014).

23. Bob Barbash, interview by the Writers Guild Oral History Project (Los Angeles: Writers Guild Foundation, 24 February 1978), 7.

24. Here I am indebted to David Hesmondhalgh's rich scholarship on this topic. See David Hesmondhalgh and Sarah Baker, *Creative Labour: Media Work in Three Cultural Industries* (London: Routledge, 2011), and David Hesmondhalgh, *The Culture Industries*, 3rd ed. (Thousand Oaks, CA: Sage, 2012).

25. Barbara Corday, interview with the author, 30 August 2013.

26. M.W., "Kanter Adds Dimension to Hyphenated Career: Writer-Prod-Dir-Emcee," *WGAw Newsletter*, December 1967, 7.

27. John Furia Jr. and David Rintels, interview by the Writers Guild Oral History Project (Los Angeles: Writers Guild Foundation, 3 May 1978), 44.

28. Robert White and Phyllis White, interview by the Writers Guild Oral History Project (Los Angeles: Writers Guild Foundation, spring 1978), 22.

29. Marc Norman, interview with the author, 9 June 2011.

30. See Gerald Horne, *Class Struggle in Hollywood 1930–1950: Moguls, Mobsters, Stars, Reds, & Trade Unionists* (Austin: University of Texas Press, 2001). I will cover these strikes in chapter 2.

31. Frank Pierson, interview with the author, 15 February 2011.

32. Copyright Act of 1909, Pub. L. No. 60–349, 35 Stat. 1075, § 62 (4 March 1909).

33. Erik Barnouw, interview by the Writers Guild Oral History Project (Los Angeles: Writers Guild Foundation, spring 1978), 11.

34. David Harmon and Nate Monaster, interview by the Writers Guild Oral History Project (Los Angeles: Writers Guild Foundation, 15 February 1978), 14–15.

35. Ernest Kinoy, interview by the Writers Guild Oral History Project (Los Angeles: Writers Guild Foundation, spring 1978), 14–15.

36. Hortense Powdermaker, *Stranger and Friend: The Way of an Anthropologist* (New York: Norton, 1967), 227–228.

37. Max Wilk, *Schmucks with Underwoods: Conversations with Hollywood's Classic Screenwriters* (Milwaukee, WI: Hal Leonard Corporation, 2004), 7.

38. Stirling Silliphant, interview by the Writers Guild Oral History Project (Los Angeles: Writers Guild Foundation, 1 March 1978), 5.

39. Maurice Tombragel, interview by the Writers Guild Oral History Project (Los Angeles: Writers Guild Foundation, 23 May 1978), 27.

40. William Ludwig, interview by the Writers Guild Oral History Project (Los Angeles: Writers Guild Foundation, 16 May 1978), 3.

41. Catherine L. Fisk, "The Role of Private Intellectual Property Rights in Markets for Labor and Ideas: Screen Credit and the Writers Guild of America, 1938–2000," *Berkeley Journal of Employment and Labor Law* 32, no. 2 (2011): 222.

42. Howard A. Rodman, interview with the author, 15 February 2011.

43. Sam Kashner, "Who's Afraid of Nichols and May?" *Vanity Fair*, January 2013, http://www.vanityfair.com/hollywood/2013/01/nichols-and-may-reunion-exclusive.

44. *Robert Towne*, directed by Sarah Morris (undistributed documentary short, 2006), 35mm and DVD, http://sarah-morris.info/?/Films/RobertTowne/.

45. On March 24, 2010, the MPAA filed joint comments with AFTRA, DGA, IATSE, the National Music Publishers Association (NMPA), the Recording Industry Association of America (RIAA), and SAG. See "Regarding Development of First Joint Federal Strategic Plan for Intellectual Property Enforcement," letter to The Honorable Victoria A. Espinel, US Intellectual Property Enforcement Coordinator, US Office of Management and Budget, 24 March 2010, http://www.mpaa.org/Resources/0c72c549–89ce-4815–9a71-de13b8e0a26f.PDF.

46. Mark Deuze, *Media Work* (Cambridge, UK: Polity, 2007), 20–27.

47. Craig Mazin, interview with the author, 12 June 2011.

48. Regarding research on local auxiliary support, see Allen J. Scott, *On Hollywood: The Place, the Industry* (Princeton: Princeton University Press, 2004), and Tom Kemper, *Hidden Talent: The Emergence of Hollywood Agents* (Berkeley: University of California Press, 2009).

49. Moore and Moore, "The Hollywood Writer" (unpublished, c. 1970), ch. 1, 1.

50. Arthur Ross, interview by the Writers Guild Oral History Project (Los Angeles: Writers Guild Foundation, 19 April 1978), 16.

51. Ludwig, Oral History Project, 3.

52. Erica Rothschild, interview with the author, 16 May 2009.

53. Harmon and Monaster, Oral History Project, 40.

54. Jorja Prover, *No One Knows Their Names: Screenwriters in Hollywood* (Madison, WI: Popular Press, 1994), 14.

55. Robin Swicord, interview with the author, 16 February 2011.

56. Betty Ulius, interview by the Writers Guild Oral History Project (Los Angeles: Writers Guild Foundation, 12 April 1978), 1.

57. Darnell M. Hunt, *The 2007 Hollywood Writers Report: Whose Stories Are We Telling?* (report commissioned by the Writers Guild of America West, Los Angeles), 6, http://www.wga.org/uploadedFiles/who_we_are/HWR07.pdf.

58. Ibid., 7.

59. Ronald Bass, interview with the author, 13 June 2011.

60. Susan Kim, interview with the author, 9 April 2012.

61. Felicia D. Henderson, "The Culture Behind Closed Doors: Issues of Gender and Race in the Writers' Room," *Cinema Journal* 50, no. 20 (Winter 2011): 151.

62. "Flipping the Script: Beyond Homophobia in Black Hollywood," panel discussion sponsored by the Writers Guild of America West, Los Angeles, 23 March 2010.

63. Dava Savel, interview with the author, 26 November 2013.

64. Neal Gabler, *An Empire of Their Own: How Jews Invented Hollywood* (New York: Crown, 1988).

65. Ring Lardner Jr., interview by Howard Suber, Suber Files, Archives, Writers Guild Foundation Shavelson-Webb Library, Los Angeles.

66. The project was left incomplete, and transcripts of the interviews were forgotten in a box in the Writers Guild Foundation Library for approximately thirty years.

67. Editorial, "Guild History Starts," *WGAw Newsletter* (February 1978), 1.

68. Erna Lazarus, interview by the Writers Guild Oral History Project (Los Angeles: Writers Guild Foundation, 15 February 1978), 13.

CHAPTER 1   THE ARTIST EMPLOYEE

1. William Manchester, *The Glory and the Dream: A Narrative History of America 1932–1972*, vol. 1 (Boston: Little, Brown & Co., 1974), 32.

2. Franklin D. Roosevelt, "On the Bank Crisis," 12 March 1933, in *FDR's Fireside Chats*, ed. Russell D. Buhite and David W. Levy (Norman: University of Oklahoma Press, 1992).

3. Nancy Lynn Schwartz, *The Hollywood Writers' Wars* (New York: McGraw-Hill, 1982), 5.

4. Ibid., 9.

5. The name of the new group was officially the "Screen Writers' Guild." In consultation with Joanne Lammers, director of the archive at the Writers Guild Foundation, and in order to keep consistency throughout the text, I use "Screen Writers Guild."

6. Charles Higham, *Merchant of Dreams: Louis B. Mayer, M.G.M., and the Secret Hollywood* (New York: Donald I. Fine, Inc., 1993), 197.

7. Ibid., 200.

8. Samuel Marx, *Mayer and Thalberg: The Make-Believe Saints* (New York: Random House, 1975), 206.

9. Philip Dunne, interview by the Writers Guild Oral History Project (Los Angeles: Writers Guild Foundation, 20 March 1978), 1.

10. James Kotsilibas-Davis, *The Barrymores: The Royal Family in Hollywood* (New York: Crown, 1981), 146.

11. Ibid.

12. Otto Friedrich, *City of Nets: A Portrait of Hollywood in the 1940s* (Berkeley: University of California Press, 1997), 72.

13. Friedrich describes the laughter as "dutiful" (ibid., 72), whereas in Higham's description everyone in the room laughed (*Merchant of Dreams*, 200).

14. Marc Norman, *What Happens Next: A History of American Screenwriting* (New York: Three Rivers Press/Random House, 2008), 156.

15. Ibid., 156.

16. Schwartz, *Hollywood Writers' Wars*, 10.

17. Lester Cole, "The Way We Were: The Beginning," *WGAw Newsletter* (February 1986): 24.

18. Mark A. Vieira, *Irving Thalberg: Boy Wonder to Producer Prince* (Berkeley: University of California Press, 2010), 306.

19. Dunne, Oral History Project, 1.

20. Brian Marlow, "Apostles to the Gentiles," *Screen Guilds' Magazine* 1, no. 1 (July 1934): 17.

21. This clause appears in multiple places, including Section 11 of the *Academy Code* and Section 10 of the *Screen Playwrights Code*. It is mentioned, as well, in the

National Labor Relations Board assessment, "In the matter of Metro-Goldwyn-Mayer Studios and Motion Picture Producers Assn., et al., and Screen Writers Guild Inc." (4 June 1938), 22–25, *Decisions and Orders of the National Labor Relations Board* 7 (1 May 1938–30 June 1938): 690.

22. "Committee Urges a Writers' Union," *New York Times*, 16 July 1916, 17.

23. "Title Insurance Grant Deed," 2 June 1921, Mary H. O'Connor Files, Writers Guild Foundation Shavelson-Webb Library, Los Angeles; Percy Heath, "The Screen Writers' Guild" *Photodramatist* 3, no. 2 (July 1921): 17.

24. Alfred Hustwick, "The Guild Forum," *Photodramatist* 3, no. 3 (August 1921): 5.

25. Another such precursor organization is the American Society of Cinematographers (ASC), which formed in 1919 and is still around today.

26. Christopher D. Wheaton, "The Screen Writers' Guild (1920–1942): The Writers' Quest for a Freely Negotiated Basic Agreement" (PhD diss., University of Southern California, 1973), 21–22.

27. Ibid., 50; Florence Peterson, *American Labor Unions: What They Are and How They Work* (New York: Harper & Brothers, 1944), 18.

28. Lardner, interview by the Writers Guild Oral History Project (Los Angeles: Writers Guild Foundation, 1978), 5.

29. Wheaton, "Screen Writers' Guild (1920–1942)," 22–23.

30. Frederica Sagor Maas, *The Shocking Miss Pilgrim: A Writer in Early Hollywood* (Lexington: University Press of Kentucky, 1999), 63.

31. Ibid., 67.

32. Richard Fine, *Hollywood and the Profession of Authorship, 1928–1940* (Ann Arbor: University of Michigan Press, 1985), 56.

33. Frances Marion, *Off with Their Heads! A Serio-Comic Tale of Hollywood* (New York: Macmillan, 1972), 64.

34. Bernard Schubert, interview by the Writers Guild Oral History Project (Los Angeles: Writers Guild Foundation, 1978), 1–2.

35. Dudley Nichols, "Conversation Piece," *Screen Guilds' Magazine* 2, no. 1 (March 1935): 5.

36. Fine, *Profession of Authorship*, 64.

37. Ben Hecht, *A Child of the Century* (New York: Simon and Schuster, 1954), 466.

38. *The Writer Speaks: Julius Epstein*, DVD, 1994, Writers Guild Foundation Shavelson-Webb Library, Los Angeles.

39. See Lea Jacobs and Richard Maltby, "Rethinking the Production Code," *Quarterly Review of Film and Video* 15, no. 4 (1995): 1–3.

40. Ibid.

41. Hecht, *A Child of the Century*, 479.

42. Fine, *Profession of Authorship*, 85.

43. In reality, fewer than a handful of these scripts were ever used. *Authors' League Bulletin* 11, no. 7 (October 1923): 8.

44. Fine, *Profession of Authorship*, 12.

45. John Schultheiss, "The Eastern Writer in Hollywood," *Cinema Journal* 11, no. 1 (Autumn 1971): 13.

46. Fitzgerald, quoted in Gene D. Phillips, *Fiction, Film, and F. Scott Fitzgerald* (Chicago: Loyola University Press, 1986), 27.

47. Wilder quoted in Joseph Leo Blotner, *Faulkner: A Biography* (New York: Random House, 1974), 773.

48. Maurice Zolotow, *Billy Wilder in Hollywood* (New York: Putnam, 1977), 72.

49. *The Writer Speaks: Julius Epstein*.

50. Edmund North, interview by the Writers Guild Oral History Project (Los Angeles: Writers Guild Foundation, 14 March 1978), 1–2.

51. Devery Freeman, interview by the Writers Guild Oral History Project (Los Angeles: Writers Guild Foundation, 4 April 1978), 4–5.

52. Bob Thomas, *Thalberg: Life and Legend* (New York: Doubleday & Co., 1969), 186.

53. William Ludwig, interview by the Writers Guild Oral History Project (Los Angeles: Writers Guild Foundation, 16 May 1978), 4.

54. *The Writer Speaks: Julius Epstein*.

55. Donald Ogden Stewart, "Writing for the Movies," *Focus on Film*, no. 5 (Winter 1970): 52.

56. Fine, *Profession of Authorship*, 141.

57. Schwartz, *Hollywood Writers' Wars*, 8.

58. David King Dunaway, *Huxley in Hollywood* (New York: Harper & Row, 1989), 98.

59. Fine, *Profession of Authorship*, 13.

60. North, Oral History Project, 1–2.

61. Wheaton, "Screen Writers' Guild (1920–1942)," 61.

62. Ibid., 80.

63. Lizzie Francke, *Script Girls: Women Screenwriters in Hollywood* (London: BFI, 1994), 41.

64. Marion, *Off with Their Heads!*, 240.

65. John Howard Lawson, letter to Louise Silcox, 19 April 1933, Writers Guild History Files, Writers Guild Foundation Shavelson-Webb Library, Los Angeles.

66. Schwartz, *Hollywood Writers' Wars*, 49–50.

67. George Wasson, letter to J. J. Gain at Fox Film Corporation Studio, 12 May 1933, Writers Guild History Files, Writers Guild Foundation Shavelson-Webb Library, Los Angeles.

68. Wasson to Gain regarding Sonya Levien's contract, 16 May 1933, Writers Guild History Files, Writers Guild Foundation Shavelson-Webb Library, Los Angeles.

69. *The Writer Speaks: Fay Kanin*, DVD, 18 May 1998, Writers Guild Foundation Shavelson-Webb Library, Los Angeles.

70. Thomas, *Thalberg*, 267.

71. Ian Hamilton, *Writers in Hollywood, 1915–1951* (New York: Carroll & Graf, 1990), 87.

72. Quoted in Greg Mitchell, "How Hollywood Fixed an Election," *American Film* (November 1988): 30.

73. Arthur M. Schlesinger Jr., *The Coming of the New Deal* (Boston: Houghton Mifflin, 1959), 98–99.

74. Tom Kemper, *Hidden Talent: The Emergence of Hollywood Agents* (Berkeley: University of California Press, 2009), 22.

75. Larry Ceplair and Steven Englund, *The Inquisition in Hollywood: Politics in the Film Community 1930–1960* (Urbana: University of Illinois Press, 1979), 29.

76. *Variety*, 17 October 1933, 7.

77. *Variety*, 2 January 1934, 2.

78. Ceplair and Englund, *Inquisition in Hollywood*, 31.

79. Ibid., 32.

80. Marion, *Off with Their Heads!*, 240.

81. See *A.L.A. Schecter Poultry Corp. v. United States*, 295 U.S. 495 (1935).

82. Harry Tugend, interview by the Writers Guild Oral History Project (Los Angeles: Writers Guild Foundation, c. spring 1978), 5.

83. It was, in fact, the first year that the statuettes were referred to as "Oscars," although the awards had been distributed since 1927.

84. Michael Charles Nielsen and Gene Mailes, *Hollywood's Other Blacklist: Union Struggles in the Studio System* (London: BFI, 1995), 25.

85. *Variety*, 29 April 1936, 27.

86. Thomas, *Thalberg*, 267–268.

87. Dalton Trumbo, *Time of the Toad: A Study of Inquisition in America* (1948; rpt., New York: Harper, 1972), 36.

88. Schwartz, *Hollywood Writers' Wars*, 67.

89. Ibid., 68.

90. Dunne, Oral History Project, 2–3; James O. Kemm, *Rupert Hughes: A Hollywood Legend* (Beverly Hills, CA: Pomegranate Press, 1997), 248. John Bright referred to Howard Emmet Rogers as "the Grey Eminence, because he was the only totally pale Southern Californian I had ever seen." John Bright, interview by the Writers Guild Oral History Project (Los Angeles: Writers Guild Foundation, 26 July 1978), 7.

91. Editorial, *Los Angeles Examiner*, 27 April 1936.

92. "Screen Head Sounds Plea," *Los Angeles Times*, 30 April 1936, A1.

93. *Screen Guilds' Magazine*, May 1936, 28.

94. Dudley Nichols, "Cooking a Goose," *Screen Guilds' Magazine*, May 1936, 6.

95. Freeman, Oral History Project, 1.

96. Samson Raphaelson, interview by the Writers Guild Oral History Project (Los Angeles: Writers Guild Foundation, 1978), 1.

97. Ibid., 1–2.

98. Schwartz, *Hollywood Writers' Wars*, 66.

99. Ibid., 71. Dore Schary described Ryskind as a man who "in his younger days had been a flaming . . . liberal"; interview by the Writers Guild Oral History Project (Los Angeles: Writers Guild Foundation, 1978), 1.

100. Mary McCall, interview by the Writers Guild Oral History Project (Los Angeles: Writers Guild Foundation, 7 March 1979), 1.

101. Ceplair and Englund, *Inquisition in Hollywood*, 39.

102. Dunne, Oral History Project, 3.

103. Schary, Oral History Project, 2.

104. Erwin Gelsey, interview by the Writers Guild Oral History Project (Los Angeles: Writers Guild Foundation, 1978), 1.

105. Wheaton, "Screen Writers' Guild (1920–1942)," 135.

106. *Variety*, 16 September 1936, 2.

107. Hecht, *A Child of the Century*, 471.

108. *Variety*, 15 June 1938, 7.

109. Schwartz, *Hollywood Writers' Wars*, 73–74.

110. David L. Goodrich, *The Real Nick and Nora: Frances Goodrich and Albert Hackett, Writers of Stage and Screen Classics* (Carbondale: Southern Illinois University Press, 2001), 101; John Bright, *Worms in the Winecup: A Memoir* (Lanham, MD: Scarecrow Press, 2002), 15.

111. Roland Flamini, *Thalberg: The Last Tycoon and the World of MGM* (New York: Crown, 1994), 206.

112. Ibid., 207.

113. Schwartz, *Hollywood Writers' Wars*, 113.

114. Michael J. Utvich, "WGA Fiftieth Anniversary Program," 7 September 1981, Special Collections, Writers Guild Foundation Shavelson-Webb Library, Los Angeles.

115. Wheaton, "Screen Writers' Guild (1920–1942)," 136.

116. Ibid., 135.

117. *The Writer Speaks: Julius Epstein.*

118. National Labor Relations Board, R-402 to R-420 (4 June 1938), 6.

119. Leo C. Rosten, *Hollywood: The Movie Colony, the Movie Makers* (New York: Harcourt Brace, 1941), 318.

120. *Variety*, 8 June 1938, 21.

121. Goodrich, *The Real Nick and Nora*, 103; Schwartz, *Hollywood Writers' Wars*, 124.

122. *Variety*, 15 June 1938, 7.

123. "All Writers Join Move On Closed Shop," *Motion Picture Daily*, 18 April 1936. The Screen Actors Guild had a 90 percent closed shop. Directors and assistant directors were given an 80 percent closed shop. Only the American Society of Cinematographers and the Screen Publicists Guild were given virtually 100 percent closed shops—and that was only after they had threatened to strike. *Variety*, 30 August 1939, 4.

124. *Variety*, 14 February 1940, 5.

125. Sheridan Gibney, interview by the Writers Guild Oral History Project (Los Angeles: Writers Guild Foundation, 6 March 1978), 1–2.

126. *Variety*, 8 May 1940, 7.

127. Wheaton, "Screen Writers' Guild (1920–1942)," 162.

128. Gibney, Oral History Project, 13.

129. Ibid., 2.

130. Tugend, Oral History Project, 11.

131. Rosten, *Hollywood: The Movie Colony*, 176.

132. Bright, Oral History Project, 2.

133. Catherine L. Fisk, "The Role of Private Intellectual Property Rights in Markets for Labor and Ideas: Screen Credit and the Writers Guild of America, 1938–2000," *Berkeley Journal of Employment and Labor Law* 32, no. 2 (2011): 257.

CHAPTER 2   TWO FRONT LINES

1. Larry Ceplair and Steven Englund, *The Inquisition in Hollywood: Politics in the Film Community 1930–1960* (Urbana: University of Illinois Press, 1979), 252.

2. *The Hollywood Reporter*, 7 May 1947.

3. Nancy Lynn Schwartz, *The Hollywood Writers' Wars* (New York: McGraw-Hill, 1982), 257.

4. Philip Dunne, interview by the Writers Guild Oral History Project (Los Angeles: Writers Guild Foundation, 20 March 1978), 15.

5. James O. Kemm, *Rupert Hughes: A Hollywood Legend* (Beverly Hills, CA: Pomegranate Press, 1997), 289–290.

6. Schwartz, *Hollywood Writers' Wars*, 253.

7. Ibid., 457.

8. Louis Sahagun and Robert W. Welkos, "Ring Lardner Jr., Last of the Hollywood 10, Dies," *Los Angeles Times*, 2 November 2000.

9. Ceplair and Englund, *Inquisition in Hollywood*, 262.

10. House of Representatives, *Hearings Before the Committee on Un-American Activities*, 80th Congress, First Session, Public Law 601, Section 121, Subsection Q (2), 1947.

11. Ceplair and Englund, *Inquisition in Hollywood*, 265.

12. For more on Jews in Hollywood during this era, see Neal Gabler, *An Empire of Their Own: How Jews Invented Hollywood* (New York: Crown, 1988), 370.

13. Quotation from the *Washington Post* dated 21 October 1947, in *The Screen Writer*, December 1947 (Los Angeles: Screen Writers Guild), 10.

14. Quotation from the *New York Times* dated 2 November 1947 in *The Screen Writer*, December 1947 (Los Angeles: Screen Writers Guild), 11.

15. Larry Ceplair, "SAG and the Motion Picture Blacklist," *Screen Actor* 39 (January 1998): 23.

16. Association of Motion Picture Producers, the Motion Picture Association of America, and the Society of Independent Motion Picture Producers, "The Waldorf Statement,"

press release, 3 December 1947, Archives, Writers Guild Foundation Shavelson-Webb Library, Los Angeles.

17. James M. Cain, letter to the executive board of the Screen Writers Guild, 16 February 1948, Special Collections, Writers Guild Foundation Shavelson-Webb Library, Los Angeles.

18. William Ludwig, interview by the Writers Guild Oral History Project (Los Angeles: Writers Guild Foundation, 16 May 1978), 9–10.

19. Ben Urwand argues that moguls took directions from Georg Gyssling, vice consul in the German consulate based in Los Angeles, and were therefore collaborating with the Nazis. Other historians, including Thomas Doherty, offer a more convincing argument that considers the nuances of Hollywood decision-making and examines some actions that were not so virtuous but were not pure collaborations with Hitler or the Nazis. See Urwand, *The Collaboration: Hollywood's Pact with Hitler* (Cambridge, MA: Harvard University Press, 2013), and Doherty, *Hollywood and Hitler, 1933–1939* (New York: Columbia University Press, 2013).

20. Christopher D. Wheaton, "The Screen Writers' Guild (1920–1942): The Writers' Quest for a Freely Negotiated Basic Agreement" (PhD diss., University of Southern California, 1973), 115, quoting Ford in *TAC: A Magazine of Theatre, Radio, Music, Dance* (October 1938), 3.

21. Schwartz, *Hollywood Writers' Wars*, 176.

22. Ibid., 178.

23. Marc Norman, *What Happens Next: A History of American Screenwriting* (New York: Three Rivers Press/Random House, 2008), 209.

24. "Employment Status of Writers as of May 15, 1945," *The Screen Writer*, June 1945, 38; "Employment Status of Writers as of June 15, 1945," *The Screen Writer*, July 1945, 40; "Employment Status of Writers as of Nov. 5, 1945," *The Screen Writer*, November 1945, 38; "Employment Status of Writers as of Dec. 15, 1945," *The Screen Writer*, December 1945, 37.

25. This service was the brainchild of Rex Stout, president of the Authors' League of America.

26. Ceplair and Englund, *Inquisition in Hollywood*, 187.

27. War Activities Committee of the Motion Picture Industry, "War Activities Committee Report on American Motion Picture Industry's Gift to U.S. Army of 16 mm Film Programs for Showing in Combat Areas Overseas to U.S. Army, Navy, Marine Corps and other 'Persons in Uniform,'" 1943, Archives, Writers Guild Foundation Shavelson-Webb Library, Los Angeles.

28. Screen Writers Guild, "Report on the Activities of the Hollywood Writers Mobilization," 24 October 1944, Archives, Writers Guild Foundation Shavelson-Webb Library, Los Angeles, 1.

29. Ibid., 4.

30. Screen Writers Guild, draft of the *Manual for Writers*, sent to Robert Riskin, Chief of the Bureau of Motion Pictures, Office of War Information, Overseas Division, January 1944, Archives, Writers Guild Foundation Shavelson-Webb Library, Los Angeles, Introduction.

31. Ibid., 6.

32. Ibid., 11.

33. Ibid., 9.

34. Ibid., 8.

35. Judy Stone, *Eye on the World: Conversations with International Filmmakers* (Los Angeles: Silman-James Press, 1997), 628.

36. As laid out in President Franklin D. Roosevelt's State of the Union address before Congress in 1941, these are: freedom of speech, freedom of worship, freedom from want, and freedom from fear.

37. Harold Medford, "Report from a GI Typewriter," *The Screen Writer*, June 1945, 17–19.

38. Bernard Gordon, letter to the editor, *Los Angeles Times*, 2 June 2002.

39. Patrick Goldstein, "Cornered Rats and Personal Betrayals," *Los Angeles Times*, 20 October 1997.

40. Michael Kanin, interview by the Writers Guild Oral History Project (Los Angeles: Writers Guild Foundation, spring 1978), 5.

41. Phillip Dunne interviewed by Thomas Stemple, box 25, OH 36, vol. 1, Darryl F. Zanuck Project, Oral History Collection, American Film Institute, Louis B. Mayer Library, Los Angeles, 103.

42. Screen Writers Guild, "Report on the Activities of the Hollywood Writers Mobilization," 2.

43. Schwartz, *Hollywood Writers' Wars*, 202–203.

44. Neal Gabler, *Walt Disney: The Triumph of the American Imagination* (New York: Random House, 2006), 364.

45. Telegram to the executive board of the Screen Writers Guild from 45 members of the Screen Writers Guild, undated, Archives, Writers Guild Foundation Shavelson-Webb Library, Los Angeles.

46. For more on this tension between the IATSE and the CSU, see Brett L. Abrams, "The First Hollywood Blacklist: The Major Studios Deal with the Conference of Studio Unions, 1941–47," *Southern California Quarterly 77*, no. 3 (1995): 215–253.

47. Reynold Humphries, *Hollywood's Blacklist: A Political and Cultural History* (Edinburgh: Edinburgh University Press, 2011), 32.

48. Screen Writers Guild Planning Committee, "Film Industry Planning Committee for Mass Meeting, June 19, 1944," 19 May 1944, Archives, Writers Guild Foundation Shavelson-Webb Library, Los Angeles.

49. This recommendation was adopted at a Screen Writers Guild membership meeting. Screen Writers Guild, "Membership Meeting Notes," 10 April 1944, Archives, Writers Guild Foundation Shavelson-Webb Library, Los Angeles.

50 Carey McWilliams, "The Inside Story of the Hollywood Strike," *PM Examiner*, 2 September 1945, 9.

51. In the matter of Columbia Pictures Corporation, Loew's Incorporated, Paramount Pictures Inc., RKO Radio Pictures, Inc., Republic Productions, Inc., Twentieth

Century–Fox Film Corporation, Universal Pictures Company, Inc., Warner Bros. Pictures, Inc. and Screen Set Designers, Illustrators & Decorators, Local 1421, AFL and International Alliance of Theatrical Stage Employees and Moving Picture Machine Operators of the United States and Canada, Local 44, AFL. National Labor Relations Board Case No. 21-RE-20 (1945), 4.

52. John Bright, interview by the Writers Guild Oral History Project (Los Angeles: Writers Guild Foundation, 26 July 1978), 14.

53. Erna Lazarus, interview by the Writers Guild Oral History Project (Los Angeles: Writers Guild Foundation, 15 February 1978), 3.

54. Daniel Taradash, *The Writer Speaks: Daniel Taradash*, DVD, 1998, Writers Guild Foundation Shavelson-Webb Library, Los Angeles.

55. Mel Shavelson, *The Writer Speaks: Mel Shavelson*, DVD, 25 June 1996, Writers Guild Foundation Shavelson-Webb Library, Los Angeles.

56. Bright, Oral History Project, 14.

57. Ludwig, Oral History Project, 11.

58. Bright, Oral History Project, 14.

59. Lardner, interview by the Writers Guild Oral History Project (Los Angeles: Writers Guild Foundation, 1978), 7.

60. Ludwig, Oral History Project, 16.

61. Dunne, Oral History Project, 9.

62. Ceplair, "SAG and the Motion Picture Blacklist," 22.

63. Ibid., 21.

64. George Lipsitz, *Rainbow at Midnight: Labor and Culture in the 1940s* (Urbana and Chicago: University of Illinois Press, 1994), 99.

65. Screen Writers Guild, memo to Eric Johnson, c. 12 October 1945, Archives, Writers Guild Foundation Shavelson-Webb Library, Los Angeles.

66. Screen Writers Guild, "Hollywood Strike Strategy Committee Memo," 28 October 1945, Archives, Writers Guild Foundation Shavelson-Webb Library, Los Angeles.

67. Abraham Polonsky, "How the Blacklist Worked in Hollywood," interview by James Pasternak and William Howton, *Film Culture* 50–51 (1970): 45.

68. Other Hollywood-based publications emerged around the same time as *The Screen Writer*, including the *Hollywood Quarterly*. Published out of UCLA, the *Quarterly* had what Schwartz calls "an undercurrent of conscience." Schwartz, *Hollywood Writers' Wars*, 230.

69. Editorial, *The Screen Writer*, June 1945, 37.

70. Editorial, *The Screen Writer*, September 1945, 51.

71. As of June 1945, there were 236 SWG members on active duty, and 32 had returned. By December 1945, 171 were still in the services, and 125 had returned. See the "Employment Status of Writers" statistics in the issues of *The Screen Writer* for June, July, November, and December 1945.

72. Robert R. Presnell, "The Great Parenthesis," *The Screen Writer*, September 1945, 13.

73. Lester Koenig, "Back from the Wars," *The Screen Writer*, August 1945, 27.

74. James Hilton, "A Novelist Looks at the Screen," *The Screen Writer*, November 1945, 31.

75. Audrey Wood, "Too Fast and Too Soon," *The Screen Writer*, August 1948, 35–38.

76. George Corey, "The Screen Writer and Television," *The Screen Writer*, August 1948, 16–22.

77. J. D. Marshall, *Blueprint on Babylon* (Tempe, AZ: Phoenix House, 1978), 14.

78. James Wong Howe, "The Cameraman Talks Back," *The Screen Writer*, July 1945, 36–37.

79. Arch Oboler, "Look—Then Listen," *The Screen Writer*, December 1945, 26–30.

80. David Bordwell, Janet Staiger, and Kristin Thompson, *The Classical Hollywood Cinema: Film Style and Mode of Production to 1960* (New York: Columbia University Press, 1985), 334.

81. Charles Grayson, "Communication: Writers' War," *The Screen Writer*, August 1946, 39.

82. Budd Schulberg, "The Celluloid Noose," *The Screen Writer*, August 1946, 15.

83. Editorial, *The Screen Writer*, July 1945, 37.

84. Jean Renoir, "Chaplin Among the Immortals," *The Screen Writer*, July 1947, 1–4.

85. Eric Johnston, letter to Emmet Lavery, and Emmet Lavery, letter to Eric Johnston, in "SWG Bulletin: The French-American Film Agreement" *The Screen Writer*, August 1946, 45–51.

86. Editorial, *The Screen Writer*, July 1945, 38.

87. Raymond Chandler, "Writers in Hollywood," *Atlantic Monthly*, November 1945, 50–54.

88. Philip Dunne, "An Essay on Dignity," *The Screen Writer*, December 1945, 2.

89. Ibid., 4.

90. Thomas M. Pryor, "About the Writer and Why He Does Not Get More Notice," *New York Times*, 5 August 1945, as quoted in the editorial "A Note on Recognition," *The Screen Writer*, September 1945, 53.

91. Selection from an article in the *Providence Journal* as quoted in the editorial "A Note on Recognition," *The Screen Writer*, September 1945, 54.

92. Lardner, Oral History Project, 6.

93. It is unclear why there is a discrepancy between the number of attendees and the number of votes. One must assume that either some members left before the vote and/or that some members abstained from voting. Editorial, *The Screen Writer*, August 1946, 3.

94. James M. Cain, "Just What Is AAA?" *The Screen Writer*, October 1946, 1–4.

95. Lardner, Oral History Project, 7.

96. William R. Wilkerson, editorial, *Hollywood Reporter*, 19 August 1946.

97. Ezra Goodman, *The Fifty-Year Decline and Fall of Hollywood*, 3rd ed. (New York: Simon and Schuster, 1961), 24–25.

98. Selections from articles in the *Chicago Tribune*, 9 August and 14 September 1946, as quoted in "AAA Press Survey," *The Screen Writer*, October 1946, 37, 47.

99. Draft of correspondence from Philip Dunne, Howard Estabrook, Sheridan Gibney, Mary McCall Jr., Marguerite Roberts, Frank Partos, F. Hugh Herbert, David Hertz, and Waldo Salt to members of the Screen Writers Guild, undated, Executive Director Files, Special Collections, Writers Guild Foundation Shavelson-Webb Library, Los Angeles.

100. Lardner, Oral History Project, 6.

101. "Hollywood's World View," *New Movies*, National Board of Review, July 1946, as quoted in *The Screen Writer*, August 1946, 30.

102. Howard Koch, "Mr. Rankin Has Made Me Self Conscious," *The Screen Writer*, September 1945, 9.

103. Lewis R. Foster, letter to Dalton Trumbo, editor, *The Screen Writer*, December 1945, 38.

104. Editors' response to Lewis R. Foster, *The Screen Writer*, December 1945, 39.

105. Garrett Graham, "Communications: A Plea for Urbanity," *The Screen Writer*, August 1946, 37.

106. Philip Dunne, "SWG—Trade Union or Writers' Protective Association," *The Screen Writer*, October 1946, 6.

107. Editorial, "Reds in Hollywood," *Chicago Tribune*, 20 January 1947. Editorials in the *Tribune* were notoriously anti-Semitic at the time.

108. Emmet Lavery, "You Never Can Tell," *The Screen Writer*, August 1946, 34–35.

109. IATSE Office of Roy Brewer, "IATSE's Reply," *The Screen Writer*, February 1947, 46.

110. Jack Warner, quoted in Schwartz, *Hollywood Writers' Wars*, 254.

111. Ben Roberts and Ivan Goff, interview by the Writers Guild Oral History Project (Los Angeles: Writers Guild Foundation, 28 April 1978), 3.

112. M. G. Pomerance, executive secretary of the Screen Writers Guild, telegram to the Honorable Harry S. Truman, President of the United States, 19 September 1945, Executive Director Files, Special Collections, Writers Guild Foundation Shavelson-Webb Library, Los Angeles.

113. Correspondence between Maurice Rapf, Screen Writers Guild, and J. E. Benton, Los Angeles Ambassador Hotel, 18–20 June 1946, Executive Director Files, Special Collections, Writers Guild Foundation Shavelson-Webb Library, Los Angeles.

114. Arthur Ross, interview by the Writers Guild Oral History Project (Los Angeles: Writers Guild Foundation, 19 April 1978), 2.

115. Philip Dunne, letter to Emmet Lavery, president of the Screen Writers Guild, 12 September 1947, Special Collections, Writers Guild Foundation Shavelson-Webb Library, Los Angeles.

116. Dalton Trumbo, *Time of the Toad: A Study of Inquisition in America.* (1949; rpt., New York: Harper, 1972), 36.

117. Ibid., 37.

118. Ceplair and Englund, *Inquisition in Hollywood*, 418.

119. Schwartz, *Hollywood Writers' Wars*, 271.

120. Sheridan Gibney, interview by the Writers Guild Oral History Project (Los Angeles: Writers Guild Foundation, 6 March 1978), 7.

121. Ceplair and Englund, *Inquisition in Hollywood*, 286.

122. Ibid., 286–287.

123. Dunne, interview by Thomas Stemple, 106.

124. Dunne, Oral History Project, 11.

125. Victor Navasky, *Naming Names*, rev. ed. (New York: Hill and Wang, 2003), 369.

126. Dunne, Oral History Project, 11–12

127. Ibid., 16–17.

128. Eric Johnson, as quoted by Dalton Trumbo in *Time of the Toad*, 35.

129. In 1950, Valentine Davies (*Miracle on 34th Street*, *The Glenn Miller Story*), who was a board member and had served as president of the SWG from 1949 to 1950, refused to sign a loyalty oath. Stanley Rubin, telegram to Valentine Davies, 23 October 1950, Archives, Writers Guild Foundation Shavelson-Webb Library, Los Angeles.

130. "The Screen Writers' Guild Is Facing a Crisis," *The Screen Writer*, November 1947, 1.

131. Navasky, *Naming Names*, 176.

132. Gibney, Oral History Project, 6.

133. Editorial, *The Screen Writer*, October 1948, 13.

134. Navasky, *Naming Names*, 174.

135. The SWG lost this first case on a technicality. The second trial was settled out of court. Harry Tugend, interview by the Writers Guild Oral History Project (Los Angeles: Writers Guild Foundation, c. spring 1978), 15.

136. Editorial, "A Molotov among Us," *Hollywood Reporter*, December 17, 1947, 1.

137. Editorial, *The Screen Writer*, September 1948, 18.

138. Biberman and Dmytryk served six-month sentences.

139. Carl Foreman quoted in Schwartz, *Hollywood Writers' Wars*, 265.

140. Board of the Screen Writers Guild, "Screen Writers Guild Anti-Communist Oath," 3 December 1951, Executive Director Files, Special Collections, Writers Guild Foundation Shavelson-Webb Library, Los Angeles.

141. Gibney, Oral History Project, 12.

142. Paul Jarrico and Marsha Hunt, interview by Elizabeth Farnsworth, *NewsHour*, PBS, 24 October 1997.

143. Marsha Hunt, interview by Glen Lovell in "50 Years: SAG Remembers the Blacklist," special issue, *National Screen Actor* 39, no. 3 (January 1998): 12.

144. Devery Freeman, interview by the Writers Guild Oral History Project (Los Angeles: Writers Guild Foundation, 4 April 1978), 8.

145. Walter Bernstein, personal interview with author, 16 July 2009, New York, NY.

146. Joan Scott, interviewed by Howard Suber, tape 6, Suber Files, Archives, Writers Guild Foundation Shavelson-Webb Library, Los Angeles.

147. David Robb, "Blacklist Ended Lardner, Schulberg Relationship," *Hollywood Reporter*, 3–5 November 2000, 64.

148. Gibney, Oral History Project, 9.

149. Borden Chase, letter to the executive board of the Screen Writers Guild, 2 April 1951, Special Collections, Writers Guild Foundation Shavelson-Webb Library, Los Angeles.

150. Navasky, *Naming Names*, 369–370.

151. Larry Markes, interview by the Writers Guild Oral History Project (Los Angeles: Writers Guild Foundation, spring 1978), 21–22.

152. Greg Krizman, "Hollywood Remembers the Blacklist," in "50 Years: SAG Remembers the Blacklist," special issue, *National Screen Actor* 39, no. 3 (January 1998): 32.

153. Lardner, Oral History Project, 8.

154. Jon Lewis, "'We Do Not Ask You to Condone This': How the Blacklist Saved Hollywood," *Cinema Journal* 39, no. 2 (2000): 3–30.

155. Schwartz, *Hollywood Writers' Wars*, 255.

156. Catherine L. Fisk, "The Role of Private Intellectual Property Rights in Markets for Labor and Ideas: Screen Credit and the Writers Guild of America, 1938–2000," *Berkeley Journal of Employment and Labor Law* 32, no. 2 (2011): 274–275.

157. Polonsky, *Film Culture*, 47.

158. David Robb, "TV's Blacklist: You Are There," *Hollywood Reporter*, 14–16 November 1997, 78.

159. Gladwin Hill, "Movie Companies Settle Red Suits," *New York Times*, 4 January 1952.

160. "Hollywood Suits Due to Be Withdrawn," *Motion Picture Exhibitor Magazine*, New York State edition, 16 January 1952, Press Clippings, Writers Guild Foundation Shavelson-Webb Library, Los Angeles.

161. Nedrick Young, "'Please Don't Pound the Gavel at Me': The Testimony of Nedrick Young," in "Hollywood Blacklisting," ed. Gordon Hitchens, special double issue, *Film Culture* 50–51 (Fall–Winter 1970): 8.

162. Affidavit of John Howard Lawson in *Nedrick Young v. Motion Picture Association of America, Inc.*, 299 F.2d 119 (D.C. Cir. 1962), 95.

163. Larry M. Wertheim, "*Nedrick Young, et al. v. MPAA, et al.:* The Fight against the Hollywood Blacklist," *Southern California Quarterly* 57, no. 4 (Winter 1975): 383–418.

164. Freeman, Oral History Project, 13.

165. Transcript of "Foreman Awards Screen Laurel," *WGAw News*, May 1976, 22.

166. Michael Wilson, "Acceptance Speech," Writers Guild of America Laurel Awards, 1976, Archives, Writers Guild Foundation Shavelson-Webb Library, Los Angeles.

167. Sadly, Jarrico died in a car crash on his way home from the event.

168. Joan Scott, interviewed by Howard Suber, tape 5.

CHAPTER 3   THE INFANT PRODIGY

1. Lynn Spigel, *Make Room for TV: Television and the Family Ideal in Postwar America* (Chicago: University of Chicago Press, 1992).

2. "New Television Writers Union Opens Offices," *Los Angeles Times*, 26 August 1952, Press Clippings, Special Collections, Writers Guild Foundation Shavelson-Webb Library, Los Angeles.

3. "Writers Call Strike against TV-Alliance: Seek 100G Fund," *Daily Variety*, 6 August 1952; "TV Strike Spurned by Radio Writers: Guild Calls Action of Authors League Illegal and Declares It Will Not Support Tie-Up," *New York Times*, 18 August 1952.

4. "Authors League Unions to Set Course in Strike," *Variety*, 1951, Press Clippings, Special Collections, Writers Guild Foundation Shavelson-Webb Library, Los Angeles.

5. Charles Isaacs, "Early TV Writers Faced Blacklist," *Los Angeles Times*, 3 November 1997. Isaacs says that there was only one series (*Fireside Theater*) recorded on film, but in the early 1950sthere were a number, including *I Love Lucy* and *Amos & Andy*.

6. "New Television Writers Union Opens Offices."

7. David Harmon and Nate Monaster, interview by the Writers Guild Oral History Project (Los Angeles: Writers Guild Foundation, 15 February 1978), 3.

8. "Mary McCall Won't Run for Reelection as Prexy of SWG," *Variety*, 3 September 1952, New York City edition; "TV Writers Reject: Video Scribes Pushing for Union Entirely Their Own; Issue List of Objectives," *Hollywood Reporter*, 15 October 1952.

9. Joan Moore and Burton Moore, "The Hollywood Writer" (unpublished, c. 1970), ch. 3, Writers Guild Foundation Shavelson-Webb Library Archives, Los Angeles.

10. "TV Writers Reject."

11. "New Desilu Hearing Completed," *Television Writer* 2, no. 2 (May 1953): 2.

12. Philip Dunne, letter to Alice Penneman at the Screen Writers Guild, 31 January 1951, and Alice Penneman, letter to Philip Dunne, 1 February 1951, Special Collections, Writers Guild Foundation Shavelson-Webb Library, Los Angeles.

13. Philip Dunne, "An Essay on Dignity," *The Screen Writer*, December 1945, 5.

14. Stanley Rubin, interview by the Writers Guild Oral History Project (Los Angeles: Writers Guild Foundation, 9 May 1979), 11.

15. Michael Kanin, interview by the Writers Guild Oral History Project (Los Angeles: Writers Guild Foundation, spring 1978), 6–7.

16. Ibid., 7.

17. William Weaver, "Television Harnessed to Benefit Pictures," *Motion Picture Herald*, 10 May 1952, Press Clippings, Special Collections, Writers Guild Foundation Shavelson-Webb Library, Los Angeles.

18. Ernest Kinoy, interview by the Writers Guild Oral History Project (Los Angeles: Writers Guild Foundation, spring 1978), 7.

19. *The Writer Speaks: David Dortort*, DVD, 4 June 2007, Writers Guild Foundation Shavelson-Webb Library, Los Angeles.

20. Erna Lazarus, interview by the Writers Guild Oral History Project (Los Angeles: Writers Guild Foundation, 15 February 1978), 11.

21. Jon Kraszewski, *The New Entrepreneurs: An Institutional History of Television Anthology Writers* (Middletown, CT: Wesleyan University Press, 2010), 27.

22. "Boost Granted in Writers Salaries," *Longview [WA] Daily News*, 24 January 1952.

23. "Writers Get Extra Pay for Re-use of TV Scripts by Webs," *Daily Variety*, 20 May 1952, Press Clippings, Special Collections, Writers Guild Foundation Shavelson-Webb Library, Los Angeles.

24. Memorandum by Mary McCall to the membership of the Screen Writers Guild, "S.W.G. in 1952," Special Collections, Writers Guild Foundation Shavelson-Webb Library, Los Angeles

25. Ibid.

26. "Boost Granted in Writers Salaries."

27. "Radio, Pix Scribes Grumble at Low Pay for Telepix," *Daily Variety*, 15 May 1952, Press Clippings, Special Collections, Writers Guild Foundation Shavelson-Webb Library, Los Angeles.

28. Karl Tunberg quoted in Moore and Moore, "Hollywood Writer," 27n1.

29. William Boddy, *Fifties Television: The Industry and Its Critics* (Urbana: University of Illinois Press, 1990), 86.

30. Robert Schiller, interview with the author, 29 January 2007.

31. Leonard Stern, interview with the author, 14 January 2010.

32. Norman Lear, interview with the author, 20 August 2013.

33. Carl Reiner, interview with the author, 29 August 2013.

34. "Deported Reuben Ship 'Forces' Reinstatement in Screen Writers Guild," *Variety*, 10 September 1953.

35. "SWG Continues Harboring Reds, Brewer Charges," *Hollywood Reporter*, 9 November 1953.

36. Ibid.

37. "Prexy Mary McCall, Dudley Nichols Lead SWG Opposition to MPIC 'Loyalty Board,'" *Daily Variety*, 3 July 1952.

38. "Referendum Ballots Mailed to Members," *Daily Variety*, 3 July 1952. The article recounts that the MPIC loyalty plan was on the table at the special membership meeting on 2 July, but it could not be voted on because a quorum was not present. Overall sentiment at the meeting was that the SWG would not approve the plan. At the meeting, "Miss McCall, Dudley Nichols, Edward Huebsch and John Howard Lawson spearheaded the fight against the opposition of the loyalty plan. Leading proponents of the plan included Sheridan Gibney, Virginia Kellogg and Leonard Spigelgass."

39. See *The Radio Writer*, bulletin of the Radio Writers Guild, published August 1947–February 1952. Radio Writers Guild, Periodicals, Writers Guild Foundation Shavelson-Webb Library, Los Angeles.

40. Larry Marks, "Television, Anyone? Western V.P. Reports," *The Radio Writer* 3, no. 8 (8 February 1952): 8.

41. "M'Carran [*sic*] Lists Radio Writers As 'Subversives,'" *New York Compass*, 27 August 1952.

42. Sam Moore, interview by the Writers Guild Oral History Project (Los Angeles: Writers Guild Foundation, 18 June 1979), 7. Moore was a radio writer on the West Coast.

43. Rex Stout, letter to "All Members of the Authors League of America," advertisement in *Daily Variety*, 11 August 1952.

44. "RWG Officially Refuses to Join in Video Strike; Walkout Termed Illegal," *Hollywood Reporter*, 18 August 1952.

45. Robert White and Phyllis White, interview by the Writers Guild Oral History Project (Los Angeles: Writers Guild Foundation, spring 1978), 15–16.

46. It is hard to know whether the structure would have changed as the union grew, since the TWA did not last longer than two years.

47. "Screen Writers Guild, TV Alliance Negotiate to End Six-Week Strike," *Daily Variety*, 15 September 1952.

48. "SWG Votes to Limit Use of Proxies; Elects F. Hugh Herbert Prexy," *Variety*, 18 November 1953.

49. "Writers in TV Control Battle: TWA's NLRB Petition May Stall Screen Writers Guild's New Web Pact for Full Year," *Daily Variety*, 13 October 1952.

50. "Writers for TV Films End 14 Week Strike," *Los Angeles Times*, 17 November 1952, 1, 5.

51. "NOTICE TO ALL TELEVISION WRITERS: You Do Not Need to Join TWA!" advertisement in *Hollywood Reporter*, 1 July 1953.

52. "SWG Votes to Limit Use of Proxies."

53. Richard L. Breen, "SWG: The Challenge," *Film Daily*, 35th anniversary issue, 13 August 1953.

54. "SWG Prexy Candidates Differ on Loyalty Oath," *Variety*, 29 October 1953.

55. "TWA Prexy Opposing Own Board's Proposal to Bar Commie Members," *Variety*, 2 September 1953.

56. "'I Love Lucy' Union Rejected," *Los Angeles Times*, 19 July 1953, 2.

57. Isaacs, "Early TV Writers Faced Blacklist."

58. White and White, Oral History Project, 15.

59. F. Hugh Herbert, letter from the Screen Writers Guild to the members of the Radio Writers Guild, 6 April 1954, page 4, Special Collections, Writers Guild Foundation Shavelson-Webb Library, Los Angeles.

60. Hy Freedman, interview by the Writers Guild Oral History Project (Los Angeles: Writers Guild Foundation, 6 April 1978), 4–5.

61. Kraszewski, *New Entrepreneurs*, 18. The Authors League had a deficit of $40,000, which made the choice to separate ties more obvious. "Authors League Seeks Stronger Central Power," *Variety*, 17 June 1952.

62. F. Hugh Herbert, president of WGA West, letter to Adolph Deutsch, president of the Screen Composers Association, 15 October 1954, Screen Composers Association Records, Margaret Herrick Library, Academy of Motion Picture Arts and Sciences, Beverley Hills, CA.

63. Moore and Moore, "Hollywood Writer," 29.

64. White and White, Oral History Project, 16.

65. "Chevigny Hopes to Get TWA into ALA 'to Replace RWG,'" *Hollywood Reporter*, 3 August 1953; "Radio Writers Feud Goes On," *Variety*, 16 September 1953.

66. "Authors League Seeks Stronger Central Power," *Variety*, 17 June 1952.

67. The Writers Guild Library did not become part of the foundation and open its doors until 1984, but talk of the library began in 1948. Art Arthur, letter to members of the executive board, 12 January 1948, Special Collections, Writers Guild Foundation Shavelson-Webb Library, Los Angeles. All writers (as well as aspiring writers and the community) have benefited from the work of the foundation over the years; at the time, however, the screenwriters were wary of their new partners. Although in later years the WGA East would have a small foundation, the Writers Guild Foundation was founded out of the coffers of Hollywood screenwriters.

68. Kinoy, Oral History Project, 7.

69. Ibid.

70. Stein, interview with the author.

71. Richard Levinson and William Link, *Stay Tuned: An Inside Look at the Making of Prime-Time Television* (New York: Ace Books, 1981), 12–13.

72. Boddy, *Fifties Television*, 1.

73. Maurice Tombragel, interview by the Writers Guild Oral History Project (Los Angeles: Writers Guild Foundation, 23 May 1978), 11.

74. Edmund North, interview by the Writers Guild Oral History Project (Los Angeles: Writers Guild Foundation, 14 March 1978), 8.

75. Harmon and Monaster, Oral History Project, 4–5, 9.

76. Ibid., 8, 10.

77. Moore and Moore, "Hollywood Writer," 30.

78. RKO stopped production in 1957, and then there were seven companies. Christopher H. Sterling and Timothy R. Haight as cited in Peter Lev, *The Fifties: Transforming the Screen 1950–1959* (Berkeley: University of California Press, 2006), 302.

79. In a battle over the screening of the Italian film *Il Miracolo* (co-written by Roberto Rossellini and Fredrico Fellini), the Supreme Court decided in *Joseph Burstyn, Inc. v. Wilson* (1952) that film censorship was in violation of the First Amendment. See Laura Wittern-Keller and Raymond J. Haberski Jr., *The Miracle Case: Film Censorship and the Supreme Court*, Landmark Law Cases and American Society (Lawrence: University Press of Kansas, 2008).

80. John Michael Hayes, interview with Patrick McGilligan in *Backstory 3: Interviews with Screenwriters of the 60s* (Berkeley: University of California Press, 1997), 181.

81. For a brilliant, well-researched overview, see Christopher Anderson, *Hollywood TV: The Studio System in the Fifties* (Austin: University of Texas Press, 1994).

82. Kraszewski, *New Entrepreneurs*, 139.

83. Stirling Silliphant, interview with Patrick McGilligan in *Backstory 3*, 341.

84. *The Writer Speaks: David Dortort.*

85. Bob Chandler, "Deadlock a Pix Biz Poser," *Variety*, 27 October 1959.

86. Ibid. See also Jonathan Kandell, "Lew Wasserman, 89, Is Dead; Last of Hollywood's Moguls," *New York Times*, 4 June 2002, http://www.nytimes.com/2002/06/04/business/lew-wasserman-89-is-dead-last-of-hollywood-s-moguls.html?pagewanted=all&src=pm.

87. Michael Conant, as cited in Lev, *The Fifties*, 138.

88. Chandler, "Deadlock a Pix Biz Poser."

89. "Writers Ordered Out on Strike Ineligible for State Unemployment," *Hollywood Reporter*, 18 January 1960. *Variety* estimated that the number was closer to between $190 million and $250 million, based on approximately 2,500 films available from the studios to sell to television at a historical average price of $70,000–$100,000 per film. "What Are the Post-48's Worth?" *Variety*, 21 January 1960.

90. Mel Tolkin, interview by the Writers Guild Oral History Project (Los Angeles: Writers Guild Foundation, 26 July 1978), 1–2.

91. Harmon and Monaster, Oral History Project, 11–12.

92. "Writers Make Stiff Demands: 70% Wage Hike, TV Pay and 'Rights' Are the High Points," *Variety*, 27 April 1959.

93. "Writer Strike against Film Producers Slated," *Los Angeles Times*, 2 October 1959.

94. Thomas McDonald, "Hollywood in Tension: Writers, Producers Reach Pay Scale as a Strike Is Voted—Newcomers," *New York Times*, 8 November 1959.

95. Richard R. St. Johns, memo to all Alliance members, "Expiration of Writers Guild Contract," Alliance of TV Film Producers, 27 October 1959, United Artists Corporation Records 1919–1965, ZIV–United Artists, Inc. Legal Files, 1951-1963, box 7, folder 9, Wisconsin Center for Film and Theater Research, University of Wisconsin, Madison.

96. Michael Franklin quoted in "WGA to Skouras: Join 'Struggle,'" *Variety*, 31 December 1959.

97. "Writers Press Guild to Strike Major Studios on Jan. 7," *Hollywood Reporter*, 29 December 1959.

98. Harmon and Monaster, Oral History Project, 19–20.

99. "Writers Ordered Out on Strike Ineligible for State Unemployment," *Hollywood Reporter*, 18 January 1960.

100. Ten of these series were at Warner Bros., three were at Twentieth Century–Fox, eight were at Screen Gems/Columbia, and one was at Disney. Paramount, MGM, and Allied Artists also had television productions in development. Bob Chandler, "Oddity If Writers Guild Strikes Majors: Members Working for Same Bosses' Telepix Would Support War Chest against Theatrical Features," *Variety*, 11 November 1959.

101. "Writers Ordered Out on Strike Ineligible."

102. Oliver Crawford, interview by the Writers Guild Oral History Project (Los Angeles: Writers Guild Foundation, 9 March 1978), 2.

103. The lower estimates are from "Writers Guild Strike Spreads to Film Studios," *Los Angeles Times*, 17 January 1960; the higher estimates are from "Writers Ordered Out on Strike Ineligible."

104. "Movie Studios Lay Off over 100 Secretaries in Writers Strike," *Wall Street Journal*, 18 January 1960.

105. "Prexies and Writers Sked Meet," *Daily Variety*, 18 January 1960.

106. "Pact Impass with Nets So WGA in Huddle," *Daily Variety*, 8 February 1960.

107. "Prexies and Writers Sked Meet."

108. Bob Chandler, "'Hyphen' Service Defined by WGA," *Daily Variety*, 29 January 1960.

109. Stephen Lord, interview by the Writers Guild Oral History Project (Los Angeles: Writers Guild Foundation, 21 February 1978), 1.

110. Harmon and Monaster, Oral History Project, 29–30.

111. Sy Salkowitz, interview by the Writers Guild Oral History Project (Los Angeles: Writers Guild Foundation, 4 April 1978), 12–13.

112. North, Oral History Project, 10.

113. Freedman, Oral History Project, 10.

114. Frank Moss, interview by the Writers Guild Oral History Project (Los Angeles: Writers Guild Foundation, 22 February 1978), 1–2.

115. Kay Lenard, interview by the Writers Guild Oral History Project (Los Angeles: Writers Guild Foundation, 14 March 1978), 4.

116. William Ludwig, interview by the Writers Guild Oral History Project (Los Angeles: Writers Guild Foundation, 16 May 1978), 11.

117. John Bright, interview by the Writers Guild Oral History Project (Los Angeles: Writers Guild Foundation, 26 July 1978), 24–25.

118. "TV-Film Writers, Producers Fail in Strike Peace Hopes," *Los Angeles Mirror-News*, 28 April 1960.

119. "Film Studios and Writers OK Contract," *Los Angeles Mirror-News*, 11 June 1960.

120. "Screen Writers New Privileges: (1) B.O. Royalties in France, Spain; (2) Firmer Control as to Credit," *Variety*, 22 June 1960.

121. Ibid.

122. Michael Franklin, memo to WGA members, "Attention!: Royalty Plan," 1 March 1963, WGA History Files, Special Collections, Writers Guild Foundation Shavelson-Webb Library, Los Angeles.

123. "Writers Accept 6-Year Pact," *Hollywood Citizen News*, 20 June 1960.

124. Frank Pierson, interview with the author, 15 February 2011.

125. Herb Meadow, interview by the Writers Guild Oral History Project (Los Angeles: Writers Guild Foundation, 15 March 1978), 15.

126. Harmon and Monaster, Oral History Project, 7.

127. North, Oral History Project, 3.

128. Kanin, Oral History Project, 16.

129. Jay Presson Allen, interview with Patrick McGilligan in *Backstory* 3, 25–26.

130. Hal Kanter, interview by the Writers Guild Oral History Project (Los Angeles: Writers Guild Foundation, 21 June 1978), 5–6.

131. Michael Franklin, interview by the Writers Guild Oral History Project (Los Angeles: Writers Guild Foundation, 20 March1978), 10.

132. Rubin, Oral History Project, 10–11.

133. Thomas Schatz, "New Hollywood," in *Film Theory Goes to the Movies*, ed. Jim Collins, Hilary Radner, and Ava Preacher Collins (New York: Routledge, 1992), 8–36.

134. Lisa Rosen, "Take Five: 3 Wise Men," *Written By: The Magazine of the Writers Guild of America, West*, Summer 2013, 12.

135. Justin Wyatt, *High Concept: Movies and Marketing in Hollywood* (Austin: University of Texas Press, 1994), 71.

136. "MGM/UA under Kerkorian Meant 20 Years of Change," *Los Angeles Times*, 8 March 1990, http://articles.latimes.com/1990–03–08/business/fi-2987_1_mgm-grand.

CHAPTER 4   MAVERICKS

1. *The Writer Speaks: William Goldman*, DVD, 27 May 2010, Writers Guild Foundation Shavelson-Webb Library, Los Angeles.

2. Frank Pierson, interview with the author, 15 February 2011.

3. Sherwood Schwartz, interview by the Writers Guild Oral History Project (Los Angeles: Writers Guild Foundation, 3 May 1978), 2–4.

4. John Furia Jr. and David Rintels, interview by the Writers Guild Oral History Project (Los Angeles: Writers Guild Foundation, 3 May 1978), 44–45.

5. Patrick McGilligan, *Backstory 4: Interviews with Screenwriters of the 1970s and 1980s* (Berkeley: University of California Press, 2006), 4.

6. James Crawford, "Film Credit" (Ph.D. diss., University of Southern California, 2013), 236.

7. Catherine L. Fisk, "The Role of Private Intellectual Property Rights in Markets for Labor and Ideas: Screen Credit and the Writers Guild of America, 1938–2000." *Berkeley Journal of Employment and Labor Law* 32, no. 2 (2011): 218.

8. Virginia Wright Wexman, "One Man, One Film: The Directors Guild of American and the Cultural Construction of the Artist" (paper delivered to the Society for Cinema & Media Studies Conference, Chicago, 8 March 2013).

9. *The Writer Speaks: Daniel Taradash*, DVD, 1998, Writers Guild Foundation Shavelson-Webb Library, Los Angeles.

10. Andrew Sarris, "Notes on the Auteur Theory in 1962," in *Film Theory and Criticism: Introductory Readings*, 6th ed., ed. Gerald Mast, Marshall Cohen, and Leo Braudy (New York: Oxford University Press, 2004), 561–564.

11. Fisk, "Role of Private Intellectual Property Rights," 274–275.

12. Michael Franklin, interview with the author, 8 August 2013.

13. Fisk, "Role of Private Intellectual Property Rights," 257.

14. Crawford, "Film Credit," 287.

15. Jesse Heistand, "The 'Credit' Card," *Hollywood Reporter*, 31 March 2005.

16. Pierson, interview.

17. Len Chassman, interview by the Writers Guild Oral History Project (Los Angeles: Writers Guild Foundation, 8 August 1978), 20–21.

18. Pierson, interview.

19. Herb Meadow, interview by the Writers Guild Oral History Project (Los Angeles: Writers Guild Foundation, 15 March 1978), 25.

20. Mel Brooks, interview with the author, 15 August 2013.

21. Ibid.

22. Carl Reiner, interview with the author, 29 August 2013.

23. Director's Guild of America, "Possessory Credit Timeline," *DGA Magazine*, February 2004, http://www.dga.org/Craft/DGAQ/All-Articles/0402-Feb-2004/Possessory-Credit-Timeline.aspx.

24. See Timothy Corrigan's notion of "the commerce of auteurism" in "Auteurs and the New Hollywood," in *The New American Cinema*, ed. Jon Lewis (Durham, NC: Duke University Press, 1998), 38–63.

25. Bernard Weinraub, "Screenwriters May Walk Out Over Film Credit and Respect," *New York Times*, 16 January 2001, http://www.nytimes.com/2001/01/16/business/screenwriters-may-walk-out-over-film-credit-and-respect.html?pagewanted=all&src=pm.

26. George Eckstein, interview by the Writers Guild Oral History Project (Los Angeles: Writers Guild Foundation, spring 1978), 1.

27. Meadow, Oral History Project, 24.

28. Richard Levinson and William Link, *Stay Tuned: An Inside Look at the Making of Prime-Time Television* (New York: Ace Books, 1981), 184–186.

29. Ibid., 14.

30. David Isaacs, interview with the author, 30 July 2013.

31. Cheri Steinkellner, interview with the author, 12 August 2013.

32. Ron Clark, interview with the author, 26 August 2009.

33. Frank Pierson, interview.

34. George Eckstein, Oral History Project, 5.

35. Ernest Kinoy, interview by the Writers Guild Oral History Project (Los Angeles: Writers Guild Foundation, spring 1978), 20.

36. M.W., "Kanter Adds Dimension to Hyphenated Career: Writer-Prod-Dir-Emcee," *WGAw Newsletter*, December 1967, 7.

37. Carey Wilber, interview by the Writers Guild Oral History Project (Los Angeles: Writers Guild Foundation, 25 July 1978), 5. Wilber is cited in the materials as Carey Wilbur.

38. Ben Roberts and Ivan Goff, interview by the Writers Guild Oral History Project (Los Angeles: Writers Guild Foundation, 28 April 1978), 22.

39. Stephen Farber, "Rift Remains after Strike by Writers," *New York Times*, 30 June 1973, 67.

40. Sy Salkowitz, interview by the Writers Guild Oral History Project (Los Angeles: Writers Guild Foundation, 4 April 1978), 13.

41. Sherwood Schwartz, Oral History Project, 8.

42. Leonard Stern, interview with the author, 14 January 2010.

43. Leonard Stern, interview by the Writers Guild Oral History Project (Los Angeles: Writers Guild Foundation, 17 May 1978), 9. These issues are still a part of the organization's mission statement today. See "The History of the Caucus," Caucus for Producers, Writers & Directors, last modified 2001, http://www.caucus.org/about/shorthistory.html.

44. Some writers are also members of the Producers Guild of America, just as others are also members of the DGA and SAG.

45. *American Broadcasting Companies, Inc., et al., Petitioners, v. Writers Guild of America, West, Inc., et al.; Association of Motion Picture and Television Producers, Inc., Petitioner, v. Writers Guild of America, West, Inc., et al.; National Labor Relations Board, Petitioner, v. Writers Guild of America, West, Inc., et al.* Case Record No. 437 U.S. 411 (1978). Opinion delivered by Justice White. Others voting in favor were Harry Blackmun, Lewis F. Powell, William Rehnquist, and Chief Justice Warren E. Burger. Dissenting were Justices John Paul Stevens, Potter Stewart, William J. Brennan, and Thurgood Marshall.

46. Ibid.

47. Ibid.

48. M.W., "Hyphenate Sam Rolfe," 1.

49. Stirling Silliphant, interview by the Writers Guild Oral History Project (Los Angeles: Writers Guild Foundation, 1 March 1978), 4.

50. Patricia Falken Smith, interview by the Writers Guild Oral History Project (Los Angeles: Writers Guild Foundation, 16 March 1978), 15.

51. Saul Turteltaub, interview with the author, 16 August 2013.

52. Marc Norman, *What Happens Next: A History of American Screenwriting* (New York: Three Rivers Press/Random House, 2008), 390.

53. McGilligan, *Backstory* 4, 5.

54. William Goldman, *Adventures in the Screen Trade* (New York: Grand Central Publishing, 1986).

55. Paul Schrader as quoted in Norman, *What Happens Next*, 397.

56. Geoff King, *New Hollywood Cinema* (New York: Columbia University Press, 2002), 90.

57. Mark Norman, interview with the author, 9 June 2011.

58. For more on the rise of independent films and the mainstreaming of the indie, see Alisa Perren's excellent *Indie, Inc.: Miramax and the Transformation of Hollywood in the 1990s* (Austin: University of Texas Press, 2012).

59. Stanley Rubin, interview by the Writers Guild Oral History Project (Los Angeles: Writers Guild Foundation, 9 May 1979), 20.

60. *The Writer Speaks: Fay Kanin*, DVD, 18 May 1998, Writers Guild Foundation Shavelson-Webb Library, Los Angeles.

61. Fred Silverman, interview with the author, 16 August 2013.

62. J. B. Bird, "Roots," Archive of American Television, Television Academy Foundation, 2013, http://www.emmytvlegends.org/interviews/shows/roots.

63. *Writers on Writing: William Blinn*, DVD, 23 April 2009, Writers Guild Foundation Shavelson-Webb Library, Los Angeles.

64. *Writers on Writing: William Blinn.*

65. Fred Silverman, interview.

66. Ibid. Norman Lear echoed this longing for the Fin-Syn structure and smaller corporate overhead in his interview with me, 20 August 2013.

67. John Caldwell, *Televisuality: Style, Crisis, and Authority in American Television* (New Brunswick, NJ: Rutgers University Press, 1995), 57.

68. Norman Lear, interview.

69. Television Academy, "Hall of Fame 2011: Inductee Susan Harris (Exclusive Interview)," *YouTube* (recorded 20 January 2011), http://www.youtube.com/watch?v=aIj2Mw59DPQ&noredirect=1.

70. Allan Burns, interview with the author, 7 August 2013.

71. Robert Schiller, interview with the author, 12 January 2012.

72. Norman Lear, interview.

73. David Isaacs, interview.

74. Alvin Sargent, interview with the author, 25 August 2009.

75. Michael Franklin, memo from the WGA to All Signatories to the 1973 WGA MBA, 8 April 1974, Archives, Writers Guild Foundation Shavelson-Webb Library, Los Angeles. The memo does not note whether these women were staff writers or freelancers.

76. Ibid.

77. Michael Franklin, interview.

78. Jean Rouverol Butler, interview by Howard Suber, Suber Files, tape 6, Archives, Writers Guild Foundation Shavelson-Webb Library, Los Angeles.

79. Norman Lear, interview.

80. WGA Women's Committee, "Women's Committee Statistics Report," 7 November 1974, Archives, Writers Guild Foundation Shavelson-Webb Library, Los Angeles.

81. Ibid.

82. Barbara Corday, interview with the author, 30 August 2013.

83. Ibid.

84. Both quotations from Leonora Thuna, letter to the editor, "Story Eds Should Become Aware of Women Writers," *WGAw Newsletter*, June 1983, 17.

85. William T. Bielby and Denise D. Bielby, *The 1987 Hollywood Writers' Report: A Survey of Ethnic, Gender, and Age Employment Factors* (West Hollywood, CA: Writers Guild of America, West, 1987).

86. Ibid.

87. Cheri Steinkellner, interview.

88. James R. Webb, "Screenplays and the Black Writer," reprinted from the *Stanford Alumni Almanac*, March 1969, in "POV: Point of View," *WGAw Newsletter*, May 1969, 1, 8.

89. Ibid.

90. Carey Wilber, Oral History Project, 3.

91. Bill Boulware, interview with Oliver Williams, "POV: A Writer Who's Black . . . and Working: An Interview," *WGAw Newsletter*, June 1983, 28–29.

92. Len Riley, "POV: All-White or All-American?" *WGAw Newsletter*, June 1980, 26–30.

93. Jennifer Holt, *Empires of Entertainment: Media Industries and the Politics of Deregulation, 1980–1996* (New Brunswick, NJ: Rutgers University Press, 2011), 3.

94. Ibid, 15.

95. The Nielsen Company–NTI in 1980 and 1990, cited in "TV Basics," TVB (New York: Television Bureau of Advertising, 2010), 2, http://www.tvb.org/media/file/TVB_FF_TV_Basics.pdf; Larry Gross, "My Media Studies: Cultivation to Participation," *Television & New Media* 10, no. 1 (January 2009): 66–68, doi:10.1177/1527476408325105.

96. Cheri Steinkellner, interview.

97. David Isaacs, interview.

98. Will Tusher, "Producers Once Again Unified," *Variety*, 8 February 1982, 1.

99. Ibid., 12.

100. Grace Reiner, interview with author, 23 June 2009.

101. Ibid.

102. Dale Pollack, "Writers Pondering Strike Issue," *Los Angeles Times*, 15 February 1985, http://articles.latimes.com/1985-02–15/entertainment/ca-3397_1_strike-issue.

103. Standard & Poor's, *Industry Surveys* 1985, L18, as cited in Holt, *Empires of Entertainment*, 16; Alan J. Scott, *On Hollywood: The Place, the Industry* (Princeton, NJ: Princeton University Press, 2004).

104. Susan Christopherson, "Labor: The Effects of Media Concentration on the Film and Television Workforce," in *Contemporary Hollywood Film Industry*, ed. Paul McDonald and Janet Wasko (New York: Wiley-Blackwell, 2008), 160.

105. Peter Lefcourt, moderator, "Seven Letters to the Editor: A Roundtable Discussion on Politics in the Writers Guild of America," *Written By: The Magazine of the Writers Guild of America, West*, April 2005, http://www.wga.org/writtenby/writtenbysub.aspx?id=872.

106. Ibid.

107. Edmund Morris, letter to the editor, *WGAw Newsletter*, May 1985, 26–27.

108. Grace Reiner, interview.

109. Ernest Lehman, "From the Guild President," *WGAw Newsletter*, November 1985, 1, 8–9.

110. Howard Rodman, interview with the author, 15 February 2011.

111. Cheri Steinkellner, interview.

112. "Writers Strike Chronology," *Los Angeles Times*, 4 August 1988. Accessed at http://articles.latimes.com/1988-08-04/news/mn-10237_1_writers-guild.

113. See Chad Raphael, "The Political Economic Origins of Reali-TV," *Jump Cut: A Review of Contemporary Media*, no. 41 (May 1997): 102–109.

114. The WGA made slight gains on creative rights and foreign sales. The AMPTP secured a sliding residual scale for hour-long reruns.

115. Chuck Slocum, interview with the author, 14 January 2010.

116. Marc Norman, interview.

117. George Axelrod, interview by Patrick McGilligan, *Backstory* 3: Interviews with Screenwriters of the 60s (Berkeley: University of California Press, 1997), 69.

118. Ronald Bass, interview with the author, 13 June 2011.

119. Joe Eszterhas, interview by Michael Fleming, "Playboy Interview: Joe Eszterhas," *Playboy*, 1 April 1998, 58.

120. Ronald Bass, interview.

121. Caldwell, *Televisuality*, 105.

122. Saul Turteltaub, interview.

CHAPTER 5   CONFEDERATION

1. Tom Fontana, interview with author, 23 October 2009.

2. A series of film-worthy twists, turns, mysteries, and dramas led to leadership upheavals within the WGA West, including the successive departures of two presidents, Victoria Riskin (*My Antonia*), the first female president of the WGAw (2001–2004), and Charles Holland (*Murder One*), the first African-American president of the Writers Guild (January–March 2004).

3. John Auerbach, "Writers United?" *Cinema Journal* 45, no. 2 (Winter 2006): 97.

4. Carl DiOrio, "Mangan to Exit WGA East," *Hollywood Reporter*, 31 August 2007.

5. Tom Fontana, interview.

6. Howard A. Rodman, "WGA Strike One Year Later: Rodman," *Deadline Hollywood*, 28 February 2009, http://www.deadline.com/2009/02/wga-strike-one-year-later-howard-rodman/.

7. Susan Christopherson, "Labor: The Effects of Media Concentration on the Film and Television Workforce," in *The Contemporary Hollywood Film Industry*, ed. Paul McDonald and Janet Wasko (New York: Wiley-Blackwell, 2008), 162.

8. Andy Meisler, "The Man Who Keeps *E.R.*'s Heart Beating," *New York Times*, 26 February 1995.

9. Denise Mann, "It's Not TV, It's Brand Management TV: The Collective Author(s) of the *Lost* Franchise," in *Production Studies: Cultural Studies of Media Industries*, ed. Vicki Mayer, Miranda J. Banks, and John T. Caldwell (London: Routledge, 2009), 99–114.

10. Norman Lear, interview with the author, 20 August 2013.

11. Barbara Corday, interview with the author, 30 August 2013.

12. See Mara Einstein, *Media Diversity: Economics, Ownership, and the FCC* (London: Routledge, 2004).

13. Administrative Procedure Act (APA), 5 U.S.C. § 706 6(2)(A) (2006).

14. Jennifer Holt, *Empires of Entertainment: Media Industries and the Politics of Deregulation, 1980–1996* (New Brunswick, NJ: Rutgers University Press, 2011), 150.

15. Charles Slocum, interview with the author, 24 January 2010.

16. Charles Slocum, "Seven Steps to Wisdom," *Written By: The Magazine of the Writers Guild of America, West*, October 2002.

17. This instability was occurring across media industries beyond film and television. See Mark Deuze, *Media Work* (Cambridge, UK: Polity, 2007).

18. Tom Fontana, interview.

19. This is a summary list of the major regulatory provisions. The Telecommunications Act also revoked regulations on radio station ownership and cracked down on content violations with the inclusion of the Communications Decency Act, a new ratings system, and the requirement that all new television sets include the V-chip, a technology intended to allow parents to manage their children's viewing based on content ratings. For a detailed analysis, see Jeff Chester, *Digital Destiny: New Media and the Future of Democracy* (New York: New Press, 2007).

20. Emanuel Levy, *Cinema of Outsiders: The Rise of American Independent Film* (New York: NYU Press, 2001), 510n38. Later companies like Lions Gate Entertainment followed this pattern to great success.

21. Another example is Fox Atomic. For more discussion of this movement, see Chuck Tryon, *Reinventing Cinema: Movies in the Age of Media Convergence* (New Brunswick, NJ: Rutgers University Press, 2009), 171.

22. Gary Indiana, "Gus Van Sant," *BOMB* 45 (Fall 1993), http://bombsite.com/issues/45/articles/1699#.

23. Alisa Perren, *Indie, Inc.: Miramax and the Transformation of Hollywood in the 1990s* (Austin: University of Texas Press, 2012).

24. Levy, *Cinema of Outsiders*, 3.

25. Disney subsequently sold Miramax in 2010—not back to the Weinstein Company, but rather to the oil money/private equity firm Filmyard Holdings.

26. There were also a number of short-lived series (*The Critic*) or series shown briefly on primetime that then transitioned to Saturday morning (*Batman: The Animated Series, The Tick, Life with Louie*).

27. WGA memo, "WGA Reaches Groundbreaking Contract Agreement with Fox Television: Primetime Animation Writers Reach Contractual Parity with Their Live-Action Counterparts Los Angeles," 14 August 1999, Special Collections, Writers Guild Foundation Shavelson-Webb Library Archives, Los Angeles.

28. David A. Goodman, interview with the author, 24 April 2009.

29. Sydnye White, "Documentary by Design," *Cinema Journal* 45, no. 2 (Winter 2006): 94.

30. Bill Carter, "Reality Shows Alter the Way TV Does Business," *New York Times*, 25 January 2003.

31. John Koch, "On the Dock of the Bay," *Written By: The Magazine of the Writers Guild of America, West*, May 2005, 17.

32. Del Reisman, "Spring through the Guilds and Honorary Societies," *Weekly Variety*, 18–24 November 1996.

33. John Zuur Platten quoted in Suzanne Oshry, "Getting in the Game," *Written By: The Magazine of the Writers Guild of America, West*, October 2004, 52.

34. Christy Marx quoted in ibid., 55.

35. Charles Slocum, interview.

36. The memo suggested a "charm school" that would have promising writers "undergo an intensive image makeover." The goal was to increase the visibility of writers and to improve their professional status. Ron Tammariello, internal memo to Brian Walton and Paul Nawrocki, 1995, Writers Guild Foundation Shavelson-Webb Library Archives, Los Angeles.

37. See Michael Z. Newman and Elana Levine, "The Showrunner as *Auteur*," in *Legitimating Television: Media Convergence and Cultural Status*, ed. Michael Z. Newman and Elana Levine (New York: Routledge, 2011), 38–58.

38. David Goodman, interview.

39. Mann, "It's Not TV, It's Brand Management TV," 99–114.

40. Michael Curtin, "Matrix Media," in *Television Studies after TV: Understanding Television in the Post-Broadcast Era*, ed. Graeme Turner and Jinna Tay (London: Routledge, 2009), 13.

41. Http://transition.fcc.gov/ownership/california100306/statement_patric_verrone.pdf.

42. Robin Schiff, interview with the author, 21 April 2009.

43. Grace Reiner, interview with author, 23 June 2009. Howard A. Rodman said of her: "Grace Reiner is a force of nature, and has the entire MBA in her head, like a character from Fahrenheit 451" (Howard A. Rodman, personal communication with the author, 15 August 2010).

44. David Robb, "WGA to Decide Walton Verdict," *Hollywood Reporter*, 4 August 1998.

45. Daniel Petrie Jr., memo to the membership of the WGA West, "A Referendum Defeated 921–821," September 1998, Archives, Writers Guild Foundation Shavelson-Webb Library, Los Angeles.

46. Elias Davis, interview with the author, 29 September 2009.

47. Anonymous, interview with the author, 26 April 2012.

48. Grace Reiner, interview.

49. Marc Norman quoted in Michael T. Jarvis, "Putting Faces to Some Famous Words," *Los Angeles Times*, 31 October 2003, E10.

50. William Goldman quoted in ibid.

51. Charles Slocum, interview.

52. Pelle Snickars and Patrick Vonderau, "Introduction," in *The YouTube Reader*, ed. Pelle Snickars and Patrick Vonderau (Stockholm: National Library of Sweden, 2009), 10.

53. Ross McCall, interview with the author, 16 May 2009.

54. Greg Thomas Garcia quoted in Neely Tucker, "Reality Looms: Writers' Strike Could Change Pace of Television," *Washington Post*, 1 November 2007.

55. Mark Gunn, interview with the author, 22 March 2009.

56. Patric Verrone, interview with the author, 26 April 2012.

57. David Young, interview with the author, 29 May 2012.

58. Jim Benson, "*Top Model* Takes Strikers Off Payroll," *Broadcasting & Cable*, 7 November 2006, http://www.broadcastingcable.com/article/106484-Top_Model_Takes_Strikers_Off_Payroll.php.

59. Stephen J. Cannell on behalf of the Caucus of Television Producers, Writers and Directors, statement read before the Public Hearing on Media Ownership, *F.C.C. Hearings Concerning Media Consolidation*, 3 October 2006, Los Angeles, http://apps.fcc.gov/ecfs/comment/view?id=5513687633.

60. Taylor Hackford on behalf of the Directors Guild of America, ibid., http://apps.fcc.gov/ecfs/document/view?id=6518528813.

61. Mike Mills on behalf of the Recording Artists Coalition, ibid., http://apps.fcc.gov/ecfs/document/view?id=6518524527.

62. John Connolly, AFTRA national vice president, ibid., http://apps.fcc.gov/ecfs/document/view?id=6518524524.

63. Anne-Marie Johnson on behalf of the Screen Actors Guild, ibid., http://apps.fcc.gov/ecfs/document/view?id=6518524529.

64. Mona Mangan, executive director, WGA East, ibid., http://transition.fcc.gov/ownership/california100306/statement_mona_mangan.pdf.

65. Patric Verrone, president of the WGA West, ibid., http://transition.fcc.gov/ownership/california100306/statement_patric_verrone.pdf.

66. Marshall Herskovitz, on behalf of the Producers Guild of America, ibid., http://transition.fcc.gov/ownership/california100306/statement_marshall_herskovitz.pdf.

67. Statement of Commissioner Deborah Taylor Tate, Re: Promoting Diversification of Ownership in the Broadcasting Services, et al. (MB Docket Nos. 07–294, 06–121, 02–277, 01–235, 01–317, 00–244 and 04–228), *2006 Quadrennial Media Ownership Review*, FCC 07–216 (2006), 120, http://hraunfoss.fcc.gov/edocs_public/attachmatch/FCC-07-217A5.pdf.

68. Dissenting Statement of Commissioner Michael J. Copps, ibid., 106, http://hraunfoss.fcc.gov/edocs_public/attachmatch/FCC-07–217A3.pdf.

69. Oshry, "Getting in the Game," 52.

70. Eric Bangeman, "Growth of Gaming in 2007 Far Outpaces Movies, Music," *ars technica*, 25 January 2008, http://arstechnica.com/gaming/2008/01/growth-of-gaming-in-2007-far-outpaces-movies-music/.

71. Anonymous, "Renaissance Scribes: Enter the Many Media Writers," *Game Writers Quarterly* 1, no. 3 (Fall 2006): 4.

72. David Young, interview.

73. David Goodman, interview.

74. This kind of split among membership seriously weakened the Screen Actors Guild in its 2011 negotiations.

75. The structure proved so effective that, even to this day, the WGA East continues to hold meetings with strike captains in order to hear about the issues and concerns of its membership.

76. Bruce Rosenblum, "AMPTP: State of Network Television," Television Critics Association Summer 2007 Press Tour, 13 July 2007, Beverly Hills, CA.

77. Mark Gunn, interview.

78. Susan Kim, interview with the author, 9 April 2012.

79. Michael Winship, interview with the author, 9 April 2012.

80. David Goodman, interview.

81. Roger Wolfson, "How the WGA Won: A Behind-the-Scenes Look at the WGA Strike," *Huffington Post*, 12 February 2008, http://www.huffingtonpost.com/roger-wolfson/how-the-wga-won-a-behind-_b_86178.html.

82. Bill Scheft, interview with the author, 6 April 2013.

83. Michael Winship, interview.

84. Wolfson, "How the WGA Won."

85. Janet Abbate, *Inventing the Internet* (Cambridge, MA: MIT Press, 2000).

86. *United Hollywood*, http://www.unitedhollywood.com and http://www.unitedhollywood.blogspot.com (sites discontinued).

87. Dante Atkins, "It's Not 1988 Anymore: The WGA Strike, the Internet and Media Decentralization," *Flow TV*, 22 May 2008, http://flowtv.org/2008/05/it%E2%80%99s-not-1988-anymore-the-wga-strike-the-internet-and-media-decentralization-dante-atkins-founder-unitedhollywoodcom/.

88. Courtney Lilly, interview with the author, 16 May 2009.

89. Scott Collins, "Strike Coverage Was Hazardous Duty," *Los Angeles Times*, 18 February 2008, http://www.latimes.com/entertainment/la-et-channel18feb18,0,1028014.story#axzz2iPhPf6Fi.

90. Jennie Chamberlain and Daniel Chamberlain, "We Write, You Wrong," *Flow TV*, 22 May 2008, http://flowtv.org/2008/05/%E2%80%9Cwe-write-you-wrong%E2%80%9D-jennie-chamberlain-screenwriter-daniel-chamberlain-usc/.

91. Brian Stelter, "On YouTube, Creative Venting," Media Decoder Blog, *New York Times*, 7 November 2007, http://mediadecoder.blogs.nytimes.com/2007/11/07/on-youtube-creative-venting/?_r=0.

92. Frank Lesser and Rob Dubbin, "Sorry, Internet," *YouTube* video, 2007, http://www.youtube.com/watch?v=npqx8CsBEyk.

93. Greg Daniels et al., "*The Office* Is Closed," *YouTube* video, 2007, http://www.youtube.com/watch?v=b6hqP0c0_gw.

94. Peter Rader quoted in Ryan J. Meehan and Katherine L. Miller, "Both Sides Now," *Harvard Crimson*, 15 November 2007, http://www.thecrimson.com/article/2007/11/15/both-sides-now-no-your-tivo/#.

95. George Hickenlooper, Alan Sereboff, Kamala Lopez, and Jill Kushner, *Speechless* #16, United Hollywood video, November 2007, http://www.deadline.com/2007/11/speechless-16-amy-ryanpatricia-clarkson/.

96. John Eggerton, "Nielsen: Cable, Internet Benefited from WGA Strike," *Broadcasting & Cable*, 2 April 2008, http://www.broadcastingcable.com/article/113129-Nielsen_Cable_Internet_Benefited_from_WGA_Strike.php.

97. Michael Winship, interview.

98. The final deals the two unions made with the AMPTP were similar, with one important exception. Members agreed to a fixed payment for content streamed online for three years, but in the third year writers were promised 2 percent of distributors' gross in all years that the content is streamed. See the Nielsen Company's publication *Television in Transition: The Impact of the Writers' Strike* (New York: Nielsen, 2008).

99. Dave McNary, "No Edits on WGA Strike," *Variety*, 24 August 2008, http://variety.com/2008/scene/news/no-edits-on-wga-strike-1117991065/.

100. Jeff Zucker, "A Time For Change," keynote address, National Association of Television Programming Executives Conference and Exhibition, Las Vegas, NV, 29 January 2008.

101. Anonymous, interview with the author, 26 April 2012.

102. Craig Mazin, interview with the author, 12 June 2011.

103. Mark Gunn, interview.

104. Ross McCall, interview.

105. Del Reisman, interview with the author, 2 April 2009.

106. Deuze, *Media Work*, 51.

107. Robert Seidman, "Hulu Growth Stalling Already?" *TV by the Numbers*, 3 June 2009, http://tvbythenumbers.zap2it.com/2009/06/03/hulu-growth-stalling-already/19992/.

108. Jason Sklar, interview with the author, 19 May 2009.

109. Erica Rothschild, interview with the author, 16 May 2009.

110. Tom Fontana, interview.

111. Howard Rodman, interview with the author, 15 February 2011.

112. Walter Bernstein, interview with the author, 16 July 2009.

CONCLUSION

1. In earlier research I have interviewed other media practitioners.

2. Examples of this kind of lay theory can be found in John Thornton Caldwell, *Production Culture: Industrial Reflexivity and Critical Practice in Film and Television* (Durham, NC: Duke University Press, 2008).

3. In particular, see articles by James Schamus (*The Wedding Banquet, Crouching Tiger, Hidden Dragon*), Howard A. Rodman (*Joe Gould's Secret, Savage Grace*), José Rivera (*a.k.a. Pablo, The Motorcycle Diaries, The 33*), Sydnye White (*Detroit S.W.A.T.*), John Auerbach (*Stepfather II*), and Jan Oxenberg (*Once and Again, Parenthood, Pretty Little Liars*) in "In Focus: Writing for the American Screen," *Cinema Journal* 45, no. 2 (Winter 2006).

4. Catherine L. Fisk, "The Role of Private Intellectual Property Rights in Markets for Labor and Ideas: Screen Credit and the Writers Guild of America, 1938–2000," *Berkeley Journal of Employment and Labor Law* 32, no. 2 (2011): 228*n*59.

5. National Association for the Advancement of Colored People, Television Diversity Hearings, 29 November 1999, Los Angeles, CA. For further discussion, see National Association for the Advancement of Colored People, *Out of Focus—Out of Sync, Take 4: A Report on the Television Industry* (December 2008); accessible at http://naacp.3cdn.net/b7cf63e85b9742c1c6_w4m6vqs00.pdf.

6. Kimberly Myers, interview with the author, 30 August 2013.

7. Aline Brosh McKenna, interview with the author, 16 August 2013.

8. Chris Levinson, interview with the author, 14 August 2013.

9. Willa Paskin, "David Simon: Most TV Is Unwatchable," *Salon*, 23 September 2012, http://www.salon.com/2012/09/23/david simon_most_tv_is_unwatchable/.

10. Matthew Weiner, "Series Showrunners" (panel discussion, Academy of Television Arts and Sciences Foundation Faculty Seminar, North Hollywood, CA, 9 November 2010).

11. Aline Brosh McKenna, interview.

12. Philip Dunne, *Take Two: A Life in Movies and Politics* (New York: McGraw-Hill, 1980), 43.

13. Brett Martin, "Inside the Breaking Bad Writers' Room: How Vince Gilligan Runs the Show," *The Guardian*, 20 September 2013, http://www.theguardian.com/tv-and-radio/2013/sep/20/breaking-bad-writers-room-vince-gilligan?CMP=twt_fbo.

14. John August, interview with the author, 6 August 2013.

15. Craig Mazin, interview with the author, 12 June 2011.

16. Dave McNary, "WGA West Earnings Up 4% for 2012; TV Earnings Up 10.1% While Screen Work Continues to Slide," *Variety*, 1 July 2013, http://variety.com/2013/film/news/wga-west-earnings-up-4-for-2012–1200503571/.

17. Ibid. McNary notes that employment for features went down to 6.7 percent, the third year in a row of declines at the major studios.

18. Frank Pierson, interview with the author, 15 February 2011. Pierson himself started in television, then wrote for film, but returned to writing television at the end of his career, scripting episodes of both *The Good Wife* and *Mad Men*.

19. Ronald Bass, interview with the author, 13 June 2011.

20. Toby Miller, Nitin Govil, John McMurria, and Richard Maxwell write, "Hollywood is assuredly operating on a global scale. The impact may be visible on screen, but it is also felt at a bodily level by the labour that makes it happen." Toby Miller, Nitin Govil, John McMurria, and Richard Maxwell, *Global Hollywood* (London: BFI, 2001), 219.

21. Editorial, *The Screen Writer*, July 1945, 38.

22. Hal Kanter, interview by the Writers Guild Oral History Project (Los Angeles: Writers Guild Foundation, 21 June 1978), 8.

23. *The Writer Speaks: Fay Kanin*, DVD, 18 May 1998, Writers Guild Foundation Shavelson-Webb Library, Los Angeles.

24. *The Writer Speaks: David Dortort*, DVD.

APPENDIX B: METHODOLOGY

1. Hortense Powdermaker, *Hollywood: the Dream Factory* (New York: Little, Brown and Company, 1950); Leo C. Rosten, *Hollywood: The Movie Colony, the Movie Makers* (New York: Harcourt Brace, 1941).

2. William T. Bielby and Denise D. Bielby's yearly statistical *Hollywood Writers' Report* series (West Hollywood, CA: Writers Guild of America, West); Todd Gitlin, *Inside Prime Time* (New York: Pantheon, 1983); John Thornton Caldwell, *Production Culture: Industrial Reflexivity and Critical Practice in Film and Television* (Durham, NC: Duke University Press, 2008); Denise Mann, "It's Not TV, It's Brand Management TV: The Collective Author(s) of the *Lost* Franchise," in *Production Studies: Cultural Studies of Media Industries*, ed. Vicki Mayer, Miranda J. Banks, and John T. Caldwell (London: Routledge, 2009), 99–114.

3. Horace Newcomb and Robert S. Alley, *The Producer's Medium: Conversations with Creators of American TV* (New York: Oxford University Press, 1983).

4. Thomas Schatz, *The Genius of the System: Hollywood Filmmaking in the Studio Era* (New York: Pantheon Books, 1988); Jennifer Holt, *Empires of Entertainment: Media Industries and the Politics of Deregulation, 1980–1996* (New Brunswick, NJ: Rutgers University Press, 2011); Alisa Perren, *Indie, Inc.: Miramax and the Transformation of Hollywood in the 1990s* (Austin: University of Texas Press, 2012).

5. See Nancy Lynn Schwartz, *The Hollywood Writers' Wars* (New York: McGraw-Hill, 1982), 257; Ian Hamilton, *Writers in Hollywood, 1915–1951* (New York: Carroll & Graf, 1990); Joan Moore and Burton Moore, "The Hollywood Writer" (unpublished ms., c. 1970, Writers Guild Foundation Shavelson-Webb Library Archives, Los Angeles); Marc Norman, *What Happens Next: A History of American Screenwriting* (New York: Three Rivers Press/Random House, 2008); Christopher D. Wheaton, "The Screen Writers' Guild (1920–1942): The Writers Quest for a Freely Negotiated Basic Agreement" (PhD diss., University of Southern California, 1973).

6. Editorial, "Guild History Starts," *WGAw Newsletter* (February 1978).

7. Mark Williams, "Considering Monty Margetts's *Cook's Corner: Oral History and Television History*," in *Television, History, and American Culture: Feminist Critical Essays*, ed. Mary Beth Haralovich and Lauren Rabinovitz (Durham, NC: Duke University Press, 1999), 52.

8. Craig Mazin, interview with the author, 12 June 2011.

9. Gitlin, *Inside Primetime*, 14.

10. Felicia Henderson has done fascinating research on television production by studying writers and the writers' room. See Henderson, "The Culture Behind Closed Doors: Issues of Gender and Race in the Writers' Room," *Cinema Journal* 50, no. 20 (Winter 2011): 145–152.

11. Paul Veyne, *Writing History: Essay on Epistemology*, trans. Mina Moore-Rinvolucri (Middletown, CT: Wesleyan University Press, 1984): 235; cited in Robert Sklar, "Does Film History Need a Crisis?" *Cinema Journal* 44, no. 1 (2004): 135.

12. James Schamus, "In Focus: Writing for the American Screen," *Cinema Journal* 45, no. 2 (Winter 2006): 85.

BIBLIOGRAPHY

Abbate, Janet. *Inventing the Internet.* Cambridge, MA: MIT Press, 2000.

Abrams, Brett L. "The First Hollywood Blacklist: The Major Studios Deal with the Conference of Studio Unions, 1941–47." *Southern California Quarterly* 77, no. 3 (1995): 215–253.

Anderson, Christopher. *Hollywood TV: The Studio System in the Fifties.* Austin: University of Texas Press, 1994.

Bielby, William T., and Denise D. Bielby. *The 1987 Hollywood Writers' Report: A Survey of Ethnic, Gender, and Age Employment Factors.* West Hollywood, CA: Writers Guild of America, West, 1987.

Blotner, Joseph Leo. *Faulkner: A Biography.* New York: Random House, 1974.

Boddy, William. *Fifties Television: The Industry and Its Critics.* Urbana: University of Illinois Press, 1990.

Bordwell, David, Janet Staiger, and Kristin Thompson. *The Classical Hollywood Cinema: Film Style and Mode of Production to 1960.* New York: Columbia University Press, 1985.

Bright, John. *Worms in the Winecup: A Memoir.* Lanham, MD: Scarecrow Press, 2002.

Caldwell, John Thornton. *Production Culture: Industrial Reflexivity and Critical Practice in Film and Television.* Durham, NC: Duke University Press, 2008.

———. *Televisuality: Style, Crisis, and Authority in American Television.* New Brunswick, NJ: Rutgers University Press, 1995.

Ceplair, Larry, and Steven Englund. *The Inquisition in Hollywood: Politics in the Film Community 1930–1960.* Urbana: University of Illinois Press, 1979.

Chester, Jeff. *Digital Destiny: New Media and the Future of Democracy.* New York: New Press, 2007.

Christopherson, Susan. "Labor: The Effects of Media Concentration on the Film and Television Workforce." In *The Contemporary Hollywood Film Industry,* edited by Paul McDonald and Janet Wasko, 155–166. New York: Wiley-Blackwell, 2008.

Conor, Bridget. *Screenwriting: Creative Labour and Professional Practice.* London: Routledge, 2014.

———. "Subjects at Work: Investigating the Creative Labour of British Screenwriters." In *Behind the Screen: Inside European Production Cultures,* edited by Petr Szczepanik and Patrick Vonderau, 207–220. London: Palgrave Macmillan, 2013.

Corrigan, Timothy. "Auteurs and the New Hollywood." In *The New American Cinema,* edited by Jon Lewis, 38–63. Durham, NC: Duke University Press, 1998.

Counter, J. Nicholas, III. "Foreword: Key Issues Facing Producers and Distributors in the Motion Picture and Television Industry." In *Under the Stars: Essays on Labor Relations in Arts and Entertainment*, edited by Lois S. Gray and Ronald L. Seeber, vii–xii. Ithaca, NY: ILR/Cornell University Press, 1996.

Crawford, James. "Film Credit." Ph.D. diss., University of Southern California, 2013. ProQuest (Publication No. 14349).

Curtin, Michael. "Matrix Media." In *Television Studies after TV: Understanding Television in the Post-Broadcast Era*, edited by Graeme Turner and Jinna Tay, 9–19. London: Routledge, 2009.

Deuze, Mark. *Media Work*. Cambridge, UK: Polity, 2007.

Doherty, Thomas. *Hollywood and Hitler, 1933–1939*. New York: Columbia University Press, 2013.

Dunaway, David King. *Huxley in Hollywood*. New York: Harper & Row, 1989.

Dunne, Philip. *Take Two: A Life in Movies and Politics*. New York: McGraw-Hill, 1980.

Einstein, Mara. *Media Diversity: Economics, Ownership, and the FCC*. London: Routledge, 2004.

Fine, Richard. *Hollywood and the Profession of Authorship, 1928–1940*. Ann Arbor: University of Michigan Press, 1985.

Fisk, Catherine L. "The Role of Private Intellectual Property Rights in Markets for Labor and Ideas: Screen Credit and the Writers Guild of America, 1938–2000." *Berkeley Journal of Employment and Labor Law* 32, no. 2 (2011): 215–278.

Flamini, Roland. *Thalberg: The Last Tycoon and the World of MGM*. New York: Crown, 1994.

Francke, Lizzie. *Script Girls: Women Screenwriters in Hollywood*. London: BFI, 1994.

Friedrich, Otto. *City of Nets: A Portrait of Hollywood in the 1940s*. Berkeley: University of California Press, 1997.

Gabler, Neal. *An Empire of Their Own: How Jews Invented Hollywood*. New York: Crown, 1988.

———. *Walt Disney: The Triumph of the American Imagination*. New York: Random House, 2006.

Gitlin, Todd. *Inside Prime Time*. New York: Pantheon, 1983.

Goldman, William. *Adventures in the Screen Trade*. New York: Grand Central Publishing, 1986.

Goodman, Ezra. *The Fifty-Year Decline and Fall of Hollywood*. 3rd ed. New York: Simon and Schuster, 1961.

Goodrich, David L. *The Real Nick and Nora: Frances Goodrich and Albert Hackett, Writers of Stage and Screen Classics*. Carbondale: Southern Illinois University Press, 2001.

Gross, Larry. "My Media Studies: Cultivation to Participation." *Television & New Media* 10, no. 1 (January 2009): 66–68.

Hamilton, Ian. *Writers in Hollywood, 1915–1951*. New York: Carroll & Graf, 1990.

Hecht, Ben. *A Child of the Century*. New York: Simon and Schuster, 1954.

Henderson, Felicia D. "The Culture Behind Closed Doors: Issues of Gender and Race in the Writers' Room." *Cinema Journal* 50, no. 20 (Winter 2011): 145–152.

Hesmondhalgh, David. *The Culture Industries*. 3rd ed. Thousand Oaks, CA: Sage, 2012.

———, and Sarah Baker. *Creative Labour: Media Work in Three Cultural Industries*. Culture, Economy, and the Social. London: Routledge, 2011.

Higham, Charles. *Merchant of Dreams: Louis B. Mayer, M.G.M., and the Secret Hollywood*. New York: Donald I. Fine, Inc., 1993.

Holt, Jennifer. *Empires of Entertainment: Media Industries and the Politics of Deregulation, 1980–1996*. New Brunswick, NJ: Rutgers University Press, 2011.

Horne, Gerald. *Class Struggle in Hollywood 1930–1950: Moguls, Mobsters, Stars, Reds, and Trade Unionists*. Austin: University of Texas Press, 2001.

Humphries, Reynold. *Hollywood's Blacklist: A Political and Cultural History*. Edinburgh: Edinburgh University Press, 2011.

Jacobs, Lea, and Richard Maltby. "Rethinking the Production Code." *Quarterly Review of Film and Video* 15, no. 4 (1995): 1–3.

Kemm, James O. *Rupert Hughes: A Hollywood Legend*. Beverly Hills, CA: Pomegranate Press, 1997.

Kemper, Tom. *Hidden Talent: The Emergence of Hollywood Agents*. Berkeley: University of California Press, 2009.

King, Geoff. *New Hollywood Cinema*. New York: Columbia University Press, 2002.

Kotsilibas-Davis, James. *The Barrymores: The Royal Family in Hollywood*. New York: Crown, 1981.

Kraszewski, Jon. *The New Entrepreneurs: An Institutional History of Television Anthology Writers*. Middletown, CT: Wesleyan University Press, 2010.

Lev, Peter. *The Fifties: Transforming the Screen 1950–1959*. Berkeley: University of California Press, 2006.

Levine, Elana. "Toward a Paradigm for Media Production Research: Behind the Scenes at *General Hospital*." *Critical Studies in Media Communication* 18, no. 1 (2001): 66–82.

Levinson, Richard, and William Link. *Stay Tuned: An Inside Look at the Making of Prime-Time Television*. New York: Ace Books, 1981.

Levy, Emanuel. *Cinema of Outsiders: The Rise of American Independent Film*. New York: NYU Press, 2001.

Lewis, Jon. "'We Do Not Ask You to Condone This': How the Blacklist Saved Hollywood." *Cinema Journal* 39, no. 2 (2000): 3–30.

Lipsitz, George. *Rainbow at Midnight: Labor and Culture in the 1940s*. Urbana and Chicago: University of Illinois Press, 1994.

Loos, Anita. *Kiss Hollywood Goodbye*. New York: Viking, 1974.

Maas, Frederica Sagor. *The Shocking Miss Pilgrim: A Writer in Early Hollywood*. Lexington: University Press of Kentucky, 1999.

Manchester, William. *The Glory and the Dream: A Narrative History of America 1932–1972*. Vol. 1. Boston: Little, Brown & Co., 1974.

Mann, Denise. "It's Not TV, It's Brand Management TV: The Collective Author(s) of the *Lost* Franchise." In *Production Studies: Cultural Studies of Media Industries*, edited by Vicki Mayer, Miranda J. Banks, and John T. Caldwell, 99–114. London: Routledge, 2009.

Marion, Frances. *Off with Their Heads! A Serio-Comic Tale of Hollywood*. New York: Macmillan, 1972.

Marshall, J. D. *Blueprint on Babylon*. Tempe, AZ: Phoenix House, 1978.

Marx, Samuel. *Mayer and Thalberg: The Make-Believe Saints*. New York: Random House, 1975.

Mayer, Vicki, Miranda J. Banks, and John Thornton Caldwell, eds. *Production Studies: Cultural Studies of Media Industries*. London: Routledge, 2009.

McGilligan, Patrick. *Backstory 3: Interviews with Screenwriters of the 60s*. Berkeley: University of California Press, 1997.

——. *Backstory 4: Interviews with Screenwriters of the 1970s and 1980s.* Berkeley: University of California Press, 2006.

Miller, Toby, Nitin Govil, John McMurria, and Richard Maxwell. *Global Hollywood.* London: BFI, 2001.

Mitchell, Greg. "How Hollywood Fixed an Election." *American Film* (November 1988): 30.

Moore, Joan, and Burton Moore. "The Hollywood Writer." Unpublished manuscript, c. 1970. Writers Guild Foundation Shavelson-Webb Library Archives, Los Angeles.

Navasky, Victor. *Naming Names.* Rev. ed. New York: Hill and Wang, 2003.

Newcomb, Horace, and Robert S. Alley. *The Producer's Medium: Conversations with Creators of American TV.* New York: Oxford University Press, 1983.

Newman, Michael Z., and Elana Levine. "The Showrunner as *Auteur*." In *Legitimating Television: Media Convergence and Cultural Status*, edited by Michael Z. Newman and Elana Levine, 38–58. New York: Routledge, 2011.

Nichols, Dudley. "Conversation Piece." *The Screen Guilds Magazine* 2, no. 1 (March 1935): 5.

Nickens, Daryl G., ed., for the Writers Guild Foundation. *Doing It for Money: The Agony and Ecstasy of Writing and Surviving in Hollywood.* Los Angeles: Tallfellow Press, 2006.

Nielsen, Michael Charles, and Gene Mailes. *Hollywood's Other Blacklist: Union Struggles in the Studio System.* London: BFI, 1995.

Norman, Marc. *What Happens Next: A History of American Screenwriting.* New York: Three Rivers Press/Random House, 2008.

Perren, Alisa. *Indie, Inc.: Miramax and the Transformation of Hollywood in the 1990s.* Austin: University of Texas Press, 2012.

Peterson, Florence. *American Labor Unions: What They Are and How They Work.* New York: Harper & Brothers, 1944.

Phillips, Gene D. *Fiction, Film, and F. Scott Fitzgerald.* Chicago: Loyola University Press, 1986.

Polonsky, Abraham. "How the Blacklist Worked in Hollywood." Interview by James Pasternak and William Howton. *Film Culture* 50–51 (1970): 45.

Powdermaker, Hortense. *Hollywood, the Dream Factory.* New York: Little, Brown and Company, 1950.

——. *Stranger and Friend: The Way of an Anthropologist.* New York: Norton, 1967.

Prover, Jorja. *No One Knows Their Names: Screenwriters in Hollywood.* Madison, WI: Popular Press, 1994.

Raphael, Chad. "The Political Economic Origins of Reali-TV." *Jump Cut: A Review of Contemporary Media*, no. 41 (May 1997): 102–109.

Redvall, Eva Novrup. *Writing and Producing Television Drama in Denmark: From "The Kingdom" to "The Killing."* New York: Palgrave Macmillan, 2013.

Rodman, Howard A. "What a Screenplay Isn't." *Cinema Journal* 45, no. 2 (Winter 2006): 86–89.

Roosevelt, Franklin D. "On the Bank Crisis." *Fireside Chats.* 12 March 1933.

Ross, Andrew. *No Collar: The Humane Workplace and Its Hidden Costs.* Philadelphia: Temple University Press, 2002.

Rosten, Leo C. *Hollywood: The Movie Colony, the Movie Makers.* New York: Harcourt Brace, 1941.

Sarris, Andrew. "Notes on the Auteur Theory in 1962." In *Film Theory and Criticism: Introductory Readings*, 6th ed., edited by Gerald Mast, Marshall Cohen, and Leo Braudy, 585–588. New York: Oxford University Press, 2004.

Schamus, James. "In Focus: Writing for the American Screen." *Cinema Journal* 45, no. 2 (Winter 2006): 85.

Schatz, Thomas. *The Genius of the System: Hollywood Filmmaking in the Studio Era*, New York: Pantheon Books, 1988.

——. "New Hollywood." In *Film Theory Goes to the Movies*, edited by Jim Collins, Hilary Radner, and Ava Preacher Collins, 8–36. New York: Routledge, 1992.

Schlesinger, Arthur M., Jr. *The Coming of the New Deal*. Boston: Houghton Mifflin, 1959.

Schultheiss, John. "The Eastern Writer in Hollywood." *Cinema Journal* 11, no. 1 (Autumn 1971): 13.

Schwartz, Nancy Lynn. *The Hollywood Writers' Wars*. New York: McGraw-Hill, 1982.

Scott, Allen J. *On Hollywood: The Place, the Industry*. Princeton: Princeton University Press, 2004.

Snickars, Pelle, and Patrick Vonderau. "Introduction." In *The YouTube Reader*, edited by Pelle Snickars and Patrick Vonderau, 9–21. Stockholm: National Library of Sweden, 2009.

Spigel, Lynn. *Make Room for TV: Television and the Family Ideal in Postwar America*. Chicago: University of Chicago Press, 1992.

Stewart, Donald Ogden. "Writing for the Movies." *Focus on Film* (Winter 1970): 52.

Stone, Judy. *Eye on the World: Conversations with International Filmmakers*. Los Angeles: Silman-James Press, 1997.

Swanson, Neely. "Women Can't Create and White Men Can't Jump." *Baseline Intelligence*, 4 February 2010, http://www.baselineintel.com/research-wrap?dctail/C7/women_cant_create_and_white_men_cant_jump.

Tinic, Serra. *On Location: Canada's Television Industry in a Global Market*. Toronto: University of Toronto Press, 2005.

Towne, Robert. "On Moving Pictures," *Chinatown and The Last Detail: 2 Screenplays*. New York: Grove Press, 1997.

Thomas, Bob. *Thalberg: Life and Legend*. New York: Doubleday & Co., 1969.

Trumbo, Dalton. *Time of the Toad: A Study of Inquisition in America*. 1949. Rpt., New York: Harper, 1972.

Tryon, Chuck. *Reinventing Cinema: Movies in the Age of Media Convergence*. New Brunswick, NJ: Rutgers University Press, 2009.

Urwand, Ben. *The Collaboration: Hollywood's Pact with Hitler*. Cambridge, MA: Harvard University Press, 2013.

Veyne, Paul. *Writing History: Essay on Epistemology*. Translated by Mina Moore-Rinvolucri. Middletown, CT: Wesleyan University Press, 1984.

Vieira, Mark A. *Irving Thalberg: Boy Wonder to Producer Prince*. Berkeley: University of California Press, 2010.

Wheaton, Christopher D. "The Screen Writers' Guild (1920–1942): The Writers' Quest for a Freely Negotiated Basic Agreement." PhD diss., University of Southern California, 1973.

White, Sydnye. "Documentary by Design." *Cinema Journal* 45, no. 2 (Winter 2006): 92–95.

Wilk, Max. *Schmucks with Underwoods: Conversations with Hollywood's Classic Screenwriters.* Milwaukee, WI: Hal Leonard Corporation, 2004.

Williams, Mark. "Considering Monty Margetts's *Cook's Corner: Oral History and Television History.*" In *Television, History, and American Culture: Feminist Critical Essays*, edited by Mary Beth Haralovich and Lauren Rabinovitz. Durham, NC: Duke University Press, 1999.

Wittern-Keller, Laura, and Raymond J. Haberski Jr. *The Miracle Case: Film Censorship and the Supreme Court.* Landmark Law Cases and American Society. Lawrence: University Press of Kansas, 2008.

Wyatt, Justin. *High Concept: Movies and Marketing in Hollywood.* Austin: University of Texas Press, 1994.

Zolotow, Maurice. *Billy Wilder in Hollywood.* New York: Putnam, 1977.

INDEX

Page references in **boldface** refer to illustrations

313

ABOUT THE AUTHOR

MIRANDA J. BANKS is an assistant professor of Visual and Media Arts at Emerson College, where she teaches film and television history and media industries studies. She is co-editor of *Production Studies: Cultural Studies of Media Industries* (2009). Her work has appeared in *Television & New Media, Popular Communication*, and *Montage/AV*. She studied at Stanford University as an undergraduate and earned her MA and PhD from the Department of Film, Television, and Digital Media at UCLA.